THE ENGLISH POETS

T. H. WARD.

VOL. I.

EARLY POETRY:

CHAUCER to DONNE.

THE

ENGLISH POETS

SELECTIONS

WITH CRITICAL INTRODUCTIONS

BY VARIOUS WRITERS

AND A GENERAL INTRODUCTION BY

MATTHEW ARNOLD

EDITED BY

THOMAS HUMPHRY WARD

VOL. I

CHAUCER to DONNE

Granger Index Reprint Series

BOOKS FOR LIBRARIES PRESS
FREEPORT, NEW YORK

First Published 1885
Reprinted 1971

INTERNATIONAL STANDARD BOOK NUMBER:
0-8369-6244-3

LIBRARY OF CONGRESS CATALOG CARD NUMBER:
77-149119

PRINTED IN THE UNITED STATES OF AMERICA

PREFACE.

THE aim of this book is to supply an admitted want—that of an anthology which may adequately represent the vast and varied field of English Poetry.

Nothing of the kind at present exists. There are great collections of the whole works of the poets, like that of Chalmers; there are innumerable volumes of 'Beauties' of a more or less unsatisfactory kind; there are Selections from single poets; there are a few admirable volumes, like that of Mr. Palgrave, which deal with special departments of our poetical literature. The only book which attempts to cover the whole ground and to select on a large scale is Campbell's; and Campbell's, though the work of a true poet and, according to the standard of his time, a critic of authority, can no longer be regarded as sufficient. It is indeed impossible that a selection of the kind should be really well done, should be done with an approach to finality, if it is the work of one critic alone. The history of English poetry is so wide, its various sections and stages have become the objects of so special a study, that a book which aims at selecting the best from the whole field and pronouncing its judgments with some degree of authority, must not be the work of one writer, but of many. It was on this plan that M. Crépet's excellent book, *Les poètes français*, was constructed twenty years ago; and what he there did for French poetry we here wish to do for English poetry—to present a collection of what is best in it, chosen and judged by those whose tastes and studies specially qualify them for the several tasks they have undertaken.

Our design has not been to present a complete collection of all that may fairly be called masterpieces—if it had been so, the volumes would of necessity have been three times as many as they are. Still less has it been to give a complete history of English poetry—if it had been so, many names that we have passed over would have been admitted. It has been, to collect as many of the best and most characteristic of their writings as should fully represent the great poets, and at the same time to omit no one who is poetically considerable. There are writers who were famous in their day and who played a great part in the history of English literature, but who have faded from public notice and are no longer generally read; men like Sidney, and Cowley, and Waller. Again, there are writers who never were well known, but who wrote a few beautiful poems as it were by accident; men like some of the minor Elizabethans, or Lovelace, or Christopher Smart. We have endeavoured to do justice to both these classes; to gather from the former what may serve to explain why they were famous, and from the latter whatever they wrote that is of real poetical excellence.

We have not included the writings of living poets, nor the drama, properly so called. Had we admitted the drama we should have been compelled to double our space; besides, in spite of Charles Lamb, we may venture to say that by the nature of the case a play lends itself to selection less than any other form of literature. But where a play is only a play in name, like *Comus* or the *Gentle Shepherd*, we have not excluded it; and songs from the dramatists have of course been admitted.

Two points seem to require a word of notice—the order and the orthography. The first is approximately chronological; for in this matter it was found impossible to follow any rigid rule. To go uniformly by the date, either of birth or publication, would be in many cases misleading ; for we often find a poet not beginning to write till after the death of some younger contemporary, and oftener still we find his poems only posthumously collected. A vague *floruit circa* is the only date that is often possible in literary history. With regard to the orthography, the principle adopted has been, to print according to contemporary spelling up to the time of Wyatt and Surrey—the time of the Renascence—and since that date to adopt the uniform modern spelling. The exceptions that we have made are in the case of the Scotch poets (though with them it is a matter rather of language than of orthography), and of Spenser, who is so intentionally archaic that his spelling is peculiar, and is a part of himself. Spenser accordingly we have printed from Dr. Morris's text.

It remains for the Editor to express his cordial thanks to those who have so kindly co-operated with him; and he may be permitted to mention specially the names of Professor Skeat, who has revised the whole of the text of the poets down to Douglas; of Mr. Edmund W. Gosse, whose great knowledge of English poetry, especially of that of the seventeenth and eighteenth centuries, has been of the greatest service to the book; and of Mr. Matthew Arnold, who, besides his direct contributions, has from time to time given most valuable advice.

CONTENTS.

PAGE

INTRODUCTION.

'THE future of poetry is immense, because in poetry, where it is worthy of its high destinies, our race, as time goes on, will find an ever surer and surer stay. There is not a creed which is not shaken, not an accredited dogma which is not shown to be questionable, not a received tradition which does not threaten to dissolve. Our religion has materialised itself in the fact, in the supposed fact; it has attached its emotion to the fact, and now the fact is failing it. But for poetry the idea is everything; the rest is a world of illusion, of divine illusion. Poetry attaches its emotion to the idea; the idea *is* the fact. The strongest part of our religion to-day is its unconscious poetry.'

Let me be permitted to quote these words of my own, as uttering the thought which should, in my opinion, go with us and govern us in all our study of poetry. In the present work it is the course of one great contributory stream to the world-river of poetry that we are invited to follow. We are here invited to trace the stream of English poetry. But whether we set ourselves, as here, to follow only one of the several streams that make the mighty river of poetry, or whether we seek to know them all, our governing thought should be the same. We should conceive of poetry worthily, and more highly than it has been the custom to conceive of it. We should conceive of it as capable of higher uses, and called to higher destinies, than those which in general men have assigned to it hitherto. More and more mankind will discover that we have to turn to poetry to interpret life for us, to console us, to sustain us. Without poetry, our science will appear incomplete; and most of what now passes with us for religion and philosophy will be replaced by poetry. Science, I say, will appear incomplete without it. For finely and truly does Wordsworth call poetry 'the impassioned expression which is in the countenance of all science;' and what is a countenance without its expression? Again, Wordsworth finely and truly calls poetry 'the breath and finer spirit of all knowledge:' our religion, parading evidences such as those on which the popular mind relies now; our philosophy, pluming itself on its reasonings about causation and finite and infinite being; what are they but the shadows and dreams and false shows of knowledge? The day will come when we shall wonder at ourselves for having trusted to them, for having taken them seriously; and the more we perceive their hollowness, the more we shall prize 'the breath and finer spirit of knowledge' offered to us by poetry.

But if we conceive thus highly of the destinies of poetry, we must also set our standard for poetry high, since poetry, to be capable of fulfilling such high destinies, must be poetry of a high order of excellence. We must accustom ourselves to a high standard and to a strict judgment. Sainte-Beuve relates that Napoleon one day said, when somebody was spoken of in his presence as a charlatan: 'Charlatan as much as you please; but where is there *not* charlatanism?' 'Yes,' answers Sainte-Beuve, 'in politics, in the art of governing mankind, that is perhaps true. But in the order of thought, in art, the glory, the eternal honour is that charlatanism shall find no entrance; herein lies the inviolableness of that noble portion of man's being.' It is admirably said, and let us hold fast to it. In poetry, which is thought and art in one, it is the glory, the eternal honour, that charlatanism shall find no entrance ; that this noble sphere be kept inviolate and inviolable. Charlatanism is for confusing or obliterating the distinctions between excellent and inferior, sound and unsound or only half-sound, true and untrue or only half-true. It is charlatanism, conscious or unconscious, whenever we confuse or obliterate these. And in poetry, more than anywhere else, it is unpermissible to confuse or obliterate them. For in poetry the distinction between excellent and inferior, sound and unsound or only half-sound, true and untrue or only half-true, is of paramount importance. It is of paramount importance because of the high destinies of poetry. In poetry, as a criticism of life under the conditions fixed for such a criticism by the laws of poetic truth and poetic beauty, the spirit of our race will find, we have said, as time goes on and as other helps fail, its consolation and stay. But the consolation and stay will be of power in proportion to the power of the criticism of life. And the criticism of life will be of power in proportion as the poetry conveying it is excellent rather than inferior, sound rather than unsound or half-sound, true rather than untrue or half-true.

The best poetry is what we want; the best poetry will be found to have a power of forming, sustaining, and delighting us, as nothing else can. A clearer, deeper sense of the best in poetry, and of the strength and joy to be drawn from it, is the most precious benefit which we can gather from a poetical collection such as the present. And yet in the very nature and conduct of such a collection there is inevitably something which tends to obscure in us the consciousness of what our benefit should be, and to distract us from the pursuit of it. We should therefore steadily set it before our minds

b 2

at the outset, and should compel ourselves to revert constantly
to the thought of it as we proceed.

Yes; constantly, in reading poetry, a sense for the best, the
really excellent, and of the strength and joy to be drawn from
it, should be present in our minds and should govern our
estimate of what we read.   But this real estimate, the only
true one, is liable to be superseded, if we are not watchful,
by two other kinds of estimate, the historic estimate and the
personal estimate, both of which are fallacious.   A poet or
a poem may count to us historically, they may count to us on
grounds personal to ourselves, and they may count to us really.
They may count to us historically.   The course of develop-
ment of a nation's language, thought, and poetry, is profoundly
interesting; and by regarding a poet's work as a stage in this
course of development we may easily bring ourselves to make
it of more importance as poetry than in itself it really is, we
may come to use a language of quite exaggerated praise in
criticising it; in short, to over-rate it.   So arises in our poetic
judgments the fallacy caused by the estimate which we may call
historic.   Then, again, a poet or a poem may count to us on
grounds personal to ourselves.   Our personal affinities, likings,
and circumstances, have great power to sway our estimate of
this or that poet's work, and to make us attach more import-
ance to it as poetry than in itself it really possesses, because
to us it is, or has been, of high importance.   Here also we
over-rate the object of our interest, and apply to it a language
of praise which is quite exaggerated.   And thus we get the
source of a second fallacy in our poetic judgments,—the fallacy
caused by an estimate which we may call personal.

Both fallacies are natural.   It is evident how naturally the
study of the history and development of a poetry may incline
a man to pause over reputations and works once conspicuous

but now obscure, and to quarrel with a careless public for skipping, in obedience to mere tradition and habit, from one famous name or work in its national poetry to another, ignorant of what it misses, and of the reason for keeping what it keeps, and of the whole process of growth in its poetry. The French have become diligent students of their own early poetry, which they long neglected; the study makes many of them dissatisfied with their so-called classical poetry, the court-tragedy of the seventeenth century, a poetry which Pellisson long ago reproached with its want of the true poetic stamp, with its *politesse stérile et rampante*, but which nevertheless has reigned in France as absolutely as if it had been the perfection of classical poetry indeed. The dissatisfaction is natural; yet a lively and accomplished critic, M. Charles d'Héricault, the editor of Clément Marot, goes too far when he says that 'the cloud of glory playing round a classic is a mist as dangerous to the future of a literature as it is intolerable for the purposes of history.' 'It hinders,' he goes on, 'it hinders us from seeing more than one single point, the culminating and exceptional point; the summary, fictitious and arbitrary, of a thought and of a work. It substitutes a halo for a physiognomy, it puts a statue where there was once a man, and hiding from us all trace of the labour, the attempts, the weaknesses, the failures, it claims not study but veneration; it does not show us how the thing is done, it imposes upon us a model. Above all, for the historian this creation of classic personages is inadmissible; for it withdraws the poet from his time, from his proper life, it breaks historical relationships, it blinds criticism by conventional admiration, and renders the investigation of literary origins unacceptable. It gives us a human personage no longer, but a God seated immovable amidst his perfect work, like Jupiter on Olympus; and hardly will it be possible for the young student, to whom such work is exhibited at such a distance from him, to believe that it did not issue ready made from that divine head.'

All this is brilliantly and tellingly said, but we must plead for a distinction. Everything depends on the reality of a poet's classic character. If he is a dubious classic, let us sift him; if he is a false classic, let us explode him. But if he is a real classic, if his work belongs to the class of the very best (for this is the true and right meaning of the word *classic*, *classical*), then the great thing for us is to feel and enjoy his work as deeply as ever we can, and to appreciate the wide difference between it and all work which has not the same high character. This is what is salutary, this is what is formative; this is the great benefit to be got from the study of poetry. Everything which interferes with it, which hinders it, is injurious. True, we must read our classic with open eyes, and not with eyes blinded with superstition; we must perceive when his work comes short, when it drops out of the class of the very best, and we must rate it, in such cases, at its proper value. But the use of this negative criticism is not in itself, it is entirely in its enabling us to have a clearer sense and a deeper enjoyment of what is truly excellent. To trace the labour, the attempts, the weaknesses, the failures of a genuine classic, to acquaint oneself with his time and his life and his historical relationships, is mere literary dilettantism unless it has that clear sense and deeper enjoyment for its end. It may be said that the more we know about a classic the better we shall enjoy him; and, if we lived as long as Methuselah and had all of us heads of perfect clearness and wills of perfect steadfastness, this might be true in fact as it is plausible in theory. But the case here is much the same as the case with the Greek and Latin studies of our schoolboys. The elaborate philological groundwork which we require them to lay is in theory an admirable preparation for appreciating the Greek and Latin authors worthily. The more thoroughly we lay the groundwork, the better we shall be able, it may be said, to enjoy the authors. True, if time were not so short, and schoolboys' wits not so soon tired and their power of attention exhausted; only, as it is, the elaborate philological preparation goes on, but the authors are little known and less enjoyed. So with the investigator of 'historic origins' in poetry. He ought to enjoy the true classic all the better for his investigations; he often is distracted from the enjoyment of the best, and with the less good he overbusies himself, and is prone to overrate it in proportion to the trouble which it has cost him.

The idea of tracing historic origins and historical relationships cannot be absent from a compilation like the present. And naturally the poets to be exhibited in it will be assigned to those persons for exhibition who are known to prize them highly, rather than to those who have no special inclination towards them. Moreover the very occupation with an author, and the business of exhibiting him, disposes us to affirm and amplify his importance. In the present work, therefore, we are sure of frequent temptation to adopt the historic estimate, or the personal estimate, and to forget the real estimate; which latter, nevertheless, we must employ if we are to make poetry yield us its full benefit. So high is that benefit, the benefit of clearly feeling and of deeply enjoying the really excellent, the truly classic in poetry, that we do well, I say, to set it fixedly before our minds as our object in studying poets and poetry, and to make the desire of attaining it the one principle to which, as the *Imitation* says, whatever we may read or come to know, we always return. *Cum multa legeris et cognoveris, ad unum semper oportet redire principium.*

The historic estimate is likely in especial to affect our judgment and our language when we are dealing with ancient poets; the personal estimate when we are dealing with poets our contemporaries, or at any rate modern. The exaggerations due to the historic estimate are not in themselves, perhaps, of very much gravity. Their report hardly enters the general ear; probably they do not always impose even on the literary men who adopt them. But they lead to a dangerous abuse of language. So we hear Cædmon, amongst our own poets, compared to Milton. I have already noticed the enthusiasm of one accomplished French critic for 'historic origins.' Another eminent French critic, M. Vitet, comments upon that famous document of the early poetry of his nation, the *Chanson de Roland*. It is indeed a most interesting document. The *joculator* or *jongleur* Taillefer, who was with William the Conqueror's army at Hastings, marched before the Norman troops, so said the tradition, singing 'of Charlemagne and of Roland and of Oliver, and of the vassals who died at Roncevaux;' and it is suggested that in the *Chanson de Roland* by one Turoldus or Théroulde, a poem preserved in a manuscript of the twelfth century in the Bodleian Library at Oxford, we have certainly the matter, perhaps even some of the words, of the chaunt which Taillefer sang. The poem has vigour and freshness; it is not without pathos. But M. Vitet is not satisfied with seeing in it a document of some poetic value, and of very high historic and linguistic value; he sees in it a grand and beautiful work, a monument of epic genius. In its general design he finds the grandiose conception, in its details he finds the constant union of simplicity with greatness, which are the marks, he truly says, of the genuine epic, and distinguish it from the artificial epic of literary ages. One thinks of Homer; this is the sort of praise which is given to Homer, and justly given. Higher praise there cannot well be, and it is the praise due to epic poetry of the highest order only, and to no other. Let us try, then, the *Chanson de Roland* at its best. Roland, mortally wounded, lays himself down under a pine-tree, with his face turned towards Spain and the enemy:—

> 'De plusurs choses à remembrer li prist,
> De tantes teres cume li bers cunquist,
> De dulce France, des humes de sun lign,
> De Carlemagne sun seignor ki l'nurrit[1].'

That is primitive work, I repeat, with an undeniable poetic quality of its own. It deserves such praise, and such praise is sufficient for it. But now turn to Homer:—

> Ὥς φάτο· τοὺς δ' ἤδη κατέχεν φυσίζοος αἶα
> ἐν Λακεδαίμονι αὖθι, φίλῃ ἐν πατρίδι γαίῃ[2].

We are here in another world, another order of poetry altogether; here is rightly due such supreme praise as that which M. Vitet gives to the *Chanson de Roland*. If our words are to have any meaning, if our judgments are to have any solidity, we must not heap that supreme praise upon poetry of an order immeasurably inferior.

Indeed there can be no more useful help for discovering what poetry belongs to the class of the truly excellent, and can therefore do us most good, than to have always in one's mind lines and expressions of the great masters, and to apply them as a touchstone to other poetry. Of course we are not to require this other poetry to resemble them; it may be very

---

[1] 'Then began he to call many things to remembrance,—all the lands which his valour conquered, and pleasant France, and the men of his lineage, and Charlemagne his liege lord who nourished him.'—*Chanson de Roland*, iii. 939–942.

[2] 'So said she; they long since in Earth's soft arms were reposing,
   There, in their own dear land, their father land, Lacedæmon.'
   Iliad, iii. 243–4 (translated by Dr. Hawtrey).

dissimilar. But if we have any tact we shall find them, when we have lodged them well in our minds, an infallible touch-stone for detecting the presence or absence of high poetic quality, and also the degree of this quality, in all other poetry which we may place beside them. Short passages, even single lines, will serve our turn quite sufficiently. Take the two lines which I have just quoted from Homer, the poet's comment on Helen's mention of her brothers ;— or take his

> Ἄ δειλώ, τί σφῶϊ δόμεν Πηλῆϊ ἄνακτι
> θνητῷ; ὑμεῖς δ' ἐστὸν ἀγήρω τ' ἀθανάτω τε.
> ἦ ἵνα δυστήνοισι μετ' ἀνδράσιν ἄλγε' ἔχητον[1];

the address of Zeus to the horses of Peleus ;—or, take finally, his

> Καὶ σέ, γέρον, τὸ πρὶν μὲν ἀκούομεν ὄλβιον εἶναι[2]·

the words of Achilles to Priam, a suppliant before him. Take that incomparable line and a half of Dante, Ugolino's tre-mendous words:—

> ' Io no piangeva; sì dentro impietrai.
> Piangevan elli . . .[3] '

take the lovely words of Beatrice to Virgil:—

> ' Io son fatta da Dio, sua mercè, tale,
> Che la vostra miseria non mi tange,
> Nè fiamma d' esto incendio non m' assale . . .[4] '

take the simple, but perfect, single line:—

> ' In la sua volontade è nostra pace[5].'

---

[1] 'Ah, unhappy pair, why gave we you to King Peleus, to a mortal? but ye are without old age, and immortal. Was it that with men born to misery ye might have sorrow?'—*Iliad*, xvii. 443-5.

[2] 'Nay, and thou too, old man, in former days wast, as we hear, happy.' —*Iliad*, xxiv. 543.

[3] 'I wailed not, so of stone grew I within;—*they* wailed.'—*Inferno*, xxxiii. 39, 40.

[4] 'Of such sort hath God, thanked be his mercy, made me, that your misery toucheth me not, neither doth the flame of this fire strike me.'—*Inferno*, ii. 91-3.

[5] 'In His will is our peace.'—*Paradiso*, iii. 85.

Take of Shakespeare a line or two of Henry the Fourth's expostulation with sleep :—

> ' Wilt thou upon the high and giddy mast
> Seal up the ship-boy's eyes, and rock his brains
> In cradle of the rude imperious surge . . .'

and take, as well, Hamlet's dying request to Horatio :—

> ' If thou didst ever hold me in thy heart,
> Absent thee from felicity awhile,
> And in this harsh world draw thy breath in pain
> To tell my story . . .'

Take of Milton that Miltonic passage :—

> ' Darken'd so, yet shone
> Above them all the arch-angel; but his face
> Deep scars of thunder had intrench'd, and care
> Sat on his faded cheek . . .'

add two such lines as :—

> ' And courage never to submit or yield
> And what is else not to be overcome . . .'

and finish with the exquisite close to the loss of Proserpine, the loss

> ' . . . . . . which cost Ceres all that pain
> To seek her through the world.'

These few lines, if we have tact and can use them, are enough even of themselves to keep clear and sound our judgments about poetry, to save us from fallacious estimates of it, to conduct us to a real estimate.

The specimens I have quoted differ widely from one another, but they have in common this : the possession of the very highest poetical quality. If we are thoroughly penetrated by their power, we shall find that we have acquired a sense enabling us, whatever poetry may be laid before us, to feel the degree in which a high poetical quality is present or wanting there. Critics give themselves great labour to draw out what in the abstract constitutes the characters of a high quality of poetry. It is much better simply to have recourse to concrete examples;—to take specimens of poetry of the high, the very highest quality, and to say: The characters of a high quality of poetry are what is expressed *there.* They are far better recognised by being felt in the verse of the master, than by being perused in the prose of the critic. Nevertheless if we are urgently pressed to give some critical account of them, we may safely, perhaps, venture on laying down, not indeed how and why the characters arise, but where and in what they arise. They are in the matter and substance of the poetry, and they are in its manner and style. Both of these, the substance and matter on the one hand, the style and manner on the other, have a mark, an accent, of high beauty, worth, and power. But if we are asked to define this mark and accent in the abstract, our answer must be: No, for we should thereby be darkening the question, not clearing it. The mark and accent are as given by the substance and matter of that poetry, by the style and manner of that poetry, and of all other poetry which is akin to it in quality.

Only one thing we may add as to the substance and matter of poetry, guiding ourselves by Aristotle's profound observation that the superiority of poetry over history consists in its possessing a higher truth and a higher seriousness ($\phi\iota\lambda o\sigma o\phi\acute{\omega}\tau\epsilon\rho o\nu$ καὶ $\sigma\pi o\nu\delta a\iota\acute{o}\tau\epsilon\rho o\nu$). Let us add, therefore, to what we have said, this: that the substance and matter of the best poetry acquire their special character from possessing, in an eminent degree, truth and seriousness. We may add yet further, what is in itself evident, that to the style and manner of the best poetry their special character, their accent, is given by their diction, and, even yet more, by their movement. And though we distinguish between the two characters, the two accents, of superiority, yet they are nevertheless vitally connected one with the other. The superior character of truth and seriousness, in the matter and substance of the best poetry, is inseparable from the superiority of diction and movement marking its style and manner. The two superiorities are closely related, and are in steadfast proportion one to the other. So far as high poetic truth and seriousness are wanting to a poet's matter and substance, so far also, we may be sure, will a high poetic stamp of diction and movement be wanting to his style and manner. In proportion as this high stamp of diction and movement, again, is absent from a poet's style and manner, we shall find, also, that high poetic truth and seriousness are absent from his substance and matter.

So stated, these are but dry generalities; their whole force lies in their application. And I could wish every student of poetry to make the application of them for himself. Made by himself, the application would impress itself upon his mind far more deeply than made by me. Neither will my limits allow me to make any full application of the generalities above propounded; but in the hope of bringing out, at any rate, some significance in them, and of establishing an important principle more firmly by their means, I will, in the space which remains to me, follow rapidly from the commencement the course of our English poetry with them in my view.

Once more I return to the early poetry of France, with which our own poetry, in its origins, is indissolubly connected. In the twelfth and thirteenth centuries, that seed-time of all modern language and literature, the poetry of France had a clear predominance in Europe. Of the two divisions of that poetry, its productions in the *langue d'oil* and its productions in the *langue d'oc*, the poetry of the *langue d'oc*, of southern France, of the troubadours, is of importance because of its effect on

Italian literature;—the first literature of modern Europe to strike the true and grand note, and to bring forth, as in Dante and Petrarch it brought forth, classics. But the predominance of French poetry in Europe, during the twelfth and thirteenth centuries, is due to its poetry of the *langue d'oil*, the poetry of northern France and of the tongue which is now the French language. In the twelfth century the bloom of this romance-poetry was earlier and stronger in England, at the court of our Anglo-Norman kings, than in France itself. But it was a bloom of French poetry; and as our native poetry formed itself, it formed itself out of this. The romance-poems which took possession of the heart and imagination of Europe in the twelfth and thirteenth centuries are French; 'they are,' as Southey justly says, 'the pride of French literature, nor have we anything which can be placed in competition with them.' Themes were supplied from all quarters; but the romance-setting which was common to them all, and which gained the ear of Europe, was French. This constituted for the French poetry, literature and language, at the height of the Middle Age, an unchallenged predominance. The Italian Brunetto Latini, the master of Dante, wrote his *Treasure* in French because, he says, 'la parleure en est plus délitable et plus commune à toutes gens.' In the same century, the thirteenth, the French romance-writer, Christian of Troyes, formulates the claims, in chivalry and letters, of France, his native country, as follows :—

> 'Or vous ert par ce livre apris,
> Que Gresse ot ·de chevalerie
> Le premier los et de clergie;
> Puis vint chevalerie à Rome,
> Et de la clergie la some,
> Qui ore est en France venue.
> Diex doinst qu'ele i soit retenue,
> Et que li lius li abelisse
> Tant que de France n'isse
> L'onor qui s'i est arestée!'

'Now by this book you will learn that first Greece had the renown for chivalry and letters; then chivalry and the primacy in letters passed to Rome, and now it is come to France. God grant it may be kept there; and that the place may please it so well, that the honour which has come to make stay in France may never depart thence!'

Yet it is now all gone, this French romance-poetry, of which the weight of substance and the power of style are not unfairly represented by this extract from Christian of Troyes. Only by means of the historic estimate can we persuade ourselves now to think that any of it is of poetical importance.

But in the fourteenth century there comes an Englishman nourished on this poetry, taught his trade by this poetry, getting words, rhyme, metre from this poetry; for even of that stanza which the Italians used, and which Chaucer derived immediately from the Italians, the basis and suggestion was probably given in France. Chaucer (I have already named him) fascinated his contemporaries, but so too did Christian of Troyes and Wolfram of Eschenbach. Chaucer's power of fascination, however, is enduring; his poetical importance does not need the assistance of the historic estimate, it is real. He is a genuine source of joy and strength which is flowing still for us and will flow always. He will be read, as time goes on, far more generally than he is read now. His language is a cause of difficulty for us; but so also, and I think in quite as great a degree, is the language of Burns. In Chaucer's case, as in that of Burns, it is a difficulty to be unhesitatingly accepted and overcome.

If we ask ourselves wherein consists the immense superiority of Chaucer's poetry over the romance-poetry, why it is that in passing from this to Chaucer we suddenly feel ourselves to be in another world, we shall find that his superiority is both in the substance of his poetry and in the style of his poetry.

His superiority in substance is given by his large, free, simple, clear yet kindly view of human life,—so unlike the total want, in the romance-poets, of all intelligent command of it. Chaucer has not their helplessness; he has gained the power to survey the world from a central, a truly human point of view. We have only to call to mind the Prologue to *The Canterbury Tales.* The right comment upon it is Dryden's : ' It is sufficient to say, according to the proverb, that *here is God's plenty.*' And again: ' He is a perpetual fountain of good sense.' It is by a large, free, sound representation of things, that poetry, this high criticism of life, has truth of substance ; and Chaucer's poetry has truth of substance.

Of his style and manner, if we think first of the romance-poetry and then of Chaucer's divine liquidness of diction, his divine fluidity of movement, it is difficult to speak temperately. They are irresistible, and justify all the rapture with which his successors speak of his ' gold dew-drops of speech.' Johnson misses the point entirely when he finds fault with Dryden for ascribing to Chaucer the first refinement of our numbers, and says that Gower also can show smooth numbers and easy rhymes. The refinement of our numbers means something far more than this. A nation may have versifiers with smooth numbers and easy rhymes, and yet may have no real poetry at all. Chaucer is the father of our splendid English poetry, he is our ' well of English undefiled,' because by the lovely charm of his diction, the lovely charm of his movement, he makes an epoch and founds a tradition. In Spenser, Shakespeare, Milton, Keats, we can follow the tradition of the liquid diction, the fluid movement, of Chaucer; at one time it is his liquid diction of which in these poets we feel the virtue, and at another time it is his fluid movement. And the virtue is irresistible.

Bounded as is my space, I must yet find room for an example

of Chaucer's virtue, as I have given examples to show the virtue of the great classics. I feel disposed to say that a single line is enough to show the charm of Chaucer's verse; that merely one line like this:

> ' O martyr souded¹ in virginitee !'

has a virtue of manner and movement such as we shall not find in all the verse of romance-poetry;—but this is saying nothing. The virtue is such as we shall not find, perhaps, in all English poetry, outside the poets whom I have named as the special inheritors of Chaucer's tradition. A single line, however, is too little if we have not the strain of Chaucer's verse well in our memory; let us take a stanza. It is from *The Prioress's Tale*, the story of the Christian child murdered in a Jewry:—

> ' My throte is cut unto my nekke-bone
> Saidè this child, and as by way of kinde
> I should have deyd, yea, longè time agone;
> But Jesu Christ, as ye in bookès finde,
> Will that his glory last and be in minde,
> And for the worship of his mother dere
> Yet may I sing *O Alma* loud and clere.'

Wordsworth has modernised this Tale, and to feel how delicate and evanescent is the charm of verse, we have only to read Wordsworth's first three lines of this stanza after Chaucer's:—

> ' My throat is cut unto the bone, I trow,
> Said this young child, and by the law of kind
> I should have died, yea, many hours ago.'

The charm is departed. It is often said that the power of liquidness and fluidity in Chaucer's verse was dependent upon a free, a licentious dealing with language, such as is now impossible; upon a liberty, such as Burns too enjoyed, of making words like *neck*, *bird*, into a dissyllable by adding to them, and words

---

¹ The French *soudé;* soldered, fixed fast.

like *cause, rhyme*, into a dissyllable by sounding the *e* mute. It is
true that Chaucer's fluidity is conjoined with this liberty, and is
admirably served by it; but we ought not to say that it was
dependent upon it. It was dependent upon his talent. Other
poets with a like liberty do not attain to the fluidity of Chaucer;
Burns himself does not attain to it. Poets again, who have a
talent akin to Chaucer's, such as Shakespeare or Keats, have
known how to attain to his fluidity without the like liberty.

And yet Chaucer is not one of the great classics. His poetry
transcends and effaces, easily and without effort, all the romance-
poetry of Catholic Christendom; it transcends and effaces all
the English poetry contemporary with it, it transcends and
effaces all the English poetry subsequent to it down to the
age of Elizabeth. Of such avail is poetic truth of substance,
in its natural and necessary union with poetic truth of style.
And yet, I say, Chaucer is not one of the great classics. He
has not their accent. What is wanting to him is suggested
by the mere mention of the name of the first great classic
of Christendom, the immortal poet who died eighty years
before Chaucer,—Dante. The accent of such verse as

'In la sua volontade è nostra pace . . .'

is altogether beyond Chaucer's reach; we praise him, but we
feel that this accent is out of the question for him. It may
be said that it was necessarily out of the reach of any poet
in the England of that stage of growth. Possibly; but we are
to adopt a real, not a historic, estimate of poetry. However we
may account for its absence, something is wanting, then, to
the poetry of Chaucer, which poetry must have before it can be
placed in the glorious class of the best. And there is no doubt
what that something is. It is the σπουδαιότης, the high and
excellent seriousness, which Aristotle assigns as one of the

grand virtues of poetry. The substance of Chaucer's poetry, his view of things and his criticism of life, has largeness, freedom, shrewdness, benignity; but it has not this high seriousness. Homer's criticism of life has it, Dante's has it, Shakespeare's has it. It is this chiefly which gives to our spirits what they can rest upon; and with the increasing demands of our modern ages upon poetry, this virtue of giving us what we can rest upon will be more and more highly esteemed. A voice from the slums of Paris, fifty or sixty years after Chaucer, the voice of poor Villon out of his life of riot and crime, has at its happy moments (as, for instance, in the last stanza of *La Belle Heaulmière*[1]) more of this important poetic virtue of seriousness than all the productions of Chaucer. But its apparition in Villon, and in men like Villon, is fitful; the greatness of the great poets, the power of their criticism of life, is that their virtue is sustained.

To our praise, therefore, of Chaucer as a poet there must be this limitation; he lacks the high seriousness of the great classics, and therewith an important part of their virtue. Still,

---

[1] The name *Heaulmière* is said to be derived from a head-dress (helm) worn as a mark by courtesans. In Villon's ballad, a poor old creature of this class laments her days of youth and beauty. The last stanza of the ballad runs thus :—

> ' Ainsi le bon temps regretons
> Entre nous, pauvres vieilles sottes,
> Assises bas, à croppetons,
> Tout en ung tas comme pelottes;
> A petit feu de chenevottes
> Tost allumées, tost estainctes.
> Et jadis fusmes si mignottes !
> Ainsi en prend à maintz et maintes.'

'**Thus** amongst ourselves we regret the good time, poor silly old things, low-seated on our heels, all in a heap like so many balls ; by a little fire of hemp-stalks, soon lighted, soon spent. And once we were such darlings ! So fares it with many and many a one.'

the main fact for us to bear in mind about Chaucer is his sterling value according to that real estimate which we firmly adopt for all poets. He has poetic truth of substance, though he has not high poetic seriousness, and corresponding to his truth of substance he has an exquisite virtue of style and manner. With him is born our real poetry.

But for my present purpose I need not dwell on our Elizabethan poetry, or on the continuation and close of this poetry in Milton. We all of us profess to be agreed in the estimate of this poetry; we all of us recognise it as great poetry, our greatest, and Shakespeare and Milton as our poetical classics. The real estimate, here, has universal currency. With the next age of our poetry divergency and difficulty begin. An historic estimate of that poetry has established itself; and the question is, whether it will be found to coincide with the real estimate.

The age of Dryden, together with our whole eighteenth century which followed it, sincerely believed itself to have produced poetical classics of its own, and even to have made advance, in poetry, beyond all its predecessors. Dryden regards as not seriously disputable the opinion ' that the sweetness of English verse was never understood or practised by our fathers.' Cowley could see nothing at all in Chaucer's poetry. Dryden heartily admired it, and, as we have seen, praised its matter admirably; but of its exquisite manner and movement all he can find to say is that ' there is the rude sweetness of a Scotch tune in it, which is natural and pleasing, though not perfect.' Addison, wishing to praise Chaucer's numbers, compares them with Dryden's own. And all through the eighteenth century, and down even into our own times, the stereotyped phrase of approbation for good verse found in our early poetry has been, that it even approached the verse of Dryden, Addison, Pope, and Johnson.

Are Dryden and Pope poetical classics? Is the historic estimate, which represents them as such, and which has been so long established that it cannot easily give way, the real estimate? Wordsworth and Coleridge, as is well known, denied it; but the authority of Wordsworth and Coleridge does not weigh much with the young generation, and there are many signs to show that the eighteenth century and its judgments are coming into favour again. Are the favourite poets of the eighteenth century classics?

It is impossible within my present limits to discuss the question fully. And what man of letters would not shrink from seeming to dispose dictatorially of the claims of two men who are, at any rate, such masters in letters as Dryden and Pope; two men of such admirable talent, both of them, and one of them, Dryden, a man, on all sides, of such energetic and genial power? And yet, if we are to gain the full benefit from poetry, we must have the real estimate of it. I cast about for some mode of arriving, in the present case, at such an estimate without offence. And perhaps the best way is to begin, as it is easy to begin, with cordial praise.

When we find Chapman, the Elizabethan translator of Homer, expressing himself in his preface thus: ' Though truth in her very nakedness sits in so deep a pit, that from Gades to Aurora and Ganges few eyes can sound her, I hope yet those few here will so discover and confirm, that, the date being out of her darkness in this morning of our poet, he shall now gird his temples with the sun,'—we pronounce that such a prose is intolerable. When we find Milton writing : ' And long it was not after, when I was confirmed in this opinion, that he, who would not be frustrate of his hope to write well hereafter in laudable things, ought himself to be a true poem,'—we pronounce that such a prose has its own grandeur, but that it is obsolete and inconvenient. But when we find Dryden telling us: ' What Virgil wrote in the vigour of his age, in plenty and at ease, I have undertaken to translate in my declining years; struggling with wants, oppressed with sickness, curbed in my genius, liable to be misconstrued in all I write,'—then we exclaim that here at last we have the true English prose, a prose such as we would all gladly use if we only knew how. Yet Dryden was Milton's contemporary.

But after the Restoration the time had come when our nation felt the imperious need of a fit prose. So, too, the time had likewise come when our nation felt the imperious need of freeing itself from the absorbing preoccupation which religion in the Puritan age had exercised. It was impossible that this freedom should be brought about without some negative excess, without some neglect and impairment of the religious life of the soul; and the spiritual history of the eighteenth century shows us that the freedom was not achieved without them. Still, the freedom was achieved; the preoccupation, an undoubtedly baneful and retarding one if it had continued, was got rid of. And as with religion amongst us at that period, so it was also with letters. A fit prose was a necessity; but it was impossible that a fit prose should establish itself amongst us without some touch of frost to the imaginative life of the soul. The needful qualities for a fit prose are regularity, uniformity, precision, balance. The men of letters, whose destiny it may be to bring their nation to the attainment of a fit prose, must of necessity, whether they work in prose or in verse, give a predominating, an almost exclusive attention to the qualities of regularity, uniformity, precision, balance. But an almost exclusive attention to these qualities involves some repression and silencing of poetry.

We are to regard Dryden as the puissant and glorious founder, Pope as the splendid high-priest, of our age of prose

and reason, of our excellent and indispensable eighteenth cen‑
tury. For the purposes of their mission and destiny their
poetry, like their prose, is admirable. Do you ask me whether
Dryden's verse, take it almost where you will, is not good?

> ‘A milk-white Hind, immortal and unchanged,
> Fed on the lawns and in the forest ranged.’

I answer: Admirable for the purposes of the inaugurator of an
age of prose and reason. Do you ask me whether Pope's
verse, take it almost where you will, is not good?

> ‘To Hounslow Heath I point, and Banstead Down;
> Thence comes your mutton, and these chicks my own.’

I answer: Admirable for the purposes of the high-priest of
an age of prose and reason. But do you ask me whether such
verse proceeds from men with an adequate poetic criticism of
life, from men whose criticism of life has a high seriousness,
or even, without that high seriousness, has poetic largeness,
freedom, insight, benignity? Do you ask me whether the ap‑
plication of ideas to life in the verse of these men, often a
powerful application, no doubt, is a powerful *poetic* application?
Do you ask me whether the poetry of these men has either the
matter or the inseparable manner of such an adequate poetic
criticism; whether it has the accent of

> ‘Absent thee from felicity awhile . . .’

or of

> ‘And what is else not to be overcome . . .’

or of

> ‘O martyr souded in virginitee!’

I answer: It has not and cannot have them; it is the poetry of
the builders of an age of prose and reason. Though they may
write in verse, though they may in a certain sense be masters of

the art of versification, Dryden and Pope are not classics of our poetry, they are classics of our prose.

Gray is our poetical classic of that literature and age; the position of Gray is singular, and demands a word of notice here. He has not the volume or the power of poets who, coming in times more favourable, have attained to an independent criticism of life. But he lived with the great poets, he lived, above all, with the Greeks, through perpetually studying and enjoying them; and he caught their poetic point of view for regarding life, caught their poetic manner. The point of view and the manner are not self-sprung in him, he caught them of others; and he had not the free and abundant use of them. But whereas Addison and Pope never had the use of them, Gray had the use of them at times. He is the scantiest and frailest of classics in our poetry, but he is a classic.

And now, after Gray, we are met, as we draw towards the end of the eighteenth century, we are met by the great name of Burns. We enter now on times where the personal estimate of poets begins to be rife, and where the real estimate of them is not reached without difficulty. But in spite of the disturbing pressures of personal partiality, of national partiality, let us try to reach a real estimate of the poetry of Burns.

By his English poetry Burns in general belongs to the eighteenth century, and has little importance for us.

> ‘Mark ruffian Violence, distain'd with crimes,
> Rousing elate in these degenerate times;
> View unsuspecting Innocence a prey,
> As guileful Fraud points out the erring way;
> While subtle Litigation's pliant tongue
> The life-blood equal sucks of Right and Wrong!’

Evidently this is not the real Burns, or his name and fame would have disappeared long ago. Nor is Clarinda's love-poet,

Sylvander, the real Burns either. But he tells us himself : 'These English songs gravel me to death. I have not the command of the language that I have of my native tongue. In fact, I think that my ideas are more barren in English than in Scotch. I have been at *Duncan Gray* to dress it in English, but all I can do is desperately stupid.' We English turn naturally, in Burns, to the poems in our own language, because we can read them easily; but in those poems we have not the real Burns.

The real Burns is of course in his Scotch poems. Let us boldly say that of much of this poetry, a poetry dealing perpetually with Scotch drink, Scotch religion, and Scotch manners, a Scotchman's estimate is apt to be personal. A Scotchman is used to this world of Scotch drink, Scotch religion, and Scotch manners; he has a tenderness for it; he meets its poet half way. In this tender mood he reads pieces like the *Holy Fair* or *Halloween*. But this world of Scotch drink, Scotch religion, and Scotch manners is against a poet, not for him, when it is not a partial countryman who reads him; for in itself it is not a beautiful world, and no one can deny that it is of advantage to a poet to deal with a beautiful world. Burns's world of Scotch drink, Scotch religion, and Scotch manners, is often a harsh, a sordid, a repulsive world; even the world of his *Cotter's Saturday Night* is not a beautiful world. No doubt a poet's criticism of life may have such truth and power that it triumphs over its world and delights us. Burns may triumph over his world, often he does triumph over his world, but let us observe how and where. Burns is the first case we have had where the bias of the personal estimate tends to mislead ; let us look at him closely, he can bear it.

Many of his admirers will tell us that we have Burns, convivial, genuine, delightful, here :—

> ' Leeze me on drink ! it gies us mair
>   Than either school or college;
> It kindles wit, it waukens lair,
>   It pangs us fou o' knowledge.
> Be 't whisky gill or penny wheep
>   Or ony stronger potion,
> It never fails, on drinking deep,
>   To kittle up our notion
>   By night or day.'

There is a great deal of that sort of thing in Burns, and it is
unsatisfactory, not because it is bacchanalian poetry, but because
it has not that accent of sincerity which bacchanalian poetry,
to do it justice, very often has. There is something in it of
bravado, something which makes us feel that we have not
the man speaking to us with his real voice; something, there-
fore, poetically unsound.

With still more confidence will his admirers tell us that we
have the genuine Burns, the great poet, when his strain asserts
the independence, equality, dignity, of men, as in the famous
song *For a' that and a' that :*—

> ' A prince can mak' a belted knight,
>   A marquis, duke, and a' that;
> But an honest man's aboon his might,
>   Guid faith he mauna fa' that !
>   For a' that, and a' that,
>   Their dignities, and a' that,
>   The pith o' sense, and pride o' worth,
>   Are higher rank than a' that.'

Here they find his grand, genuine touches; and still more, when
this puissant genius, who so often set morality at defiance, falls
moralising :—

> ' The sacred lowe o' weel-placed love
>   Luxuriantly indulge it;
> But never tempt th' illicit rove,
>   Tho' naething should divulge it.

> I waive the quantum o' the sin,
> The hazard o' concealing,
> But och! it hardens a' within,
> And petrifies the feeling.'

Or in a higher strain :—

> 'Who made the heart, 'tis He alone
> Decidedly can try us;
> He knows each chord, its various tone;
> Each spring, its various bias.
> Then at the balance let's be mute,
> We never can adjust it;
> What's *done* we partly may compute,
> But know not what's resisted.'

Or in a better strain yet, a strain, his admirers will say, unsurpassable :—

> 'To make a happy fire-side clime
> To weans and wife,
> That's the true pathos and sublime
> Of human life.'

There is criticism of life for you, the admirers of Burns will say to us; there is the application of ideas to life! There is, undoubtedly. The doctrine of the last-quoted lines coincides almost exactly with what was the aim and end, Xenophon tells us, of all the teaching of Socrates. And the application is a powerful one; made by a man of vigorous understanding, and (need I say?) a master of language.

But for supreme poetical success more is required than the powerful application of ideas to life; it must be an application under the conditions fixed by the laws of poetic truth and poetic beauty. Those laws fix as an essential condition, in the poet's treatment of such matters as are here in question, high seriousness;—the high seriousness which comes from absolute sincerity. The accent of high seriousness, born of absolute sincerity, is what gives to such verse as

> 'In la sua volontade è nostra pace...'

to such criticism of life as Dante's, its power. Is this accent felt in the passages which I have been quoting from Burns? Surely not; surely, if our sense is quick, we must perceive that we have not in those passages a voice from the very inmost soul of the genuine Burns; he is not speaking to us from these depths, he is more or less preaching. And the compensation for admiring such passages less, from missing the perfect poetic accent in them, will be that we shall admire more the poetry where that accent is found.

No; Burns, like Chaucer, comes short of the high seriousness of the great classics, and the virtue of matter and manner which goes with that high seriousness is wanting to his work. At moments he touches it in a profound and passionate melancholy, as in those four immortal lines taken by Byron as a motto for *The Giaour*, but which have in them a depth of poetic quality such as resides in no verse of Byron's own:—

> ‘Had we never loved sae kindly,
> Had we never loved sae blindly,
> Never met, or never parted,
> We had ne'er been broken-hearted.’

But a whole poem of that quality Burns cannot make; the rest, in the *Farewell to Nancy*, is verbiage.

We arrive best at the real estimate of Burns, I think, by conceiving his work as having truth of matter and truth of manner, but not the accent or the poetic virtue of the highest masters. His genuine criticism of life, when the sheer poet in him speaks, is ironic; it is not:

> ‘Thou Power Supreme, whose mighty scheme
> These woes of mine fulfil,
> Here firm I rest, they must be best
> Because they are Thy will!’

It is far rather: *Whistle owre the lave o't!* Yet we may say of him as of Chaucer, that of life and the world, as they come before him,

his view is large, free, shrewd, benignant,—truly poetic, there-
fore; and his manner of rendering what he sees is to match
But we must note, at the same time, his great difference from
Chaucer. The freedom of Chaucer is heightened, in Burns, by
a fiery, reckless energy; the benignity of Chaucer deepens, in
Burns, into an overwhelming sense of the pathos of things;—of
the pathos of human nature, the pathos, also, of non-human
nature. Instead of the fluidity of Chaucer's manner, the manner
of Burns has spring, bounding swiftness. Burns is by far the
greater force, though he has perhaps less charm. The world of
Chaucer is fairer, richer, more significant than that of Burns;
but when the largeness and freedom of Burns get full sweep, as
in *Tam o' Shanter*, or still more in that puissant and splendid
production, *The Jolly Beggars*, his world may be what it will,
his poetic genius triumphs over it. In the world of the *Jolly
Beggars* there is more than hideousness and squalor, there
is bestiality; yet the piece is a superb poetic success. It has
a breadth, truth, and power which make the famous scene in
Auerbach's Cellar, of Goethe's *Faust*, seem artificial and tame
beside it, and which are only matched by Shakespeare and
Aristophanes.

Here, where his largeness and freedom serve him so admi-
rably, and also in those poems and songs, where to shrewdness
he adds infinite archness and wit, and to benignity infinite
pathos, where his manner is flawless, and a perfect poetic·whole
is the result,—in things like the address to the Mouse whose
home he had ruined, in things like *Duncan Gray, Tam Glen,
Whistle and I'll come to you, my lad, Auld lang syne* (the list might
be made much longer),—here we have the genuine Burns, of
whom the real estimate must be high indeed. Not a classic,
nor with the excellent σπουδαιότης of the great classics, nor with
a verse rising to a criticism of life and a virtue like theirs;

but a poet with thorough truth of substance and an answering truth of style, giving us a poetry sound to the core. We all of us have a leaning towards the pathetic, and may be inclined perhaps to prize Burns most for his touches of piercing, sometimes almost intolerable, pathos ; for verse like :

> ' We twa hae paidl't i' the burn
>   From mornin' sun till dine;
> But seas between us braid hae roar'd
>   Sin auld lang syne . . .'

where he is as lovely as he is sound. But perhaps it is by the perfection of soundness of his lighter and archer master-pieces that he is poetically most wholesome for us. For the votary misled by a personal estimate of Shelley, as so many of us have been, are, and will be,—of that beautiful spirit building his many-coloured haze of words and images

> ' Pinnacled dim in the intense inane '—

no contact can be wholesomer than the contact with Burns at his archest and soundest. Side by side with the

> ' On the brink of the night and the morning
>   My coursers are wont to respire,
> But the Earth has just whispered a warning
>   That their flight must be swifter than fire . . .'

of *Prometheus Unbound*, how salutary, how very salutary, to place this from *Tam Glen :*—

> ' My minnie does constantly deave me
>   And bids me beware o' young men ;
> They flatter, she says, to deceive me ;
>   But wha can think sae o' Tam Glen ? '

But we enter on burning ground as we approach the poetry of times so near to us, poetry like that of Byron, Shelley, and Wordsworth, of which the estimates are so often not only personal, but personal with passion. For my purpose, it is enough

to have taken the single case of Burns, the first poet we come
to of whose work the estimate formed is evidently apt to be
personal, and to have suggested how we may proceed, using
the poetry of the great classics as a sort of touchstone, to
correct this estimate, as we had previously corrected by the
same means the historic estimate where we met with it. A
collection like the present, with its succession of celebrated
names and celebrated poems, offers a good opportunity to us
for resolutely endeavouring to make our estimates of poetry
real. I have sought to point out a method which will help
us in making them so, and to exhibit it in use so far as to
put any one who likes in a way of applying it for himself.

At any rate the end to which the method and the estimate are
designed to lead, and from leading to which, if they do lead to
it, they get their whole value,—the benefit of being able clearly
to feel and deeply to enjoy the best, the truly classic, in poetry,—
is an end, let me say it once more at parting, of supreme im-
portance. We are often told that an era is opening in which
we are to see multitudes of a common sort of readers, and
masses of a common sort of literature ; that such readers do not
want and could not relish anything better than such literature,
and that to provide it is becoming a vast and profitable industry.
Even if good literature entirely lost currency with the world, it
would still be abundantly worth while to continue to enjoy it by
oneself. But it never will lose currency with the world, in spite
of momentary appearances ; it never will lose supremacy. Cur-
rency and supremacy are insured to it, not indeed by the
world's deliberate and conscious choice, but by something far
deeper,—by the instinct of self-preservation in humanity.

Matthew Arnold.

CHAUCER.

[GEOFFREY CHAUCER, born in London probably about 1310 died at West-
minster in 1400. He was the son of a vintner; was page in Prince Lionel's
household, served in the army, was taken prisoner in France. He was
afterwards valet and squire to Edward III and went as king's commissioner
to Italy in 1372, and later. He was Controller of the Customs in the port
of London from 1381 to 1386, was M.P. for Kent in 1386, Clerk of the
King's Works at Windsor in 1389, and died poor. Mr. Furnivall divides
his poetical history into four periods. (1) up to 1371, including the early
poems, viz the *A. B. C*, the *Compleynte to Pité*, the *Boke of the Duchesse*, and
the *Compleynte of Mars*; (2) from 1372 to 1381, including the *Troylus and
Criseyde, Anelida*, and the *Former Age*; (3) the best period, from 1381 to
1389, including the *Parlement of Foules*, the *Hous of Fame*, the *Legende of
Goode Women*, and the chief of the *Canterbury Tales*; (4) from 1390 to 1400,
including the latest *Canterbury Tales*, and the Ballades and Poems of Reflec-
tion and later age, of which the last few, like the *Steadfastness*, show failing
power.]

It is natural that a book which aims at including the best that
has been done in English verse should begin with Chaucer, to
whom no one has ever seriously denied the name which Dryden
gave him, of the Father of English poetry. The poems of an
earlier date, the *Brut* and the *Ormulum*, the Romances and the
Homilies, have indeed an interest of their own ; but it is a purely
antiquarian interest, and even under that aspect it does not exist
for the reader of Chaucer, who cannot in any sense be said to have
been inspired by them. English poetry, distinguished on the one
hand from the 'rym dogerel' of the romancers, which is not poetry,
and on the other from *Beowulf*, which is poetry but not, in the
ordinary sense, English, begins in the reign of Edward III, with
Chaucer and his lesser contemporaries. In them we see at a

glance that the step has been taken which separates the rhymer from the poet, the 'maker,' who has something new to say, and has found the art of saying it beautifully. The poet, says an Elizabethan critic, 'can express the true and lively of everything which is set before him, and which he taketh in hand to describe'—words that exactly meet Chaucer's case, and draw the line between himself and his predecessors. In the half century before Chaucer there had indeed been isolated poems—a lyric or two of real freshness and beauty—but not till that time of heightened national life, of wider culture, and of more harmonised society into which he was born, was there a sufficiency either of ideas or of accessible poetical material on English ground to shape and furnish an imaginative development like his. To him first among the writers of English it was given to catch and to express 'the true and lively' throughout a broad life of human range and feeling. Before him there had been story-telling, there had been stray notes of poetry : but in Chaucer England brought forth her first poet, as modern times count poetry ; her first skilled and conscious work-man, who, coming in upon the stores of natural fact open to all alike, was enabled to communicate to whatever he touched that colour, that force, that distinction, in virtue of which common life and common feelings turn to poetry. And having found her poet, she did not fail to recognise him. Very soon, as Gower's 'Venus' says of him in the often-quoted lines,

> ' Of di'ës and of songës glad
> The whiche he for my sakë made
> The land fulfilled is over al.'

The themes of his books run glibly from the tongue of his own 'Sergeaunt of Lawe,' like matter familiar to all. His literary contemporaries felt and confessed in him the Poet's mysterious gifts, and his height above themselves. The best English poetical opinion, in the mouth of Spenser, Sidney, Milton, Dry-den, has continuously acknowledged him ; while the more our later world turns back to him, and learns to read and under-stand him, the stronger grows his claim in even our critical modern eyes, not only to the antiquarian charm of the story-teller and the 'translateur,' but to the influence and honours of the poet.

Chaucer then is for us the first English poet, and as such has all the interest that attaches to a great original figure. But he makes no parade of his originality; on the contrary, like all mediæval writers, he translates, and borrows, and is anxious to reveal his authorities, lest he should be thought to be palming off mere frivolous inventions of his own. Other men's work is to him an ever open storehouse to be freely used, now for foundation, now for ornament. Hence with a writer like Chaucer the examination of his sources is at once more possible and more fruitful than is the case with a later poet. We know that every writer is in a great measure the creation of the books he has read and the times he has lived in ; but with a modern writer, or one like Virgil, it is impossible to disengage these influences with any real success. Not so with Chaucer and the poets of a young, unformed civilisation ; they bear on their foreheads the traces of their origin. They reflect simply and readily the influence of the moment ; happiness or sorrow, success or failure, this book or that—each has its instant effect on their work, so that it becomes a matter of real importance for him who would appreciate an early poet to know what he read and how he lived. Accordingly, from very early times, from the time of Stowe, Speght, and the Thynnes, those who have cared for Chaucer have shown a curiosity about the influences that formed him. A century ago, Tyrwhitt did as much as one man could to set the study of these influences on a sound footing, and in our own day the labours of the Chaucer Society and of Professor Ten Brink and other Germans have furnished us with a nearly complete apparatus for conducting it. With infinite industry, such as is shown in Mr. Furniva l's Six-Text edition of the poet, they have given us what materials exist for settling Chaucer's text ; they have separated, on evidence both internal and derived from the circumstances of his life and times, his genuine work from the spurious pieces that tradition had thrust upon him ; and they have skilfully tracked his poems to their sources. On ground so prepared we may tread firmly, and even in a short sketch like the present, which attempts no more than to present results that are generally agreed upon, it is possible to speak with some approach to certainty.

Chaucer was a great reader, and in more than one well-known passage he tells us what he felt for books.

> ' On bookës for to rede I me delyte,
> And to hem yive I feyth and ful credence,'

he says, in the prologue to the *Legende of Goode Women*. Books are to him the soil from which knowledge springs :—

> * For out of oldë feldës, as men saith,
> Cometh al this newë corn from yeer to yere,
> And out of oldë bokës, in good faith,
> Cometh al this newë science that men lere.'

He reads 'the longë day ful fast' ; and it is no vain fancy which would discover in the book-loving ' Clerke of Oxenford' some traits that the poet has transferred from his own character. He knew Latin, French, and Italian, and was familiar with the best that had been written in those languages. His Latin studies included Boethius, whose book *De Consolatione Philosophiae* he translated into English ; Macrobius, as far as the *Somnium Scipionis* is concerned ; Livy and others of the great Roman prose writers, and many of the poets, ' Ovide, Lucan, Stace,' with Virgil and probably Claudian. But it must be remembered that he read Latin not as we read it, but as we read a modern foreign language, rapidly rather than exactly, with more desire to come by a rough and ready way to the sense than to be clear about the structure of the sentences. He cared very little either for grammar or for prosody ; he talks of Æneas and Anchïses, and some would believe that he makes of Lollius, the correspondent of Horace, 'myn auctour Lollius,' a historian of the Trojan war.[1] In the same way, of the historical study of Latin literature, of the conscious attempt to realise the life of classical times, there is no trace in Chaucer. His favourite Latin writers were unquestionably Boethius and Ovid, as they were the favourites of the middle ages in general ; Boethius, of whom a recent editor has counted nineteen imitations before the end of the fifteenth century, and Ovid, whose *Ars Amandi* and *Metamorphoses* were the storehouse of the mediæval love-poet and story-teller. Nothing, on the other hand, shows more clearly the limitations of Chaucer's genius than his attitude towards Virgil.

[1] Horace to Lollius, Epp. I. 2. 1—
> ' Trojani belli scriptorem, maxime Lolli,
> Dum tu declamas Romae, Praeneste relegi.'

Dr. Latham supposes that Chaucer mistook the name of the person addressed for the historian, and Prof. Ten Brink suggests that he read—
> ' Trojani belli scriptor*um* maxime, Lolli,
> Dum tu declamas Romae, Praeneste *te* legi.'

The false quantity would be no argument against this ingenious supposition ; but what is more to the point is that the context shows Horace to be writing about a third person. Besides, it is not certain that Chaucer had read Horace.

No 'long study and great love' had made him search the volume
of that 'honour and light of other poets' as Dante was made to
search it ; on the contrary, he prefers the romantic exaggerations
of Statius, and it is for the rhetorical Lucan that he reserves the
epithet of 'the gret poete.' Among the Good Women of the
Legende comes Dido, it is true, and her story is taken more from
the Æneid than from the Heroides. But what a change has
passed over the tale since the religious Roman, charged with the
sense of destiny, called away his hero from the embraces of the
love-lorn queen to the work of founding the empire of the world !

> 'The fresshë lady, of the citee qucene,
> Stood in the temple, in her estat royalle,
> So richëly, and eke so faire withalle,
> So yong, so lusty, with her eighen glade,
> That yf the God that heven and erthë made
> Wolde han a love, for beautë and goodnesse,
> And womanhode, and trouthe, and semlynesse,
> Whom sholde he loven but this lady swete?
> Ther nys no woman to him half so mete.'

Such is Dido ; while the grave Trojan, for whom in Virgil the
gods are contending, becomes in Chaucer's hands a mere vulgar
deceiver, a 'grete gentilman' indeed to outward seeming, that has
the gifts of pleasing, and can

> 'Wel doon al his obeÿsaunce
> To hire at festeÿngës and at daunce,'

but hollow at heart, false in his oaths and in his tears ; in a word,
a cool, unscrupulous seeker of *bonnes fortunes.* And again, at the
central point of all, what has become of the 'conscious heaven'
and 'pronuba Juno'?

> 'For ther hath Æneas yknyled soo,
> And tolde her al his herte and al his woo;
> And sworn so depë to hire to be trewe
> For wele or woo, and chaungë for noo newe,
> And as a fals lover so wel kan pleyne
> That sely Dido rewed on his peyne,
> And toke him for housbonde, and was his wife
> For evermor, whil that hem lastë lyfe.'

Chaucer, in fact, is purely mediæval in his rendering of antiquity,
and among the ancient writers he turns with the greatest sympathy
to those in whom the romantic element is strongest. The spirit

of the Renascence is stirring within him, but it is not in his
relation to the ancients that we detect it ; it is rather in his
'humanism'—in his openness of mind, in his fresh delight in
visible and sensible things, in his sense of the variety of human
character and motive, and of the pity of human fate.

French poetry plays a far larger part in Chaucer's work than do
the classical writers. Whether or not his name implies that he
was partly French in blood, he certainly spent some time in
France, first as a prisoner of war (A.D. 1359) and afterwards on the
king's business. He began life as a page in the household of the
Duke of Clarence, where French was no doubt spoken as much as
English ; and his attention was early drawn to that trouvère-
literature which in the days of his youth formed the chief reading
of the court circles. In point of fact, all his writings up to 1372
(the date of his first visit to Italy) are either translations or
imitations, more or less close, of French poems ; and even after he
had returned, impressed with the ineffaceable charm of Italy, he
still looked to France for much of his material. One of his
earliest and one of his very latest poems, the *A. B. C.* and the
Compleynte of Venus, are translations from De Deguileville and
Gransson ; the *Boke of the Duchesse* derives much from a poem
of Machault ; the Ballads and Roundels, of which a few remain
to us, probably out of very many, are French in form ; and it is
in a poem of Eustache Deschamps that we find what appears
to be the first model of the ten-syllabled rhyming couplet which
Chaucer made his own, and which has since become one of the
most distinctive forms of English verse. The comic stories in the
Canterbury Tales are mostly based on the *fabliaux*, a department
of literature which has always seemed to belong pre-eminently to
the countrymen of la Fontaine. But among French poems, that
which made the deepest mark on him was the 'Roman de la
Rose,' the first and principal specimen of what M. Sandras, Chau-
cer's French critic, has happily called the psychological epic.
This poem, as is well known, was begun by Guillaume de Lorris
under Louis IX, and continued at immense length by Jean de
Meung forty years later, under Philip the Fair ; the former poet's
work being an elaborate and thrice-refined love allegory, and that
of the latter being a fierce satire against all that the Middle Age
was accustomed to reverence—women, nobles, priests. The two
parts of the poem, however, agreed in form ; that is, they sub-
stituted for the heroic romances of the preceding centuries those

allegorical abstractions, those 'indirect crook'd ways,' with which scholasticism had infected European thought. L'Amant, in his search for the Rose of Beauty, Déduit, Papelardie, l'Oiseuse, Faux-Semblant, are, as a French critic puts it, 'members of the family of Entities and Quiddities that were born to the realist doctors.' The vogue of the 'Roman' was immense, and Chaucer, that 'grant translateur,' translated it, as the Prologue to the *Legende* bears witness, and as Lydgate also affirms in his catalogue of the master's works. The most recent critics, with Mr. Bradshaw and Professor Ten Brink at their head, have indeed denied Chaucer's claim to that version of the *Romaunt* which till lately has always passed for his ; and in obedience to their opinion we have separated from the body of Chaucer's acknowledged writings the passage of that poem that we are able to quote ; but the question is one which, as far as Chaucer's debt to French literature is concerned, is of little importance. Translate the *Romaunt* he certainly did, and the impression it made upon him was deep and lasting. On the one hand it furnished him with a whole allegorical mythology, as well as with his stock landscape, his stock device of the Dream, and even (we may at least imagine) confirmed him in the choice of the flowing eight-syllabled couplet for the *Hous of Fame* ; and on the other, it furnished him with those weapons of satire which he used with such effect in the Pardoner's prologue and elsewhere.

Twenty years ago a vigorous attempt was made in M. Sandras' *Étude sur Chaucer* to show that the English poet, though a man of original genius, was in point of matter, from first to last, an imitator of the *trouvères*. A more rational criticism has since then put the case in a truer light, and shown not only the bold independence of his models which Chaucer exhibited from the beginning, but the fact that it was only in early life that he got his chief models from France. The great event of his life was undoubtedly his first Italian journey, during which, if we are to trust an old tradition that has never been disproved, he met Petrarch at Padua. From this time onward he wrote with a firmer pen and with a closer adherence to truth, and the foreign examples that he henceforth followed were not French but Italian, not Guillaume de Lorris and Machault, but Dante, Boccaccio, and, to a certain extent, Petrarch. He does not, it is true, altogether depart from his old methods ; the dream of the *Romaunt* reappears in the *Parlement* and in the *Hous of Fame* ; the May morning and the daisy introduce the *Legende*. But there is no comparison between the workmanship of the two periods, and whereas that of the first is loose and disjointed, that of the second—except perhaps in the case of the *Hous of Fame*, which is more than half comic, a sort of travesty of the Divina Commedia, and therefore not to be judged by strict rules—that of the second is compact, well-ordered, and guided by the true artist's mastery over his materials. Italy in fact gave to Chaucer at precisely the right moment just that stimulus and that external standard which he required for the true completion of his work; and rendered him in its own way the same service that the study of Greek rendered to Europe in general a century later. His debt to Italy was both direct and indirect. From Dante, whose genius was so wholly unlike his own, he took a great number of isolated passages (the *Troylus* and the *Parlement* especially are full of reminiscences of the great Florentine) ; and he took also, as we said, the hint for the *Hous of Fame*, that most notable burlesque poem, where the serious meaning lies so near to the humorous outside. From Petrarch,

> ' Whos rethorykë sweete
> Enlumined al Itaille of poetrye,'

he took, besides minor borrowings, the *Clerkes Tale*, almost exactly translating it from the laureate's Latin rendering of Boccaccio's story. From Boccaccio, whom by a strange irony of literary fortune he seems not to have known by name, he freely translated his two longest and, in a sense, greatest poems, *Troylus and Criseyde* and *The Knightes Tale* ; and it is possible, though by no means certain, that the framework of the Canterbury Tales was suggested by the Decameron. But more important than this direct debt was what he indirectly owed to these great writers. He first learnt from them the art of constructing a story, that art which, as he afterwards developed it, has made of him unquestionably our chief narrative poet. It was from them—for, strange to say, he had read Virgil without learning it—that he first learnt the necessity of self-criticism ; of that severe process, so foreign to the mediæval mind, which deliberates, sifts, tests, rejects, and alters, before a work is sent out into the world.

So much for Chaucer's books and their effect on him. Were there however no more in him than what his books put into him, he would be of no greater importance to us than Gower or Lydgate. It takes more than learning, more than a gift for

selection and adaptation, to make a poet. Those intimate verses
which we have quoted from the *Legende* themselves, proceed to
tell us of a passion which is stronger in him than the passion for
reading. ' I reverence my books,' he says,

> ' So hertëly that there is gamë noon
> That fro my bokës maketh me to goon
> But yt be seldom on the holy day,
> Save certeynly whan that the moneth of May
> Is comen, and that I here the foulës synge,
> And that the flourës gynnen for to springe,
> Farewel my boke, and my devocioun!'

What he here calls May, with its birds and flowers, really means
Nature as a whole ; not external nature only, but the world with
its rich variety of sights and sounds and situations, especially its
most varied product, *Man*. As to his feeling for external nature,
indeed, it might be called limited ; it is only to the birds and the
flowers, the ' schowres swote' and the other genial gifts of spring
that it seems to extend. Not only is there no trace in him of
that 'religion of Nature' which is so powerful a factor in modern
poetry, but there is nothing that in the least resembles those
elaborate backgrounds in which the genius of Spenser takes such
delight. Nay, in the poet to whom we owe the immortal group
of pilgrims, there is little even of that minute local observation
of places and their features, that memory for the grave-covered
plains of Arles or the shattered banks of the Adige, which made
a part of Dante's genius, and gives such vividness to the phantom
landscape of his poem. While the Inferno has been mapped out
for centuries, it is only to-day, after long discussion, that our
scholars are able to make a map of the pilgrimage to Canterbury.
But although the distinctive sense of landscape is for the most
part absent, how keen is the poet's eye for colour, for effective
detail ! Who but Chaucer, while avoiding altogether the inven-
tory style of the ordinary romancer, a style on which he himself
poured ridicule in his *Sir Thopas*, could have brought such
a glittering barbaric presence before us as this of the King of
Inde ?—

> ' The gret Emetrius, the King of Inde,
> Upon a stedë bay trapped in stele ,
> Covered with cloth of gold diapred wele,
> Came riding like the god of armës, Mars.
> His cote-armure was of a cloth of Tars

> Couchëd with perlës white and round and grete;
> His sadel was of brent gold new ybete;
> His mantelet upon his shouldre hanging
> Bret ful of rubies red as fyr sparkling;
> His crispë heer like ringës was yronne,
> And that was yelwe and glitered as the sonne …
> And as a leon he his looking cast.'

Or such a sketch in black and white as this first glimpse of Creseide ?—

> ‘ Among these other folkë was Creseide
> In widowes habit blak: but nathëles
> Right as our firstë lettre is now an **A**
> In beautee first so stood she makëles¹;
> Her goodly looking gladed all the prees².
> Nas never seen thing to be praised derre,
> Nor under cloudë blak so bright a sterre,
> As was Creseide, they sayden everichone
> That her behelden in her blakkë wede.'

Or such an intense and concentrated piece of colour as his Chanticlere ?—

> ‘ His comb was redder than the fyn coral
> And batayled as it were a castel wal;
> His bil was blak and as the geet³ it schon;
> Like asure were his leggës and his ton⁴;
> His naylës whiter than the lily flour,
> And like the burnischt gold was his colour.'

As for the world of man and human character, it is here admittedly that Chaucer's triumphs have been greatest. In this respect his fame is so well established that there is little need to dwell on qualities with which he makes his first and deepest impression, and which moreover will be abundantly illlustrated by the extracts which follow. In his treatment of external nature, there are limits beyond which Chaucer cannot go—the limits of his time, of a more certain, a more easily satisfied age than ours. But in his sympathy with man, with human action and human feeling, his range is very great and his handling infinitely varied. The popular opinion of centuries has fixed upon the Prologue to the *Canterbury Tales* as his masterpiece, because it is there that this dramatic power of his, this realistic gift which can grasp at will

---

¹ without mate or peer.   ² crowd.   ³ jet.   ⁴ toes.

almost any phase of character or incident, noble or trivial, passionate or grotesque, finds its fullest scope. Other fourteenth century writers can tell a story (though none indeed so well as he), can be tragic, pathetic, amusing; but none else of that day can bring the actual world of men and women before us with the movement of a Florentine procession-picture and with a colour and a truth of detail that anticipate the great Dutch masters of painting. To pass from the framework of other mediæval collections, even from the villa and gardens of the *Decameron*, to Chaucer's group of pilgrims, is to pass from convention to reality. To reality; for, as Dryden says in that Preface which shows how high he stood above the critical level of his age, in the Prologue 'we have our forefathers and great-grandames all before us, as they were in Chaucer's days; their general characters are still remaining in mankind, and even in England, though they are called by other names than those of Monks and Friars, and Canons, and Lady Abbesses, and Nuns: for mankind is ever the same, and nothing lost out of nature, though everything is altered.'

It is not enough for a poet to observe, however: what he observes must first be transformed by feeling before it can become matter for poetry. What distinguishes Chaucer is that he not only observes truly and feels keenly, but that he keeps his feeling fresh and unspoiled by his knowledge of books and of affairs. As the times went he was really learned, and he passed a varied active existence in the Court, in the London custom-house, and in foreign missions on the king's service. From his life his poetry only gained; the Knight, the Friar, the Shipman—nay, even young Troylus and Constance and 'Emilye the schene,'—are what they are by virtue of his experience of actual human beings. But it is even more notable that the study of books, in an age when study so often led to pedantry, left him as free and human as it found him; and that his joy in other men's poetry, and his wish to reproduce it for his countrymen, still gave way to the desire to render it more beautiful and more true. Translator and imitator as he was, what strikes us in his work from the very earliest date is his independence of his models. Even when he wrote the *Boke of the Duchesse*, at a time when he was a mere novice in literature, he could rise and did rise above his material, so that one enthusiastic Chaucerian, in his desire to repel M. Sandras' charge of 'imitation servile,' flatly refuses to believe that Chaucer ever read Machault's 'Dit' at all. This indeed is too patriotic criticism; but it is certainly true to say that Chaucer worked up Machault and Ovid in this poem, as he worked up his French and Italian materials generally, so as thoroughly to subordinate them to his own purpose. The most striking instance of this free treatment of his model is, of course, his rendering of the *Troylus* and the *Knightes Tale* from Boccaccio. The story of Palamon and Arcite possessed a great fascination for Chaucer, and it seems certain that he wrote it twice, in two quite distinct forms. With the earlier, in stanzas, which has perished except for what he has embodied in one or two other writings, we are not concerned; but it is open to any one to compare the Knightes Tale, in the final shape in which Chaucer's mature hand has left it to us, with the immense romantic epic of Boccaccio. Tyrwhitt's blunt common-sense long since pointed out the ethical inferiority of the *Teseide*; and we may point in the same way to the judgment that Chaucer has shown in stripping off episodes, in retrenching Boccaccio's mythological exuberance, in avoiding frigid personifications, and in heightening the interest of the end by the touches which he adds in his magnificent description of the Temple of Mars. In the 'Troylus' the difference between the two poets is even deeper, for it is a difference as much moral as artistic. Compare those young Florentine worldlings—for such they are—Troilo and Pandaro, with the boyish, single-minded, enthusiastic, pitiable Troylus, and his older friend who stands by to check his passionate excesses with a proverb and again a proverb, like Sancho by the side of the Knight of la Mancha; worldly experience controlling romance! Compare Griseida, that light-o'-love, that heroine of the *Decameron*, with the fragile, tender-hearted and remorseful Cryseyde, who yields through sheer weakness to the pleading and the sorrow of 'this sodeyn Diomede' as she has yielded to her Trojan lover!

> 'Ne me ne list this sely womman chyde
> Ferther than the storië wol devyse;
> Hire name, allas! is published so wyde,
> That for hire gilte it ought ynough suffise;
> And if I mighte excuse her any wyse,
> For she so sory was for her untrouthe,
> Ywis I wolde excuse hire yet for routhe.'

'Routhe' indeed, pity for inevitable sorrow, is a note of Chaucer's mind which for ever distinguishes him from Boccaccio, and marks him out as the true forerunner of the poet of *Hamlet* and *Othello*.

To him the world and human character are no simple things, nor are actions to be judged as the fruit of one motive alone. Who can wonder if, possessed with this new sense of the complexity of human destiny, he should sometimes have failed to render it with the clearness of an artist dealing with a simpler theme? Those critics are probably right who pronounce the *Troylus* inferior to the *Filostrato* in point of literary form ; but their criticism, to be complete, should add that it is far more interesting in the history of poetry.

The first of a poet's gifts is to feel ; the second is to express. Chaucer possesses this second gift as abundantly as he possesses the first. The p int which contemporary and later poets almost invariably note in him is, not his power of telling a story, not his tragedy, his humour, or his character-drawing, but his *language.* To Lydgate he is

> 'The noble rethor poete of Britayne;'

his great achievement has been

> 'Out of our tongue to avoyde all rudënesse,
> And to reform it with colours of swetenesse.'

To Occleve he was 'the floure of eloquence,'

> 'The firstë fynder of our faire langage.'

Dunbar, at the end of the fifteenth century, speaks of his 'fresh enamel'd termës celical' ; and long afterwards Spenser gave him the immortal epithet of 'the well of English undefiled.' Chaucer, like Dante, had the rare fortune of coming in upon an unformed language, and, so far as one man could, of forming it. He grew up among the last generation in England that used French as an official tongue. It was in 1362, when Chaucer was just entering manhood, that the session of the House of Commons was first opened with an English speech. Hence it is easy to see the hollowness of the charge, so often brought against him since Verstegan first made it, that 'he was a great mingler of English with French,' that 'he corrupted our language with French words.' Tyrwhitt long since refuted this charge ; and if it wanted further refutation, we might point to *Piers Plowman's Vision*, the work of a poet of the people, written for the people in their own speech, but containing a greater proportion of French words than Chaucer's writings contain. And yet Chaucer is a courtier, a Londoner, perhaps partly French by extraction; above all, he is a translator, and some influence from the language he is translating passes into his own verse. The truth is that in his hands for the first time our language appears as it is; in structure of course purely Germanic, but rich, assimilative, bold in its borrowings, adopting and adapting at its pleasure any words of any language that might come in its way. How Chaucer used this noble instrument is not to be demonstrated; it is to be felt. *De sensibus non est disputandum*; it is vain to discuss matters of personal experience, to point to qualities in a poet's verse which must really be judged by the individual ear. Otherwise we might dwell on Chaucer's use of his metre, which varies in such subtle response to his subject and his mood; or on his skill in rhyming, though, as he says, 'ryme in Englisch hath such skarsetë'; or on the 'linked sweetness' of the love-passages in the *Troylus*; or on the grandeur of his tragic descriptions, where the sound gives so solemn an echo to the sense :—

> 'First on the wal was peynted a forest,
> In which ther dwelleth neither man ne best,
> With knotty knarry bareyne treës olde
> Of stubbës scharpe and hidous to byholde
> In which ther ran a swymbel in a swough.'

These qualities come into view at a first reading of Chaucer; and why should the pleasure to be gained from them be kept for the few? 'How few there are who can read Chaucer so as to understand him perfectly,' says Dryden, apologising for 'translating' him. In our day, with the wider spread of historical study, with the numerous helps to old English that the care of scholars has produced for us, with the purification that Chaucer's text has undergone, this saying of Dryden's ought not to be true. It ought to be not only possible, but easy, for an educated reader to learn the few essentials of Chaucerian grammar, and for an ear at all trained to poetry to tune itself to the unfamiliar harmonies. For those who make the attempt the reward is certain. They will gain the knowledge, not only of the great poet and creative genius that these pages have endeavoured to sketch, but of the master who uses our language with a power, a freedom, a variety, a rhythmic beauty, that, in five centuries, not ten of his successors have been found able to rival.

EDITOR.

The Boke of the Duchesse.

[The following passage is given as a specimen of Chaucer's earliest or
French period. The date is 1369.]

Me thoghtë thus, that hyt was May,
And in the dawnynge, ther I lay,
Me mette [1] thus in my bed al naked,
And loked forth, for I was waked
With smalë foulës, a grete hepe,
That had afrayed me out of slepe,
Thorgh noyse and swetnesse of her songe.
And as me mette, they sate amonge
Upon my chambre roof wythoute,
Upon the tylës al aboute ;
And songen everych in hys wyse
The mostë solempnë servise
By noote, that ever man, Y trowe,
Had herd.   For somme of hem songe lowe,
Somme high, and al of oon acorde.
To tellë shortly at oo word,
Was never herd so swete a steven,
But hyt hadde be a thyng of heven,
So mery a soun, so swete entewnes,
That, certes, for the toune of Tewnes,
I nolde but I had herd hem synge,
For al my chambre gan to rynge,
Thorgh syngynge of her armonye ;
For instrument nor melodye
Was no-wher herd yet half so swete,
Nor of acorde ne half so mete.
For ther was noon of hem that feynede
To synge, for eche of hem hym peynede [2]

[1] I dreamed.   [2] took trouble.

To fynde out mery crafty notys ;
They ne sparede not her throtys.
And, sooth to seyn, my chambre was
Ful wel depeynted, and with glas
Were alle the wyndowes wel yglased
Ful clere, and nat an hoole ycrased,
That to beholde hyt was grete joye.
For holy al the story of Troye
Was in the glasynge ywrought thus ;
Of Ector, and of kyng Priamus,
Of Achilles, and of kyng Lamedon,
And eke of Medea and of Jason,
Of Paris, Eleyne, and of Lavyne ;
And alie the walles, with coloures fyne
Were peynted, bothë text and glose,
And al the Romaunce of the Rose.
My windowës were shet echon,
And throgh the glas the sonnë shon
Upon my bed with bryghtë bemys,
With many gladë, gildë stremys ;
And eke the welken was so faire,
Blewe, bryghtë, clerë was the ayre,
And ful atempre, for sothe, hyt was ;
For nother to cold nor hoote yt nas,
Ne in al the welkene was a clowde.

TROYLUS AND CRISEYDE.

[Troylus sees Criseyde in the Temple, and loves her at first sight.]

But though that Grekës hem of Troye in shetten [1],
And hire cité beseged al aboute,
Hire olde usagës woldë thai noght letten,
As for to honoure hire goddës ful devoute,
But aldermost in honour, out of doute,
They had a relyk hight Palladioun,
That was hire trist aboven everichoun.

[1] shut.

And so byfel, whan comen was the tyme
Of Aperil, whan clothed is the mede
With newë grene, of lusty Veer the prime,
And swotë smellen floures, white and rede;
In sondry wisë schewed, as I rede,
The folk of Troye hire observaunces olde,
Palladyones festë for to holde.

And to the temple, in alle hire bestë wise,
In general ther wentë many a wyght
To herken of Palladyoun servise,
And namëly so mony a lusty knyght,
So many a lady fresshe, and mayden bryght,
Ful wele araied, bothë moste and leste,
Ye, bothë for the seson and the feeste.

Among thise other folk was Criseyda,
In wydewes habit blak; but nathëles,
Right as oure firstë lettre is now an A,
In beauté first so stood sche makëles[1];
Hire goodly lokyng gladded al the prees:
Nas nevere seyn thyng to ben preysed derre[2],
Nor under cloudë blak so bright a sterre,

As was Criseyde, as folk seyde everychon,
That hire byhelden in hire blakë wede;
And yet sche stood ful low and stille allone
Byhynden other folk in litel brede[3],
And neygh the dore, ay under schames drede,
Symple of atyre, and debonair of cheere,
Wyth ful asseured lokynge and manere.

This Troylus, as he was wont to gyde
His yongë knyhtës, ladde hem up and down,
In thilkë largë temple on every syde,
Byholdynge ay the ladies of the town;
Now here now ther, for no devocioun

[1] matchless.   [2] dearer.   [3] a little way.

Hadde he to non to reven[1] him his reste,
But gan to preyse and lakken[2] whom him leste.

And in his walk ful fast he gan to wayten,
If knyght or sqwyer of his compaynye
Gan for to sigh, or lete his eyen bayten[3]
On any woman that he koude aspye;
He woldë smyle, and holden it folye,
And seye him thus :—'God wot sche slepeth softe
For love of the, whan thow turnest ful ofte.

'I have herd telle, pardieux, of your lyvynge,
Ye lovers, and youre lewde[4] observaunces,
And which a[5] labour folk han in wynnynge
Of love, and in the kepynge which doutaunces;
And when your preye is lost, wo and penaunces;
O, verrey foolës! nice and blynde be ye;
Ther is not oon kan war by other be.'

And with that worde he gan caste up his browe,
Ascaunces[6], lo! is this nought wysly spoken?
At whiche the God of Love gan loken rowe[7]
Right for despit, and shoop for to ben wroken[8].
He kydde[9] anon his bowë nas not broken:
For, sodenly he hitte him attë fulle,
And yet as proude a pacok can he pulle.

O blynde world! O blynd intencioun!
How often falleth al the effecte contraire
Of surquidrye[10] and foul presumpcioun,
For kaught is proud, and kaught is debonaire!
This Troylus is clomben on the staire,
And litel weneth that he schal descenden;
But alday[11] fayleth thinge that fooles wenden.

---

[1] deprive.   [2] criticise.   [3] feast.   [4] unlearned, foolish.
[5] what.   [6] as much as to say.   [7] stern.   [8] aimed at vengeance.
[9] shewed.   [10] arrogance.   [11] every day.

As proudë Bayard[1] gynneth for to skyppe
Out of the wey, so priketh him his corn,
Til he a lassch have of the longë whippe,
Than thynketh he, 'Thogh I praunce al byforn
First in the trayse, ful fat and newë shorn,
Yet am I but an hors, and horses lawe
I mote endure, and with my feerës[2] drawe.'

So ferd it by this fiers and proudë knyght,
Though he a worthi kyngës sonnë were,
And wendë no thinge had had swichë myght,
Ayeins his wille, that scholde his hertë stere[3];
That with a look his hertë wex a feere,
That, he that now was moost in pride above,
Wex sodeynly most subgit unto love.

Forthy[4] ensaumple taketh of this man,
Ye wisë, proude, and worthy folkës alle,
To scornen Love, whiche that so soonë kan
The fredom of youre hertës to him thralle ;
For evere was, and evere schal befalle,
That Love is he that allë thing may bynde ;
For may no man fordon the lawe of kynde[5].

That this be soth hath proved and doth yit ;
For this trowe I ye knowen alle and some,
Men reden not that folk han gretter wit
Than thei that hath ben most with love ynome[6];
And strengest folk ben therwith overcome,
The worthiest and the grettest of degree ;
This was and is, and yit men schal it see.

And treweliche it sit wel to be so,
For alderwysest han therwith ben plesed,
And thai that han ben aldermost in wo,
With love han ben conforted most and esed ;
And oft it hath the cruel herte apesed,
And worthi folk made worthier of name,
And causeth most to dreden vice and schame.

---

[1] 'Bay,' a common name for a horse.   [2] fellows.
[3] steer.   [4] therefore.   [5] nature.   [6] taken prisoner.

C 2

And sith it may not godely ben withstonde,
And is a thing so vertuous in kynde,
Refuseth not to Love for to ben bonde,
Syn, as him selven list, he may yow bynde,
The yerde[1] is bet that bowen wol and wynde
Than that that brest[2]; and therfor I yow rede
To folowen him that so wel kan yow lede.

*   *   *   *   *   *

[Pandarus, the uncle of Criseyde and the friend of Troylus, has told her of
    Troylus' love.   She is left alone, and sees him returning from battle.]

With this he tok his leve, and home he wente;
A, Lord! so he was glad, and wel bygon!
Criseyde aros, no longer she ne stente,
But streght into hire closet wente anon,
And set hire down, as stille as any ston,
And every word gon up and down to wynde,
That he hadde seyde, as it come hire to mynde,

And wex somdel[3] astoned in hire thought,
Right for the newë cas; but when that she
Was ful avysed, tho fond she right nought
Of peril, why she aught aferëd be:
For man may love of possibilité
A woman so, his hertë may to-breste[4],
And she nought love ayeyn, but if hire leste.

But as she sat allon and thoughte thus,
Ascry aroos at scarmich[5] al withoute,
And men cried in the street, 'Se Troilus
Hath right now put to flyght the Grekës route.'
With that gan al hire meyné[6] for to shoute:
'A! go we se, caste up the yatës wide,
For thorwgh this strete he moot to paleys ryde;'

---

[1] wand.
[2] bursts, breaks.
[3] somewhat.
[4] break.
[5] a battle-cry arose.
           attendants.

For oother way is to the gatës noon,
Of Dardanus, ther[1] open is the cheyne:
With that come he, and alle his folk anon,
An esy pace rydynge, in routës tweyne,
Right as his happy day was[2], sothe to seyne:
For which men seyn may nought distourbed be
That shal bytyden of necessité.

This Troilus sat on his bayë stede
Al armed save his hed ful richely,
And wonded was his hors, and gan to blede,
On whiche he rood a paas[3] ful softëly:
But swiche a knyghtly sightë trewëly
As was on hym, was nought, withouten faile,
To loke on Mars, that god is of batayle.

So like a man of armës and a knyght,
He was to sen, fulfild of heigh prowesse;
For bothe he hadde a body, and a myght
To don that thyng, as wele as hardynesse;
And ek to sen hym in his gere hym dresse,
So fressh, so yong, so weldy semëd he,
It was an heven upon hym for to se.

His helm to-hewen was in twenty places,
That by a tyssew heng his bak byhynde,
His shelde to-dasshed was with swerdes and maces,
In which men myghtë many an arwe fynde,
That thyrled haddë horn, and nerf, and rynde;
And ay the peple criede, 'Here cometh oure joye,
And, next his brother, holder up of Troye.'

For which he wex a litel rede for schame
Whan he the peple upon him herdë crien,
That to byholde it was a noble game,
How sobreliche he castë down his eighen:
Criseyd anon gan al his chere aspyen,
And leet so softe it in hire herte synken,
That to hire self she seyde, 'Who yaf me drynken[4]?'

---

[1] where.
[2] as though it were a lucky day for him.
[3] at foot's pace.
[4] who has given me a love-potion?

For of hire owën thought she wex al rede,
Remembrynge hire right thus, ‘Lo! this is he,
Which that myn uncle swerth he moot be dede,
But I on hym have mercy and pité:’
And with that thought, for pure ashamëd she
Gan in hire hed to pulle, and that as faste,
While he and al the peple forby paste.

And gan to caste, and rollen up and down
Within hire thought his excellent prowesse,
And his estat, and also his renoun,
His wit, his shappe, and ek his gentilnesse;
But moost hire favour was for his distresse
Was al for hire, and thought it as a rowthe [1]
To sleen swich oon, if that he mentë trouthe.

Now myghte som envÿous jangle thus,
‘This was a sodeyn love, how myghte it be
That she so lightly lovede Troylus,
Right for the firstë sightë?’ Ye, pardé?
Now who so seith so, moot he never ythe [2]!
For every thyng a gynnyng hath it nede
Er al be wrought, withouten any drede.

For I sey nought that she so sodeynly
Yaf hym hire love, but that she gan enclyne
To like hym firste, and I have told yow why;
And efter that, his manhod and his pyne
Made love withinne hire hertë for to myne;
For which by proces, and by goode servyse,
He gat hire love, and in no sodeyn wyse.

●   ●   ✱   ✱   ✱   ●

[1] pity.   [2] y-thé: succeed, prosper.

[Troylus' long courtship is at last rewarded with the
love of Criseyde.]

O soth is seyd, that helëd for to be,
As of a fevere, or other gret syknesse,
Men mostë drynke, as men may oftë se,
Ful bittre drynk : and for to han gladnesse
Men drynken of peynës, and gret distresse :
I mene it here, as for this aventure,
That thorwgh a peyne hath fonden al his cure.

And now swetnessë semeth morë swete,
That bitternesse assayed was byforn ;
For out of wo in blissë now they flete,
Non swich they felten syn that they were born ;
Now is this bet than bothë two be lorn !
For love of God ! take every womman hede,
To werken thus, if it cometh to the nede.

Criseyde, al quyt from every drede and teene,
As she that justë cause hadde hym to triste,
Made hym swich feste, it joië was to seene,
When she his trouthe and clene ententë wiste :
And as aboute a tre, with many a twiste,
Bytrent and writh[1] the sootë wodëbynde,
Gan ich of hem in armës other wynde.

And as the new abaysëd nyghtyngale,
That stynteth first, when she bygynneth synge,
When that she hereth any herdës tale,
Or in the heggës any wight sterynge ;
And, after, syker[2] doth hire vois out rynge ;
Right so Criseyde, when hire dredë stente,
Opned hire herte, and told hym hire entente.

---

[1] entwines and wreathes.   [2] sure, clear.

And right as he that seth his deth yshapen,
And deyen mot, in aught that he may gesse,
And sodeynly rescous doth hym escapen[1],
And from his deth is brought in sykernesse ;
For al this world, in swich present gladnesse
Was Troilus, and hath his lady swete :
With worsë hap God lat us nevere mete !

*   *   *   *   *   *

In suffisaunce, in blisse, and in syngynges,
This Troilus gan al his lyf to lede :
He spendeth, jousteth, maketh festeyinges,
He yeveth frely ofte, and chaungeth wede[2] ;
He halt aboute hym alway, out of drede,
A world of folk, as com hym wel of kynde[3],
The fressheste and the beste he koudë fynde.

That swich a vois was of hym and a neven[4],
Thoroughout the world, of honour and largesse,
That it up rong unto the yate of heven ;
And as in love he was in swich gladnesse,
That in his herte he demëd, as I gesse,
That ther nys lovere in this world at ese,
So wel as he, and thus gan love hym plese.

The goodlyhed or beauté, which that kynde
In any other lady hadde iset,
Kan nought the mountaunce of a knotte unbynde
About his herte, of al Criseydes net :
He was so narwe ymasked[5], and yknet,
That it undon on any manner syde,
That nyl nought ben, for aught that may betide.

And by the hond ful oft he woldë take
This Pandarus, and into gardyn lede,
And swich a feste, and swiche a proces make
Hym of Criseyde, and of hire wommanhede,
And of hire beauté, that, withouten drede,

---

[1] makes him free.   [2] dress.   [3] as well suits his nature.
          [4] name.   [5] enmeshed.

It was an heven his wordës for to here,
And thanne he woldë synge in this manere :—

'Love [1], that of erth and se hath governaunce !
Love, that his hestës hath in heven hye !
Lovë, that with an holsom alliaunce
Halt peples joynëd, as hym list hem gye [2] !
Lovë, that knetteth law and compaignye,
And couples doth in vertu for to dwelle !
Bynd this acorde, that I have told and telle !

' That, that the world, with faith which that is stable,
Dyverseth so, his stoundës [3] concordynge ;—
That elementz, that ben so discordable,
Holden a bond perpetualy durynge ;—
That Phebus mot his rosy carte forth brynge,
And that the mone hath lordschip over the nyght ;—
Al this doth Love, ay heryed [4] be his myght !

' That, that the se, that gredy is to flowen,
Constreyneth to a certeyn endë so
Hise flodës, that so fiersly they ne growen
To drenchen erth and al for evermo ;
And if that Love aught lete his brydel go,
Al that now loveth asonder sholdë lepe,
And lost were al that Love halt now to hepe [5].

' Soo, woldë Gode, that auctour is of kynde [6],
That with his bond Love, of his vertu, liste
To cerclen hertës alle, and fastë bynde,
That from his bond no wighte the wey out wyste !
And hertës colde, hem wolde I that he twiste,
To make hem love, and that hem liste ay rewe
On hertës soore, and kepe hem that ben trewe.'

* * * * * *

[1] This song is paraphrased from Boethius, Cons. 2, met. 8.
[2] guide. [3] times. [4] praised. [5] holds together. [6] nature.

[Criseyde is to be sent away to her father Calchas, in the Grecian camp, in exchange for Antenor, who has been taken prisoner. She vows fidelity, and tells Troylus why she loves him, promising to return on the tenth night.]

'For trusteth wel that your estat real,
Ne veyn delite, nor oonly worthinesse
Of yow in werre or tournay marcial,
Ne pomp, array, nobley, or ek richesse,
Ne madë me to rewe on youre distresse,
But moral virtu, grounded upon trowthe,
That was the cause I first hadde on yow routhe.

'Eke gentil herte, and manhode that ye hadde,
And that ye hadde (as me thought) in despite
Every thyng that souned in-to [1] badde,
As rudënesse, and poeplish [2] appetite,
And that your reson brideled your delite,
This made, aboven every creature,
That I was youre, and shal whil I may dure.

'And this may length of yerës nought fordo,
Ne remuable fortunë deface ;
But Juppiter, that of his myght may do
The sorwful to be glad, so yeve us grace,
Er nyghtës ten to meten in this place,
So that it may youre herte and myn suffise !
And fareth now wel, for tyme is that ye rise.'

*   *   *   *   *   *

[Troylus wanders about, waiting for Criseyde's return.]

And therwithalle, his meynye for to blende [3],
A cause he fond in townë for to go,
And to Criseydes hous they gonnen wende ;

---

[1] tended towards.   [2] vulgar.   [3] to deceive his companions.

But Lord ! this sely Troilus was wo !
Hym thoughte his sorwful hertë braste atwo ;
For when he saugh hire dorres sperred [1] alle,
Wel neigh for sorwe adoun he gan to falle.

Therwith, when he was ware, and gan biholde,
How shet was every wyndow of the place,
As frost hym thoughte his hertë gan to colde ;
For which, with chaunged deedlich palë face,
Withouten word, he forth bygan to pace ;
And, as God wolde, he gan so fastë ryde,
That no wight of his contenaunce espyde.

Than seyde he thus :—'O paleys desolat !
O hous of housses, whilom best yhight !
O paleys empty and disconsolat !
O thou lanterne, of which queynt is the light !
O paleys, whilom day, that now art nyght !
Wel oughtestow to falle, and I to dye,
Syn she is went that wont was us to gye [2].

'O paleys, whilom crowne of houses alle,
Enlumyned with sonne of allë blisse !
O rynge, fro which the ruby is out falle !
O cause of wo, that cause has ben of blisse !
Yit syn I may no bet, fayn wolde I kysse
Thy coldë dorës, dorste I for this route ;
And farewel shryne, of which the seint is oute !

Therwith he caste on Pandarus his yë,
With chaunged face, and pitous to beholde ;
And when he myght his tymé aright espyë,
Ay as he rood, to Pandarus he tolde
His newë sorwe, and ek his joyes olde,
So pitously, and with so dede an hewe,
That every wight myght on his sorwes rewe.

[1] bolted   [2] guide.

Fro thennes-forth he rydeth up and down,
And every thynge com hym to remembraunce,
As he rood forth by places of the town,
In which he whilom had al his plesaunce :—
'Lo ! yond saugh I myn owën lady daunce ;
And in that temple, with hire eyën clere,
Me caughtë first my rightë lady deere.

'And yonder have I herd ful lustily
My deerë hertë laughe ; and yonder pleye
Saugh Ich hire oonës ek ful blisfully ;
And yonder oonës to me gan she seye,
'Now goodë swetë ! love me wel, I preye ;
And yond so gladly gan she me beholde,
That to the deth myn herte is to hir holde.

'And at that corner in the yonder hous,
Herde I myn alderlevest[1] lady deere,
So wommanly, with vois melodyous,
Syngen so wel, so goodely and so clere,
That in my soulë yit me thynkth I here
The blisful sown ; and in that yonder place
My lady first me took unto hire grace.'

Than thought he thus, 'O blisful lord Cupide !
When I the processe have[al] in memórie,
How thow me hast werreyed[2] on every syde,
Men myght a book make of it lyk a stórie !
What nede is thee to seke on me victórie,
Syn I am thyn, and holly at thi wille ?
What joye hastow thyn owën folk to spille ?

'Wel hastow, lord, ywroke on me thyn ire,
Thow myghty god ! and dredeful for to greve !
Now mercy, god ! thow woost wel I desire
Thy gracë moost, of allë lustës leeve !
And lyve and dye I wol in thy beleve ;
For which I naxe[3] in guerdon but a boone,
That thow Criseydë ayein me sendë soone.

---

[1] best beloved.   [2] made war on.   [3] ask not.

'Destreyne hire herte as fastë to retourne,
As thow doost myn to longen hire to see ;
Than woot I wel that she nyl naught sojournc :
Now blisful lord ! so cruwel thow ne be
Unto the blod of Troye, I preyë the,
As Juno was unto the blod Thebane,
For which the folk of Thebës caughte hire bane.'

And efter this he to the yatës wente,
Ther as Criseyde out rood a ful good pas,
And up and doun ther made he many a wente,
And to himself ful ofte he seyde, ' Allas !
Fro hennës rood my blisse and my solas !
As woldë blisful God now for his joye,
I myght hire seen ayein com into Troye !

'And to the yonder hille I gan hire gyde ;
Allas ! and ther I took of hire my leeve ;
And yond I saugh hire to hire fader ryde,
For sorwe of which myn hertë shal to-cleve ;
And hider hom I com when it was eve ;
And here I dwelle, out-cast from allë joye,
And shal, til I may seen her eft[1] in Troye.'

And of hym-self ymagynëd he ofte,
To be defet[2], and pale, and waxen lesse
Than he was wont, and that men seydë softe,
'What may it be ? who kan the sothë gesse,
Why Troylus hath al this hevynesse ?'
And al this nas but his melencolye,
That he hadde of hym-self swich fantasye.

Another tyme ymagynen he wolde,
That every wyght that wentë by the weye
Hadde of him routhe, and that they seyën sholde,
'I am right sory, Troilus wol deye.'
And thus he drof a day yit forth or tweye,
As ye han herd ; swich lyf right gan he lede,
As he that stood bitwixen hope and drede.

---

[1] again   [2] cast down.

For which hym liked in his songës shewe
Thencheson [1] of his wo, as he best myghte,
And made a song of wordës but a fewe,
Somwhat his woful hertë for to lighte :
And when he was from every mannës sighte,
With softë vois, he of his lady deere,
That absent was, gan synge as ye may here.

'O sterre, of which I lost have al the lightë,
With hertë soore wel oughte I to bewaylle,
That ever derk in tormente, nyght by nyghtë,
Towarde my deth, with wynde in steere [2] I saylle ;
For which the tenthë nyght if that I faile
The gidynge of thi bemës brighte an houre,
My ship and me Caribdes wol devoure.'

This songe when he thus songen haddë soone
He fel ayein into his sikës olde ;
And every nyght, as was his wone to doone,
He stood, the bryghtë monë to beholde ;
And al his sorwe he to the moonë tolde,
And seyde, 'Iwis, when thow art hornëd newe
I shal be glad, if al the world be trewe.

'I saugh thyn hornës olde ek by the morwe,
Whan hennës rood my rightë lady deere,
That cause is of my torment and my sorwe ;
For which, O bryghte Lucina the cleere !
For love of God ! renne fast aboute thy spere [3] ;
For when thyn hornës newë gynnen sprynge,
Than shal she come that may my blisse brynge.'

The day is moore, and longer ever nyght
Than they ben wont to be, hym thoughtë tho ;
And that the sonnë wente his course unright,
By longer weye than it was wont to go ;
And seyde, 'Iwis, me dredeth everemo
The sonnës sonë, Pheton, be on lyve [4],
And that his fader cart amys he dryve.'

---

[1] the cause.   [2] with a fair wind.   [3] sphere.   [4] alive.

Upon the walles fast ek wolde he walke,
And on the Grekes oost he woldë se ;
And to hymself right thus he woldë talke :—
'Lo, yonder is myn owen lady free,
Or ellës yonder, ther the tentës bee,
And thennës comth this cyr that is so soote [1],
That in my soule I feele it doth me boote.

'And haidyly, this wynd that moore and moore
Thus stoundemele [2] encresseth in my face,
Is of my ladys depë sykës sore ;
I preve it thus, for in noon other place
Of al this town, save oonly in this space,
Feele I no wynd that souneth so lyke peyne ;
It seith 'Allas ! whi twynned be we tweyne ?'

This longë tyme he dryveth forth right thus,
Til fully passed was the nynthë nyght ;
And ay bysyde hym was this Pandarus,
That bisily dide al his fullë myght
Hym to confort, and make his hertë light ;
Yevynge hym hope alwey, the tenthë morwe
That she shal come, and stenten al his sorwe.

*   *   *   *   *   *

[Criseyde, in her father's tent, is wooed by Diomede, and gradually
yields to him.]

Retournynge in hir soule ay up and doun
The wordës of this sodeyn Diomede,
His gret estate, and peril of the town,
And that she was allon, and haddë nede
Of frendes help ; and thus bygan to brede [3]
The causë whi, the sothë for to telle,
That sche tok fully purpos for to dwelle [4].

[1] sweet.   [2] from time to time.   [3] to arise.
          [4] to remain with her father, instead of returning to Troy.

The morwe com, and gostly for to speke,
This Diomede is com unto Criseyde ;
And shortly, lest that ye my talë breke,
So wel he for hymselfë spak and seyde,
That alle hire sykës soore adown he layde :
And finaly, the sothë for to seyne,
He refte hire of the grete of al hire peyne.

And efter this, the storie telleth us,
That she him yaf the fairë bayë steede,
The which she onës wan of Troilus ;
And eke a broch (and that was litel nede)
That Troilus[1] was, she yaf this Diomede ;
And ek the bet from sorw hym to releve,
She made hym were a pensel[2] of hire sleve.

I fynde ek in storyës elleswhere,
When thorugh the body hirt was Dyomede
Of Troilus, tho weep she many a teere,
When that she saugh hise wydë woundes blede,
And that she took to kepen hym good hede,
And for to hele hym of his sorwes smerte,
Men seyn, I not[3], that she yaf hym hire herte.

But trewelyche, the storye telleth us,
Ther made never womman morë wo
Than she, when that she falsede Troylus ;
She seyde, 'Allas ! for now is clene ago[4]
My name of trouthe in love for evermo ;
For I have falsed oon the gentileste
That evere was, and oon the worthieste.

'Allas ! of me unto the worldës ende
Shal neither ben ywriten nor ysonge
No good word, for thise bokës wol me shende :
Irolled schal I ben on many a tonge ;
Thorughout the world my bellë schal be ronge ;

---

[1] Troilus's.   [2] a banner (made).   [3] ne wot = know not.   [4] gone.

And wommen most wol haten me of alle ;
Allas ! that swich a cas me sholdë falle !

'They wol seyn, in as muche as in me is,
I have hem don dishonoure, walaway !
Al be I not the firste that dide amys,
What helpeth that to don my blame away ?
But syn I se ther is no better way,
And that to late is now for me to rewe,
To Dyomede algate [1] I wol be trewe.

'But, Troilus, syn I no better may,
And syn that thus departen ye and I,
Yet preye I God so yeve yow right good day ;
As for the gentilestë trewëly,
That evere I say [2], to serven faithfully,
And best kan ay his lady honour kepe ;'
And with that word she braste anon to wepe.

'And certes, yow to haten shal I nevere,
And frendës love, that shal ye han of me,
And my good word, al shold I lyven evere ;
And trewëly I wol right sory be,
For to sen yow in adversité ;
And giltëlees I wot wel I yow leeve,
And al shal passe, and thus tak I my leve.'

But trewëly how longe it was betweyne,
That she forsok hym for this Dyomede,
Ther is non auctour telleth it, I wene ;
Tak every man now to his bokës hede,
He shal no timë fynden, out of drede ;
For though that he bigan to wowe hire soone,
Er he hire wan, yet was ther more to doone.

Ne me ne list this sely womman chyde
Ferther than the storië wol devyse ;
Hire name, allas ! is publyshed so wyde,
That for hire gilte it ought ynough suffise ;
And if I myght excuse hire any wyse,

---

[1] always, anyhow.   [2] saw.

For she so sory was for hire untrouthe,
Iwis I wold excuse hire yet for routhe.

*   *   *   *   *   *

[Troylus discovers Criseyde's infidelity, and meets his death,
fighting desperately.]

The wrath, as I bigan yow for to seye,
Of Troilus, the Grekës boughten deere ;
For thousandës his hondës maden dye,
As he that was withouten any peere,
Save Ector in his tyme, as I kan here ;
But, walawey ! save only Goddës wille,
Dispitously hym slough the fiers Achille.

And when that he was slayn in this manere,
His lightë gost ful blisfully is went
Up to the holownesse of the seventh spere,
In convers letynge everych element[1] ;
And ther he saugh, with ful avysëment,
The erratyk sterrës, herkenynge armonye,
With sownës ful of hevenyssh melodye.

And down from thennës faste he gan avyse
This litel spot of erth, that with the se
Embracëd is ; and fully gan despise
This wreched world, and held al vanyté,
To respect of the pleyn felicité
That is in hevene above : and at the laste,
Ther he was slayn, his lokyng down he caste.

And in hymself he lough right at the wo
Of hem that wepten for his deth so faste,
And dampned al our werk that folweth so
The blyndë lust, the which that may not laste,
And sholden al our herte on hevene caste ;

[1] From the seventh or uttermost heaven all the others would appear
convex, or *convers.*

And forth he wentë, shortly for to telle,
Ther as Mercurie sorted hym to dwelle.

Swich fyn hath, lo! this Troilus for love !
Swich fyn hath al his gretë worthynesse !
Swich fyn hath his estat reäl[1] above !
Swich fyn his lust, swich fyn hath his noblesse !
Swich fyn hath falsë worldës brotelnesse[2] !
And thus bigan his lovynge of Cryseyde,
As I have told, and in this wise he deyde.

O yongë fresshë folkës, he or she,
In which that love up groweth with your age,
Repeireth hom fro worldly vanyté,
And of your herte up casteth the visage
To thilkë God, that after his ymage
Yow made, and thynketh al nys but a faire,
This world that passeth soon, as flourës faire.

And loveth hym the which that, right for love,
Upon a crois, our soulës for to beye,
First starf[3] and roos, and sit[4] in heven above,
For he nyl falsen no wight, dar I seye,
That wol his herte al holly on hym leye ;
And syn he best to love is, and most meke,
What nedeth feyned loves for to seke ?

Lo ! here of payens corsed oldë rites !
Lo ! here what alle hire goddës may availle !
Lo ! here this wreched worldës appetites !
Lo ! here the fyn and guerdon for travaille,
Of Jove, Apollo, of Mars, and swich rascaille !
Lo ! here the forme of oldë clerkës speche
In poetrie, if ye hire bokës seche.

[1] royal.　　[2] brittleness.　　[3] died.　　[4] sits.

The Parlement of Foules.

[Chaucer dreams that he sees the birds assembled on St. Valentine's Day to
choose their mates, the Goddess Nature presiding. Among the mates
is a formel, or female eagle, wooed by three tercels : the formel being
probably Anne of Bohemia, and the tercel royal King Richard II.]

And in a launde, upon an hille of floures,
Was set this noble goddessë Nature ;
Of braunches were hir hallës and hir boures
Ywrought, after hir crafte and hir mesure ;
Ne ther nas fowl that cometh of engendrure,
That there ne werë prest [1], in hir presence,
To take hir dome [2], and yeve hir audience.

*   *   *   *   *   *

There myghtë men the royal egle fynde,
That with his sharpë look perceth the Sonne ;
And other egles of a lower kynde,
Of which that clerkës wel devysen konne ;
There was the tiraunt with his fethres donne
And grey, I mene the goshauke that doth pyne [3]
To briddës, for his outrageous ravyne.

The gentil faucoun [4], that with his feet distreyneth
The kyngës hond ; the hardy sperhauk eke,
The quaylës foo ; the merlyon that peyneth
Hymself ful ofte the larke for to seke ;
There was the dowvë, with hir eyën meke ;
The jalouse swanne, ayens hys deth that syngeth ;
The owle eke, that of dethe the bodë bryngeth.

---

[1] ready.   [2] judgment.
[3] causes torment.   [4] the peregrine.

The crane the geaunt, with his trompes soune :
The thefe the chough, and eke the janglyng pye ;
The scornyng jay, the eles foo the heroune ;
The falsë lapwyng, ful of trecherye ;
The starë, that the counseyl kan bewrye[1];
The tamë ruddok[2], and the coward kyte ;
The cok, that orlogge ys of thropës lyte[3].

The sparow, Venus sone, and the nyghtyngale
That clepeth forth the fresshë levës newe :
The swalow, mordrer of the beës smale,
That maken hony of flourës fressh of hewe ;
The wedded turtel, with hys hertë trewe ;
The pecok, with his aungels fethers bryghte ;
The fesaunt, scorner of the cok by nyghte.

The waker[4] goos, the cukkow ever unkynde,
The papinjay, ful of delycacye ;
The drakë, stroyer of his owën kynde ;
The storkë, wreker of avowterie ;
Tho hootë cormeraunt, ful of glotonye ;
The ravene and the crowe, with voys of care ;
The throstel old, the frosty feldëfare.

* * * * * *

[The question as to which tercel is to have the formel eagle is referred to
the Parliament of Birds. Some of the opinions given are as follows.]

The watir foulës han her hedës leyd
Togedir, and of shorte avysëment,
Whan everych had hys large golee[5] seyd,
They seyden sothly al by on assent,
How that the goos, with hir faconde gent[6],
That soo desireth to pronounce our nede,
Shal telle our tale, and preyde to God hir spede.

---

[1] that talks and reveals secrets.   [2] robin.   [3] that is clock to
small villages.   [4] wakeful.   [5] mouthful.   [6] gentle eloquence.

And for these watir foulës tho began
The goos to speke, and in hir cakëlynge,
She seydë, 'Pes now, tak kepe[1] every man,
And herkneth which a resoun I shal forth bringe!
My wyt ys sharpe, I love no taryinge!
I sey I rede[2] hym, though he were my brother,
But she wol love hym, lat hym love another.'

'Loo! here a parfyte resoun of a goos!'
Quod the sperhaukë. 'Never mote she thee[3]!
Loo, suche hyt ys to have a tongë loos!
Now pardé, fool, yet were hit bet[4] for the
Have holde thy pes, than shewed thy nycëté;
Hyt lyth not in hys wyt, nor in hys wille;
But sooth ys seyd, a fool kan noght be stille.'

The laughtre aroos of gentil foulës alle,
And ryght anoon the sede-foul[5] chosen hadde
The turtel trewe, and ganne hir to hem calle;
And prayden hir to seyë the soth sadde
Of thys matere, and asked what she radde[6].
And she answerde, that pleynly hir entente
She woldë shewe, and sothly what she mente.

'Nay, God forbede a lover shuldë chaunge!'
The turtel seyde, and wex for shame al reed:
'Thoogh that hys lady evermore be straunge,
Yet let hym serve hir ever, tyl he be deed.
Forsoth, I preysë noght the gooses reed;
For though she deyed, I wolde noon other make[7];
I wol ben hirs til that the deth me take.'

'Wel bourded[8],' quod the dukë, 'by my hat!
That men shulde alwey loven causëles,
Who kan a resoun fynde, or wyt in that?
Daunceth he murye[9] that ys murtheles?
Who shulde rechche[10] of that ys rechcheles?

---

[1] pay attention.   [2] advise.   [3] may she thrive.   **[4] better.**
[5] the fowls that feed on grain.   [6] advised.   [7] mate.   **[8] jested.**
[9] merrily.   [10] reck, care.

Ye! quek! yet,' quod the dukë, 'wel and faire!
There ben moo sterrës, God woot, than a paire.'

'Now fy, cherl!' quod the gentil tercëlet,—
'Out of the dunghil com that word ful ryght;
Thou kanst noght see which thing is wel beset;
Thou farest be love as owlës doon by lyght,—
The day hem blent, ful wel they see by nyght;
Thy kynde ys of so lowe a wrechednesse,
That what love is thou kanst not see ne gesse.'

Thoo gan the cukkow put hym forth in pres[1]
For foule that eteth worm, and seydë blyve[2] :—
'So I,' quod he, 'may have my make in pes,
I rechë not how longë that ye strive.
Lat ech of hem be soleyn al her lyve,
This ys my reed, syne they may not acorde;
This shortë lessoun nedeth noght recorde.'

'Yee, have the glotoun fild ynogh hys paunche,
Thanne are we wel!' seydë the merlyoun[3] :—
'Thou mordrere of the haysogge[4] on the braunche
That broghtë the forth! thou rewful glotoun!
Lyve thou soleyn, wormës corrupcioun!
For no fors ys of lak of thy nature[5] ;
Goo, lewëd be thou while the world may dure!'

'Now pes,' quod Nature, 'I commaundë here,
For I have herd al your opynioun,
And in effect yet be we never the nere;
But fynally, this ys my conclusioun,—
That she hir self shal have the eleccioun
Of whom hir lyst, who-so be wrooth or blythe;
Hym that she cheest[6], he shal han hir as swithe[7].'

[1] among the crowd. [2] quickly. [3] the merlin. [4] hedge-sparrow.
[5] failure of thy whole species would not matter. [6] chooses. [7] swiftly

The Hous of Fame.

[Chaucer dreams that he is carried up by an eagle to the House of Fame, midway between heaven, earth, and sea. The eagle thus explains why Jove does him this honour.]

'But er I bere thee mochë ferre[1],
I wol thee tellë what I am,
And whider thou shalt, and why I cam
To do thys, so that thou [thee] take
Good herte, and not for ferë quake.'
'Gladly,' quod I. 'Now wel,' quod he:
'First, I, that in my feet have thee,
Of which thou hast a fere and wonder,
Am dwellyng with the god of thonder,
Whiche that men callen Jupiter,
That dooth me flee ful oftë fer
To do al hys comaundëment.
And for this cause he hath me sent
To thee : now herkë, be thy trouthe !
Certeyn he hath of thee routhe,
That thou so longë trewëly
Hast served so ententyfly[2]
Hys blyndë nevew Cupido,
And fairë Venus also,
Withoutë guerdoun ever yit,
And nevertheles hast set thy wit,
(Although [that] in thy hede ful lyt is)
To makë songës, bokes, and dytees,
In ryme, or ellës in cadence,
As thou best conne, in reverence
Of Love, and of hys servantes eke,
That have hys servyse soght, and seke ;

---

[1] further.   [2] attentively.

And peynest the to preyse hys art,
Although thou haddest never part ;
Wherfore, al-so God me blesse,
Jovës halt [1] hyt gret humblesse,
And vertu eke, that thou wolt make
A nyght ful ofte thyn hede to ake,
In thy studyë so thou writest,
And evermo of love enditest,
In honour of hym and preysynges,
And in his folkës furtherynges,
And in hir matere al devisest,
And noght hym nor his folk dispisest,
Although thou maist goo in the daunce
Of hem that hym lyst not avaunce.
Wherfore, as I seyde, ywys,
Jupiter considereth this ;
And also, beausir, other thynges ;
That is, that thou hast no tydynges
Of Lovës folke, yf they be glade,
Ne of noght ellës that God made ;
And noght oonly fro fer contree,
That ther no tydyng cometh to thee,
Not of thy verray neyghëbores,
That dwellen almost at thy dores,
Thou herest neyther that nor this,
For when thy labour doon al ys,
And hast made al thy rekënynges,
Instede of reste and newë thynges,
Thou goost home to thy house anoon,
And, also [2] domb as any stoon,
Thou sittest at another booke,
Tyl fully dasewyd [3] ys thy looke,
And lyvest thus as an heremyte,
Although thyn abstynence ys lyte.
And therfore Jovës, through hys grace,
Wol that I bere thee to a place,
Which that hight the Hous of Fame,
To do thee som disport and game,

---

[1] holds, deems.   [2] quite as.   [3] dazed.

> In som recompensacioun
> Of labour and devocioun
> That thou hast had, loo ! causëles,
> To·Cupido the rechchëles.

PROLOGUE TO THE LEGENDE OF GOODE WOMEN.

[The poet loves books, but loves the daisy more.]

And as for me, though than I kon but lyte[1],
On bokës for to rede I me delyte,
And to hem yive I feyth and ful credence,
And in myn herte have hem in reverence
So hertëly, that ther is gamë noon
That fro my bokës maketh me to goon,
But yt be seldom on the holy day,
Save, certeynly, when that the moneth of May
Is comen, and that I here the foulës synge,
And that the flourës gynnen for to sprynge,
Farewel my boke, and my devocioun !
Now have I than suche a condicioun,
That of allë the flourës in the mede,
Than love I most thise flourës white and rede,
Suche as men callen daysyes in her toun.
To hem have I so gret affeccioun,
As I seyde erst, whan comen is the May,
That, in my bed ther daweth[2] me no day,
That I nam up and walkyng in the mede,
To seen this floure ayein the sonnë sprede,
Whan it up ryseth erly by the morwe ;
That blisful sight softeneth al my sorwe,
So glad am I, whan that I have presence
Of it, to doon it allë reverence,
As she that is of allë flourës flour,
Fulfillëd of al vertue and honour,

---

[1] little.   [2] dawneth.

And ever ilike[1] faire, and fressh of hewe.
And I love it, and ever ylike newe,
And ever shal, til that myn hertë dye ;
Al swere I nat, of this I wol nat lye,
Ther lovedë no wight hotter in his lyve.
And, whan that hit ys eve, I rennë blyve[2],
As sone as ever the sonnë gynneth weste,
To seen this flour, how it wol go to reste,
For fere of nyght, so hateth she derknesse !
Hire chere is pleynly sprad in the brightnesse
Of the sonnë, for ther yt wol unclose.
Allas, that I ne had Englyssh, ryme, or prose,
Suffisant this flour to preyse aryght !
But helpeth, ye that han konnyng and myght,
Ye lovers, that kan make of sentëment ;
In this case oghten ye be diligent,
To forthren me somwhat in my labour,
Whethir ye ben with the leef or with the flour[3],
For wel I wot, that ye han herbiforn
Of makynge ropen[4], and lad awey the corn ;
And I come after, glenyng here and there,
And am ful glad yf I may fynde an ere
Of any goodly word that ye han left.
And thogh it happen me rehercen eft
That ye han in your fresshë songës sayd,
Forbereth me, and beth not evil apayd[5],
Syn that ye see I do yt in the honour
Of love, and eke in service of the flour,
Whom that I serve as I have wit or myght.
She is the clerenesse and the verray lyght,
That in this derkë worlde me wynt[6] and ledyth,
The hert in-with my sorwful brest yow dredith,
And loveth so sore, that ye ben verrayly
The maistresse of my wit, and nothing I.
My word, my werkes, ys knyt so in your bond
That, as an harpe obeieth to the hond

[1] alike. [2] run quickly.
[3] See the introduction to the poem of that name, p. 84.
[4] reaped the fruit of poetry. [5] be not ill pleased. [6] winds, turns.

That maketh it soune after his fyngerynge,
Ryght so mowe[1] ye oute of myn hertë bringe
Swich vois, ryght as yow lyst, to laughe or pleyne;
Be ye myn gide, and lady sovereyne.
As to my erthely God, to yow I calle,
Bothe in this werke, and in my sorwes alle.

*   *   *   *   *   *

[He falls asleep, and dreams that he sees the God of Love leading in Queen Alcestis, clad like the daisy.]

Whan that the sonne out of the south gan weste,
And that this flour gan close, and goon to reste,
For derknesse of the nyght, the which she dredde,
Home to myn house ful swiftly I me spedde
To goon to reste, and erly for to ryse,
To seen this flour sprede, as I devyse.
And in a litel herber that I have,
That benched was on turvës fresshe ygrave,
I bad men sholdë me my couchë make;
For deyntee of the newë someres sake[2],
I bad hem strawen flourës on my bed.
Whan I was leyd, and had myn eyen hed[3],
I fel on slepe, in-with an houre or twoo,
Me mette[4] how I lay in the medewe thoo[5],
To seen this flour that I love so and drede;
And from a-fer come walkyng in the mede
The God of Love, and in his hande a quene,
And she was clad in reäl[6] habit grene;
A fret of gold she haddë next her heer,
And upon that a whit coroune she beer,
With flourouns smale, and [that] I shal nat lye,
For al the world ryght as a dayësye
Ycorouned ys with whitë levës lyte[7],
So were the flowrouns of hire coroune white;
For of oo perlë, fyne, oriental,
Hire whitë corounë was imaked al,

---

[1] can.   [2] for the sake of the rarity of the new summer.   [3] hid.
[4] I dreamed.   [5] then.   [6] royal.   [7] little

For which the whitë coroune above the grene
Made hirë lyke a dayesie for to sene,
Considered eke hir fret of golde above.
Yclothed was this myghty God of Love
In silke, enbrouded ful of grenë greves[1],
In-with a fret of redë rosë leves,
The fresshest syn the world was first begonne.
His giltë here was coroned with a sonne
In stede of gold, for hevynesse and wyghte[2];
Therwith me thoght his facë shoon so brighte
That wel unnethës[3] myghte I him beholde;
And in his hand me thoghte I saugh him holde
Twoo firy dartës, as the gledës[4] rede,
And aungelyke hys wyngës saugh I sprede.
And, al be that men seyn that blynd ys he,
Algate me thoghtë that he myghtë se ;
For sternëly on me he gan byholde,
So that his loking dooth myn hertë colde.
And by the hande he held this noble quene,
Coroned with white, and clothëd al in grene,
So womanly, so bénigne, and so meke,
That in this world, thogh that men woldë seke,
Half of hire beauté shuldë men nat fynde
In creäture that formed ys by kynde[5].
And therfore may I seyn, as thynketh me,
This song in preysyng of this lady fre.

Hyde, Absalon, thy giltë tresses clere ;
Ester, ley thou thy mekenesse al adown ;
Hyde, Jonathas, al thy frendly manere ;
Penelopee, and Marcia Catoun[6],
Make of your wifhode no comparysoun ;
Hyde ye your beautes, Ysoude[7] and Eleyne,
My lady comith, that al this may disteyne[8].

---

[1] groves: 'embroidered with green branches.'
[2] because gold would be heavy.   [3] scarcely.   [4] sparks.
[5] nature.   [6] i.e. wife of Cato.   [7] Iseult.
[8] stain; make foul by comparison.

Thy fairë body lat yt nat appere,
Lavyne ; and thou Lucresse of Romë toune,
And Polixene, that boghten love so dere,
And Cleopatre, with al thy passyoun,
Hyde ye your trouthe of love, and your renoun,
And thou, Tesbé, that hast of love suche peyne,
My lady comith, that al this may disteyne.

Hero, Dido, Laudomia, alle yfere[1],
And Phillis, hangyng for thy Demophoun,
And Canace, espied by thy chere[2],
Ysiphile betraysed with Jasoun,
Maketh of your trouthë neyther boost ne soun,
Nor Ypermystre, or Adriane[3], ye tweyne,
My lady cometh, that all this may dysteyne.

The Prologue to the Canterbury Tales.

Whan that Aprillë with his schowrës swoote
The drought of Marche had perced to the roote,
And·bathed every veyne in swich licour,
Of which vertue engendred is the flour ;
Whan Zephirus eek with his swetë breethe
Enspired hath in every holte and heethe
The tendre croppës, and the yongë sonne
Hath in the Ram his halfë cours i-ronne,
And smalë fowlës maken melodie,
That slepen al the night with open eye,
So priketh hem nature in here corages[4] :—
Than longen folk to gon on pilgrimages,
And palmers for to seeken straungë strondes,
To ferne halwes, kouthe[5] in sondry londes ;
And specially, from every schirës ende
Of Engelond, to Caunterbury they wende,

---

[1] together.   [2] discovered by thy look.   [3] Ariadne.
    [4] their hearts.   [5] distant saints, known.

The holy blisful martir for to seeke,
That hem hath holpen whan that they were seeke[1].
Byfel that, in that sesoun on a day,
In Southwerk at the Tabard as I lay,
Redy to wenden on my pilgrimage
To Caunterbury with ful devout corage,
At night was come into that hostelrye
Wel nyne and twenty in a compainye,
Of sondry folk, by aventure i-falle
In felaweschipe, and pilgryms were thei alle,
That toward Caunterbury wolden ryde ;
The chambres and the stables weren wyde,
And wel we werën esed attë beste[2].
And schortly, whan the sonnë was to reste,
So hadde I spoken with hem everychon,
That I was of here felaweschipe anon,
And madë forward erly for to ryse,
To take our wey ther as I yow devyse.
But nathëles, whil I have tyme and space,
Or[3] that I forther in this talë pace,
Me thinketh it acordaunt to resoun,
To tellë yow al the condicioun
Of eche of hem, so as it semede me,
And whiche they weren, and of what degre ;
And eek in what array that they were inne :
And at a knight than wol I first bygynne.

A KNIGHT ther was, and that a worthy man,
That from the tymë that he first bigan
To ryden out, he lovede chyvalrye,
Trouthe and honour, fredom and curteisye.
Ful worthy was he in his lordës werre,
And therto hadde he riden, noman ferre[4],
As wel in Cristendom as in hethënesse,
And evere honoured for his worthinesse.
At Alisaundre he was whan it was wonne,
Ful oftë tyme he hadde the bord bygonne[5]

---

[1] sick.   [2] treated in the best way.   [3] Before.   [4] further.
[5] Either 'been served first at table,' or 'begun the tournament.'

Aboven allë naciouns in Pruce.
In Lettowe hadde he reysed[1] and in Ruce,
No cristen man so ofte of his degre.
In Gernade attë siegë hadde he be
Of Algesir, and riden in Belmarie.
At Lieys was he, and at Satalie,
Whan they were wonne ; and in the Greetë see
At many a noble arive[2] hadde he be.
At mortal batailles hadde he ben fiftene,
And foughten for our feith at Tramassene
In lystës thriës, and ay slayn his foo.
This ilkë worthy knight hadde ben also
Somtymë with the lord of Palatye,
Ageyn another hethen in Turkye :
And evermore he hadde a sovereyn prys[3].
And though that he was worthy, he was wys,
And of his port as meke as is a mayde.
He nevere yit no vileinye ne sayde
In al his lyf, unto no maner wight.
He was a verray perfight gentil knight.
But for to tellen you of his array,
His hors was good, but he ne was nought gay.
Of fustyan he werede a gepoun[4]
Al bysmotered[5] with his habergeoun[6].
For he was late ycome from his viage,
And wentë for to doon his pilgrimage.
  With him ther was his sone, a yong SQUYER,
A lovyere, and a lusty bacheler,
With lokkës crulle[7] as they were leyd in presse.
Of twenty yeer of age he was, I gesse.
Of his stature he was of even lengthe,
And wonderly delyver[8], and gret of strengthe.
And he hadde ben somtyme in chivachye[9],
In Flaundres, in Artoys, and Picardye,
And born him wel, as of so litel space,
In hope to stonden in his lady grace.

---

[1] campaigned.   [2] disembarkation.   [3] high fame.   [4] tunic.
[5] soiled.   [6] coat of mail.   [7] curled.   [8] active.
[9] military service.

Embrowded was he, as it were a mede
Al ful of fresshë floures, white and reede.
Syngynge he was, or floytynge¹, al the day ;
He was as fressh as is the moneth of May.
Schort was his goune, with sleevës longe and wyde.
Wel cowde he sitte on hors, and fairë ryde.
He cowdë songës make and wel endite,
Juste and eek daunce, and wel purtreye and write.
So hote he lovedë, that by nightertale²
He sleep nomore than doth a nightyngale.
Curteys he was, lowly, and servysable,
And carf³ byforn his fader at the table.

   A YEMAN hadde he, and servauntz nomoo
At that tyme, for him lustë⁴ rydë soo ;
And he was clad in coote and hood of grene.
A shef of pocok arwës brighte and kene
Under his belte he bar ful thriftily.
Wel cowde he dresse his takel yemanly ;
His arwes drowpede nought with fetheres lowe.
And in his hond he bar a mighty bowe.
A not-heed⁵ hadde he with a broun visage.
Of woodë-craft wel cowde he al the usage.
Upon his arm he bar a gay bracer⁶,
And by his side a swerd and a bokeler,
And on that other side a gay daggere,
Harneysed wel, and scharp as poynt of spere ;
A Cristofre on his brest of silver schene.
An horn he bar, the bawdrik was of grene ;
A forster⁷ was he sothly, as I gesse.

   Ther was also a Nonne, a PRIORESSE,
That of hire smylyng was ful symple and coy ;
Hire grettest ooth ne was but by seynt Loy⁸ ;
And sche was cleped madame Eglentyne.
Ful wel sche sang the servisë divyne,
Entuned in hire nose ful semëly ;
And Frensch sche spak ful faire and fetysly⁹,

---

¹ fluting.   ² night-time.   ³ carved.
⁴ it was his pleasure.   ⁵ crop-head.   ⁶ guard for the arms.
⁷ forester.   ⁸ St. Eligius.   ⁹ neatly.

After the scole of Stratford attë Bowe,
For Frensch of Parys was to hire unknowe.
At metë wel i-taught was sche withalle ;
Sche leet no morsel from hire lippës falle,
Ne wette hire fyngres in hire saucë deepe.
Wel cowde sche carie a morsel, and wel keepe,
That no dropë ne fille upon hire breste.
In curteisie was set ful moche hire leste.
Hire overlippë wypede sche so clene,
That in hire cuppë was no ferthing sene
Of grecë, whan sche dronken hadde hire draughte.
Ful semëly after hir mete sche raughte [1],
And sikerly sche was of gret disport,
And ful plesaunt, and amyable of port,
And peynede hir [2] to countrefetë cheere
Of court, and ben estatlich of manere,
And to ben holden digne of reverence.
But for to speken of hir conscience,
Sche was so charitable and so pitous,
Sche woldë weepe if that sche saw a mous
Caught in a trappe, if it were deed or bledde.
Of smalë houndës hadde sche, that sche fedde
With rosted flessh, or mylk and wastel breed [3].
But sore weep sche if oon of hem were deed,
Or if men smot it with a yerdë smerte :
And al was conscience and tendre herte.
Ful semëly hire wympel [4] i-pynched was ;
Hir nose tretys [5] ; hir eyën greye as glas ;
Hir mouth ful smal, and therto softe and reed
But sikerly sche hadde a fair forheed.
It was almost a spannë brood, I trowe ;
For hardily sche was not undergrowe.
Ful fetys was hir cloke, as I was war.
Of smal coral aboute hir arm sche bar
A peire of bedës gauded [6] al with grene ;
And theron heng a broch of gold ful schene,

---

[1] reached.   [2] took trouble.   [3] cake (*gasteau*).   [4] gorget.
   [5] well shaped.   [6] The *gaudies* were the larger beads.

On which was first i-write a crownëd A,
And after, *Amor vincit omnia.*
Another NONNE with hir haddë sche,
That was hir chapeleyne, and PRESTES thre.

A MONK ther was, a fair for the maistryë [1],
An out-rydere, that lovedë veneryë ;
A manly man, to ben an abbot able.
Ful many a deynté hors hadde he in stable :
And whan he rood, men mighte his bridel heere
Gynglen in a whistlyng wynd as cleere,
And eek as lowde as doth the chapel belle.
Ther as this lord was kepere of the celle,
The reule of seynt Maure or of seint Beneyt,
Bycause that it was old and somdel streyt,
This ilkë monk leet oldë thingës pace,
And held after the newë world the space.
He yaf nat of that text a pullëd hen [2],
That seith, that hunters been noon holy men ;
Ne that a monk, whan he is recchëles [3]
Is likned to a fissch that is waterles ;
This is to seyn, a monk out of his cloystre.
But thilkë text held he not worth an oystre.
And I seide his opinioun was good.
What [4] schulde he studie, and make himselven wood [5],
Upon a book in cloystre alway to powre.
Or swynkë with his handës, and laboure,
As Austyn bit [6] ? How schal the world be servëd ?
Lat Austyn have his swynk to him reservëd.
Therfor he was a pricasour [7] aright ;
Greyhoundes he hadde as swifte as fowel in flight ;
Of prikyng and of huntyng for the hare
Was al his lust, for no cost wolde he spare.
I saugh his slevës purfiled attë honde
With grys [8], and that the fyneste of a londe.
And for to festne his hood under his chynne
He hadde of gold y-wrought a curious pynne :

---

[1] to a sovereign degree.   [2] valued it less than a plucked hen.
[3] or, *resetless*, away from his seat or station.   [4] why.   [5] mad.
[6] bids (biddeth).   [7] hunter.   [8] grey fur.

E 2

A love-knot in the grettere ende ther was.
His heed was balled, that schon as eny glas,
And eek his face, as he hadde ben ánoynt.
He was a lord ful fat and in good poynt ;
His eyën steepe[1], and rollyng in his heede,
That stemëde as a forneys of a leede[2];
His bootës souple, his hors in gret estat.
Now certeinly he was a fair prelat ;
He was not pale as a for-pyned[3] goost.
A fat swan lovede he best of eny roost.
His palfrey was as broun as is a berye.

 A FRERE there was, a wantown and a merye,
A lymytour[4], a ful solempnë man.
In alle the ordres foure is noon that can
So moche of daliaunce and fair langage.
He hadde i-mad ful many a mariage
Of yongë wymmen, at his owën cost.
Unto his ordre he was a noble post.
Ful wel biloved and famulier was he
With frankeleyns over-al in his cuntre,
And eek with worthy wommen of the toun :
For he hadde power of confessioun,
As seyde himself, morë than a curat,
For of his ordre he was licentiat[5].
Ful swetëly herde he confessioun,
And plesaunt was his absolucioun ;
He was an esy man to yeve penaunce
Ther as he wistë han[6] a good pitaunce ;
For unto a poure ordre for to yive
Is signë that a man is wel i-schrive.
For if he yaf, he dorstë make avaunt,
He wistë that a man was repentaunt.
For many a man so hard is of his herte,
He may not wepe although him sorë smerte.
Therfore in stede of wepyng and preyeres,
Men moot yive silver to the pourë freres.

---

[1] bright. [2] under a cauldron. [3] worn out. [4] a beggar over a certain district. [5] held a licence from the Pope. [6] wherever he knew he would have.

His typet was ay farsëd ful of knyfes
And pynnës, for to yivë fairë wyfes.
And certeynly he hadde a mery note ;
Wel couthe he synge and pleyen on a rote [1].
Of yeddynges [2] he bar utterly the prys.
His nekkë whit was as the flour-de-lys.
Therto he strong was as a champioun.
He knew the tavernes wel in every toun,
And everych hostiler and tappestere,
Bet then a lazer, or a beggestere,
For unto such a worthy man as he
Acorded not, as by his faculté,
To han with sikë lazars aqueyntaunce.
It is not honest, it may not avaunce,
For to delen with no such poraille [3],
But al with riche, and sellers of vitaille.
And overal, ther as profyt schulde arise,
Curteys he was, and lowly of servyse.
Ther nas no man nowher so vertuous.
He was the bestë beggere in his hous,
For though a widewe haddë noght oo schoo,
So plesaunt was his *In principio* [4],
Yet wolde he have a ferthing or he wente.
His purchas [5] was wel better than his rente.
And rage he couthe as it were right a whelpe,
In lovë-dayës [6] couthe he mochel helpe.
For ther he was not lik a cloysterer,
With a thredbare cope as is a poure scoler,
But he was lik a maister or a pope.
Of double worsted was his semy-cope,
That rounded as a belle out of the presse.
Somwhat he lipsede, for his wantownesse,
To make his Englissch swete upon his tunge ;
And in his harpyng, whan that he hadde sunge,
His eyën twynkled in his heed aright,
As don the sterrës in the frosty night.

---

[1] harp, or fiddle.   [2] songs.   [3] paupers.   [4] St. John i. 1, the usual friars' greeting.   [5] what he got by begging.   [6] days of arbitration.

This worthy lymytour was cleped Huberd.

A MARCHAUNT was ther with a forkëd berd,
In mottëleye, and high on hors he sat,
Upon his heed a Flaundrisch bevere hat ;
His botës clapsed faire and fetysly.
His resons he spak ful solempnëly,
Sownynge alway thencres of his wynnynge.
He wolde the see were kept for [1] eny thinge
Betwixë Middelburgh and Orëwelle.
Wel couthe he in eschaungë scheeldës [2] selle.
This worthi man ful wel his wit bisette ;
Ther wistë no wight that he was in dette,
So estatly was he of governaunce,
With his bargayns, and with his chevysaunce [3].
For sothe he was a worthy man withalle,
But soth to sayn, I not how men him calle.

A CLERK ther was of Oxenford also,
That unto logik haddë longe i-go.
As lenë was his hors as is a rake,
And he was not right fat, I undertake ;
But lokëde holwe, and therto soberly.
Ful thredbar was his overest courtepy [4].
For he hadde geten him yit no benefice,
Ne was so worldly for to have office.
For him was levere have at his beddës heede
Twenty bookës, clad in blak or reede,
Of Aristotle and his philosophyë,
Then robës riche, or fithele, or gay sawtryë [5].
But al be that he was a philosophre,
Yet haddë he but litel gold in cofre ;
But al that he mighte of his frendës hente,
On bookës and on lernyng he it spente,
And busily gan for the soulës preye
Of hem that yaf him wherwith to scoleye ;
Of studie took he most cure and most heede.
Not oo word spak he morë than was neede,

---

[1] for fear of.   [2] coins stamped with a shield : *écus.*
[3] gains.   [4] short cloak.   [5] psaltery, harp.

And that was seid in forme and reverence
And schort and quyk, and ful of high sentence.
Sownynge in[1] moral vertu was his speche,
And gladly wolde he lerne, and gladly teche.

* * * * * *

  A good man was ther of religioun,
And was a pourë PERSOUN of a toun ;
But riche he was of holy thought and werk.
He was also a lerned man, a clerk,
That Cristës gospel trewëly wolde preche ;
His parischens devoutly wolde he teche.
Benigne he was, and wonder diligent,
And in adversité ful pacient ;
And such he was i-provëd oftë sithes[2].
Ful loth were him to cursë for his tythes.
But rather wolde he yeven, out of dowte,
Unto his pourë parisschens aboute,
Of his offrynge, and eek of his substaunce.
He cowde in litel thing han suffisaunce.
Wyd was his parische, and houses fer asonder,
But he ne laftë not for reyne ne thonder,
In siknesse nor in meschief to visite·
The ferreste in his parissche, moche and lite,
Upon his feet, and in his hond a staf.
This noble ensample to his scheep he yaf,
That first he wroughte, and afterward he taughte,
Out of the gospel he tho wordës caughte,
And this figure he addede eek therto,
That if gold rustë, what schal yren doo ?
For if a prest be foul, on whom we truste,
No wonder is a lewëd man to ruste ;
And schame it is, if that a prest tak keep,
A [filthy] schepherde and a clenë scheep ;
Wel oughte a prest ensample for to yive,
By his clennesse, how that his scheep schulde lyve.
He settë not his benefice to hyre,
And leet his scheep encombred in the myre,

       [1] tending towards.   [2] oft-times.

And ran to Londone, unto seyntë Poules,
To seeken him a chaunterie for soules[1],
Or with a bretherhede to ben withholde;
But dwelte at hoom, and keptë wel his folde,
So that the wolf ne made it not myscarye;
He was a schepherd and no mercenarie.
And though he holy were, and vertuous,
He was to sinful man nought despitous,
Ne of his spechë daungerous[2] ne digne,
But in his teching discret and benigne.
To drawë folk to heven by fairnesse
By good ensample, this was his busynesse:
But it were eny persone obstinat,
What so he were, of high or lowe estat,
Him wolde he snybbë scharply for the nonës.
A better preest, I trowe, ther nowher non is.
He waytede after no pompe and reverence,
Ne makede him a spiced[3] conscience,
But Cristës lore, and his apostles twelve,
He taughte, but first he folwede it himselve.

The Tale of the Man of Lawe.

[Custance is falsely charged with the murder of Dame Hermengild.
The Knight who charges her is struck down for his perjury.]

Allas! Custance! thou hast no champioun
Ne fyghtë canstow nought, so weylawey!
But he, that starf for our redempcioun,
And bond Sathan (and yit lyth ther[4] he lay)
So be thy strongë champioun this day!
For, but if crist open miracle kythe[5],
Withouten gilt thou shalt be slayn as swythe[6].

---

[1] an endowment for saying masses.   [2] haughty.
[3] nice, fastidious.   [4] where.   [5] show.   [6] quickly

She sette her doun on knees, and thus she sayde,
'Immortal god, that sauedest Susanne
Fro falsë blame, and thow, merciful mayde,
Mary I menë, doughter to Seint Anne,
Bifore whos child aungelës singe Osanne,
If I be giltlees of this felonye,
My socour be, for elles I shal dye!'

Haue ye not seyn som tyme a palë face,
Among a prees, of him that hath be lad
Toward his deth, wher as him gat no grace,
And swich a colour in his face hath had,
Men myghtë knowe his face, that was bistad[1],
Amongës alle the faces in that route :
So stant Custance, and looketh hir aboute.

O queenës, lyuinge in prosperitee,
Duchesses, and ladyës euerichone,
Haueth som rewthe on hir aduersitee ;
An emperourës doughter stant allone ;
She hath no wight to whom to make hir mone.
O blood roial ! that stondest in this drede,
Fer ben thy frendës at thy gretë nede !

This Alla king hath swich compassioun,
As gentil herte is fulfild of pitee,
That from his yën ran the water doun.
'Now hastily do fecche a book,' quod he,
'And if this knyght wol sweren how that she
This womman slow, yet wole we vs auyse
Whom that we wole that shal ben our Iustyse.'

A Briton book, writen with Euangyles,
Was fet[2], and on this book he swor anoon
She gilty was, and in the menë whyles
A hand him smot vpon the nekkë-boon,
That doun he fel atonës as a stoon,
And both his yën braste out of his face
In sight of euery body in that place.

---

[1] in sore peril.   [2] fetched.

A voys was herd in general audience,
And seyde, 'thou hast disclaundered giltelees
The doughter of holy chirche in hey presence;
Thus hastou doon, and yet holde I my pees.'
Of this meruaille agast was al the prees;
As masëd folk they stoden euerichone,
For drede of wrechë[1], saue Custance allone.

Gret was the drede and eek the repentance
Of hem that hadden wrong suspeccioun
Vpon this sely innocent Custance;
And, for this miracle, in conclusioun,
And by Custances mediacioun,
The king, and many another in that place,
Conuerted was, thanked be Cristës grace!

This falsë knyght was slayn for his vntrewthe
By Iugëment of Alla hastily;
And yet Custance hadde of his deth gret rewthe.
And after this Iesus, of his mercy,
Made Alla wedden ful solempnëly
This holy mayden, that is so bright and sheene,
And thus hath Crist ymaad Custance a queene.

*   *   *   *   *   *

[Through the intrigues of Donegild, the queen mother, a forged letter is
sent in the king's name bidding Custance to be banished and turned
adrift in an open boat.]

Wepen both yonge and olde in al that place,
Whan that the king this cursëd letter sente,
And Custance, with a deedly palë face,
The ferthë day toward hir ship she wente.
But nathëles she taketh in good entente
The wille of Crist, and, kneling on the stronde,
She seydë, 'lord! ay wel-com be thy sonde[2]!

---

[1] vengeance.   [2] sending, visitation.

He that me keptë fro the falsë blame
Whyl I was on the londe amongës yow,
He can me kepe from harme and eek fro shame
In saltë see, al-though I se nat how.
As strong as euer he was, he is yet now.
In him triste I, and in his moder dere,
That is to me my seyl and eek my stere[1].'

Hir litel child lay weping in hir arm,
And kneling, pitously to him she seyde,
'Pees, litel sone, I wol do thee noon harm.'
With that hir kerchef of hir heed she breyde,
And ouer his litel yën she it leyde ;
And in hir arm she lulleth it ful faste,
And in-to heuen hir yën vp she caste.

'Moder,' quod she, 'and maydë bright, Marye,
Soth is that thurgh womannës eggëment[2]
Mankynd was lorn[3] and damnëd ay to dye,
For which thy child was on a croys yrent ;
Thy blisful yën seye al his torment ;
Than is ther no comparisoun bitwene
Thy wo and any wo man may sustene.

Thou sey thy child yslayn bifor thyn yën,
And yet now lyueth my litel child, parfay !
Now, lady bryght, to whom alle woful cryën,
Thou glorie of wommanhede, thou fayrë may,
Thou hauen of refut, bryghtë sterre of day,
Rewe on my child, that of thy gentillesse
Rewest on euery rewful in distresse !

O litel child, allas ! what is thy gilt,
That neuer wroughtest sinne as yet, parde,
Why wil thyn hardë fader han thee spilt[4] ?
O mercy, derë Constable !' quod she ;
'As lat my litel child dwelle heer with thee ;
And if thou darst not sauen him, for blame,
So kis him onës in his fadres name !'

[1] rudder.   [2] incitement.   [3] lost.   [4] killed.

Ther-with she loketh bakward to the londe,
And seydë, 'far-wel, housbond rewthëlees!'
And vp she rist[1], and walketh doun the stronde
Toward the ship; hir folweth al the prees,
And euer she preyeth hir child to holde his pees;
And taketh hir leue, and with an holy entente
She blisseth hir; and in-to ship she wente.

Vitailled was the ship, it is no drede,
Habundantly for hir ful longe space,
And other necessaries that sholde nede
She hadde ynough, heried[2] be Goddes grace!
For wynd and weder almyghty God purchace
And bringe hir hoom! I can no better seye;
But in the see she dryueth forth hir weye.

* * * * * *

[King Alla and Custance meet at Rome after many years.]

Whan Alla sey his wyf, fayre he hir grette,
And weep, that it was rewthë for to see.
For at the firstë look he on hir sette
He knew wel verraily that it was she.
And she for sorwe as domb stant as a tre;
So was hir hertë shet in hir distresse
Whan she remembred his vnkyndënesse.

Twyës she swownëd in his owën syghte;
He weep, and him excuseth pitously:—
'Now God,' quod he, 'and alle his halwes[3] bryghte
So wisly[4] on my soule as haue mercy,
That of your harm as giltelees am I
As is Maurice my sone so lyk your face;
Ellës the feend me fecche out of this place!'

Long was the sobbing and the bitter peyne
Er that her woful hertës myghtë cesse;
Greet was the pitë for to here hem pleyne
Thurgh whichë pleyntës gan her wo encresse.
I prey yow al my labour to relesse;

[1] rises (**riseth**). [2] praised. [3] saints. [4] certainly.

I may nat telle her wo vn-til tomorwe,
I am so wery for to speke of sorwe.

But fynally, when that the soth is wist
That Alla giltëlees was of hir wo,
I trowe an hundred tymës been they kist,
And swich a blisse is ther bitwix hem two
That, saue the Ioye that lasteth euermo,
Ther is noon lyk that any creature
Hath seyn or shal, whyl that the world may dure.

THE CLERKES TALE.

[Chaucer moralises on the story of Patient Grisildis.]

Lenuoy de Chaucer.

Grisild is deed, and eek hir pacience,
And bothe atonës buried in Itaille ;
For which I crye in open audience,
No wedded man so hardy be tassaille
His wyuës pacience, in hope to fynde
Grisildës, for in certein he shal faille !

O noble wyuës, ful of heigh prudence,
Lat non humilitee your tongë naille,
Ne lat no clerk haue cause or diligence
To wryte of yow a storie of swich meruaille
As of Grisildis pacient and kynde ;
Lest Chicheuache yow swelwe in hir entraille[1] !

Folweth[2] Ekko, that holdeth no silence,
But euere answereth at the countretaille[3] ;

---

[1] An allusion to the old French fable of Chichevache and Bicorne, two monstrous cows, of which the former fed on patient wives and was consequently thin; the latter on patient husbands and was always fat.

[2] follow: *eth* is the termination of 2nd pers. plural imperative.

[3] in return.

Beth nat bidaffed[1] for your innocence,
But sharply tak on yow the gouernaille.
Emprinteth wel this lesson in your mynde
For commune profit, sith it may auaille.

Ye archewyuës[2], stondeth at defence,
Sin ye be stronge as is a greet camaille ;
Ne suffreth nat that men yow don offence.
And slendre wyuës, feble as in bataille,
Beth egre as is a tygre yond in Ynde ;
Ay clappeth as a mille, I yow consaille.

Ne dreed hem nat, do hem no reuerence ;
For though thyn housbonde armed be in maille,
The arwes of thy crabbed eloquence
Shal perce his brest, and eek his auentaille[3] ;
In Ialousye I rede eek thou him bynde,
And thou shalt make him couche as doth a quaille.

If thou be fair, ther folk ben in presence
Shew thou thy visage and thy apparaille ;
If thou be foul, be fre of thy dispence,
To gete thee frendës ay do thy trauaille ;
Be ay of chere as lyght as leef on lynde[4],
And lat him care, and wepe, and wringe, and waille !

The Frankeleynes Tale.

In Armoryke, that cleped is Briteyne,
Ther was a knight, that lovede and dide his peyne
To serve a lady in his bestë wise ;
And many a labour, and many a greet emprise
He for his lady wrought, er sche were wonne ;
For sche was on the fairest[5] under sonne,

---

[1] befooled.　　　[2] ruling wives.　　　[3] front of helmet.
　　[4] the linden tree.　　　[5] the one fairest.

And eek therto come of so heih kynrede,
That wel unnethës dorste this knight for drede
Telle hire his woo, his peyne, and his distresse.
But attë laste sche for his worthinesse,
And namely for his meke obeissance,
Hath suche a pité caught of his penaunce,
That prively sche fel of his acord
To take him for hir housbonde and hir lord,
(Of suche lordschipe as men han over her¹ wyves);
And, for to lede the more in blisse her lyves,
Of his fre wille he swor hir as a knight,
That never in al his lyf by day ne night
Ne schulde he upon him takë no maystrie
Ayeins hir wille, ne kythe² hir jalousye,
But hir obeye, and folwe hir wille in al,
As any lovere to his lady schal;
Save that the name of sovereynëté,
That wolde he han for schame of his degre.
Sche thanketh him, and with ful grete humblesse
Sche sayde : 'Sire, sith³ of your gentilnesse
Ye profre me to han so large a reyne,
Ne woldë never God betwixe us tweyne,
As in my gilt, were eyther werre or stryf.
Sire, I wil be your humble trewë wijf,
Have heer my trouthe, til that myn hertë brestе.'
Thus be they bothe in quiete and in reste.
For o thing, syrës, saufly dar I seye,
That frendës everich other moot obeye,
If they wille longë holden companye
Love wol nought ben constreigned by maystrye.
Whan maystrie cometh, the god of love anon
Beteth his wyngës, and fare wel, he is gon !
Love is a thing, as any spiryt, fre.
Wommen of kynde desiren liberté,
And nought to be constreigned as a thral ;
And so do men, if I sooth seyen schal.

*　　*　　*　　*　　*　　*

¹ their.　　² shew.　　³ since.

Here may men sen an humble wyse acord;
Thus hath sche take hire servaunt and hire lord,
Servaunt in love, and lord in mariage.
Than was he bothe in lordschipe and servage!
Servagë? nay, but in lordschipe above,
Sith he hath bothe his lady and his love;
His lady certës, and his wyf also,
The whiche that lawe of love accordeth to.
And whan he was in this prosperité,
Hoom with his wyf he goth to his cuntre,
Nought fer fro Penmark, ther his dwellyng was,
Wher as he lyveth in blisse and in solas.

*　　*　　*　　*　　*　　*

[Arviragus goes to England for two years on military service, and leaves
Dorigen at home.]

Now stood hir castel fastë by the see,
And often with hir frendës walked sche,
Hir to disporte upon the banke on heih,
Wher as sche many a schippe and bargë seih,
Seylinge her cours, wher as hem listë go.
But yit was ther a parcelle of hir wo,
For to hir self ful often seydë sche,
'Is there no schip, of so many as I se,
Wole bryngen hoom my lord? than were myn herte
Al waryssched [1] of this bitter peynës smerte.'
　Another tyme ther wolde sche sitte and thinke,
And caste hir eyën dounward fro the brynke;
But whan sche saugh the grisly rokkës blake,
For verray fere so wolde hire hertë quake,
That on hire feet sche mighte hir nought sustene.
Than wolde sche sitte adoun upon the grene,
And pitously into the see byholde,
And sayn right thus, with sorowful sikës [2] colde.
'Eternë God, that thurgh thy purveyaunce
Ledest the world by certein governaunce,

---

[1] cured.　　　　　　　　　　　　[2] sighs.

In ydel, as men sayn, ye nothing make.
But, Lord, these grisly feendly rokkës blake,
That semen rather a foul confusioun
Of werk, then any fayr creacioun
Of suche a parfyt wys God and a stable,
Why han ye wrought this werk unresonable?
For by this werk, south, north, ne west, ne est,
Ther nis y-fostred man, ne brid, ne best;
Hit doth no good, to my wit, but anoyeth.
Se ye nought, Lord, how mankynd it destroyeth?
An hundred thousand bodyes of mankynde
Han rokkës slayn, al be they nought in mynde;
Which mankynd is so fair part of thy werk,
That thou it madest lyk to thyn owën werk,
Than semed it, ye hadde a gret chierte[1]
Toward mankynd; but how than may it be,
That ye suche menës[2] make it to distroyen?
Whiche menës doth no good, but ever anoyen.
I wot wel, clerkës woln sayn as hem leste,
By argumentz, that al is for the beste,
Though I ne can the causes nat yknowe;
But thilkë God that madë wynd to blowe,
As kepe my lord, this is my conclusioun;
To clerkes lete I al disputison[3];
But woldë God, that al the rokkës blake
Were sonken into hellë for his sake!
These rokkës sleen myn hertë for the feere.'
Thus wolde sche sayn with many a pitous teere.

Hir freendes sawe that it nas no disport
To romen by the see, but discomfort,
And schopen[4] for to pleyen somwhere elles.
They leden hir by ryverës and by welles,
And eek in other places delitables;
They dauncen and they playe at chesse and tables[5],
So on a day, right in the morwe tyde,
Unto a gardyn that was ther besyde,

[1] charity.   [2] means, ways.   [3] disputing.
[4] planned.   [5] backgammon.

In which that thay hadde made here ordinaunce
Of vitaile, and of other purveyaunce,
They gon and pleye hem al the longë day;
And this was on the sixtë morwe of May,
Which May hadde peynted with his softë schoures
This gardyn ful of levës and of floures :
And crafte of mannës hand so curiously
Arayëd hath this gardyn trewëly,
That never nas ther gardyn of such prys,
But if it were the verrey paradys.
The odoure of flourës and the fresshë sight,
Wolde han made any pensyf hertë light
That ever was born, but if to [1] gret siknesse
Or to gret sorwe held it in distresse ;
So ful it was of beaute with plesaunce.
And after dynere gonnë they to daunce,
And synge also, save Dorigen alone.
Sche made alwey hir compleynt and hir mone,
For sche ne saugh him on the dauncë go,
That was hir housbond, and hir love also ;
But nathëles sche moste a tyme abyde,
And with good hope sche let hir sorwe slyde [2].
    Upon this daunce, amonges other men,
Daunced a squier biforen Dorigen,
That fresscher was and jolyer of array,
As to my dome, than is the month of May.
He syngeth and daunceth passyng any man,
That is or was sith that [3] this world bygan ;
Therwith he was, if men schulde him discryve,
On of the bestë farynge man on lyve,
Yong, strong, ryht vertuous, and riche, and wys,
And wel biloved, and holden in gret prys.
And schortliche, if the soth I tellen schal,
Unwytyng of this Dorigen at al,
This lusty squyer, servaunt to Venus,
Which that y-cleped was Aurelius,
Had loved hire best of any creäture
Two yeer and more, as was his aventure ;

----

[1] too.   [2] pass.   [3] since

But never durste he telle hir his grevaunce,
Withoutë cuppe [1] he drank al his penaunce.
He was dispeyred, nothing durste he seye,
Save in his songës somwhat wolde he wreye [2]
His woo, as in a general compleyning;
He sayde, he lovede and was biloved nothing.
Of suche materë made he many layes,
Songës, compleintës, roundels, virëlayes;
How that he durstë nought his sorwe telle,
But languissheth as a fury doth in helle;
And deye he moste, he seyde, as did Ekko
For Narcisus, that durste nought telle hir wo.
In other manere then [3] ye here me seye
Ne durste he nought to hir his wo bewreye,
Save that paraventure som tyme at daunces,
Ther [4] yongë folk kepen here observaunces,
Hit may wel be he lokëd on hir face
In such a wise, as man that asketh grace,
But nothing wistë sche of his entent.
Natheles it happed, er they thennës went,
Bycausë that he was hir neygheboure,
And was a man of worschipe and honour,
And haddë knowën him of tymë yore,
They felle in speche, and oftë more and more
Unto his purpos drow Aurelius;
And whan he saw his tyme, he saydë thus.
'Madame,' quod he, 'by God, that this world made,
So that I wiste it mighte your hertë glade,
I wolde that day, that your Arveragus
Wente on the see, that I Aurelius
Had went ther [4] I schulde never have come ayain;
For wel I woot my service is in vayn,
My guerdon nys but bersting of myn herte.
Madame, reweth upon my peynës smerte,
For with a word ye may me sle or save.
Her at your foot, God wold that I were grave [5]!
I have as now no leyser more to seye;
Have mercy, swete, or ye wole do me deye.'

[1] without measure.   [2] bewray, shew.   [3] than.   [4] where.   [5] buried.

Sche gan to loke upon Aurelius ;
'Is this your wil,' quod sche, 'and say ye thus ?
Never erst,' quod sche, 'ne wiste I what ye **mente,**
But now, Aurely, I knowë your entente.
By thilkë God, that yaf me soule and lyf,
Ne schal I never ben untrewë wif
In word ne werk ; as fer as I have wit,
I wol ben his to whom that I am knit.'
But after that in pley thus seydë sche :
'Tak this for fynal answer as of me.
Aurelie,' quod sche, 'by heighë God above,
Yit wol I grauntë you to ben your love,
(Sin I you se so pitously compleyne),
Lokë, what day that endëlong[1] Bryteyne
Ye remewe alle the rokkës, ston by stoon,
That thay ne lettë schip ne boot to goon ;
I say, whan ye han maad the coost so clene
Of rokkës, that ther nys no stoon y-sene,
Than wol I love yow best of any man,
Have heer my trouthe, in al that ever I can.'
'Is ther non other grace in you ?' quod he.
'No, by that Lord,' quod sche, 'that madë me,
For wel I wot that that schal never betyde.
Let such folye out of youre hertë slyde.
What deyntë schuldë man have by his lijf,
For to go love another mannës wyf ?'
Wo was Aurely whan that he this herde,
And with a sorwful herte he thus answerde.
'Madame,' quod he, 'this were an impossíble.
Than mot I deye on sodeyn deth orríble.'
And with that word he torned him anon.

＊   ＊   ＊   ＊   ＊   ＊

[Aurelius applies to a 'subtil clerke' of Orleans, who by magical arts
causes all the rocks to seem to disappear. He then goes to Dorigen,
and claims her promise.]

He taketh his leve, and sche astoniëd stood ;
In alle hir face ther nas oon drop of blood ;

[1] all along.

Sche wendë never have come in such a trappe.
'Allas!' quod sche, 'that ever this schulde happe!
For wende I never by possibilité,
That such a monstre or merveyl mightë be;
It is agayns the proces of nature.'
And hom sche goth a sorwful creäture,
For verray fere unnethë may sche go.
Sche wepeth, wayleth al a day or two,
And swowneth, that it routhë was to see;
But why it was, to no wight toldë sche,
For out of toune was goon Arviragus.
But to hir self sche spak, and saydë thus,
With facë pale, and with ful sorwful cheere,
In hir compleint, as ye schul after heere.

*   *   *   *   *   *

[Dorigen complains to Fortune.]

Thus playned Dorigen a day or tweye,
Purposyng ever that sche woldë deye;
But nathëles upon the thriddë night
Hom cam Arveragus, the worthy knight,
And askëd hir why that sche weep so sore;
And sche gan wepen ever lenger the more.
'Allas!' quod sche, 'that ever was I born!
Thus have I sayd,' quod sche, 'thus have I sworn;'
And told him al, as ye han herd bifore;
It nedeth nought reherse it you no more.
This housbond with glad cheere in frendly wise
Answerde and sayde, as I schal you devyse.
'Is ther aught ellës, Dorigen, but this?'
'Nay, nay,' quod sche, 'God helpe me so as wis[1],
This is to moche, and it were Goddes wille.'
'Ye, wyf,' quod he, 'let slepen that is stille,
It may be wel peraunter yet to day,
Ye schal your trouthë holden, by my fay.
For God so wisly[1] have mercy upon me,
I hadde wel lever y-stikid[2] for to be,

---

[1] for a certainty, certainly.   [2] stabbed.

For verray love which that I to you have,
But-if ye scholde your trouthë kepe and save.
Trouthe is the heighest thing that men may kepe.'
But with that word he gan anoon to wepe,
And sayde, ' I yow forbede up peyne of deth,
That never whil thee lasteth lyf or breth,
To no wight telle thou of this aventure.
As I may best, I wil my woo endure.
Ne make no contenaunce of hevynesse,
That folk of you may demen harm or gesse.'
And forth he cleped a squyer and a mayde.
'Go forth anoon with Dorigen,' he sayde,
'And bryngeth hir to such a place anoon.'
They take her leve, and on her wey they gon ;
But they ne wistë why sche thider wente,
He nolde no wight tellen his entente. . . . .

      This squyer, which that highte Aurelius,
On Dorigen that was so amorous,
Of adventurë happëd hir to mete
Amyd the toun, right in the quykë strete ;
As sche was boun to goon the wey forth-right
Toward the gardyn, ther as sche had hight.
And he was to the gardyn-ward also ;
For wel he spyëd whan sche woldë go
Out of hir hous, to any maner place.
But thus thay mette, of adventure or grace,
And he salueth hir with glad entente,
And askith of hir whider-ward sche wente.
And sche answerdë, half as sche were mad,
'Unto the gardyn, as myn housbond bad,
My trouthë for to holde, allas ! allas !'
Aurilius gan wondren on this cas [1],
And in his herte hadde gret compassioun
Of hir, and of hir lamentacioun,
And of Arveragus the worthy knight,
That bad hir holden al that sche hadde hight,
So loth him was his wif schuld breke hir trouthe.
And in his hert he caughte of this gret routhe,

      [1] case, circumstance.

Consideryng the best on every syde,
That fro his lust yet were him lever abyde,
Than doon so heigh a cherlissch wrecchednesse
Agayns fraunchise[1] of allë gentilesse ;
For which in fewë wordës sayde he thus.
' Madame, saith to your lord Arveragus,
That sith I se his gretë gentilesse
To you, and eek I se wel your distresse,
That him were lever han schame (and that were routhe)
Than ye to me schulde brekë thus your trouthe,
I have wel lever[2] ever to suffre woo,
Than I departe[3] the love bytwix yow two.
I yow relesse, madame, into your hond
Quyt every seurëment and every bond
That ye han maad to me as herebiforn,
Sith thilkë tymë which that ye were born.
My trouthe I plighte, I schal yow never repreve[4]
Of no byhest[5], and heer I take my leve,
As of the trewest and the bestë wif
That ever yit I knew in al my lyf.
But every wyf be war of hir byheste,
On Dorigen remembreth attë leste.
Thus can a squyer doon a gentil dede
As wel as can a knyght, withouten drede.'
  Sche thanketh him upon hir knees al bare,
And hoom unto hir housbond is sche fare,
And told him al, as ye han herd me sayd ;
And, be ye siker, he was so wel apayd[6],
That it were impossible me to write.
What schuld I lenger of this cas endite ?
Arveragus and Dorigen his wyf
In sovereyn blissë leden forth her lyf,
Never eft ne was ther anger hem bytwene ;
He cherisscheth hir as though sche were a quene,
And sche was to him trewe for evermore ;
Of these two folk ye gete of me nomore.

---

[1] generosity.　　[2] I prefer.　　[3] divide.　　[4] reprove.
　　　[5] promise.　　　　[6] paid, pleased.

THE KNIGHTES TALE.

[Palamon and Arcite first see Emelye from the prison window.]

This passeth yeer by yeer, and day by day,
Til it fel oonës, in a morwe of May,
That Emelie, that fairer was to seene
Than is the lilie on hir stalkë grene,
And fresscher than the May with flourës newe—
For with the rosë colour strof hire hewe,
I not[1] which was the fayrere of hem two—
Er it were day, as was hire wone[2] to do,
Sche was arisen, and al redy dight ;
For May wol han no sloggardye anight.
The sesoun priketh every gentil herte,
And maketh him out of his sleep to sterte,
And seith, 'Arys, and do thyn observaunce.'
This makede Emelye han remembraunce
To don honour to May, and for to ryse.
I-clothed was sche fresshe for to devyse.
Hir yelwe heer was browded in a tresse,
Byhynde hir bak, a yerdë long, I gesse.
And in the gardyn at the sonne upriste
Sche walketh up and doun, and as hir liste
Sche gadereth flourës, party whyte and reede,
To make a sotil gerland for hire heede,
And as an aungel hevenlyche sche song.
The gretë tour, that was so thikke and strong,
Which of the castel was the cheef dongeoun,
(Ther as the knightës werën in prisoun,
Of which I toldë yow, and tellen schal)
Was even joynant[3] to the gardyn-wal,
Ther as this Emelye hadde hire pleyynge.
Bright was the sonne, and cleer that morwenynge,
And Palamon, this woful prisoner,
As was his wone[2], by leve of his gayler,

---

[1] ne wot, know not.   [2] wont, custom.   [3] adjoining.

Was risen, and romede in a chambre on heigh,
In which he al the noble cité seigh,
And eek the gardyn, ful of braunches grene,
Ther as this fresshë Emely the scheene
Was in hir walk, and romede up and doun.
This sorweful prisoner, this Palamon,
Gooth in the chambre, romyng to and fro,
And to himself compleynyng of his woo ;
That he was born, ful ofte he seyde, alas !
And so byfel, by aventure or cas [1],
That thurgh a wyndow thikke, of many a barre
Of iren greet, and squar as eny sparre [2],
He caste his eyen upon Emelya,
And therwithal he bleynte [3] and cryede, a !
As though he stongen were unto the herte.
And with that crye Arcite anon up-sterte,
And seyde, ' Cosyn myn, what eyleth the,
That art so pale and deedly on to see?
Why crydestow ? who hath the doon offence?
For Goddës love, tak al in pacience
Our prisoun, for it may non other be ;
Fortune hath yeven us this adversité.
Som wikke aspect or disposicioun
Of Saturne, by som constellacioun,
Hath yeven us this, although we hadde it sworn ;
So stood the heven whan that we were born ;
We mote endure it : this is the schort and pleyn.'
    This Palamon answerde, and seyde ageyn,
' Cosyn, for sothe of this opynyoun
Thou hast a veyn ymaginacioun.
This prisoun causëd me not for to crye.
But I was hurt right now thurghout myn eye
Into myn herte, that wol my banë be.
The fairnesse of that lady that I see
Yond in the gardyn romë to and fro,
Is cause of al my crying and my wo.
I not whether sche be womman or goddesse ;
But Venus is it, sothly as I gesse.'

[1] accident or chance.   [2] bolt.   [3] blenched, started.

And therwithal on knees adoun he fil,
And seydë : 'Venus, if it be thy wil
Yow in this gardyn thus to transfigure,
Biforn me sorweful wrecchë creäture,
Out of this prisoun help that we may scape
And if so be my destiné be schape
By eterne word to deyen in prisoun,
Of our lynage have sum compassioun,
That is so lowe y-brought by tyrannye.'
And with that word Arcite gan espye
Wher as this lady romede to and fro.
And with that sighte hir beauté hurte him so,
That if that Palamon was wounded sore,
Arcite is hurt as moche as he, or more.
And with a sigh he seydë pitously :
'The fresschë beauté sleeth me sodeynly
Of hir that rometh in the yonder place ;
And but I have hir mercy and hir grace,
That I may seen hir attë lestë weye,
I nam but[1] deed ; ther nys no more to seye.'

*   *   *   *   *   *

[Arcite has been released from prison, and Palamon has escaped. They
meet in a wood near Athens.]

And with that word he fel doun in a traunce
A long tyme ; and after he upsterte[2]
This Palamon, that thoughte that thurgh his herte
He felte a cold swerd sodeynlichë glyde ;
For ire he quook[3], no lenger nolde he byde.
And whan that he hadde herd Arcitës tale,
As he were wood[4], with facë deed and pale,
He sterte him up out of the bussches thikke,
And seyde : 'Arcytë, falsë traitour wikke,
Now art thou hent[5], that lovest my lady so,
For whom that I have al this peyne and wo,
And art my blood, and to my counseil sworn,

[1] am merely.   [2] started up.   [3] quaked.
          [4] mad.   [5] caught.

As I ful ofte have told thee heer byforn,
And hast byjapëd[1] heer duk Theseus,
And falsly chaungëd hast thy namë thus ;
I wol be deed, or ellës thou schalt dye.
Thou schalt not love my lady Emelye,
But I wil love hir oonly and no mo ;
For I am Palamon, thy mortal fo.
And though that I no wepne have in this place,
But out of prisoun am astert by grace,
I dredë not that outher thou schalt dye,
Or thou ne schalt not loven Emelye.
Ches[2] which thou wilt, for thou schalt not asterte[3].'
This Arcitë, with ful despitous herte,
Whan he him knew, and hadde his talë herd,
As fers as lyoun pullede out a swerd,
And seidë thus : 'By God that sit[4] above,
Nere it[5] that thou art sik and wood for love,
And eek that thou no wepne hast in this place,
Thou schuldest nevere out of this grovë pace,
That thou ne schuldest deyen of myn hond.
For I defye[6] the seurté and the bond
Which that thou seyst that I have maad to the.
What, verray fool, think wel that love is fre !
And I wol love hir mawgre[7] al thy might.
But, for as muche thou art a worthy knight,
And wilnest to derreyne hir by batayle,
Have heer my trouthe, to-morwe I nyl not fayle,
Withouten wityng[8] of any other wight,
That heer I wol be founden as a knight,
And bryngen harneys right inough for the ;
And ches[2] the beste, and leve the worste for me.
And mete and drynkë this night wil I brynge
Inough for the, and clothes for thy beddynge.
And if so be that thou my lady wynne,
And sle me in this woode ther I am inne,
Thou maist wel han thy lady as for me.'
This Palamon answerde : 'I graunte it the.'

[1] tricked. [2] choose. [3] escape. [4] sitteth.
[5] were it not. [6] reject. [7] in spite of. [8] knowledge.

And thus they ben departed til a-morwe,
When ech of hem hadde leyd his feith to borwe
    O Cupide, out of alle charité !
O regne, that wolt no felawe han with the !
Ful soth is seyd, that lovë ne lordschipe
Wol not, his thankes[1], han no felaweschipe.
Wel fynden that Arcite and Palamoun.
Arcite is riden anon unto the toun,
And on the morwe, er it were dayës light,
Ful prively two harneys hath he dight,
Bothe suffisaunt and metë to darreyne
The batayle in the feeld betwixe hem tweyne.
And on his hors, allone as he was born,
He caryeth al this harneys him byforn ;
And in the grove, at tyme and place i-set,
This Arcite and this Palamon ben met.
Tho[2] chaungen gan the colour in here face.
Right as the honter in the regne of Trace
That stondeth at the gappë with a spere,
Whan honted is the lyoun or the bere,
And hereth him come ruschyng in the greves,
And breketh bothë bowës and the leves,
And thinketh, ' Here comth my mortel enemy,
Withoutë faile, he mot[3] be deed or I ;
For eyther I mot slen him at the gappe,
Or he mot sleen me, if that me myshappe :'
So ferden they, in chaungyng of here hewe,
As fer as everich of hem other knewe.
Ther nas no 'good day,' ne no saluyng ;
But streyt withouten word or rehersyng,
Everych of hem halp[4] for to armen other,
As frendly as he were his owën brother ;
And after that with scharpë sperës stronge
They foynen ech at other wonder longe.
Thou myghtest wenë that this Palamon
In his fightynge were as a wood[5] lyoun,
And as a cruel tygre was Arcite :
As wildë boorës gonnë they to smyte

[1] willingly.   [2] then.   [3] must, shall.   [4] helped.   [5] mad.

That frothen white as foom for irë wood.
Up to the ancle foughte they in her blood.

*   *   *   *   *   *

[The poet describes the Temples of Venus and Mars, where Arcite and
Palamon are about to offer their prayers before the final combat.]

First in the temple of Venus maystow se
Wrought on the wal, ful pitous to byholde,
The broken slepës, and the sykës [1] colde ;
The sacred teerës, and the waymentyng ;
The fyry strokës of the desiryng,
That lovës servauntz in this lyf enduren ;
The othës, that her covenantz assuren.
Plesaunce and hope, desyr, fool-hardynesse,
Beauté and youthë, bauderye, richesse,
Charmës and forcë, lesynges, flaterye,
Dispensë, busynesse, and jelousye,
That werede of yelwe goldes [2] a gerland,
And a cokkow sittyng on hir hand ;
Festës, instrumentës, caroles, daunces,
Lust and array, and alle the circumstaunces
Of love, whiche that I rekned have and schal,
By ordre weren peynted on the wal.
And mo than I can make of mencioun.
For sothly, al the mount of Citheroun,
Ther [3] Venus hath hir principal dwellyng,
Was schewed on the wal in portreying,
With al the gardyn, and the lustynesse.
Nought was foryete [4] the porter Ydelnesse,
Ne Narcisus the fayre of yore agon,
Ne yet the folye of kyng Salamon,
Ne eek the gretë strengthe of Hercules,
Thenchauntëmentz of Médea and Circes,
Ne of Turnus with the hardy fiers corage,
The richë Cresus, caytif [5] in servage [6].
Thus may ye seen that wisdom ne richesse,
Beauté ne sleightë, strengthe, ne hardynesse,

---

[1] sighs.   [2] marigolds.   [3] where.   [4] forgotten.
      [5] captive.   [6] servitude.

Ne may with Venus holdë champartye[1],
For as hir list the world than may sche gye[2],
Lo, alle thise folk i-caught were in hir las[3],
Til they for wo ful often sayde allas.
Sufficeth heer ensamples oon or tuo,
And though[4] I couthe rekne a thousend mo.
The statue of Venus, glorious for to see,
Was naked fletyng[5] in the largë see,
And fro the navel doun al covered was
With wawës[6] grene, and brighte as any glas.
A citole[7] in hir right hond haddë sche,
And on hir heed, ful semely for to see,
A rosë garland, fresch and wel smellyng,
Above hir heed hir dowvës flickeryng.
Biforn hir stood hir sonë Cupido,
Upon his schuldres wyngës hadde he two;
And blynd he was, as it is oftë seene ;
A bowe he bar and arwes brighte and kene.
Why schulde I nought as wel eek telle you al
The portreiture, that was upon the wal
Withinne the temple of mighty Mars the reede ?
Al peynted was the wal in lengthe and breede
Lik to the estres[8] of the grisly place,
That highte[9] the gretë temple of Mars in Trace,
In thilkë coldë frosty regioun,
Ther as Mars hath his sovereyn mansioun.
First on the wal was peynted a forest,
In which ther dwelleth neyther man ne best[10],
With knotty knarry bareyne treës olde
Of stubbës scharpe and hidous to byholde ;
In which ther ran a swymbel in a swough[11],
As though a storm schulde bersten every bough :
And downward on an hil under a bente[12],
Ther stood the temple of Marz armypotente,
Wrought al of burned[13] steel, of which thentré

---

[1] divided empire.   [2] guide, turn.   [3] lace, snare.   [4] never-
theless.   [5] floating.   [6] waves.   [7] harp.   [8] interior.
[9] is called.   [10] beast, animal.   [11] moaning in a gust.   [12] slope.
[13] burnished.

Was long and streyt[1], and gastly for to see.
And therout cam a rage and such a vese[2],
That it made al the gates for to rese[3].
The northern light in at the dorës schon,
For wyndowe on the wal ne was ther noon,
Thurgh which men mighten any light discerne.
The dore was al of ademaunt eterne,
I-clenched overthwart and endëlong[4]
With iren tough ; and, for to make it strong,
Every piler the temple to susteene
Was tonnë greet[5], of iren bright and schene.
Ther saugh I first the derke ymaginyng
Of felonye, and al the compassyng ;
The cruel ire, as reed as eny gleede[6] ;
The pikëpurs, and eek the palë drede ;
The smyler with the knyf under the cloke ;
The schepne[7] brennyng[8] with the blakë smoke ;
The tresoun of the murtheryng in the bed ;
The open werre, with woundës al bi-bled ;
Contek[9] with bloody knyf, and scharp manace.
Al ful of chirkyng[10] was that sory place.
The sleëre of himself[11] yet saugh I there,
His hertë-blood hath bathëd al his here ;
The nayl y-dryven in the schode[12] a-nyght ;
The coldë deth, with mouth gapyng upright.
Amyddës of the temple sat meschaunce,
With disconfort and sory contenaunce.
Yet saugh I woodnesse[13] laughying in his rage ;
Armed complaint, outhees[14], and fiers outrage.
The caroigne[15] in the bussh, with throte y-corve[16] :
A thousand slain, and not of qualme y-storve[17] ;
The tiraunt, with the prey by force y-raft[18] ;
The toun destroyed, ther was no thyng laft.
Yet sawgh I brent[19] the schippes hoppesteres[20] ;

---

[1] strait, narrow.   [2] rush.   [3] shake.   [4] across and downwards.   [5] great as a tun.   [6] live coal.   [7] stable. [8] burning.   [9] strife.   [10] shrieking.   [11] suicide.   [12] temple. [13] madness.   [14] outcry.   [15] carcase.   [16] cut.   [17] dead of sickness.   [18] reft.   [19] burnt.   [20] the dancing ships.

The huntë[1] strangled with the wildë beres[2]:
The sowe freten[3] the child right in the cradel;
The cook i-skalded, for al his longe ladel.
Nought was foryete[4] by[5] the infortune of Marte;
The cartere over-ryden with his carte,
Under the whel ful lowe he lay adoun.
Ther were also of Martes divisioun,
The barbour, and the bocher; and the smyth
That forgeth scharpë swerdës on his stith[6].
And al above depeynted[7] in a tour
Saw I conquést sittyng in gret honour,
With the scharpë swerd over his heed
Hangynge by a sotil[8] twynës threed.

GOOD COUNSEIL OF CHAUCER.

Fle fro the pres, and dwelle with sothfastnesse;
Sufficë thee thy good, though hit be smal;
For hord hath hate, and clymbyng tikelnesse[9],
Pres hath envye, and wele blent over al[10].
Savour no more then thee behovë shal;
Do wel thy-self that other folk canst rede,
And trouthe thee shal delyver, hit ys no drede[11].

Peynë thee not eche croked to redresse
In trust of hir that turneth as a bal[12],
Gret restë stant in lytil besynesse;
Bewar also to spurne ayein a nal[13],
Stryve not as doth a crokkë with a wal[14];
Dauntë thy-selfe that dauntest otheres dede,
And trouthe thee shal delyver, hit is no drede.

---

[1] hunter.   [2] bears.   [3] (I saw) the sow eat.   [4] forgotten.
[5] as regards.   [6] anvil.   [7] painted.   [8] subtle, thin.   [9] insecurity.   [10] wealth everywhere blinds people.   [11] there is no doubt.
[12] i.e. Fortune.   [13] an awl.   [14] i.e. as weak does with strong

That thee is sent receyve in buxumnesse[1],
The wrasteling of this world asketh[2] a fal ;
Heer is no hoom, heer is but wyldernesse.
Forth pilgrime, forth ! forth best, out of thy stal !
Loke up on hye, and thonkë God of al ;
Weyvë[3] thy lust, and let thy gost thee lede,
And trouthe shal thee delyver, hit is no drede.

L'Envoye[4].

Therfor, thou vache[5], leve thyn old wrecchednesse ;
Unto the worldë leve now to be thral[6] ;
Crye him mercy, that of his heigh goodnesse
Made thee of naught ; and, in especial,
Draw unto him, and pray in general
For thee, and eek for other, hevenly mede[7] ;
And trouthe schal thee delivere, it is no drede.

[1] with submission.   [2] brings.   [3] set aside.   [4] This stanza
is only in MS. Addit. 10340 (Brit. Mus).   [5] cow, poor creature.
[6] cease to be a slave to the world.   [7] reward

POEMS COMMONLY ATTRIBUTED TO CHAUCER.

THE ROMAUNT OF THE ROSE.

It has already been said (p. 7) that Chaucer translated the
Romaunt, and that a version has been current under his name for
centuries. There is only one MS. of this translation, in the
Hunterian Museum at Glasgow, so that we have no means of
comparing texts, and thus settling the difficult questions that have
been raised about it. As it stands, the poem contains various
features which, in the opinion of the most advanced school of
Chaucerian criticism, mark it out as being not Chaucer's ; the
principal difficulty being connected with the rhymes, some of
which seem to be irreconcileable with Chaucer's principles of
pronunciation. The question cannot be properly discussed here,
but in deference to what seems to be the balance of opinion
we quote the *Romaunt* under the head of 'Poems attributed to
Chaucer.' The passage given is remarkable as the original of
the 'May morning' passages which abound in Chaucer and his
successors. Whether by Chaucer or not, it is a vigorous and exact
rendering of the French.

> That it was May me thoughtë tho[1],
> It is .v. yere or more ago ;
> That it was May, thus dremëd me,
> In tyme of love and jolité,
> That al thing gynneth waxen gay,
> For ther is neither busk nor hay[2]
> In May, that it nyl shrouded been,
> And it with newë levës wreen[3].
> These wodës eek recoveren grene,
> That drie in wynter ben to sene ;
> And the erth wexith proud withallɔ,
> For swotë dewes that on it falle ;
> And the pore estat forget,
> In which that wynter had it set.

[1] then.   [2] hedge.   [3] cover.

And than bycometh the ground so proud,
That it wole have a newë shroud,
And makith so queynt his robe and faire,
That it had hewes an hundred payre,
Of gras and flouris, ynde and pers[1],
And many hewës full dyvers :
That is the robe I mene, iwis,
Through which the ground to preisen is.

The briddës, that han left her song,
While thei han suffrid cold so strong
In wedres gryl[2] and derk to sighte,
Ben in May for the sonnë brighte,
So glade, that they shewe in syngyng,
That in her hertis is sich lykyng,
That they mote syngen and be light.
Than doth the nyghtyngale hir myght,
To mak noyse, and syngen blythe.
Than is blisful many sithe[3],
The chelaundre[4], and the papyngay.
Than youngë folk entenden ay,
For to ben gay and amorous,
The tyme is than so savorous.

Hard is the hert that loveth nought
In May, whan al this mirth is wrought;
Whan he may on these braunches here
The smalë briddës syngen clere
Her blisful swetë song pitous,
And in this sesoun delytous :
Whan love affraieth[5] alle thing.

Methought a nyght, in my sleping,
Right in my bed ful redily,
That it was by the morowe erly,
And up I roos, and gan me clothe;
Anoon I wissh[6] myn hondis bothe;
A sylvre nedle forth I drough
Out of an aguler[7] queynt ynough,

---

[1] azure and blue-gray.   [2] horrible storms.   [3] times.   [4] goldfinch.
      [5] disturbs.   [6] washed.   [7] needle-case.

G 2

And gan this nedle threde anon;
For out of toun me list to gon,
The song of briddës for to here
That in thise buskës syngen clere,
And in the swete seson that leve is;
With a threde bastyng my slevis,
Alone I wente in my playing,
The smalë foulës song harknyng.
They peyned hem ful many peyre,
To synge on bowës blosmed feyre[1].
Joly and gay, ful of gladnesse,
Toward a ryver gan I me dresse,
That I herd rennë fastë by;
For fairer playing non saugh I
Than playen me by that ryvere,
For from an hille that stood ther nere,
Cam doun the streme ful stif and bold,
Cleer was the water, and as cold
As any welle is, sooth to seyn,
And somdele lasse it was than Seyn,
But it was straiter, wel-away!
And never saugh I, er that day,
The watir that so wel lyked me;
And wondir glad was I to se
That lusty place, and that ryvere;
And with that watir that ran so clere
My face I wissh. Tho saugh I wel,
The botme paved everydel[2]
With gravel, ful of stonës shene.
The medewe softë, swote, and grene,
Beet right up on the watir-syde.
Ful clere was than the morow-tyde,
And ful attempre, out of drede[3].
Tho gan I walke thorough the mede,
Dounward ay in my pleying,
The ryver-syde costeying.

---

[1] blossomed fair.   [2] everywhere.   [3] attempered, without doubt.

The Flower and the Leaf.

The Flower and the Leaf, written, according to internal evi-
dence, by a lady, and about 1450, follows out a fancy of French
origin which had already in Chaucer's time found its way into the
stock poetical material of the age, and to which he makes reference
in *The Legende of Goode Women.*

> 'But helpeth, ye that han conning and might,
> Ye lovers, that can make of sentëment;
> In this case oughtë ye be diligent
> To ferthren me somewhat in my labour,
> Whether ye been with the leafe or with the flour.'

The followers of the Flower

> ' Are such folk that loved idlenesse,
> And not deliten in no businesse,
> But for to hunte and hauke and play in medes
> And many other suchlike idle dedes:'

whereas the company of the Leaf, wearing laurel chaplets, 'whose
lusty green may not appaired be' by winter storms or frosts,
represent the brave and steadfast of all ages, the great knights and
champions, the constant lovers and pure women of past and
present times.

The poem opens with the usual spring morning, and the de-
scription of a woodland arbour hedged round with sycamore and
eglantine, and haunted with the songs of birds. Thence the poet
sees the rival companies of the Flower and the Leaf scattered over
the plain outside, and describes their dresses and equipments with
a length and wearisome detail which would alone mark off the
poem from Chaucer's work. A storm comes on, which drenches
the flower-chaplets and green dresses of Flora's train, while it
leaves those of the Leaf unharmed. These bring shelter and
friendly help to the followers of the Flower, and then the two
companies pass singing out of sight, and a 'fair lady,' herself
a servant of the Leaf, explains to the poet the meaning of the
vision.

Dryden's paraphrase of this poem, which he of course believed
to be by Chaucer, is well known.

[The author having passed a sleepless night, though why she knows not,
as she has neither sickness nor disease, wanders out early.]

And up I roos three hourës after twelfe,
Aboute the [erly] springing of the day;
And on I putte my geare and mine array,
And to a pleasaunt grove I gan to passe,
Long or the brightë Sonne up-risen was;

In which were okës grete, streight as a line,
Under the which the gras, so fresh of hew,
Was newly spronge; and an eight foot or nine
Every tree wel fro his fellow grew,
With branches brode, ladën with levës new,
That sprongen out ayen the sunnë shene,
Some very red, and some a glad light grene;

Which, as me thoughte, was right a plesant sight;
And eke the briddës songës for to here
Would have rejoyced any earthly wight;
And I that couthe not yet, in no manere,
Herë the nightingale of all the yere,
Ful busily herkned with hart and ere,
If I her voice perceive coude any-where.

And, at the last, a path of little breede[1]
I found, that gretly hadde not used be;
For it forgrowen was with grasse and weede,
That well unneth a wight [ne] might it se:
Thoght I, 'This path some whider goth, pardé!'
And so I followed, till it me brought
To right a pleasaunt herber,[2] well ywrought,

That benched was, and eke with turfës newe
Freshly turvëd, whereof the grenë gras,
So small, so thicke, so short, so fresh of hewe,
That most ylike grene wool, I wot, it was:
The hegge also that yede in this compas[3],
And closed in all the grene herbere,
With sicamour was set and eglatere[4].

*   *   *   *   *   *

[1] breadth.   [2] arbour.   [3] went round about.   [4] eglantine.

And as I stood and cast aside mine eie,
I was ware of the fairest medler-tree,
That ever yet in all my life I sic[1],
As full of blossomes as it mightë be ;
Therein a goldfinch leaping pretile
Fro bough to bough ; and, as him list, gan ete
Of buddës here and there and flourës swete.

And to the herber side ther was joyninge
This fairë tree, of which I have you told ;
And at the last the brid began to singe,
When he had eten what he etë wolde,
So passing sweetly, that by manifolde
It was more pleasaunt than I coude devise.
And when his song was ended in this wise,

The nightingale with so mery a note
Answered him, that all the woodë rong
So sodainly, that, as it were a sote[2],
I stood astonied ; so was I with the song
Thorow ravishëd, that till late and longe,
Ne wist I in what place I was, ne where ;
And ay, me thoughte, she song even by mine ere.

Wherefore about I waited busily,
On every side, if that I her mighte see ;
And, at the last, I gan full well aspie
Where she sat in a fresh grene laurer tree,
On the further side, even right by me,
That gave so passing a delicious smell,
According to the eglantere full well.

*   *   *   *   *   *

And as I sat, the briddës harkening thus,
Me thoughte that I herde voices sodainly,
The most sweetest and most delicious
That ever any wight, I trow truly,
Herd in here life ; for sothe the armony
And sweet accord was in so good musike,
That the voice[s] to angels most were[3] like.

---

[1] ᴤaw.   [2] *sot,* fool.   [3] *Old ed.* was

And at the last, out of a grove faste by,
That was right goodly and pleasant to sight,
I sie where there cam, singing lustily,
A world of ladies ; but, to tell aright
Her grete beautie, it lieth not in my might,
Ne her array ; neverthelesse I shall
Telle you a part, though I speake not of all.

The Court of Love.

The Court of Love (date about 1500) is a poem of the Chau-
cerian school, containing many echoes of Chaucer, and making
distinct reference to *The Compleynte of Pite* and *The Legende of
Goode Women.* 'Philogenet, of Cambridge Clerk,' who, in the
days of unreflecting Chaucerian criticism, was always supposed to
represent the young Chaucer himself, repairs to the Court of
Venus, where he finds Admetus and Alceste, the heroine of *The
Legende of Goode Women*, with her 'ladies good nineteene'
presiding over the Castle of Love. The Queen's handmaid
Philobone takes him in charge and shows him the wonders of the
place. He swears allegiance to the Twenty Statutes of Love, and
is then introduced to the Lady Rosial, with whom he has already
fallen in love in his dream, and whose presence inspires him v :th
long protestations of devotion. Rosial is for the time obdurate,
and sends him away again with Philobone to wait her pleasure.
After a graphic description of the Courtiers of Love, an unequal
but vigorous piece of writing, there appears to be a break in the
poem, for we find ourselves suddenly in the middle of a tender
speech of Rosial, who describes how Pite, risen from the shrine in
which Philogenet had seen her buried within the temple of Venus,
had softened her breast towards him. The poem ends with one of
the favourite bird-scenes of the time, a curious paraphrase of the
Matins for Trinity Sunday. This song in honour of Love, sung
on May morning by a chorus of birds, should be compared with
the last scenes of the *Parlement of Foules.*

The first of the following extracts, a beautiful sketch of Privy
Thought or Fancy, among the Courtiers of Love, is full of delicate
imagination, and represents the author better than the tedious
Statutes of Love, or the hymn to Venus, taken from Boethius, of

which his master, Chaucer, had before him made more successful
use. The second piece, which represents the close of the May
festival, is so characteristic of the school of poetry and of the time,
that it will bear quoting, in spite of its conventionality.

> And Prevye Thought, rejoycing of hym-self,
> Stode not fer thens in abite mervelous ;
> 'Yon is,' thought I, 'som sprite or som elf,
> His sotill image is so curious :
> How is,' quod I, 'that he is shaded thus
> With yonder cloth, I note[1] of what coloure ?'
> And nere I went and gan to lere and pore,
>
> And framed him a question full hard.
> 'What is,' quod I, 'the thyng thou lovest best ?
> Or what is bote[2] unto thy paynes hard ?
> Me think thou livest here in grete unrest,
> Thow wandrest ay from south to est and west,
> And est to north ; as fer as I can see,
> There is no place in courte may holden the.
>
> 'Whom folowest thow ? where is thy harte iset ?
> But my demaunde asoile[3] I thee require.'
> 'Me thoughte,' quod he, 'no creature may lette
> Me to ben here and where as I desire :
> For where as absence hath don out the fire,
> My mery thought it kyndelith yet agayn,
> That bodily me thinke with my souverayne
>
> 'I stand and speke, and laugh, and kisse, and halse[4],
> So that my thought comforteth me ful ofte :
> I think, God wot, though all the world be false,
> I wil be trewe ; I think also how softe
> My lady is in speche, and this on-lofte
> Bryngeth myn harte in joye and grete gladnesse ;
> This prevey thought alayeth myne hevynesse.
>
> 'And what I thinke or where to be, no man
> In all this erth can tell, iwis, but I :
> And eke there nys no swalowe swifte, ne swan

[1] know not.　　[2] remedy.　　[3] absolve, solve.　　[4] embrace.

So wight[1] of wyng, ne half so yerne[2] can flye ;
For I can ben, and that right sodenly,
In Heven, in Helle, in Paradise, and here,
And with my lady, whan I wil desire.

'I am of councell ferre and wide, I wot,
With lord and lady, and here privité
I wot it all ; and be it cold or hoot,
Thay shalle not speke withoute licence of me.
I mynde, in suche as sesonable[3] bee,
Tho[4] first the thing is thought withyn the harte,
Er any worde out from the mouth astarte.'

*　　*　　*　　*　　*　　*

And furth the cokkowe gan procede anon,
With '*Benedictus*' thankyng God in haste,
That in this May wold visite hem echon,
And gladden hem all while the feste shall laste :
And therewithal a loughter out he braste,
'I thanke it God that I shuld ende the song,
And all the service which hath ben so long.'

Thus sange thay all the service of the feste,
And that was done right erly, to my dome[5] ;
And furth goth all the courte, bothe moste and leste,
To feche the flourës fressh, and braunche and blomé ;
And namly hawthorn brought both page and grome,
With fressh garlantis, partie blewe and white,
And hem rejoysen in her grete delite.

Eke eche at other threw the flourës brighte,
The prymerose, the violet, and the goldé[6] ;
So than, as I beheld the riall sighte,
My lady gan me sodenly beholde,
And with a trewe love, plited many-folde,
She smote me thrugh the very harte as blive[7],
And Venus yet I thanke I am alive.

---

[1] swift.　　　[2] eagerly, briskly.　　　[3] ripe for, inclined to love.
[4] Then = when.　　[5] in my judgment.　　　[6] marigold.　　　[7] swiftly

WILLIAM LANGLEY,

LANGLAND.

CONTEMPORANEOUSLY with Chaucer there lived and worked one of the most remarkable of our poets, of whom we know little or nothing except from his works. And even these have been so little studied by the generality of readers, that the singular mistake has arisen of confusing the name of the work with the name of the author. It is common to see references made to 'Piers Plowman' as if he were a writer living in the fourteenth century, which is no less confusing than if we should speak of Hamlet as flourishing in the reign of Elizabeth.

Our author's name is not certainly known. That his Christian name was William there can be no doubt, though by some mistake he has sometimes been called Robert. In a note written on the fly-leaf of one of the Dublin MSS., in a hand of the fifteenth century, we are told that a certain Stacy de Rokayle, living at Shipton-under-Wychwood (about four miles from Burford in Oxfordshire), and holding land of Lord le Spenser, was the father of William de Langlond who wrote the book called Piers Plowman. The only difficulty about this testimony is the name Langland, which should rather, perhaps, be read as Langley; since the Langland family was at that date connected with Somersetshire, whilst there is actually a hamlet named Langley at no great distance from Shipton.

By a careful study of the internal evidence afforded us by the poet's works, we can make out quite sufficient to give us a clear idea of the man. We gather, chiefly from his own words, that he was born about A.D. 1332, probably at Cleobury Mortimer in Shropshire. His father and his friends put him to school (possibly in the monastery at Great Malvern), made a *clerk* or scholar of him, and taught him what holy writ meant. In 1362, at the age of about thirty, he first began work upon the poem, which was to occupy him during a great part of his after life. The real subject of the poem is the religious and social condition of the poorer classes of England during the reigns of Edward III. and Richard II. His testimony is invested with a peculiar interest by the fact that he clearly knew what he was talking about. His own experience, and his own keen powers of observation provided him with an abundant supply of material. He saw the necessity of some reform, and endeavoured to realise in his own mind the person of the coming reformer. To this ideal person he gave the name of Piers the Plowman, to signify that great results can often be achieved by comparatively humble means; and perhaps as hinting, at the same time, that if the labouring classes were to expect any great improvement to take place in their condition, they had best consider what they could do to help themselves. As years wore on, William's supposed reformer seems to have become less actual to him, and assumed, as it were, a more spiritual form to his mind. At last he fully grasps the idea that it is better to turn from any expectation of a reformer to come to the contemplation of the Saviour who has come already. At this point, his mind seizes a bolder conception; he no longer describes Piers Plowman as he had done at first, as if he were no more than what was formerly called a head harvestman, giving directions to the reapers and sowing the corn himself that he might be sure it was sown properly; but he identifies him rather with the Good Samaritan, or personified Love, who is to be of more help to mankind than Faith as typified by Abraham, or than Hope as typified by Moses. The true Good Samaritan is He who told the parable of Himself; the Reformer is no other than Christ. When Christ became incarnate, He was like a warrior doing battle in another's cause, and wearing his arms and cognisance. He put on the armour of Piers the Plowman when He took upon Himself human nature; and His victory over death was the earnest of the deliverance of mankind from all miseries, and the beginning of the improvement of the condition of the lower orders. Such ideas as these form, in fact, a part of the author's own life; they are essentially an important chapter in his autobiography.

In the first instance, he began his poem under the form of a Vision, which took at last the name of the Vision of Piers the Plowman; though it is rather a succession of visions, in some of which Piers is never seen at all. The poet describes himself as wandering on the Malvern Hills, where he falls asleep beside a murmuring brook, and dreams of a Field full of Folk, i.e. the world, of the Lady Holychurch who acts as his instructress, of the Lady Meed who corrupts justice and is ready to bribe even the king himself, of the Seven Deadly Sins, and of Piers the Plowman. Such was the first draught of his poem, to which a sort of appendix was shortly added, with the title of Do-Well, Do-bet [i.e. Do-better], and Do-best.

It would appear that he had already some acquaintance with London life ; and, soon after the writing of the first draught of the poem, he seems to have resided there permanently, taking up his abode in Cornhill, where he lived with his wife Kitte and his daughter Calote, for many long years. About A.D. 1377 he undertook the task of revising his poem ; it ended in his completely rewriting it, at the same time expanding it to so great an extent that it grew to three times its former length. Incidentally, he describes himself as a tall man, going by the nickname of Long Will ; one loath to reverence lords or ladies, or persons dressed in fur and wearing silver ornaments, and not deigning to say ' God save you ' to the serjeants whom he met. It requires no great stretch of the imagination to picture to ourselves the tall gaunt figure of Long Will, in long robes and with shaven crown, striding along Cornhill, saluting no man by the way, and minutely observant of the gay dresses to which he paid no outward reverence. It further appears that he was thoroughly versed in legal forms, and conversant with the writing out of legal documents ; such knowledge enabled him to earn small sums as a notary, and he was frequent in his attendance at Westminster Hall.

Towards the year 1393, or even a little earlier, we find him again becoming dissatisfied with the wording of his poem. Again he resolved to revise it thoroughly, but this time he is more careful about the form than· the matter. Minute corrections and alterations were made in almost every line ; a few passages were curtailed, and others somewhat lengthened. Perceiving that one long passage of his poem as it stood in the second draught was, as to its general contents, a repetition of a former passage, he so transposed his material as to bring the two passages together, interweaving them with such ingenuity that the numerous insertions seem to fall into their places naturally enough. The resulting third draught of the poem is not much longer than the second. In some points he made improvements, but the general effect of the whole is less striking and original ; this being the inevitable result of his obvious desire to tone down some of the more outspoken passages, and to express a certain leaning towards conservatism such as frequently comes with advancing years. We are bound, perhaps, to consider this latest version of the poem as being, upon the whole, the best ; but we cannot but remark that, whilst it is more mature, it is less vigorous.

Thus, during a period of more than thirty years, the poem called the Vision of Piers the Plowman, with its appendix of Do-Well, Do-bet, and Do-best, descriptive of three stages in the Christian's life and experience, grew slowly into its final shape under the author's hands. It is a poem of almost unique character, and can hardly be judged by any of the usual standards. In one respect, it reminds us of Butler's Hudibras ; it was obviously written rather to give the author an opportunity of saying many things by the way than on such a definite plan as requires a close attention on the part of a reader. The general plan has but slight coherence, and merely aims at considering what improvement can be made in men's characters, and what hope there is for the world from the teachings of Christianity. He who does a kindly action, does *well*; but he who teaches men to do good, does *better* ; whilst he who combines both, who does good himself and teaches others to do the same, does *best*. From frequently dwelling on this theme, the poet at last considers the life of Christ ; and, following the narrative of the gospels, describes His entry into Jerusalem, His betrayal and crucifixion. At this point, he supplements the gospel narrative from the apocryphal gospel of Nicodemus, describing the descent of Christ into hell, His victory over Satan and Lucifer, and His release of the souls of the patriarchs from their long prison. Then follows the glorious Resurrection of the Saviour, the descent of the Holy Ghost, and the bestowal upon men of the gifts of the Spirit. But the progress of Christianity is checked to some extent by the descent of Antichrist and the attack of the Seven Deadly Sins upon the church ; and the poem concludes by reminding us that the church is still militant, that corruptions have crept in where only truth should be preached, and that the end is not yet.

In 1399, during the brief space when the deposition of Richard II. was already imminent but had not yet been decided upon, our author wrote a poem, addressed to the king, upon the subject of the misgovernment under which England suffered. This poem, in the only extant manuscript, breaks off abruptly in the middle of a sentence ; and, though it is of considerable interest, its immediate application was speedily set aside by the rapid progress of events.

The manuscripts of Piers the Plowman, in all three versions, are very numerous, and it was once an extremely favourite poem. In the reign of Edward VI. it was for the first time printed, and went through three editions in one year. It was familiar to several of our great writers, including Lydgate, Skelton, Gascoigne, Drayton, and Spenser. The author's vocabulary is extremely copious, which occasions one difficulty in understanding his language. Some have imagined that his language contains only words of English origin, but this notion must have originated in extreme ignorance. He uses, in fact, the common midland dialect of the time, into which French words were introduced with great freedom ; and the percentage of French words employed by him is slightly greater than that which is to be found in Chaucer. The metre is the usual unrhymed alliterative metre of the older English period ; almost the *only* metre which can rightly be called *English*, since nearly all others have been borrowed from French or Italian. We commonly find about three syllables in each line, which begin with the same letter ; and such syllables are, as a rule, accented ones. The general swing of the lines has been described as anapæstic ; it is rather dactylic, with one or more unaccented syllables prefixed. The characters which William describes as appearing to him in consecutive visions have all allegorical names, and some are visionary enough ; but others may have been sketched from the life, and are as distinct as a drawing by Hogarth. The chief power of his writing resides in its homely earnestness, and in his hearty hatred of untruth in every form. In treating of theological questions, he is often obscure, minute, and tedious ; but in treating of life and manners he is keen, direct, satirical, and vivid. Some portions of the poem could well be spared ; others are of much value. It is not suited to all readers ; but most of those who explore it must be glad that they have done so. Apart from its literary merit, it is one of the most valuable linguistic monuments in the whole range of our literature.

Instead of giving, as is usual, short scraps of the poem which are almost unintelligible for lack of context, we present here, in a much abridged form, the 21st Passus or canto of the poem, the sub-ject of which will be readily perceived. It deals with Christ's entry into Jerusalem, the crucifixion, descent into hell, and resurrection.

In the following extract, the spelling has been modernised, because the language is a little difficult, as is usual in alliterative poems. It is given as a specimen of style, but has no linguistic value in its modern dress.

W. W. SKEAT.

Passus XXI. (Latest Version).

Wo-weary and wetshod · went I forth after,
As a reckless renk[1] · that recketh not of sorrow,
And yede[2] forth like a lorel[3] · all my life-time,
Till I wex[4] weary of this world · and wilned[5] eft[6] to sleep,
And leaned me till Lent · and long time I slept.
Of girls[7] and of *gloria laus* · greatly I dreamed,
And how *hosanna* by organ · old folk sung.
One, was semblable[8] to the Samaritan · and some-deal to Piers
    Plowman,
Barefoot on an ass-back · bootless came pricking,
Without spurs or spear · and sprackly[9] he looked,
As is the kind of a knight · that cometh to be dubbed,
To get his gold spurs · and galoches[10] y-couped[11].
Then was Faith in a fenestre[12] · and cried, '*Ah! fili David!*'
As doth an herald of arms · when auntres[13] come to jousts.
Old Jews of Jerusalem · for joy they sung,
    Benedictus qui venit in nomine domini.
Then I frayned[14] at Faith · what all that fare meant,
And who should joust in Jerusalem · ' Jesus,' he said,
'And fetch that[15] the fiend claimeth · Piers fruit the Plowman[16].'
'Is Piers in this place?' quoth I · and he preynte[17] upon me,
'*Liberum Dei arbitrium*,' quoth he · 'for love hath undertaken
That this Jesus, of his gentrise[18] · shall joust in Piers' arms,
In his helm and in his habergeon · *humanâ naturâ*.
That Christ be not known · for *consummatus Deus*,
In Piers' plates the Plowman[19] · this pricker[20] shall ride;
For no dint[21] shall him dere[22] · as *in Deitate patris*.'

---

[1] man.   [2] went.   [3] caitiff.   [4] became.   [5] wished.
[6] again.   [7] children.   [8] like.   [9] sprightly.   [10] shoes.
[11] curiously cut.   [12] window.   [13] adventurers.   [14] asked.
[15] that which.   [16] the fruit [souls of men] belonging to Piers Plowman
[Christ].   [17] glanced, looked.   [18] condescension.   [19] in the
plate-armour of Piers Plowman.   [20] rider.   [21] blow.   [22] harm.

'Who shall joust with Jesus?' quoth I · 'Jews, or the scribes?'
'Nay,' quoth Faith, 'but the fiend · and false-doom-to-die.
Death saith he will for-do[1] · and adown bring
All that liveth or looketh · on land and in water.
Life saith that he lieth · and hath laid his life to wed[2],
That, for all that Death can do · within three days,
To walk, and fetch from the fiend · Piers fruit the Plowman,
And lay it where him liketh · and Lucifer bind,
And for-beat[3] and bring adown · bale and death for ever!
         O mors, ero mors tua!
Then came Pilate with much people · *sedens pro tribunali*,
To see how doughtily Death should do · and deem[4] their beyer
         right[5].
The Jews and the justices · against Jesus they were,
And all the court cried · *crucifige!* loud.
Then put him forth a pilour[6] · before Pilate, and said,
'This Jesus of our Jews' temple · japed[7] and despised,
To for-do it on a day · and in three days after
Edify it eft new · here He stands that said it,
And yet make it as much[8] · in all manner [of] points
Both as long and as large · aloft and aground,
And as wide as it ever was · this we witness all!'
'*Crucifige!*' quoth a catch-poll · he can of[9] witchcraft.'
'*Tolle! tolle!*' quoth another · and took of keen thorns,
And began of a green thorn · a garland to make,
And set it sore on His head · and sith[10] said in envy,
'*Ave! Rabbi!*' quoth that ribald · and reeds shot at His eyes :
And nailed Him with three nails · naked on the rood,
And, with a pole, poison · [they] put to his lips,
And bade Him drink, His death to let[11] · and His days lengthen ;
And said, 'if He soothfast be · He will Himself help ;
And now, if Thou be Christ · God's son of heaven,
Come adown off this rood · and then will we 'lieve
That life Thee loveth · and will not let Thee die.'

---

[1] de-troy.   [2] as a pledge.   [3] I eat to death.   [4] adjudge.
[5] the right [claim] of them both.   [6] a robber put himself forward.
[7] jested.   [8] great.   [9] knows much of.   [10] then.
[11] prevent.

' *Consummatum est!* ' quoth Christ · and comsed[1] for to swoon
Piteously and pale · as prisoner that dieth.
The Lord of life and of light · then laid His eyes together,
The day for dread thereof withdrew · and dark became the sun,
The wall of the temple to-clave[2] · even in two pieces ;
The hard rock all to-rove[3] · and right dark night it seemed.
The earth quook and quashed · as [if] it quick[4] were,
And dead men for that din · came out of deep graves,
And told why that tempest · so long time dured ;
' For a bitter battle ' · the dead body said ;
' Life and Death in this darkness · the one for-doth[5] the other,
But shall no wight wit witterly[6] · who shall have the mastery
Ere Sunday, about sun-rising ' · and sank with that to earth.

*   *   *   *   *   *   *

Lo ! how the sun gan lock · her[7] light in her-self,
When she saw Him suffer death · who sun and sea made !
Lo ! the earth, for heaviness · that He would death suffer,
Quaked[8] as [a] quick thing · and al to-quashed the rocks !
Lo ! hell might not hold · but opened, when God tholed[9],
And let out Simon's[10] sons · to see Him hang on rood.
Now shall Lucifer 'lieve it · though him loath think ;
For Jesus, as a giant · with a gin[11] cometh yond,
To break and to beat adown · all that be against Him,
And to have out all · of them that Him liketh.
' Suffer we,' said Truth · ' I hear and see both
A Spirit speak to hell · and bids unspar the gates ;
     Attollite portas, principes, vestras; &c.'
A voice loud in that light · to Lucifer cried,
' Princes of this palace · prest[12] undo the gates,
For here cometh with crown · the king of all glory.'
Then sighed Satan · and said to hell,
' Such a light, against our leave · Lazarus it fetched ;
Cold care and cumbrance · is come to us all.

---

    [1] began.   [2] was cloven in twain.   [3] was reft in two.
    [4] alive.   [5] destroys.   [6] know certainly.   [7] *sun* is feminine.
    [8] *so here; above we have* quook.   [9] suffered.
    [10] In the apocryphal Gospel of Nicodemus, two sons of Simeon rise from
the dead, and reveal what they have witnessed in hell during Christ's descent
into it.   [11] device, plan.   [12] quickly.

If this king come in · mankind will be fetch,
And lead it where Lazar is · and lightly me bind.
Patriarchs and prophets · have parled[1] hereof long,
That such a lord and a light · shall lead them all hence.
But rise up, Ragamuffin ! · and reach me the bars
That Belial thy bel-sire[2] · beat[3], with thy dam[4],
And I shall let[5] this lord · and His light stop.
Ere we through brightness be blent[6] · bar we the gates !
Check we, and chain we · and each chine[7] stop,
That no light leap in · at louvre nor at loop.
And thou, Ashtaroth, hoot out · and have out our knaves,
Colting, and all his kin · our cattle[8] to save.
Brimstone boiling · burning out-cast it
All hot on their heads · that enter nigh the walls.
Set bows of brake[9] · and brazen guns,
And shoot out shot enough · His sheltrums[10] to blend[11].
Set Mahound at the mangonel[12] · and mill-stones throw,
With crooks and with calthrops · a-cloy[13] we them each one !'
'Listen !' quoth Lucifer · 'for I this lord know,
Both this lord and this light · is long ago I knew him.
May no death this Lord dere[14] · nor devil's queintise[15] ;
And, where He will, is His way · but warn Him of the perils.
If He reave me of my right · He robbeth me by mastery[16]
For, by right and by reason · the renks[17] that be here
Body and soul be mine · both good and ill.
For He Himself it said · that Sire is of hell,
That Adam and Eve · and all their issue
Should die with dool[18] · and here dwell ever,
If that they touched a tree · or took thereof an apple.
Thus this lord of light · such a law made ;
And, since He is so leal a Lord · I 'lieve that He will not
Reave us of our right · since reason them damnèd.
And, since we have been seised · seven thousand winters,
And [He] never was there-against · and now will begin,

---

[1] spoken.   [2] good father.   [3] forged.   [4] mother.   [5] stop.
[6] blinded.   [7] chink.   [8] chattels.   [9] cross bows, with powerful
levers for setting them.   [10] squadrons.   [11] blind.   [12] catapult.
[13] frustrate.   [14] harm.   [15] device.   [16] mere force.   [17] men.
[18] sorrow.

He were unwrast of[1] His word · that witness is of truth !'
'That is sooth,' said Satan · 'but I me sore doubt,
For[2] thou got them with guile · and His garden broke,
Against His love and His leave · on His land yedest[3],
Not in form of a fiend · but in form of an adder ;
And enticedest Eve · to eat by herself,
And behightest[4] her and him · after to know,
As two gods, with God · both good and ill ;
Thus with treason and with treachery · thou troiledest[5] them
      both,
And diddest[6] them break their buxomness[7] · through false
      byhest[8] ;
Thus haddest thou them out · and hither at the last.
It is not graithly[9] gotten · where guile is at the root.
Forthy[10] I dread me,' quoth the devil · 'lest Truth will them
      fetch ;
And, as thou beguiledest God's image · in going of an adder,
So hath God beguiled us all · in going of a wy[11].'

> *   *   *   *   *   *   *

'What lord art Thou?' quoth Lucifer · a voice aloud said,
'The lord of might and of main · that made all things.
Duke of this dim place · anon undo the gates,
That Christ may come in · the king's son of heaven.'
And with that breath hell brake · with all Belial's bars ;
For any wy or ward[12] · wide opened the gates.
Patriarchs and prophets · *populus in tenebris*
Sang with saint John · *ecce agnus Dei !*
Lucifer might not look · so light him ablent[13] ;
And those that our Lord loved · with that light forth flew.

> *   *   *   *   *   *   *

Ashtoreth and all others · hid them in hernes[14],
They durst not look on our Lord · the least of them all,
But let Him lead forth which Him list · and leave which Him
      liked.

---

[1] turned away from.   [2] because.   [3] went.   [4] didst
promise.   [5] didst deceive.   [6] didst cause.   [7] obedience.
[8] promise.   [9] regularly.   [10] therefore.   [11] in taking the form of a
man.   [12] despite any wight or guard.   [13] blinded.   [14] corners

Many hundreds of angels · harped then and sang,
    Culpat caro, purgat caro, Regnat Deus Dei caro.
Then piped Peace · of poetry a note,
    Clarior est solito post maxima nebula Phebus,
    Post inimicitias clarior est et amor.
' After sharpest showers,' quoth Peace · ' most sheen is the sun,
Is no weather warmer · than after watery clouds,
Nor love liefer · nor liefer friends,
Than after war and wrack · when Love and Peace be masters.
Was never war in this world · nor wickeder envy,
But Love, if him list · to laughing it brought,
And Peace, through patience · all perils stopped.'

   *   *   *   *   *   *   *

Truth trumped them, and sang · *Te Deum laudamus* ;
And then luted Love · in a loud note,
    Ecce quam bonum et quam iocundum est habitare fratres
       in unum !
Till the day dawned · these damsels danced,
That men rung to the resurrection · and with that I awaked,
And called Kitte my wife · and Calote my daughter,
' Arise ! and go reverence · God's resurrection,
And creep on knees to the cross · and kiss it for a jewel,
And rightfullest relic · none richer on earth !
For God's blessed body · it bare, for our boot[1],
And it a-feareth[2] the fiend ; · for such is the might,
May no grisly ghost · glide where it shadoweth !'

    [1] help, remedy.   [2] frightens away.

GOWER.

[JOHN GOWER seems to have been born about 1330, and died in 1408, having been blind for eight or nine years before his death. He was a gentleman of ancient family, owning estates in Kent and Suffolk. The place of his birth is unknown; he is believed to have died in the priory of St. Mary Overies, Southwark, in the church of which, now called St. Saviour's, his tomb may still be seen. The earliest of his three principal works, *Speculum Meditantis*, was in French verse, but it has not come down to posterity, nor is the precise time of its composition known. The second, *Vox Clamantis*, in Latin elegiac verse, was written between 1382 and 1384, and commemorates the rising of the commons under Wat Tyler in the former year, moralizing upon it and improving the occasion with astonishing prolixity. The third, *Confessio Amantis*, one of the best known of early English poems, was written between 1385 and 1393.]

The poetry of Gower has been variously estimated. It was a practice with the poets of the sixteenth century to link his name in a venerated trio with those of Chaucer and Lydgate, just as in the seventeenth century the names of Shakspere, Jonson, and Fletcher were often joined together as the great dramatic lights of the preceding age. In each case the effect of closer study has been to lead men to think that they have been joining gold with iron and clay. Shakspere, read attentively, rises high above the standard reached by Jonson and Fletcher ; and in a yet greater degree has the genius of Chaucer, accurately studied and rightly felt, impressed the present age with the sense of his unrivalled eminence among his contemporaries.

Gower, a man of birth and fortune, must have lived in the cultivated society of his day. Of that society, French poetry, in its various forms of Fabliau, Rondel, Romance, Epigram, Chanson, &c., was one of the chief delights and distractions. With much imitative power, with the faculty of sustained attention, with a high appreciation for his own thoughts, and remarkable linguistic facility, Gower, when he betook himself to poetry, was sure to become a copious and prolific writer. But, possessing no originality, he was equally sure to remain pent within the imprisoning bounds of fashion and conventionality, to follow, not take the lead, to interpret, not modify opinion. He seems to have been without the sense of humour ; we doubt if a single jest of his own making can be found throughout his writings. From this cause, although he may justly be called a moralist and a didactic writer, (Chaucer and Lydgate both speak of him as the 'moral' Gower), the higher intellectual rank of a satirist must be denied him. The moralist declaims, the satirist paints ; we are convinced of the deformity of vice in the one case, but we *see* it in the other. The faculties of the first dispose him to subjective estimates of men and things, those of the second to objective estimates. The one describes the offenders, the other makes them exhibit themselves. The moralist inveighs against the selfish cowardice of a degraded proletariat ; the satirist puts a few simple words in their mouths, and we know them and their kind for evermore.

> ' Curramus praecipites, et
>   *Dum jacet in ripa, calcemus Caesaris hostem.*'

Several MSS. of the *Confessio Amantis*, Gower's principal poem, contain a passage in Latin prose in which he describes the three books which he had written, all with a didactic motive, 'doctrinae causa.' The first of these, *Speculum Meditantis*, was in French verse. It was probably written between 1360 and 1370, at a period when the ladies at Edward III's court and their admirers would hardly have condescended to read a poem couched in their native English, a tongue not then believed to be suited to themes of love, mysticism, and chivalry. It was a strictly moral poem, treating of virtues and vices, and the methods of penitence and amendment ; but it has absolutely vanished ; and since from the account we have of the contents it is impossible not to believe that it was exceedingly dull, we may be reconciled to the loss. Gower's next considerable effort, the *Vox Clamantis*, a Latin elegiac poem in seven books, was suggested by the rising of the commons under Wat Tyler and others in 1381. Why he chose to write it in Latin it is impossible to say, unless we suppose that he wished to hide from the objects of them, under the veil of a learned language, the sharp censures on the classes of knights, burghers, and cultivators, which the poem contains. In a passage which is grotesque if not dramatic, the poet thus describes the ringleaders of the insurrection :—

> ' Watte vocat, cui Thomme venit, neque Symme retardat,
>   Recteque Gibbe simul Hicke venire jubent :
> Colle furit, quem Geffe juvat. nocumenta parantes,
>   Cum quibus ad damnum Wille coire vovet.
> Grigge rapit, dum Dawe strepit, comes est quibus Hobbe,
>   Lorkin et in medio non minor esse putat.'

The murder of Archbishop Sudbury by the rebels is described, but with little of that local or circumstantial colouring which we should desire. All that they succeeded in doing, says Gower, was to send him to heaven,

> ' Vivere fecerunt, quem mortificare putarunt ;
>   Quem tollunt mundo, non potuere Deo.'

For several years before the rising of the commons the fame of Chaucer's English poetry must have been growing. Mere fashion could not hold out against the commanding power of that poetry ; and Gower, when next he attempted a considerable work, found that he might as well write it in English. The *Confessio Amantis* was begun, he tells us, at the command of Richard II, who meeting him one day on the Thames, while the tide was flowing, called him into his barge, and bade him in the course of their talk to 'boke some newe thing.' Thus incited, Gower planned a work

> ' Whiche may be wisdom to the wise,
>   And play to hem that list to play.'

The long prologue is taken up with an account of the then state of the world, in which he repeats much of the censure on the various orders of men that he had introduced into the *Vox Clamantis.* He deplores the decline of virtue and good customs, and the general tendency of things to grow worse. Love itself is diseased, and no longer the pure passion that it once was. Starting from this point, he devotes the greater part of the voluminous poem which follows to an examination of the various ways in which men offend against the god of love. The seventh or penultimate book only is an exception to this remark, being a sketch of the philosophy of Aristotle. The lover is represented as a penitent, who, being half dead from a wound inflicted by Cupid, and resorting to Venus his mother, is recommended by the goddess to apply to Genius her priest, and confess to him all the sins that he has committed in the article of love. With the seven deadly sins, pride, anger, envy, &c., for his groundplan, the penitent confesses under the head of each his misdeeds as a lover, and the confessor consoles and directs him by relating the experiences of former lovers *in pari materia.* This strange medley of things human and divine, of which notable examples exist in the works of Chaucer and Boccaccio, does not mean the consecration of the world of passion by introducing religion into it, but the profanation of religion by degrading its rites and emblems to the service of earthly desire. But in this commingling of the morality of Christianity and the morality of Ovid, the two elements agree no better than fire and water ; and the sense of this, forcing itself upon the consciences of the nobler spirits that thus offended, led to those 'Retractations' and palinodes which modern critics have regarded with so much wonder and disdain. Thus it was with Chaucer ; thus with Boccaccio : to Gower perhaps, who wrote under the spell of fashion and in the groove of imitation, the precise character of the absurd confusion of ideas which reigns in his book was never sufficiently apparent to induce him to regret it.

The quarrels of poets are not relevant to the purpose of this book ; otherwise we might be tempted to enter on the much-debated question of the relations between Chaucer and Gower, and the meaning of certain inserted or suppressed passages in their writings. We will only observe that since the discovery (in Trivet's Chronicle) of the common source of the story of Constance, told by Chaucer in the Man of Lawe's tale and by Gower in the second book of the *Confessio Amantis,* the chief reason for doubting the existence of a bitter feeling between the two poets has been removed. If Chaucer had, as Tyrwhitt and Warton thought, borrowed from Gower the story of Constance, it was hard to believe that he would speak roughly of him in the prologue to the very tale which attested the literary obligation. But no such obligation existed, and therefore the words may be taken in their natural bearing[1].

That Gower was timid and a timeserver is a conclusion which it is difficult to resist, when we consider the changes made in the Prologue to the *Confessio Amantis.* In its original shape, as we

---

[1] Speaking of the stories of Canace and of Appollinus of Tyre, told by Gower in his third and eighth books, Chaucer says –

'Of suchë corsed stories I seye fy,'

and declares that not a word of this kind shall come from his pen.

have seen, it states that the poem was undertaken and made 'for kynge Richardes sake,' and prays 'that his corone longe stonde.' But in several MSS. all this is, not very skilfully, omitted or changed. In these the poem is dedicated to ' Henry of Lancaster,' and is said to have been composed in the sixteenth year of King Richard, i.e. in 1393. Henry, afterwards Henry IV, could not have been called Henry of Lancaster till after his father's death in February 1399. Soon after that date Richard II went over to Ireland ; his unpopularity in England was great ; the plot for supplanting him by Henry was set on foot, and with every month that passed the movement grew in strength. It was probably in the course of the summer of 1399 that Gower, perceiving how things were going, transformed his prologue so as to make it acceptable to the pretender whose success he anticipated. In the copies with the altered prologue he also omitted the lines of eulogy on Chaucer at the end, which the poem had originally contained. What could have prompted the omission but a feeling of estrangement? And for this estrangement the severity of the language just quoted from Chaucer supplies a probable motive.

The last considerable work of our author was the *Cronica Tripartita*, a Latin poem in three books, giving a regular history of political incidents in England from 1387 to 1399. As might be expected, the writer bears hardly throughout the poem on the unfortunate Richard. He seems to know nothing of the common story as to the manner of his death. The deposed king died, he says, in prison, from grief, and because he refused to take food.

Of Gower's shorter French poems, his *Cinkante Balades*, which exist in MS. in the library of the Duke of Sutherland, Warton has printed four. They are in stanzas of seven and eight lines, with refrains, and are written not without elegance ; the opening of one of them is here printed.

T. Arnold.

Opening of the thirtieth of Gower's 'Cinkante Balades.'

Si com la nief[1], quant le fort vent tempeste,
Pur halte mier se torne çi et la,
Ma dame, ensi[2] mon coer[3] manit en tempeste,
Quant le danger de vo parole orra,
La nief qe votre bouche soufflera,
Me fait sigler sur le peril de vie,
Quest en danger, falt[4] quil merci supplie.

Opening of the Original Prologue to the 'Confessio Amantis.'

Of hem, that writen us to-fore,
The bokës dwelle, and we therfore
Ben taught of that was writen tho.
Forthy[5] good is, that we also
In oure time amonge us here
Do write of-newë some matere
Ensampled of the oldë wise,
So that it might in suche a wise,
Whan we be dede and elleswhere,
Belevë[6] to the worldës ere
In timë comend[7] after this.
But for men sain, and soth it is,
That who that al of wisdom writ,
It dulleth ofte a mannes wit
To hem that shall it al day rede,
For thilkë cause, if that ye rede,
I woldë go the middel wey
And write a boke betwene the twey,
Somwhat of lust, somwhat of lore,
That of the lasse or of the more
Som man may like of that I write.
And for that fewë men endite

[1] nef, ship. [2] ainsi. [3] cœur. [4] faut.
[5] Therefore. [6] remain. [7] coming.

In oure Englisshe, I thenkë make
A bok for king Richardës sake,
To whom belongeth my legeaunce
With all min hertes obeisaunce,
In al that ever a legë man
Unto his king may don or can.
So ferforth I me recommaunde
To him, which all me may commaunde,
Preiend[1] unto the highe regne,
Which causeth every king to regne,
That his corone longe stonde.

   I thenke, and have it understonde,
As it befell upon a tide,
As thing, which shuldë tho betide,
Under the town of newë Troy,
Which tok of Brute his firstë joy,
In Themsë, whan it was flowend ;
As I by botë cam rowend,
So as fortune her time sette,
My legë lord perchaunce I mette,
And so befell, as I came nigh,
Out of my bote, whan he me sigh,
He bad me come into his barge.
And whan I was with him at large,
Amongës other thinges said,
He hath this charge upon me laid
And bad me do my besinesse,
That to his highë worthynesse
Some newë thing I shulde boke,
That he himself it mightë loke
After the forme of my writing.
And thus upon his commaunding
Min herte is well the morë glad
To writë so as he me bad ;
And eke my fere is well the lasse,
That non envië shall compasse ;
Without a resonable wite[2]
To feigne and blamë that I write.

---

[1] praying.   [2] cause of censure.

ALEXANDER AND THE ROBBER.

[Confessio Amantis, lib. iii.]

Of him, whom all this erthe dradde,
Whan he the world so overladde
Through werre, as it fortuned is,
King Alisaundre, I redë this,
How in a marchë[1], where he lay,
It fell parchaunce upon a day
A rover of the see was nome[2],
Which many a man had overcome,
And slain and take her good away.
This pilour[3], as the bokës say,
A famous man in sondry stede
Was of the werkës, whiche he dede.
This prisoner to-fore the kinge
Was brought, and ther upon this thinge
In audience he was accused;
And he his dede had nought excused,
And praid the king to done him right,
And said : Sire, if I were of might,
I have an herte liche unto thine,
For if thy power werë mine,
My wille is most in speciall
To rifle and geten over all
The largë worldës good about.
But for I lede a pover route[4]
And am, as who saith[5], at mischefe[6],
The name of pilour and of thefe
I bere, and thou, which routës grete
Might lede, and takë thy beyete[7],
And dost right as I woldë do,
Thy name is nothing cleped so,
But thou art namëd emperour.
Our dedës ben of oon colour,
And in effecte of oon deserte ;
But thy richesse and my poverte

---

[1] border-land, country. [2] taken. [3] pillager. [4] a poor company.
[5] as the phrase is. [6] in ill-luck. [7] advantage, acquisition.

They be nought taken evenliche,
And netheles he that is riche
This day, to-morwe he may be pover,
And in contrarie also recover
A pover man to grete richesse.
Men sain forthy, let rightwisenesse
Be peisëd[1] even in the balaunce.
   The king his hardy contenaunce
Beheld, and herde his wordës wise,
And said unto him in this wise:
Thin answere I have understonde,
Whereof my will is, that thou stonde
In my service and stille abide.
And forth withal the samë tide
He hath him terme of life witholde[2],
The more and for he shuld ben holde[3],
He made him knight and yaf him lond,
Whiche afterward was of his hond
An orped[4] knight in many a stede,
And gret prowesse of armës dede,
As the croniquës it recorden.

The Story of Constance.

[*Confessio Amantis*, lib. ii.]

But what the highë God woll spare
It may for no perill misfare.
This worthy maiden, which was there,
Stode than, as who saith, dede for fere,
To se the fest, how that it stood,
Whiche all was torned into blood.
The dissh forth with the cuppe and all
Bebled[5] they werën over all.
She sigh[6] hem die on every side,
No wonder though she wepte and cride,

---

[1] poised, weighed.   [2] retained for his life-time.   [3] and in order that he might be bound to him the more.   [4] 'horped' in the Harleian MS. It means 'bold.'   [5] besmeared.   [6] saw.

Makend many a wofull mone.
Whan all was slain but she al-one,
This oldë fend, this Sarazin,
Let take anone this Constantin,
With all the good she thider brought,
And hath ordeigned as she thought
A naked ship withoutë stere,
In which the good and her infere[1]
Vitailled full for yerës five,
Where that the wind it woldë drive,
She put upon the wawës wilde.

But he, which allë thing may shilde,
Thre yeer til that she cam to londe,
Her ship to stere hath take on honde[2],
And in Northumberlond arriveth,
And happeth thannë that she driveth
Under a castell with the flood,
Whiche upon Humber bankë stood:
And was the kingës owne also,
The whiche Allee was cleped tho,
A Saxon and a worthy knight,
But he beleveth nought aright.
Of this castell was castellaine
Elda, the kingës chamberlaine,
A knightly man after his lawe.
And when he sigh upon the wawe,
The ship drivend alonë so,
He badde anon men shulden go
To se, what it betoken may.
This was upon a somer day,
The ship was loked, and she foundë[3].
Elda within a litel stounde
It wist, and with his wife anon
Toward this yongë lady gon,
Where that they foundë gret richesse.
But she her woldë nought confesse,
Whan they her axen what she was.
And netheles, upon the cas,

---

[1] together. [2] taken in hand. [3] Constance was found.

Out of the ship with great worship
They toke her into felaship,
As they that weren of her glade.
But she no maner joië made,
But sorweth sore of that she fonde
No Cristendome in thilkë londe.
But ellës she hath all her will,
And thus with hem she dwelleth still.

Dame Hermegild, which was the wife
Of Elda, liche her owën life
Constancë loveth ; and fell so,
Spekend all day betwene hem two,
Through grace of Goddës purveiaunce,
This maiden taughtë the creaunce [1]
Unto this wif so parfitly,
Upon a day that, fastë by,
In presence of her husbonde,
Wher they go walkend on the stronde,
A blindë man, which cam ther ladde,
Unto this wife criend he badde
With bothe his hondës up, and praide
To her, and in this wise he saide ;
' O Hermegilde, which Cristes feith
Enformëd, as Constance saith,
Receivëd hast, yif me my sighte.'
Upon this worde her herte aflighte [2],
Thenkend what bestë was to done,
But netheles she herde his bone [3],
And saide,—' In trust of Cristës lawe,
Which don was on the crosse and slawe,
Thou blindë man, beholde and se.
With that to God upon his kne
Thonkend, he tok his sight anon,
Wherof they merveile everychon.
But Elda wondreth most of alle ;
This open thing whiche is befalle

---

[1] creed.   [2] felt afflicted.   [3] petition.

Concludeth him by such a way,
That he the feith no nede obey.
　　Now list what fell upon this thinge.
This Elda forth unto the kinge
A morwe tok his way and rood,
And Hermegild at home abood
Forth with Constancë well at ese.
Elda, which thought his king to plese
As he, that than unwedded was,
Of Constance all the pleinë cas
As godelich as he couthë, tolde.
The king was glad and said he wolde
Comen thider in suche a wise,
That he him might of her avise.

LYDGATE.

[JOHN LYDGATE was born at the village of Lydgate near Newmarket in Suffolk, about 1370. His death probably occurred about 1440. Apparently the latest date discoverable in any of his poems is 1433, in which year he wrote a sort of 'city poem,' celebrating the pageants, processions, and other rejoicings in the city of London on the occasion of the solemn entry of Henry VI. He was a monk in the Benedictine monastery of Bury St. Edmunds. Among his numerous writings three stand out prominently: the *Storie of Thebes*, written when he was nearly fifty; the *Troye Book*, begun under Henry IV, and finished about 1420; and the *Falls of Princes*, written between 1422 and 1433.]

Lydgate seems to have been stimulated to write partly by the example and renown of Chaucer, partly by a predilection for the French poets of that day—Christine de Pisan, Machault, Granson, &c.—and the desire to emulate them. He was a monk of that monastery of St. Edmund king and martyr, at Bury, into the interior life of which Jocelyn de Brakelonde, much helped by his modern editor[1], has enabled us to look so clearly. But Abbot Hubert and Abbot Samson had laboured and gone to their account more than two centuries before, and though his rule remained the same, the conditions of life were much changed in the interval, even for a monk of Bury. In particular, the dazzling and distracting images of *Literature* besieged his cell, and haunted his thoughts, with a persistency unknown at the earlier period. Then the vernacular literatures were in their infancy, and sober Latin was the ordinary dress of a cultivated man's thought ; now, in France and Italy, and in England, numerous works, bearing the imprint of the newest spirit of the day, decked also with sallies of wit and beautiful imagery which came directly from the heart and brain, through the familiar mother-tongue, were circulating amongst and influencing all who could think and feel. Lydgate, who by his

[1] Mr. Carlyle, in Part II of his *Past and Present.*

own account had little vocation for the cloister, whose boyhood had been mischievous[1], his youth lazy and riotous[2], and his early manhood disedifying[3], for a long time cared little about St. Edmund and the special duties of the monastic life. He had an intense admiration for Chaucer, and his first large work seems to have been *The Storie of Thebes*, which he represents as a new Canterbury tale, told by himself soon after his joining the company of pilgrims at Canterbury. It is founded on the *Thebaid* of Statius and the *Teseide* of Boccaccio, and written in the ten-syllable rhyming couplet which Chaucer had used with such effect in *The Knightes Tale.* The prologue is spirited, but when the body of the poem is reached the attention soon flags. Chaucer versifies with facility, and also with power ; Lydgate has the facility without the power. His next considerable work, on the story of Troy, was undertaken about A.D. 1412, at the request of Prince Henry, afterwards Henry V., and finished in 1420. The prince desired that the 'noble storye' of Troye should be as well known in England as elsewhere, and as well written in English—

'As in the Latyn and the Frenshe it **is.**'

Troy was then regarded as the 'antiqua mater' of every European nation. It would therefore seem very fitting, that since Wace and his English translators, following Geoffrey of Monmouth, had given in the vernacular the story of the original Trojan settlement of England under Brutus the great-grandson of Aeneas, the moving vicissitudes of the city to which Brutus and Aeneas belonged should also now be told in English. This poem is in five books, and written, like *The Storie of Thebes*, in the ten-syllable couplet. It is founded on the Latin prose history of Troy by Guido di Colonna, a Sicilian jurist of the thirteenth century. The austere old layman

---

[1] 'To my bettre did no reverence,
　　Of my sovereyns gafe no fors at al,
　　Wex obstinat by inobedience,
　　Ran into gardyns, applys ther I stal.'

[2] 'Loth to ryse, lother to bedde at eve,
　　With unwash handys reedy to dyneer,
　　My Pater-noster, my crede, or my beleeve,
　　Cast at the cok; loo! this was my manere.'

[3] 'Of religioun I weryd a blak habite,
　　Oonly outward as by apparence.'

Lydgate's Testament, among his *Minor Poems*, edited by Mr. Halliwell.

wrote many things to the disadvantage of the fair sex which are painful to the politeness of the monk, who declares that he trans-lates them unwillingly, and would give their author, were he alive, a 'bitter penance' for his crabbed language. In the third book, where the story of Troilus and Cressida is introduced, Lydgate seizes the opportunity of paying an ardent tribute of praise, love, and admiration to his 'maister Chaucer,' who had chosen that subject for a poem.

The versification of Lydgate, in this *Troy-book* and in *The Storie of Thebes*, as well as in his numerous shorter pieces, is extremely rough. If the structure of the lines is attentively considered, it will be seen that he did not regard them as consisting of ten syllables and five feet, or at least that he did not generally so regard them, but rather as made up of two halves or counter-balancing members, each containing two accents. Remembering this, the reader can get through a long passage by Lydgate or Barclay with some degree of comfort ; though, if he were to read the same passage with the expectation of meeting always the due number of syllables, his ear would be continually disappointed and annoyed. This vicious mode of versification was probably a legacy from the alliterative poets, whose popularity, especially in the North of England, was so great that their peculiar rhythm long survived after rhyme and measure had outwardly carried the day. Not to mention Layamon's *Brut*, where we see a curious mixture of rhyme and alliteration,—the former, as the poem proceeds, gradually edging out the latter,—romances and other pieces of much later date can be pointed out, in which not only rhyme and measure but even the stanza form is adopted (for instance, in the *Anters of Arthur*, published by the Camden Society, 1842), yet still alliteration is carefully practised, and the syllabic lawlessness which the alliterator held to be his privilege, maintained. In the South of England, where the influences of French and Italian literature were more powerful, alliteration was repudiated ; thus we find Chaucer making his ' Persone ' say,—

> 'I am a sotherne man,
> I cannot geste, *rom, ram, ruf*, by my letter.'

'To geste' meant to write in alliterative style, because of the great number of romances or *gestes* so written which were then in circulation.

Lydgate's last notable work was *The Falls of Princes*, founded on a French version of the Latin treatise by Boccaccio, *De Casibus Virorum Illustrium.* It is dedicated to Humphrey Duke of Gloucestei, brother to Henry V, whom he speaks of as dead, and mentions his having written his *Troy-book* at his desire. The subject of this vast poem, which is in nine books, and was printed in folio in 1558, may be gathered from the old title-page, which runs, ' The Tragedies gathered by Jhon Bochas of all such Princes as fell from theyr Estates throughe the Mutability of Fortune since the creation of Adam until his time ; wherin may be seen what vices bring menne to destruccion, wyth notable warninges howe the like may be avoyded. Translated into English by John Lidgate, Monke of Burye.' The Monk's Tale of Chaucer proceeds on the same lines ; and a company of Marian or Elizabethan poets, Sackville, Baldwin, Ferrers, &c., working out the same idea, but with a more distinct ethical purpose, produced that stupendous but forgotten work, the *Myrrour for Magistrates.* In this work Lydgate adopted the seven-line stanza so much employed by Chaucer, and also seems to have taken more pains than before to emulate the rhythmic excellence of his master's work. Hence the *Falls of Princes* is, of his three principal poems, by far the most readable. In the beginning of the eighth book he complains of age and poverty ; and one of the minor poems, written while he was employed on this work, is in the form of a letter to the Duke of Gloucester, saying that his ' purs was falle in great rerage' (arrears), and asking for money.

In his old age the *genius loci*, and the saintly memories which clung round the monastery, appear to have influenced the poet more than in his youth. We find him composing a metrical ' Life of St. Edmund,' which still reposes in MS., and writing the ' Legend of St. Alban ' for the monks of that famous monastery.

Of his minor poems a large and not uninteresting selection was edited some forty years ago for the Percy Society by Mr. Halliwell. They are mostly written in an octave stanza, not the *ottava rima*, but one in which the second rhyme embraces the second, fourth, fifth and seventh lines, whilst the third rhyme connects the sixth and eighth. A considerable number are in the ' rhyme royal,' or seven-line stanza. Two or three of them are satirical, not to say cynical ; several are descriptive ; but the majority are either versions of French or Latin fabliaux, or moralizing pieces based on proverbs and old saws. There is much that is vivid and forcible in the picture of the manners and humours of

London and Westminster given in *London Lickpenny*. *Pur le Roy* may remind us of the effusions of Elkanah Settle the city poet, unmercifully ridiculed by Pope in the *Dunciad*. If it may certainly be attributed to Lydgate, it proves that he was living in 1433, in which year occurred the visit of Henry VI to London after his coronation, when the citizens received him with extraordinary demonstrations of joy and loyalty. The pageants, dresses, uniforms, speeches, &c., are described by the poet with a wearisome minuteness. It is unlikely that Lydgate lived long after writing this poem, but the exact year of his death has never been ascertained. It happened while he was engaged in translating into rhyme royal a French version of the supposed work of Aristotle, addressed to Alexander, which is variously entitled *On the Government of Princes*, *The Secret of Secrets*, and *The Philosopher's Stone*. At the head of one of the MSS. of this work[1] (which has never been printed) there is a small picture of Lydgate : he is represented as an old man, dressed in the black habit of the Benedictines, and tendering, bare-headed and on his knees, his book to some august personage above him, who is meant either for Henry VI or St. Edmund the patron of his monastery.

T. ARNOLD.

[1] Harl. 4826.

London Lickpenny.

To London once my stepps I bent,
Where trouth in no wyse should be faynt,
To Westmynster-ward I forthwith went,
To a man of law to make complaynt ;
I sayd, 'for Marys love, that holy saynt !
Pity the poore that wold proceede' ;
But for lack of mony I cold not spede.

[After visiting all the courts at Westminster one after another, and finding
that everywhere want of cash is the one insuperable impediment, he
passes eastward to the City.]

Then unto London I dyd me hye,
Of all the land it beareth the pryse :
'Hot pescodes,' one began to crye,
'Strabery rype, and cherryes in the ryse' ;
One bad me come nere and by some spyce,
Peper and safforne they gan me bede[1],
But for lack of mony I myght not spede.

Then to the Chepe I began me drawne,
Where mutch people I saw for to stand ;
One ofred me velvet, sylke, and lawne,
An other he taketh me by the hande,
'Here is Parys thred, the fynest in the land' ;
I never was used to such thyngs indede,
And wanting mony, I might not spede.

Then went I forth by London stone,
Th[o]roughout all Canwyke streete ;
Drapers mutch cloth me offred anone ;
Then comes me one, cryed, 'Hot shepes feete' ;
One cryde 'makerell,' 'ryshes[2] grene,' an other gan greete[3] ;
On bad me by a hood to cover my head,
But for want of mony I myght not be sped.

---

[1] began to offer me.   [2] rushes.   [3] cry.

Then I hyed me into Est-Chepe;
One cryes rybbs of befe, and many a pye:
Pewter pottes they clattered on a heape;
There was harpe, pype, and mynstralsye.
'Yea, by cock! nay, by cock!' some began crye;
Some songe of Jenken and Julyan for there mede;
But for lack of mony I myght not spede.

Then into Corn-Hyll anon I yode[1],
Where was mutch stolen gere amonge;
I saw where honge myne owne hoode,
That I had lost amonge the thronge;
To by my own hood I thought it wronge,
I knew it well as I dyd my crede,
But for lack of mony I could not spede.

The taverner tooke me by the sleve,
'Sir,' sayth he, 'wyll you our wyne assay'?
I answered, 'That can not mutch me greve:
A peny can do no more then it may';
I drank a pynt, and for it did paye;
Yet sone a-hungerd from thence I yede,
And wantyng mony, I cold not spede.

Then hyed I me to Belyngsgate;
And one cryed, 'Hoo! go we hence!'
I prayd a barge-man, for God's sake,
That he wold spare me my expence.
'Thou scapst not here,' quod he, 'under two **pence**;
I lyst not yet bestow my almes dede.'
Thus, lackyng mony, I could not spede.

Then I convayd me into Kent;
For of the law wold I meddle no more;
Because no man to me tooke entent,
I dyght me to do as I dyd before.
Now Jesus, that in Bethlem was bore,
Save London, and send trew lawyers there **mede**!
For who so wantes mony with them shall not spede.

---

[1] went.

From Lydgate's 'Dietary,' or Rules for Health.

And if so be that lechis done the faile[1],
   Thanne take good hede, and usë thyngës three,
Temperat diete, temperat travaile,
   Nat malicious for none adversité ;
Meke in trouble, gladde in poverté ;
   Riche with litel, content with suffisaunce ;
Nat grucchyng[2], but mery like thi degré :
   If phisyk lak, make this thy governaunce.

     *   *   *   *   *   *

Fyre at morowe, and towards bed at eve,
   For mystis blak, and eyre[3] of pestilence ;
Betime at masse, thow shalt the better preve,
   First at thi risyng do to God reverence,
Visite the poor with intyre diligence,
   On al nedy have thow compassioun,
And God shal sendë grace and influence,
   To encreasë the and thy possessioun.

Suffre no surfetis in thy house at nyght,
   Ware of rere-soupers[4], and of grete excesse,
Of noddyng hedës, and of candel light,
   And sloth at morow, and slomberyng idelnes,
Whiche of al vices is chief porteresse ;
   Voyde al drunklew, lyers, and lechours ;
Of al unthriftës exile the mastres,
   That is to say, dyse, players, and haserdours.

After mete beware, make not to longë slepe,
   Hede, foote, and stomak preserve ay from cold ;
Be not to pensyf, of thought take no kepe ;
   After thy rent, mayntenë thyn houshold,
Suffre in tymë, in thi right be bold ;
   Swerë none othis no man to begyle ;
In thy youth be lusty, sad whan thow art olde.

---

[1] if physicians make thee fall ill.   [2] murmuring.
    [3] air.   [4] late suppers.

Dyne nat at morwe aforne thyn appetite,
   Clere eyre and walkyng makith goode digestioun,
Between meles drynk nat for no froward delite,
   But[1] thurst or travaile yeve the occasion ;
Over-salt mete doth grete oppressioun
   To feble stomakes, whan they can nat refrayne ;
For nothing more contrary to theyr complexioun,
   Of gredy handes the stomak hath grete peyne.

Thus in two thinges standith al the welthe
   Of sowle and body, whoso lust to sewe[2],
Moderat foode gevith to man his helthe,
   And al surfetis doth from hym remeue[3],
And charité unto the sowle is dewe :
   This ressayt[4] is bought of no poticarye,
Of maister Antony, nor of maister Hewe,
   To all indifferent, richest diatorye[5].

DESCRIPTION OF THE GOLDEN AGE.

[*Falls of Princes*, book vii.]

Rightwisenes chastised al robbours,
   By egall balaunce of execucion,
Fraud, falsë mede, put backward fro jurours,
   True promes holde, made no delacioun[6] ;
Forswearing shamed durst enter in no toun,
   Nor lesingmongers, because Attemperaunce
Had in that world wholy the governaunce.

That golden world could lovë God and drede,
   All the seven dedes of mercy for to use,
The rich was ready to do almës dede,
   Who asked harbour, men did him not refuse ;
No man of malice would other tho accuse,
   Defame his neighbour, because Attemperaunce
Had in that world wholy the governaunce.

---

[1] unless.   [2] follow.   [3] remove.   [4] receipt, for recipe.
      [5] dietary.   [6] no informers at work.

The true marchant by measure bought and sold,
Deceipt was none in the artificer,
Making no balkes, the plough was truely hold,
Abacke stode ldlenes, farre from labourer,
Discrecion marcial at diner and supper,
Content with measure, because Attemperaunce
Had in that world wholy the governaunce.

Of wast in clothing was that time none excesse ;
Men might the lord from his subjectës know ;
A difference made twene povertie and richesse,
Twene a princesse and other statës lowe ;
Of horned boastës no boast was tho blowe,
Nor counterfeit feining, because Attemperaunce
Had in that world wholy the governaunce.

This golden world long whylë dyd endure,
Was none allay in that metall sene,
Tyll Saturne ceased, by record of scripture,
Jupiter reygned, put out his father clëne,
Chaunged obrison into silver shene,
Al up so downe, because Attemperaunce
Was set asyde, and loste her governaunce.

OCCLEVE.

[THOMAS OCCLEVE, or HOCCLEVE (the name is spelt both ways in tne MSS. of his works), was born between 1365 and 1370. He is thought to have been of north-country parentage, deriving his name from the village of Hocclough in Northumberland. One of his minor poems, addressed to Richard duke of York, cannot well have been written before 1448, since the young prince Edward (born in 1441) and his French tutor Picard are mentioned in it. Occleve must therefore have lived to a great age, but the precise year of his death is unknown. His principal poem, *De Regimine Principum*, was written in 1411 or 1412. The asceitainable dates of his minor poems, of which only a portion has been printed, range between 1400 and 1448.]

The principal work of Thomas Occleve is the poem *De Regimine Principum*, a free version of the Latin treatise written under that title by Aegidius or Giles, a native of Rome and a disciple of St. Thomas Aquinas, which he dedicated to Philip le Hardi, son of St. Louis. This poem is in the rhyme royal, and contains between five and six thousand lines. Nearly a third part of it is taken up with a Prelude or proem, which is considerably more interesting than the work itself. A slight analysis of this proem will bring Occleve before us, both as a man and a writer, more clearly than anything else could.

After a restless night, spent in painful and fruitless musing on the insecurity of all things here below, the poet goes forth into the fields near his lodging in the Strand. A poor old man meets him, and plies him with questions as to the reason of his dejection. After naming various causes of trouble, he says—

> 'If thou fele the in any of thise ygreved,
> Or elles what, tel on in Goddes name;
> Thou seest, al day the begger is releved,
> That syt and beggith, crookyd, blynd, and lame;
> And whi? for he ne lettith for no shame
> His harmes and his povert to bewreye
> To folke, as thei goon bi hym bi the weye.'

The old man goes on to warn him against indulgence in too prolonged and solitary meditations. By these, he says, men are sometimes led on to deny the faith, as happened in the case of a heretic 'not longe agoo,' who denied that after consecration the eucharistic bread was Christ's body. For this he was burnt, though the prince (Henry) tried hard to save him, and promised to obtain his full pardon and the means of living from the king, if he would return to the faith[1]. He speaks also of the folly of extravagance in dress,—that costly and 'outragious array,' which will ruin England if it is not stopped,—on the thoughtlessness and wantonness of youth, and so on. The author, much consoled and edified, tells his mentor who he is, and how he lives. He is a writer to the Privy Seal[2], and has an annuity of twenty marks a year in the Exchequer, granted him by Henry IV. But his misfortune is that he can never depend on this being paid regularly, so that he is sometimes in danger of starving. If this be so now, what will be his plight when he is grown old, and has no other resource but the annuity? Herein lies the secret cause of his dejection. The old man, after counselling a religious resignation to the divine will, questions him still further, and finding that he is a literary man, and had known Chaucer, advises him to compose some new work and present it to the Prince, who will perhaps graciously accept it and relieve the author from his distress :

> 'Write him no thinge that sowneth unto vice,
> Kithe[3] thi love in mater of saddenesse[4],
> Loke if thou finde canst any tretice
> Grounded on his astates holsomnesse;
> Suche thing translate, and unto his highnesse,
> As humbely as thou canst, present;
> Do this, my sone.' 'Fadir, I assent.'

But he laments that 'the honour of English tounge is deed,' with whom he might have taken counsel ; then follows the celebrated passage on Chaucer, which will be found among our extracts[5]. The poet returns home, takes parchment, and writes a dedication

---

[1] This was Thomas Badby, executed in April 1410, under the statute of 1401.

[2] Among the Additional MSS. in the British Museum may be seen a large volume, No. 24,062, the documents in which, or the greater part of them, are said to be in Occleve's handwriting.

[3] Make known.   [4] a serious subject.   [5] See pp. 127, 128.

of his work to the Prince of Wales, Shakspere's Prince Hal. It is founded, he says, on Aristotle's 'boke of governaunce' (the supposed correspondence between Aristotle and Alexander which made so deep an impression on the mediæval mind), and the work of Aegidius above mentioned; he has also studied the work of Jacobus de Cessolis (Casali) called *The Chess-moralized*[1]; and the fruits of these studies he now presents to the Prince. The poem is not interesting. The various aspects under which his duty presents, or ought to present, itself to the mind of a ruler are considered successively under the heads of justice, good faith, temperance, mercy, prudence, deliberation, and so forth.

Other poems ascribed to Occleve are—the story of Gerelaus emperor of Rome and his virtuous empress, and that of Jonathas and the three jewels. Both these are from the *Gesta Romanorum:* they have never been printed, but the story of Jonathas was modernised by Browne and introduced into the *Shepherd's Pipe* (1614). Some of his minor poems were edited in 1798 by a Mr. Mason. The longest of them, *La male régle de T. Hoccleve,* exhibits a picture of the jovial and riotous life led by the poet in his younger days, which is in complete accordance with that presented in the proem to the *De Regimine.*

T. Arnold.

[1] One of the first books printed by Caxton, under the name of *The Game and Play of the Chesse.*

FROM THE PROEM TO THE 'DE REGIMINE PRINCIPUM.'

But wele awaye, so is myn hertë wo,
That the honour of English tounge is deed,
Of which I was wonte have counseil and rede.

O maister dere and fader reverent,
My maister Chaucer! floure of eloquence,
Mirrour of fructuous entendement,
O universal fadir in science,
Allas! that thou thyne excellent prudence
In thy bedde mortel myghtest not bequethë;
What eyled Dethe? allas, why wold he sle the?

O Dethe, that didest not harmë singulere
In slaughtre of hym, but alle this lond it smerteth;
But natheles yit hast thow no powere
His name to slee; his hye vertu asterteth
Unslayne fro the, whiche ay us lyfly herteth[1]
With bookës of his ornat endityng,
That is to alle this londe enlumynyng.

Hastow[2] nat eek my maistre Gower slayne?
Whos vertu I am insufficient
For to descreyve, I wote wel in certeyne:
For to sleen alle this world thow hast y-ment,
But syn oure Lord Christ was obedient
To thee, in feyth I can no better seye,
His creaturës musten thee obeye.

---

[1] encourages.   [2] Hast thou.

From the 'De Regimine Principum.'

Symple is my goste, and scars my letterure,
Unto youre excellencë for to write
Myne inward love, and yit in aventure
Wol I me put, thogh I can but lyte ;
My derë maister,—God his soulë quyte,—
And fader, Chaucer, fayne wold have me taught,
But I was dulle, and lerned lyte or naught.

Allas ! my worthy maister honorable,
This londes verray tresour and richesse,
Dethe by thy dethe hath harme irreperable
Unto us done : hir vengeable duresse
Dispoiled hath this londe of the swetnesse
Of rethoryk, for unto Tullius
Was never man so like amongës us.

Also, who was hyër in phylosofye
To Aristotle in our tunge but thow ?
The steppës of Virgile in poysye
Thou folwedest eke : men wote well ynow.
That combre-worlde[1], that the my maister slowe[2],
(Wolde I slayne werë !) dethe was to hástyf
To renne on the, and revë the thy lyf.

*   *   *   *   *   *

She myght han taryed hir vengeaunce a whyle,
Tyl sum man hadde egal to the be ;
Nay, let be that ; she wel knew that this yle
May never man forth bringe lik to the,
And hir officë nedys do must she ;
God bad hire soo, I truste as for the beste,
O maystir, maystir, God thy soulë reste !

---

[1] bane of the world; viz. death.   [2] slew.

JAMES THE FIRST

OF SCOTLAND.

[Born 1394. Captured by the English in time of peace 1405, and kept a prisoner in the Tower, in Nottingham Castle, at Croydon, and at Windsor, till 1424, when he was released. In that year he married Lady Jane Beaufort, daughter of the Earl of Somerset, and granddaughter of John of Gaunt. She was the heroine of his principal poem. *The King's Quair.* In 1437, after reigning thirteen years in Scotland, the king was assassinated at Perth. Besides *The King's Quair*, he is commonly supposed to have written one or two other poems, notably the humorous ballad *Christ's Kirk on the Green.*]

James the First of Scotland is one of the earliest and one of the best of the imitators of Chaucer, and is the first of that line of Scottish poets who kept the lamp of poetry burning during the darkness of the fifteenth century. His chief poem, *The King's Quair*, or the King's Book, seems to have been written in 1423 or 1424, about the time of his marriage ; when he was thirty years old and when Chaucer had been in his grave nearly a quarter of a century. *The King's Quair*, written in the seven-lined stanza, is about 200 stanzas long, and it tells in a style that is a curious mixture of autobiographical fact and allegorical romance the story of the captive king's courtship of the lady who became his wife, Lady Jane Beaufort. The royal prisoner, after a sleepless night spent in reading Boethius, rises at the sound of the matins bell and begins to complain of his fortune. Suddenly in the garden beneath he sees a lady, so beautiful that he who has never known love till now is instantly subdued, the nightingale and all the other birds singing in harmony with his passion. The lady disappears, and half-sleeping, half-swooning, he dreams of a strange sequel. He seems to be carried up 'fro spere to spere' to the Empire of Venus ; he wins her favour, but since his desperate case requires 'the help of other mo than one goddesse,' he is sent on with Good Hope for guide to the Palace of Minerva. The goddess of Wisdom receives him with a speech on Free Will; and finally, after an interview with the great goddess Fortune herself, he wakes to find a real messenger from Venus, 'a turture, quhite as calk,' bringing him a flowering branch, joyful evidence that his suit is to succeed :—

> '"Awake! awake! I bring, lover, I bring
>   The newis glad that blissful ben and sure
> Of thy confort; now laugh, and play, and sing,
>   That art beside so glad an aventure;
>   For in the hevyn decretit is the cure."
> And unto me the flouris did present;
> With wyngis spred hir wayis furth sche went.'

With this and with the poet's song of thankfulness *The King's Quair* ends.

No subject could be better fitted than the love-story of the captive king for a poem in the accepted *trouvère* style. The paganism of romance was fond of representing man as passive material in the hands of two supernatural powers, Fortune and Love; and poetry for two centuries was for ever returning to the theme. James the First was neither original enough to depart from the poetical conventions of his time, nor artist enough to work out his subject without confusion and repetition; and yet the personal interest of his story and its adaptability to the chosen form of treatment would be enough to save *The King's Quair* from oblivion, even without the unquestionable beauty of much of the verse. The dress is the common tinsel of the time, but the body beneath is real and human.

We have said that King James was an early and close imitator of Chaucer[1]. His nineteen years of captivity allowed him to steep himself in Chaucer's poetry, and any Chaucerian student who reads *The King's Quair* is constantly arrested by a line or a stanza or a whole episode that exactly recalls the master. It is unneces-

---

[1] The concluding stanza of the poem is as follows :—

> 'Vnto impnis of my maisteris dere,
>   *Gowere* and *Chaucere*, that on the steppis satt
> Of rethorike, quhill thai were lyvand here,
>   Superlatiue as poetis laureate,
> In moralitee and eloquence ornate,
>   I recommend my buk in lynis seven,
>   And eke thair saulis vnto the blisse of hevin.'

sary to point out, for instance, the close resemblance of the passage
which we here quote, the King's first sight of Lady Jane, to the
passage in *The Knightes Tale* (see p.   ) where Palamon and Arcite
first see Emilye. Not only the general idea but the details are
copied; for example, the King, like Palamon, doubts whether the
beautiful vision be woman or goddess. The ascent to the Empire
of Venus is like an abridgement of *The Hous of Fame*. Minerva's
discussion of Free Will is imitated from Chaucer's rendering of
the same theme, after Boethius, in *Troylus and Creseyde*. The
catalogue of beasts near the dwelling of Fortune, is an echo of
Chaucer's catalogue of birds in *The Parlement of Foules*. Isolated
instances of imitation abound ; thus

> ' Til Phebus endit had his bemës brycht,
> And bad go farewel every lefe and floure,
> *That is to say, approchen gan the night,*'

is a repetition of a well-known passage in *The Frankeleynes Tale*:—

> ' For the orizont had left the sonne his liht,
> (That is as much to sayn as it was nyht).'

A passage in *Troylus* is recalled by

> ' O besy goste, ay flikering to and fro';

and another by the King's concluding address to his book—'Go,
litel tretis.' Outside *The King's Quair*, the 'gude and godlie
ballate' here given (although it would be difficult to prove that
it belongs to King James) is obviously modelled on the 'good
counseil of Chaucer' which we have quoted above (p.   ). These
examples of the influence of Chaucer upon so rich a mind as that
of the young King of Scotland are strong evidence of the greatness
of the earlier poet and of the instantaneousness with which his
genius made itself felt.

EDITOR.

The King's Quair.

(St. 30 et seqq.)

Bewailling in my chamber thus allone,
    Despeired of all joye and remedye,
For-tiret of my thought and wo-begone,
    And to the wyndow gan I walk in hye,
To see the warld and folk that went forbye,
    As for the tyme though I of mirthis fude
    Mycht have no more, to luke it did me gude.

Now was there maid fast by the Touris wall
    A gardyn faire, and in the corneris set
Ane herbere grene, with wandis long and small
    Railit about, and so with treis set
Was all the place, and hawthorn hegis knet,
    That lyf[1] was non walkyng there forbye,
    That mycht within scarce any wight aspy.

So thick the beuis[2] and the leves grene
    Beschadit all the allyes that there were,
And myddis every herbere mycht be sene
    The scharpë grenë suetë jenepere,
Growing so fair with branchis here and there,
    That, as it semyt to a lyf without,
    The bewis spred the herbere all about.

And on the smalë grenë twistis sat
    The lytil suetë nyghtingale, and song
So loud and clere, the ympnis consecrat
    Of luvis use, now soft now lowd among,
That all the gardynis and the wallis rong
    Ryght of thaire song, and on the copill next
    Of thaire suete armony, and lo the text :—

---

[1] living thing.   [2] boughs.

'Worschippe, ye that loveris bene, this May,
 For of your bliss the kalendis are begonne,
And sing with us, away winter, away,
 Come somer, come, the suete seson and sonne,
Awake, for schame ! that have your hevynis wonne,
 And amourously lift up your hedis all,
 Thank Lufe that list you to his merci call.'

Quhen thai this song had song a littil thrawe[1],
 Thai stent a quhile, and therewith unafraid,
As I beheld, and kest myn eyen a-lawe[2],
 From beugh to beugh thay hippit and thai plaid,
And freschly in thair birdis kynd araid
 Thaire fatheris[3] new, and fret thame in the sonne,
 And thankit Lufe, that had thair makis[4] wonne.

This was the planë ditie of thair note,
 And therewithall unto myself I thought,
Quhat lufe is this, that makis birdis dote?
 Quhat may this be, how cummyth it of ought?
Quhat nedith it to be so dere ybought ?
 It is nothing, trowe I, bot feynit chere[5],
 And that one list to counterfeten chere.

Eft wold I think, O Lord, quhat may this be?
 That Lufe is of so noble mycht and kynde,
Lufing his folk, and suich prosperitee
 Is it of him, as we in bukis fynd,
May he oure hertis setten and unbynd :
 Hath he upon our hertis suich maistrye?
 Or all this is bot feynit fantasye?

For giff he be of so grete excellence,
 That he of every wight hath cure and charge,
Quhat have I gilt to him, or doon offense
 That I am thrall, and birdis gone at large ?
Sen him to serve he mycht set my corage,
 And, gif he be not so, than may I seyne
 Quhat makis folk to jangill of him in veyne ?

---

[1] space.   [2] below.   [3] feathers.   [4] mates.   [5] mirth.

Can I not ellis fynd bot giff that he
 Be lord, and, as a god, may lyve and regne,
To bynd, and louse, and maken thrallis free,
 Than wold I pray his blissful grace benigne
To hable[1] me unto his service digne,
 And evermore for to be one of tho
 Him trewly for to serve in wele and wo.

And therewith kest I doun myn eye ageyne,
 Quhare as I saw walkyng under the Toure,
Full secretely, new cumyn hir to pleyne,
 The fairest or the freschest youngë floure
That ever I sawe, methought, before that houre,
 For quhich sodayne abate, anon astert
 The blude of all my body to my hert.

And though I stood abaisit tho a lyte,
 No wonder was ; for quhy? my wittis all
Were so ouercome with plesance and delyte,
 Only through latting of myn eyen fall,
That sudaynly my hert become hir thrall,
 For ever of free wyll, for of manace[2]
 There was no takyn[3] in her suetë face.

And in my hede I drew rycht hastily,
 And eft sonës I lent it out ageyne,
And saw hir walk that verray womanly,
 With no wight mo, bot only women tueyne,
Than gan I studye in myself and seyne,
 Ah ! suete, are ye a warldly creature,
 Or hevinly thing in likeness of nature ?

Or ar ye god Cupidis owin princesse ?
 And cumyn are to louse me out of band,
Or are ye veray Nature the goddesse,
 That have depayntit with your hevinly hand
This gardyn full of flouris, as they stand?
 Quhat sall I think, allace ! quhat reverence
 Sall I minister to your excellence.

---

[1] enable. [2] pride, lit. menace. [3] token.

Giff ye a goddesse be, and that ye like
  To do me payne, I may it not astert ;
Giff ye be warldly wight, that dooth me sike[1],
  Quhy lest[2] God mak you so, my derest hert,
To do a sely prisoner thus smert,
  That lufis you all, and wote of nought but wo?
  And, therefore, merci, suete ! sen it is so.

Quhen I a lytill thrawe had maid my mone,
  Bewailing myn infortune and my chance,
Unknawin how or quhat was best to done,
  So ferre I fallyng into lufis dance,
That sodeynly my wit, my contenance,
  My hert, my will, my nature, and my mynd,
  Was changit clene rycht in ane other kind.

          *   *   *   *   *

In hir was youth, beautee, with humble aport,
  Bountee, richesse, and womanly faiture,
God better wote than my pen can report ;
  Wisdome, largesse, estate, and conyng sure
In every point, so guydit hir mesure,
  In word, in dede, in schap, in contenance,
  That nature mycht no more hir childe auance.

Throw quhich anon I knew and understude
  Wele that sche was a wardly creature,
On quhom to rest myn eyë, so much gude
  It did my wofull hert, I yow assure
That it was to me joye without mesure,
  And, at the last, my luke unto the hevin
  I threwe furthwith, and said thir versis sevin :

O Venus clere ! of goddis stellifyit,
  To quhom I yelde homage and sacrifise,
Fro this day forth your grace be magnifyit,
  That me ressauit[3] have in such [a] wise,
To lyve under your law and your seruise ;
  Now help me furth, and for your merci lede
  My hert to rest, that deis nere[4] for drede.

---

[1] causes me to sigh.   [2] did it please.   [3] received.   [4] nearly dies.

Quhen I with gude entent this orison
   Thus endit had, I stynt a lytill stound,
And eft myn eye full pitously adoun
   I kest, behalding unto hir lytill hound,
   That with his bellis playit on the ground,
     Than wold I say, and sigh therewith a lyte,
     Ah ! wele were him that now were in thy plyte !

An other quhile the lytill nyghtingale,
   That sat upon the twiggis, wold I chide,
And say rycht thus, Quhare are thy notis smale,
   That thou of love has song this morowe tyde ?
Seis thou not hir that sittis the besyde ?
   For Venus' sake, the blisfull goddesse clere,
   Sing on agane, and make my Lady chere.

FROM 'THE GUDE AND GODLIE BALLATES' (1570).

Sen throw vertew incressis dignitie,
   And vertew is flour and rute of noblés ay,
Of ony wit, or quhat estait thou be
   Ris[1] steppis few, and dreid for none effray :
   Exill al vice, and follow treuth alway ;
Lufe maist thy God, that first thy lufe began,
And for ilk inche He will thé quyte ane span.

Be not ouir proude in thy prosperitie,
   For as it cummis, sa will it pass away ;
The tyme to compt is schort, thou may weill se,
   For of grene gress sone cummis wallowit hay.
   Labour in treuth, quhilk suith is of thy fay ;
Traist maist in God, for He best gyde thé can,
And for ilk inche He will thé quyte ane span.

Sen word is thrall, and thocht is only fre,
   Thou dant[2] thy toung, that power hes and may,
Thou steik thy ene[3] fra warldis vanitie,
   Refraine thy lust, and harkin quhat I say ;
   Graip or thou slyde[4], and keip furth the hie way,
Thou hald thé fast upon thy God and man,
And for ilk inche He will thé quyte ane span.

---

[1] rise.   [2] daunt, i. e. tame, restrain.   [3] eyes.   [4] grip ere thou slide.

ROBERT HENRYSON.

142- to 148-.

[Of ROBERT HENRYSON, the charming fabulist, Chaucer's aptest and brightest scholar, almost nothing is known. David Laing conjectures him to have been born about 1425, to have been educated at some foreign university, and to have died towards the closing years of the fifteenth century. It is certain that in 1462, being then 'in Artibus Licentiatus et in Decretis Bacchalarius,' he was incorporated of the University of Glasgow; and that he was afterwards schoolmaster in Dunfermline, and worked there as a notary-public also.]

Henryson was an accomplished man and a good and genuine poet. He had studied Chaucer with the ardour and insight of an original mind, and while he has much in common with his master, he has much that is his own. His verse is usually well-minted and of full weight. Weak lines are rare in him; he had the instinct of the refrain, and was fond of doing feats in rhythm and rhyme; he is close, compact, and energetic. Again, he does not often let his learning or his imagination run away with him and divert him from his main issue. He subordinates himself to the matter he has in hand; he keeps himself to the point, and never seeks to develope for development's sake; and so, as it appears to me, he approves himself a true artist. It follows that, as a story-teller, he is seen to great advantage. He narrates with a gaiety, an ease, a rapidity, not to be surpassed in English literature between Chaucer and Burns. That, moreover, he was a born dramatist, there is scarce one of his fables but will prove. It is to be noted that he uses dialogue as a good playwright would use it; it is a means with him not only of explaining a personage but of painting a situation, not only of introducing a moral but of advancing an intrigue. He had withal an abundance of wit, humour, and good sense; he had considered life and his fellow men, nature and religion, the fashions and abuses of his epoch, with the grave, observant amiability of a true poet ; he was directly in sympathy with many things ; he loved to read and to laugh ; it was his business to moralise and teach. It was natural that he should choose the fable as a means of expressing himself. It was fortunate as well ; for his fables are perhaps the best in the language, and are worthy of consideration and regard even after La Fontaine himself.

To a modern eye his dialect is distressingly quaint and crabbed. In his hands, however, it is a right instrument, narrow in compass, it may be, but with its every note sonorous and responsive. To know the use he made of it in dialogue, he must be studied in *Robyne and Makyne,* the earliest English pastoral ; or at such moments as that of the conversation between the widows of the Cock who has just been snatched away by the Fox ; or in the incomparable *Taile of the Wolf that got the Nek-Herring throw the Wrinkis of the Fox that Begylit the Cadgear,* which, outside La Fontaine, I conceive to be one of the high-water marks of the modern apologue. In such poems as *The Three Deid Powis* [1], where he has anticipated a something of Hamlet at Yorick's grave, as *The Abbey Walk,* the *Garmond of Fair Ladies,* the *Reasoning between Age and Youth,* it is employed as a vehicle for the expression of austere thought, of quaint conceitedness, of solemn and earnest devotion, of satirical comment, with equal ease and equal success. As a specimen of classic description—as the classic appeared to the mediæval mind—I should like to quote at length his dream of Æsop. As a specimen of what may be called the choice and refined realism that informs his work, we may give a few stanzas from the prelude to his *Testament of Cresseid.* It was winter, he says, when he began his song, but, he adds, in despite of the cold,

> 'Within mine orature
> I stude, when Titan with his bemis bricht
> Withdrawin doun, and sylit [2] undercure,
>   And fair Venus, *the beauty of the nicht,*
>   *Uprais, and set unto the west full richt*
> *Hir goldin face,* in oppositioun
> Of God Phoebus, direct discending doun.

---

[1] skulls.   [2] hidden.

Throwout the glass hir bemis brast so fair
    That I micht se on everie side me by.
The northin wind had purifyit the air,
    And sched the misty cloudis fra the sky[1].
    The frost freisit, the blastis bitterly
Fra Pole Artick came quhistling loud and schill,
And causit me. remufe aganist my will.

*   *   *   *   *

I mend the fire, and beikit[2] *me about,*
    Than tuik a drink my spreitis to comfort,
And armit me weill fra the cauld thairout;
    To cut the winter nicht and mak it schort,
    I tuik ane Quair[3], and left all uther sport,
Writtin be worthie Chaucer glorious
Of fair Cresseid and lusty Troilus.'

In this charming description Henryson, by the use of simple
and natural means and by the operation of a principle of selection
that is nothing if not artistic, has produced an impression that
would not disgrace a poet skilled in the knacks and fashions of
the most pictorial school.   Indeed I confess to having read in its
connection a poem that might in many ways be imitated from it
(*La Bonne Soirée*), and to feeling and seeing more with Henry-
son than with Théophile Gautier.

W. E. HENLEY.

[1] 'The wind had swept from the wide atmosphere,
    Each vapour that obscured the sunset's ray.'   *Shelley.*
[2] bustled.   [3] book.

The Garmond of Fair Ladies

Wald my gud Lady lufe me best,
　And wirk eftir my will,
I suld ane Garmond gudliest
　Gar mak hir body till.

Off hie honour suld be hir hud,
　Upoun hir heid to weir,
Garneist with governance so gud,
　Na demyng suld hir deir.

Hir sark suld be hir body nixt,
　Of chestetie so quhyt,
With schame and dreid togidder mixt,
　The same suld be perfyt.

Hir kirtill suld be of clene constance,
　Lasit with lesum[1] lufe,
The mailyheis[2] of continuance
　For nevir to remufe.

Hir gown suld be of gudliness
　Weill ribband with renowne,
Purfillit with plesour in ilk place,
　Furrit with fyne fassoun[3].

Hir belt suld be of benignitie,
　About hir middill meit ;
Hir mantill of humilitie,
　To tholl[4] bayth wind and weit.

Hir hat suld be of fair having
　And hir tepat[5] of trewth,
Hir patelet[6] of gude pansing[7],
　Hir hals-ribbane[8] of rewth.

---

[1] lawful.　　[2] eylet-holes.　　[3] good manners.　　[4] withstand.
　　[5] tippet　　[6] ruffet.　　[7] fair thought.　　[8] neck-ribband.

Hir slevis suld be of esperance,
 To keip hir fra dispair ;
Hir gluvis of the gud govirnance,
 To hyd hir fyngearis fair.

Hir schone [1] suld be of sickernes [2],
 In syne that scho nocht slyd ;
Hir hoiss [3] of honestie, I ges,
 I suld for hir provyd.

Wald scho put on this Garmond gay,
 I durst sweir by my seill [4],
That scho woir nevir grene nor gray
 That set [5] hir half so weill.

THE TAILL OF THE LYOUN AND THE MOUS.

Ane Lyoun at his pray wery foirrun [6],
 To recreat his limmis and to rest,
Beikand [7] his breist and bellie at the sone,
 Under ane tree lay in the fair forrest,
 Swa [8] come ane trip [9] of Myis out of thair nest,
Rycht tait and trig [10], all dansand in ane gyis [11],
And ouer the Lyoun lansit [12] twyis or thrys.

He lay so still, the Myis wes nocht effeird
 Bot to and fro out ouer him tuke thair trace,
Sum tirllit at the campis [13] of his beird,
 Sum spairit nocht to claw him on the face ;
 Merie and glaid, thus dansit thay ane space,
Till at the last the nobill Lyoun woke,
And with his pow [14] the maister Mous he tuke.

---

[1] shoes.   [2] security.   [3] hosen.   [4] knowledge.   [5] suited.
[6] foundered, spent.   [7] basking; as a transitive verb.   [8] So.
[9] band.   [10] gamesome and dainty.   [11] figure.   [12] darted.
[13] long hair, locks.   [14] paw.

Scho gaif ane cry, and all the laif[1] agast
    Thair dansing left, and hid thame sone allquhair;
Scho that wes tane, cryit and weipit fast,
    And said, Allace! oftymes, that scho come thair;
'Now am I tane ane wofull presonair,
And for my gilt traistis[2] incontinent,
Of lyfe and deith to thoill[3] the jugement.'

Than spak the Lyoun to that cairfull[4] Mous,
    'Thou cative wretche, and vile unworthie thing,
Ouer malapert, and eik presumpteous
    Thow wes, to mak out ouer me thy tripping.
    Knew thow nocht weill, I wes baith lord and king
Of Beistis all?' 'Yes,' quod the Mous. 'I knaw;
But I misknew, because ye lay so law.

'Lord! I beseik thy kinglie royaltie,
    Heir quhat I say, and tak in pacience;
Considder first my simple povertie,
    And syne thy mychtie hie magnificence:
    See als how thingis done of negligence,
Nouther[5] of malice nor presumptioun,
Erar[6] suld haif grace and remissioun.

'We wir repleit, and had grit haboundance
    Of alkin[7] thingis, sic as to us effeird[8].
The sweit sesoun provokit us to dance,
    And mak sic mirth as Nature to us leird[9].
    Ye lay so still, and law upon the eird,
That, be my saull, we wend[10] ye had bene deid,
Ellis wald we nocht haif dancit ouer your heid.'

'Thy fals excuse,' the Lyoun said agane,
    'Sall nocht availl ane myte, I underta[11]:
I put the case, I had bene deid or slane
    And syne my skyn bene stoppit[12] full of stra,
    Thocht thow had found my figure lyand swa,
Because it bair the prent of my persoun,
Thow suld for feir on knees haif fallin doun.

---

[1] rest.   [2] expect.   [3] endure.   [4] sorrowful.   [5] And not.
[6] rather.   [7] all manner of.   [8] appertained.   [9] taught.
[10] thought.   [11] undertake, vow.   [12] stuffed.

'For thy trespas thow sall mak na defence,
    My nobill persoun thus to vilipend ;
Of thy feiris, nor thy awin negligence,
    For to excuse, thow can na cause pretend ;
    Thairfoir thow suffer sall ane schamefull end,
And deith, sic as to tressoun is decreit,
On to the gallous harlit[1] be the feit.'

'A mercie, Lord ! at thy gentrice[2] I ase[3] :
    As thow art king of beistis coronat[4],
Sober thy wraith, and let thy yre ouerpas,
    And mak thy mynd to mercy inclynat ;
    I grant offence is done to thyne estait,
Quhairfoir I worthie am to suffer deid,
Bot[5] gif[6] thy kinglie mercie reik[7] remeid[8].

'In everie juge mercy and reuth suld be
    As assessouris, and collaterall.
Without mercie Justice is crueltie,
    As said is in the Lawis Spirituall ;
    Quhen rigour sittis in the tribunall,
The equitie of Law quha may sustene ?
Richt few or nane, but[9] mercie gang betwene.

Alswa ye knaw the honour triumphall
    Of all[10] victour upon the strenth dependis
Of his conqueist, quhilk manlie in battell
    Throw jeopardie of weir lang defendis.
    Quhat price or loving[11] quhen the battell endis
Is said of him, that ouercummis ane man
Him[12] to defend quhilk nouther may nor can?

'Ane thousand myis to kill, and eke devoir,
    Is lytill manheid to ane strong Lyoun ;
Full lytill worschip haif ye wyn thairfoir,
    To quhais strenth is na comparisoun :
    It will degraid some part of your renoun,
To slay ane Mous quhilk may mak na defence,
Bot[13] askand mercie at your Excellence.

---

[1] dragged, trundled.   [2] nobleness, magnanimity.   [3] ask.
[4] crowned.   [5] and [6] unless.   [7] and [8] bestow pardon.   [9] unless.
[10] every.   [11] praise.   [12] For 'himself.'   [13] unless it be that ot.

Also, it semis [1] nocht your celsitude [2],
  Quhilk usis daylie meittis delitious,
To syle your teith, or lippis, with my blude,
  Quhilk to your stomok is contagious :
  Unhailsum meit is of ane sairie [3] Mous,
And that namelie untill ane strang Lyoun
Wont till be fed with gentill vennisoun.

'My lyfe is lytill worth, my deith is less,
  Yet and I leif, I may peradventure
Supple your Hienes beand in destres ;
  For oft is sene, ane man of small stature
  Reskewit hes ane Lord of hie honour,
Keipit that wes in point to be ouerthrawin [4],
Throw misfortune. Sie cace may be your awin.'

Quhen this was said, the Lyoun his language
  Paissit [5], and thocht according to ressoun,
And gart mercie his cruell yre asswage,
  And to the Mous grantit remissioun,
  Opinnit his pow, and scho on kneis fell doun,
And baith his handis unto the hevin upheld,
Cryand 'Almychtie God, mot you foryeild [6] !'

Quhen scho wes gone, the Lyoun held to hunt,
  For he had nocht, bot levit on his pray,
And slew baith tayme and wylde, as he wes wont,
  And in the cuntrie maid ane greit deray [7] ;
  Till at the last, the pepill fand the way
This cruell Lyoun how that they mycht tak,
Of hempyn cordis strang nettis couth thay mak.

And in ane rod, quhair he wes wont to ryn,
  With raipis rude fra tre to tre it band :
Syne kest ane range on raw the wod [8] within,
  With hornis blast, and kennettis [9] fast calland :
  The Lyoun fled, and throw the rone [10] rynnand,

---

[1] it does not become.   [2] highness.   [3] sorry.   [4] that was just upon the point of being overthrown.   [5] appeased.   [6] Almighty God reward you.   [7] disorder.   [8] i. e. they drove the wood.   [9] hounds.   [10] scrub.

Fell in the nett, and hankit[1] fute and heid,
For all his strenth he couth mak na remeid,
Welterand about with hiddeous rummissing[2],
    Quhyles to, quhyles fra, gif he mycht succour get;
Bot all in vane, it vailyeit him na thing,
    The mair he flang[3], the safter wes the net;
    The raipis rude wes sa about him plet[4],
On everilk syde, that succour saw he none,
Bot still lyand, and murnand maid his mone.

'O lamit Lyoun! liggand[5] heir sa law,
    Quhair is the mycht of magnificence?
Of quhome all brutall beistes in eird stude aw,
    And dreid to luke upon thy excellence!
    But[6] hoip or help, but succour or defence,
In bandis strang heir mon I ly, allace!
Till I be slane—I see nane uther grace.

'Thair is na wy[7] that will my harmis wreck[8],
    Nor creature do confort to my croun;
Quha sall me bute[9]? quha sall my bandis brek?
Quha sall me put fra pane of this presoun?'—
Be he had mide this lamentatioun,
Throw aventure[10] the lytill Mous come neir,
And of the Lyoun hard the pietuous beir[11].

And suddandlie it come in till hir mynd
    That it suld be the Lyoun did hir grace,
And said, 'Now ever I fals, and richt unkynd,
    But gif I quit sum part of thy gentrace[12]
    Thow did to me:' and on this way scho gais
To hir fellowis, and on thame fast can cry,
'Cum help, cum help;' and they come all in hy[13].

'Lo!' quod the Mous, 'this is the samin Lyoun
    That grantit grace to me quhen I wes tane;
And now is fast heir bundin in presoun,
    Brekand his heart, with sair murning and mane;
    Bot we him help of succour wait[14] he nane;

---

[1] enta gled.   [2] roaring.   [3] struggled.   [4] woven.
[5] lying.   [6] Without.   [7] No man.   [8] avenge.   [9] help.
[10] By chance.   [11] Noise.   [12] kindness.   [13] in haste.   [14] knows.

Cum help to quyte ane gude turne for ane uther ;
Go, louse him sone ;'—and they said, ' Yea, gude brother.'

They tuke na knyfe, their teith wes scharp aneuch :
  To se that sicht, forsuith it wes greit wonder,
How that thay ran amang the raipis teuch
  Befoir, behind, sum yeild [1] about, sum under,
  And schuir [2] the raipis of the nett in schunder ;
Syne bad him ryse, and he start up anone,
And thankit thame, syne on his way is gone.

    [1] went.   [2] cut.

WILLIAM DUNBAR.

[Born 145-, died 1513 (?).]

M. TAINE, in his *History of English Literature*, leaps from
Chaucer to Surrey with the remark, 'Must we quote all these
good people who speak without having anything to say?.. dozens
of translators, importing the poverties of French poetry, rhyming
chroniclers, most commonplace of men.' Of this period he men-
tions only and merely names Gower and Lydgate and Skelton.
The more genuine successors of Chaucer were the Scotch poets,
who, almost alone in our island, lit up the dusk of the 15th century
with some flashes of native power. Neither James I nor Henryson
was commonplace, and Dunbar, the most conspicuous of the
group, displays in his best work a distinct original genius.

William Dunbar was born, probably in East Lothian, between
1450 and 1460. He entered the University of St. Andrews in
1475, and took his full degree in 1479. In early life, according to
his own account, he went about from Berwick to Dover, and
passed over to Calais and Picardy, preaching and alms-gathering
as a Franciscan noviciate ; but he became dissatisfied with this
life and does not seem to have taken the vows of the order. It
has been inferred from allusions in his verse that he was for some
years employed in connection with foreign embassies. Toward
the close of the century we find him in attendance on the Scotch
Court, a poet with an established reputation, and a continual
suitor for place. In 1500 he received from the king (James IV)
a pension of £10, raised by degrees, during the next ten years to
£80 —then a respectable annuity : but he never obtained the
Church promotion, to which on somewhat irrelevant grounds he
constantly laid claim.

Dunbar revisited England in 1501, when the king's marriage
with the Princess Margaret was being negotiated. *The Thistle
and the Rose* in commemoration of that event was composed on
the 9th of May, 1503. *The Golden Targe* and the *Lament for the*

Makars were issued from Chepman's—the first Scotch—press in 1508. The poet must have accompanied the Queen, in whose favour he stood fast, to the north in 1511; for he celebrates her reception at Aberdeen. There is a record of an instalment of his pension being paid in August, 1513 : the rest is a blank, and it has been plausibly conjectured that he may, a month later, have fallen at Flodden with the King. If he lived to write the *Orison* on the passing of Albany to France (doubtfully attributed to him) the absence of any other reference to the great national disaster is remarkable. We are, however, only certain from an allusion in Lyndesay's *Papyngo* that he must have been dead in 1530.

The writings of Dunbar—on the whole the most considerable poet of our island in the interval between Chaucer and Spenser—are mainly Allegorical, Satirical, and Occasional. Allegory, a disease of the middle ages infecting most poets down to the end of the 16th century, was rife in our old Scotch verse, much of which is cast on the model of *The Romaunt of the Rose* and *The Flower and the Leaf.* In *The Golden Targe* the influence of those works is conspicuous, though much of the imitation is indirect, through *The King's Quair.* Like the royal minstrel, the poet represents himself as being roused from his slumbers by the morning, and led to the bank of a stream where presently a ship lands a hundred ladies (v. the 'world of ladies' in *The Flower and the Leaf*) in green kirtles : among them are Nature, Dame Venus, the fresh Aurora, Latona, Proserpine, &c. Then Cupid appears, leading a troop of gods to dance with the goddesses. Love detecting the poet orders his arrest. Reason defends him with the Golden Targe, till Presence comes and throws dust into the eyes of Reason and leaves Venus victrix. The plot is no more barren than those of Chaucer's own contributions to the literature of the Courts of Love : but the *Targe* is farther beset by an unusual number of the 'aureate' terms or affected Latinisms with which the Scotch poets of the century disfigured their language, planting them, as Campbell says, like children's flowers in a mock garden. The merit of the piece almost wholly consists in its riches of description; but this is enough to preserve it : the ship 'like a blossom on the spray,' the skies that 'rang with shouting of the larks,' recall Chaucer's Orient and anticipate Burns. *The Thistle and the Rose* has the same pictorial charm, with the added merit of being inspired by a genuine national enthusiasm. It is perhaps the happiest political allegory in our tongue. Heraldry has never been more skilfully handled, nor compliments more gracefully paid, nor fidelity more persuasively preached to a monarch than in this poem, which has under its southern dress a strong northern body. This remark applies to the author's work in general, and more especially to those compositions in which he mingles allegory with satire. His masterpiece, *The Dance of the Deadly Sins,* may have been suggested by passages in *Piers Plowman,* as it in turn transmitted its influence through Sackville to *The Faery Queen:* but the horrid crew of vices, summoned from their dens by lines each vigorous as the crack of a whip, are real, and Scotch, and contemporary, drawn from a knowledge of the world, not from books : these supplied Dunbar with his terminology, that with his thought. His most elaborate composition, and that which ranks next in originality to *The Dance, The Two Married Women and the Widow,* has a tincture of Boccaccio and *The Wife of Bath,* but the scene is again a northern summer eve, and the gossips are contemporaries of Queen Margaret. The poet's satire, which is here subtle, is often furious. Half his minor poems are vollies of abuse, unprecedented in English literature, unless by some of the almost contemporaneous outbursts of Skelton, mainly directed against those who had, by fair means or foul, been promoted over him ; the other half are religious and moral reveries, those of a good Catholic who lived when the first mutters of the Reformation were in the air, and are the finest devotional fragments of their age.

The special characteristics of Dunbar's genius are variety and force. His volume is a medley in which tenderness and vindictiveness, blistering satire and exuberant fancy meet. His writings are only in a minor degree bound up with the politics of his age, and though they reflect its fashions, they for the most part appeal to wider human sympathies. He has not wearied us with any very long poem. His inspiration and his personal animus find vent within moderate bounds, but they are constantly springing up at different points and assuming various attitudes. At one time he is a quiet moralist praising the golden mean, at another he is as fierce as Juvenal. Devoid of the subtlety and the dramatic power of Chaucer, his attacks, often coarse, are always direct and sincere. His drawing, like that of the *Ballads,* is in 'he fore-ground : there is no chiaroscuro in his pages, no more than in those of his countrymen from Barbour to Burns. The story of the battle between *The Tailor and Souter* might have been written by Rabelais : *The Devil's Inquest* is the original of *The Devil's Drive:* the meditation on *A Winter's Walk* is not un-worthy of Cowper, nor the best stanzas in *The Merle and the Nightingale* of Wordsworth.

Like Erasmus, Dunbar railed against the friars and their indulgences ' quorum pars fuit :' but there is no reason to suspect that he was more or less than a large-hearted Roman Catholic in his creed. He had none of the protagonist spirit which is required to assail the traditions of a thousand years. Of a generally buoyant temper he appears, like most satirists, to have taken at times a view of the world, in which the Epicurean gloom dominates the Epicurean gaiety. ' All earthly joy returns in pain' is the refrain of one of his poems ; ' Timor mortis conturbat me' of another. The shadow of the ' atra dies' falls aslant his most luxuriant moods. In the sonnet beginning :—

> ' What is this life but ane straucht way to deid,
>   Whilk has a time to pass and nane to dwell';

there is something of the satiety of a disappointed worldling ; but in others—

> ' Be merry, man, and tak not sare in mind
>   The wavering of this wretched warld of sorrow,'—

we have the manlier temper : on the one side *Vanitas vanitatum, et omnia vanitas,* on the other the *Philosophie Douce.*

J. NICHOL.

Note. In the following extracts, the text of Mr. David Laing, Ed. 1834, has been generally adhered to. Where there are different readings, that has been adopted which gives the best metre.

From 'The Thrissill and the Rois.'

Quhen Merche wes with variand windis past
  And Appryle had, with her silver schouris,
Tane leif at Nature with ane orient blast,
  And lusty May, that muddir is of flouris,
  Had maid the birdis to begyn thair houris [1]
Amang the tendir odouris reid and quhyt,
Quhois armony to heir it wes delyt :

In bed at morrow, sleiping as I lay,
  Me thocht Aurora, with hir cristall ene
In at the window lukit by the day,
  And halsit me, with visage paill and grene ;
  On quhois hand a lark sang fro the splene [2],
Awalk, luvaris, out of your slomering
Sé hou the lusty morrow dois up spring.

Me thocht fresche May befoir my bed up studc,
  In weid depaynt of mony diverss hew,
Sobir, benyng, and full of mansuetude
  In brycht atteir of flouris forgit new
  Hevinly of color, quhyt, reid, broun and blew,
Balmit in dew, and gilt with Phebus bemys ;
Quhyll all the house illumynit of her lemys [3].

Slugird, scho said, awalk annone for schame,
  And in my honour sum thing thou go wryt ;
The lark hes done the mirry day proclame,
  To raise up luvaris with confort and delyt ;
  Yit nocht incressis thy curage to indyt,
Quhois hairt sum tyme hes glaid and blisfull bene,
Sangis to mak undir the levis grene.

  *   *   *   *   *   *

[1] morning orisons.   [2] from the heart.   [3] rays.

Than callit scho all flouris that grew on feild
   Discirnyng all thair fassionis and effeiris
Upone the awfull Thrissil scho beheld
   And saw him kepit with a busche of speiris ;
   Considering him so able for the weiris
A radius croun of rubeis scho him gaif,
And said, In feild go furth and fend the laif[1] :

And sen thou art a King, thou be discreit ;
   Herb without vertew thow hald nocht of sic pryce
As herb of vertew and of odour sueit ;
   And lat no nettill vyle, and full of vyce,
   Hir fallow[2] to the gudly flour-de-lyce ;
Nor latt no wyld weid, full of churlicheness,
Compair hir till the lilleis nobilness.

Nor hald non udir flour in sic denty[3]
   As the fresche Rois, of cullour reid and quhyt :
For gife thow dois, hurt is thyne honesty ;
   Considring that no flour is so perfyt,
   So full of vertew, plesans, and delyt,
So full of blisful angeilik bewty,
Imperiall birth, honour and dignité.

FROM 'THE GOLDYN TARGE.'

Bryght as the stern of day begouth to schyne
Quhen gone to bed war Vesper and Lucyne,
   I raise, and by a rosere[4] did me rest :
Up sprang the goldyn candill matutyne,
With clere depurit bemes cristallyne
   Glading the mery foulis in thair nest ;
   Or Phebus was in purpur cape revest
Up raise the lark, the hevyn's menstrale fyne
In May, in till a morow myrthfullest.

Full angellike thir birdis sang thair houris
Within thair courtyns grene, in to thair bouris,
   Apparalit quhite and red, wyth blomes suete ;

---

[1] rest.   [2] match herself.   [3] favour.   [4] rose bush.

Anamalit was the felde with all colouris,
The perly droppis schuke in silvir schouris ;
  Quhill all in balme did branch and levis flete[1],
  To part fra Phebus did Aurora grete[2] ;
Hir cristall teris I saw hyng on the flouris
  Quhilk he for lufe all drank up with his hete.

For mirth of May, wyth skippis and wyth hoppis,
The birdis sang upon the tender croppis,
  With curiouse notis, as Venus chapell clerkis ;
The rosis yong, new spreding of their knoppis[3]
War powderit brycht with hevinly beriall droppis
  Throu bemes rede, birnyng as ruby sperkis ;
  The skyes rang for schoutyng of the larkis.

The Dance of the Sevin Deidly Synnis.

Off Februar the fyiftene nycht,
Full lang befoir the dayis lycht,
  I lay in till a trance ;
And than I saw baith Hevin and Hell :
Me thocht, amangis the feyndis fell,
  Mahoun gart cry ane Dance
Off Schrewis[4] that were nevir schrevin,
Aganis the feist of Fasternis evin[5]
  To mak thair observance ;
  He bad gallandis ga graith a gyiss[6]
And kast up gamountis[7] in the Skyiss
  As varlotis dois in France.

 * * * * * *

Heilie Harlottis on hawtane wyiss
Come in with mony sindrie gyiss,
  Bot yit luche[8] nevir Mahoun,
Quhill[9] preistis come in with bair schevin nekkis,
Than all the Feyndis lewche, and made gekkis[10],
  Blak-belly and Bawsy Broun.

 * * * * * *

[1] gloat. [2] weep. [3] buds. [4] Outcasts. [5] Fasterns Evening,
the eve of Lent. [6] prepare a guise or mask. [7] gambols
[8] laughed. [9] till. [10] mocks.

Lat sé, quoth he, now quha begynnis,
With that the fowll Sevin Deidly synnis
    Begowth to leip at anis.
And first of all in Dance was Pryd,
With hair wyld bak, and bonet on syd,
    Lyk to mak vaistie[1] wanis[2];
And round abowt him, as a quheill,
Hang all in rumpillis to the heill
    His kethat[3] for the nanis:
Mony prowd trumpour with him trippit
Throw skaldand[4] fyre, ay as thay skippit
    Thay gyrnd with hyddous granis.

Than Yre come in with sturt and stryfe;
His hand wes ay upoun his knyfe,
    He brandeist lyk a beir[5]:
Bostaris, braggaris, and barganeris,
Eftir him passit in to pairis,
    All bodin[6] in feir of weir
In jakkis, and scryppis and bonettis of steill
Thair leggis wer chenyeit to the heill,
    Frawart was their affeir:
Sum upoun uder with brandis beft[7],
Sum jagit uthers to the heft
    With knyvis that scherp cowd scheir.

Nixt in the Dance followite Invy,
Fild full of feid[8] and fellony,
    Hid malyce and dispyte.
For pryvie hatrent that tratour trymlit;
Him followit mony freik[9] dissymlit
    With fenyeit wordis quhyte:
And flattereris in to menis facis;
And bak-byttaris in secreit placis,
    To ley that had delyte;
And rownaris[10] of false lesingis,
Allace! that courtis of noble kingis
    Of thame can nevir be quyte.

---

[1] waste.   [2] abodes.   [3] robe.   [4] northern participial form.
[5] observe that *ei* represents several southern vowel sounds.   [6] arrayed.
[7] struck.   [8] feud.   [9] petulant fellow.   [10] whisperers.

Nixt him in Dans come Cuvatyce
Rute of all evill, and grund of vyce,
   That nevir cowd be content :
Catyvis, wrechis, and ockeraris [1],
Hud-pykis [2], hurdaris [3], and gadderaris [4],
   All with that warlo went :
Out of thair throttis thay schot on udder
Hett moltin gold, me thocht, a fudder [5]
   As fyre-flawcht [6] maist fervent ;
Ay as thay tumit [7] them of schot,
Feyndis fild thame new up to the thrott
   With gold of allkin [8] prent.

Syne Sweirnes [9], at the secound bidding,
Come lyk a sow out of a midding,
   Full slepy wes his grunyie [10],
Mony sweir bumbard belly huddroun [11],
Mony slute daw [12], and slepy duddroun [13],
   Him servit ay with sounyie [14].
He drew thame furth in till a chenyie
And Belliall with a brydill renyie
   Evir lascht thame on the lunyie [15] :
In Dans thay war so slaw of feit,
Thay gaif thame in the fyre a heit,
   And made them quicker of counyie [16].

Than Lichery, that lathly corse,
Came berand [17] lyk a bagit horse,
   And Ydilness did him leid ;
Thair wes with him ane ugly sort,
And mony stynkand fowll tramort [18]
   That had in syn bene deid :
Quhen they were enterit in the Dance,
Thay wer full strenge of countenance,
   Lyke tortchis byrnand reid,

*   *   *   *   *

[1] usurers.   [2] misers.   [3] hoarders.   [4] gatherers.   [5] load,
properly of 128 lbs. weight.   [6] wild-fire.   [7] emptied   [8] of all kinds.
[9] sloth.   [10] grunt.   [11] tun-bellied sloven.   [12] slothful wench.
[13] slut.   [14] care.   [15] loins.   [16] apprehension.   [17] snorting.   [18] corpse.

Than the fowll monstir Gluttony
Of wame unsasiable and grèdy,
　　To Dance he did him dress :
Him followit mony fowll drunckart,
With can and collep[1], cop and quart,
　　In surffet and excess ;
Full mony a waistless wally-drag[2],
With wamis unweildable, did furth wag,
　　In creische[3] that did incress
Drynk ! ay thay cryit with many a gaip,
The Feyndis gaif thame hait leid to laip
　　Thair leveray[4] wes na less.

　　　*　　　*　　　*　　　*　　　*

Na menstrallis playit to thame but dowt,
For gle-men thair wer haldin owt,
　　Be day, and eik by nycht :
Except a menstrall that slew a man,
Swa till his heretage he wan,
　　And enterit by breif of richt.

Than cryd Mahoun for a Heleand Padyane[5]:
Syne ran a Feynd to feche Makfadyane,
　　Far northwart in a nuke ;
Be he the Correnoch had done schout,
Ersche men so gadderit him abowt,
　　In Hell grit rowme thay tuke ;
Thae tarmegantis, with tag and tatter,
Full lowd in Ersche begowth to clatter
　　And rowp[6] lyk revin and ruke.
The Devill sa devt wes with thair yell,
That in the depest pot of hell,
　　He smorit[7] thame with smuke.

---

[1] drinking cups.　　[2] outcast.　　[3] grease.　　[4] reward
　[5] Highland pageant.　　[6] croak.　　[7] smothered.

From 'The Lament for the Makaris Quhen he was Seik.'

I that in heill[1] wes and glaidness,
Am trublit now with gret seikness,
And feblit with infirmitie ;
    Timor Mortis conturbat me.

Our plesance heir is all vane glory
This fals Warld is bot transitory
The flesche is brukle[2], the Feynd is slé ;
    Timor Mortis conturbat me.

The stait of Man dois change and vary
Now sound, now seik, now blyth, now sary,
Now dansand mirry, now like to die ;
    Timor Mortis conturbat me.

No Stait in Erd heir standis sicker,
As with the wynd wavis the wickir[3],
So wavis this warldis vanité ;
    Timor Mortis conturbat me.

Unto the Deid gois all Estaitis
Princis, Prellattis, and Potestaitis,
Baith riche and puire of all degré ;
    Timor mortis conturbat me.

He takis the knychtis in to feild,
Anarmit under helme and scheild,
Victour he is at all mellie ;
    Timor Mortis conturbat me.

    *   *   *   *   *

I see that Makaris amang the laif[4]
Playis heir thair padyanis, syne gois to graif ;
Spairit is nocht thair faculté ;
    Timor Mortis conturbat me.

---

[1] health.   [2] brittle. .   [3] osier.   [4] poets among the rest.

He hes done peteouslie devour
The noble Chawcer of makaris flouir
The Monk of Bery, and Gower, all thré ;
    Timor Mortis conturbat me.

    *   *   *   *   *   *

He hes Blind Hary, and Sandy Traill
Slaine with his schot of mortall haill
Quhilk Patrick Johnestoun mycht nocht flé ·
    Timor Mortis conturbat me.

He hes reft Merseir his endyte,
That did in luve so lifly write,
So schort, so quyk, of sentence hie ;
    Timor Mortis conturbat me.

He hes tane Roull of Abirdene,
And gentil Roull of Corstorphine ;
Two bettir fallowis did no man sé ;
    Timor Mortis conturbat me.

In Dumfermelyne he hes tane Brown
With Maister Robert Henrisoun
Schir Johne the Ross embraist hes hé ;
    Timor Mortis conturbat me.

And he hes now tane, last of aw,
Gud gentill Stobo and Quintyne Schaw
Of quhome all wichtis hes petie ;
    Timor Mortis conturbat me.

Gud Maister Walter Kennedy,
In poynt of dede lyis veraly,
Gret reuth it were that so suld be ;
    Timon Mortis conturbat me.

Sen he has all my Brether tane,
He will nocht lat me leif alane,
On forse I mon his nyxt pray be ;
    Timor Mortis conturbat me.

Sen for the Deid remeid is non,
Best is that we for deid dispone,
Eftir our deid that leif may we ;
    Timor Mortis conturbat me.

GAWAIN DOUGLAS.

[GAWAIN DOUGLAS (born 1474–75) was a younger son of the famous Earl of Angus, called 'Bell the Cat.' Though even elementary education was rare in his noble family,

> ('Thanks to St. Bothan, son of mine,
> Save Gawain, ne'er could pen a line,')

Gawain devoted himself to study, matriculated at the University of St. Andrews in 1489, and took his degree in 1494. He published his *Palice of Honour* in 1501, and finished his translation of the *Aeneid* in 1513. He seems now to have abandoned poetry, and after many stormy intrigues, was consecrated Bishop of Dunkeld in 1515. He was carried down the 'drumly' stream of Scotch politics, and died in exile in London in 1522. The date of his unpublished poem *King Hart* is uncertain; it was probably composed between 1501 and 1512. An admirable edition of Douglas' works has lately been made, in four volumes, by Mr. John Small of Edinburgh.]

GAWAIN DOUGLAS attempted the poet's art amidst the clash of arms ; he was learned in an age and among a people that despised literature. The revival of letters, when it reached Scotland, was crushed out by the nobles, who hated dominies and Italians. Classical literature and Erasmus had a pupil in the young Archbishop of St. Andrews, a Stuart who fell under the English arrows, when 'groom fought like noble, squire like knight' around the king at Flodden. Gawain Douglas, noble by birth and ambitious of nature, ceased to court poetry, after poetry had done her best for him,—had helped the recommendations of the English Court to win him a bishopric from Leo X. The lilies and laurels of Italy, the sweet Virgilian measures, were soon blighted and silenced by the wind and hail of Scotland, by clerical austerity, and the storms of war that in those days beat round even episcopal palaces. Among all the poets beheld by Douglas in vision (in the *Palice of Honour*), but two or three were countrymen of his own.

The chief original poem of Douglas, *The Palice of Honour*, is an allegory of the sort which had long been in fashion. Moral ideas in allegorical disguises, descriptions of spring, and scraps of mediaeval learning were the staple of such compositions. Like the other poets, French and English, of the last two centuries, Douglas woke on a morning of May, wandered in a garden, and beheld various masques or revels of the goddesses, heroes, poets, virtues, vices (such as 'Busteousness'), and classical and Biblical worthies. In his vision he characteristically confused all that he happened to know of the past, made Sinon and Achitophel comrades in guilt and misfortune, while Penthesilea and Jeptha's daughter ranged together in Diana's company, and 'irrepreuabill Susane' rode about in the troop of 'Cleopatra and worthie Mark Anthone.' The diverting and pathetic combinations of this sort still render Douglas's poems rich in surprises, and he occasionally does poetical justice on the wicked men of antiquity, as when he makes Cicero knock down Catiline with a folio. To modern readers his allegory seems to possess but few original qualities. His poem, indeed, is rich with descriptions of flowers and stately palaces, his style, like Venus's throne, is 'with stones rich over fret and cloth of gold,' his pictures have the quaint gorgeousness and untarnished hues that we admire in the paintings of Crivelli. But these qualities he shares with so many other poets of the century which preceded his own, that we find him most original when he is describing some scene he knew too well, some hour of storm and surly weather, the bleakness of a Scotch winter, or a 'desert terribill,' like that through which 'Childe Roland to the dark tower came.' (See extracts 1 and 2.)

A poem of Douglas's which was not printed during his lifetime, *King Hart*, is also allegorical. King Hart, or the heart of man, dwells in a kind of city of Mansoul ; he is attended by five servants—the five senses,—besieged and defeated by Dame Pleasance, visited by Age, deserted by Youthhead, Disport, and Fresh Delight. There is nothing particularly original in an allegory of which the form was common before, and not unfrequently employed after the age of Douglas. (Compare 'the Bewitching Mistress Heart' in *The Legal Proceedings against Sin in Man-shire*, 1640.)

The little piece of verse called *Conscience* is not bad in its quibbling way. When the Church was young and flourishing, *Conscience* ruled her. Men wearied of *Conscience*, and cut off the *Con*, leaving *Science*. Then came an age of ecclesiastical learning, which lasted till the world 'thought that Science was too long a jape,' and got rid of *Sci.* Nothing was left now but *ens,* worldly substance, 'riches and gear that gart all grace go hence.' The Church in Scotland did not retain even *ens* long after the age of Douglas. Grace, on the other hand, waxed abundant.

The work by which Douglas lives, and deserves to live, is his translation of the *Aeneid.* It is a singular fruit of a barren and unlearned time, and, as a romantic rendering of the *Aeneid,* may still be read with pleasure. The two poets whom Douglas most admired of all the motley crowd who pass through *The Palice of Honour* were Virgil and Chaucer. Each of these masters he calls an *a per se.* He imitated the latter in the manner of his allegorical verse, and he translated the former with complete success. We must not ask the impossible from Douglas,—we must not expect exquisite philological accuracy ; but he had the 'root of the matter,' an intense delight in Virgil's music and in Virgil's narrative, a perfect sympathy with 'sweet Dido,' and that keen sense of the human life of Greek, Trojan, and Latin, which enabled him in turn to make them live in Scottish rhyme. If he talks of 'the nuns of Bacchus,' and if his Sibyl admonishes Aeneas to 'tell his beads,' Douglas is merely using what he thinks the legitimate freedom of the translator. He justifies his method, too, by quotations from Horace and St. Gregory. He is giving a modern face to the ancient manners, a face which his readers would recognise. In his prologues, his sympathy carries him beyond orthodox limits, and he defends the behaviour of Aeneas to Dido against the attacks of Chaucer. He is so earnest a 'humanist' that he places himself in the mental attitude of Virgil, and avers that Aeneas only deserted Dido at the bidding of the gods :—

> ' Certes, Virgill schawis Enee did na thing,
> Frome Dido of Cartaige at his departing,
> Bot quhilk the goddes commandit him to forne;
> And gif that thair command maid him mansworne,
> That war repreif to thair divinitee
> And na reproche unto the said Enee.'

But though Douglas is a humanist in verse, all the Bishop asserts himself in prose. In his prose note he observes that Enee falit then gretly to the sueit Dido, quhilk falt reprefit nocht the goddessis divinite, for they had na divinite. as said is before.' Though he adores the Olympians in verse, Douglas adopts the Euhemeristic theory in prose : 'Juno was bot ane woman, dochter to Saturn, sistir and spows to Jupiter king of Crete.' In spite of these edifying notes, Douglas's conscience pricked him, 'for he to Gentiles' bukis gaif sik keip.' Even if he knew Greek, he probably would not have translated Homer, as a friend asked him to do. The prologue to the Thirteenth Book of the *Aeneid* (i.e. of the book 'ekit' to Virgil by Mapheus Vegius,) proves that there were moments when he thought even Virgil a perilous and unprofitable heathen.

The language of Douglas, as he observes (Prologue to the First Book), is 'braid and plane,' that is to say, it is good broad Scotch, and still 'plain' enough to a Scotch reader. He does not, how-ever, 'clere all sudroun refuse,' when no Scotch word served his turn, and he frankly admits that

'the ryme
Causis me to mak digressioun sum tyme.'

Douglas's rank is that of an accomplished versifier, who deserted poetry with no great regret for the dangerous game of politics.

A. LANG.

A Desert Terrible.

[From *The Palice of Honour.*]

My rauist spreit[1] in that desert terribill,
Approchit neir that vglie flude horribill,
Like till[2] Cochyte the riuer infernall,
With vile water quhilk maid a hiddious trubil,
Rinnand ouirheid, blude reid, and impossibill
That it had been a riuer naturall;
With brayis[3] bair, raif[4] rochis like to fall,
Quhairon na gers[5] nor herbis were visibill,
Bot swappis[6] brint with blastis boriall.

This laithlie flude rumland as thonder routit,
In quhome the fisch ȝelland[7] as eluis schoutit,
Thair ȝelpis wilde my heiring all fordeifit,
Thay grym monstures my spreits abhorrit and doutit.
Not throw the soyl bot muskane[8] treis sproutit,
Combust, barrant, vnblomit and vnleifit,
Auld rottin runtis quhairin na sap was leifit,
Moch, all waist, widderit with granis moutit,
A ganand[9] den, quhair murtherars men reifit[10].

Quhairfoir my seluin was richt sair agast,
This wildernes abhominabill and waist,
(In quhome nathing was nature comfortand)
Was dark as rock, the quhilk the sey vpcast.
The quhissilling wind blew mony bitter blast,
Runtis rattillit and vneith[11] micht I stand.
Out throw the wod I crap on fute and hand,
The riuer stank, the treis clatterit fast.
The soyl was nocht bot marres[12], slike[13], and sand.

---

[1] ravished spirit.   [2] to.   [3] braes, slopes.   [4] riven.
[5] grass.   [6] sedges.   [7] screaming.   [8] rotten.   [9] proper.
[10] rob.   [11] scarcely.   [12] marsh.   [13] slime.

A Scottish Winter Landscape.

[From the *Prologue to the Aeneid*, Bk. vii.]

The frosty regioun ringis of the ʒeir,
The tyme and sessoune bitter cald and paill,
Thai schort days that clerkis clepe brumaill ;
Quhen brym [1] blastis of the northyne art [2]
Ourquhelmit had Neptunus in his cart,
And all to schaik the levis of the treis,
The rageand storm ourwalterand wally seis [3] ;
Reveris ran reid on spait with watteir broune,
And burnis hurlis all thair bankis downe,
And landbrist rumland [4] rudely wyth sic beir [5],
So loud ne rummist wyld lioun or beir.
Fludis monstreis, sic as meirswyne or quhailis [6],
For the tempest law [7] in the deip devallyis [8].
Mars occident, retrograide in his speir,
Provocand stryff, regnit as lord that ʒeir ;
Rany Orioune wyth his stormy face
Bewalit of the schipman by his rays ;
Frawart Saturne, chill of complexioune,
Throw quhais aspect derth and infectioune
Bene causit oft, and mortale pestilens,
Went progressiue the greis [9] of his ascens ;
And lusty Hebe, Junois douchtir gay,
Stud spulʒeit [10] of hir office and array.
The soill ysowpit into wattir wak [11],
The firmament ourkest with rokis blak,
The ground fadyt, and fauch wolx [12] all the **feildis,**
Montayne toppis sleikit wyth snaw ourheildis,
On raggit rolkis of hard harsk quhyne stane [13],
With frosyne frontis cauld clynty clewis [14] schane ;
Bewtie wes lost, and barrand schew the landis,
With frostis haire [15] ourfret the feildis standis.

---

[1] violent.   [2] quarter of the heaven.   [3] overwhelming the wavy seas.
[4] the flood roaring.   [5] cry, noise.   [6] porpoises or whales.   [7] low.
[8] descends.   [9] degrees.   [10] spoiled.   [11] wet.   [12] became
reddish.   [13] rough whin-stones.   [14] stony cliffs.   [15] hoar.

Soure bittir bubbis[1], and the schowris snell
Semyt on the sward ane similitude of hell,
Reducyng to our mynd, in every steid,
Goustly schaddois of eild and grisly deid,
Thik drumly scuggis[2] dirknit so the hevyne.
Dym skyis oft furth warpit feirfull levyne[3],
Flaggis of fyir, and mony felloun flawe,
Scharp soppis of sleit, and of the snypand[4] snawe.
The dowy[5] dichis war all donk and wait,
The law vaille flodderit all wyth spait,
The plane stretis and every hie way
Full of fluschis, doubbis[6], myre and clay.

*   *   *   *   *   *   ●

Our craggis, and the front of rochis seyre,
Hang gret isch schoklis lang as ony spere ;
The grund stude barrand, widderit, dosk and gray,
Herbis, flouris, and gersis wallowit away ;
Woddis, forestis, wyth nakyt bewis blout[7],
Stud strypyt of thair weyd in every hout[8].
So bustuysly Boreas his bugill blew,
The deyr full dern[9] dovne in the dalis drew ;
Smal byrdis, flokand throw thik ronnis[10] thrang,
In chyrmyng and with cheping changit thair sang,
Sekand hidlis and hirnys[11] thaim to hyde
Fra feirfull thudis of the tempestuus tyde.
The wattir lynnis[12] routtis, and every lynde
Quhyslyt and brayt of the swouchand wynde.
Puire laboraris and byssy husband men
Went wayt and wery draglyt in the fen ;
The silly scheip and thair lytill hyrd gromis
Lurkis vndir le of bankis, wodys, and bromys ;
And wthir[13] dantit gretar bestial,
Within thair stabillis sesyt into stall,
Sic as mulis, horsis, oxin and ky,
Fed tuskit baris[14], and fat swyne in sty,

---

[1] blasts.   [2] gloomy shadows.   [3] lightning.   [4] nipping.
[5] dreary.   [6] pools.   [7] naked.   [8] holt, wood.   [9] secretly.
[10] brambles.   [11] corners.   [12] waterfalls.   [13] other.   [14] boars.

Sustenit war by mannis gouernance
On hervist and on symmeris purviance.
Widequhair with fors so Eolus schouttis schyll
In this congelyt sessioune scharp and chyll,
The callour air, penetrative and puire,
Dasyng the bluide in every creature,
Maid seik[1] warm stovis, and beyne[2] fyris hoyt,
In double garmont cled and wyly coyt[3],
Wyth mychty drink, and meytis confortive,
Agayne the storme wyntre for to strive.

The Fête Champêtre.

[From *The Palice of Honour.*]

Our horsis pasturit in ane plesand plane,
Law at the fute of ane faire grene montane,
Amid ane meid schaddowit with ceder treis,
Saif fra all heit, thair micht we weill remane.
All kinde of herbis, flouris, frute, and grane,
With euerie growand tre thair men micht cheis,
The beriall[4] stremis rinnand ouir stanerie greis[5]
Made sober noyis, the schaw[6] dinnit agane
For birdis sang, and sounding of the beis.

The ladyis fair on diuers instrumentis,
Went playand, singand, dansand ouir the bentis[7],
Full angellike and heuinlie was thair soun.
Quhat creature amid his hart imprentis,
The fresche bewtie, the gudelie representis,
The merie speiche, fair hauingis[8], hie renoun
Of thame, wald set a wise man half in swoun,
Thair womanlines wryithit[9] the elementis,
Stoneist[10] the heuin, and all the eirth adoun.

---

[1] made men seek.   [2] genial.   [3] secret under-garment.
[4] like beryl.   [5] gravelly ledges.   [6] thicket.   [7] open fields.
[8] manners.   [9] disturbed.   [10] astonished.

A Ballade in Commendation of Honour.

[From *The Palice of Honour.*]

O hie honour, sweit heuinlie flour degest[1],
Gem verteous, maist precious, gudliest.
For hie renoun thow art guerdoun conding[2],
Of worschip kend the glorious end and rest,
But quhome[3] in richt na worthie wicht may lest.
Thy greit puissance may maist auance all thing,
And pouerall to mekill auaill sone bring[4].
I the require sen thow but peir[5] art best,
That efter this in thy hie blis we ring.

Of grace thy face in euerie place sa schynis,
That sweit all spreit baith heid and feit inclynis,
Thy gloir afoir[6] for till imploir remeid.
He docht[7] richt nocht, quhilk out of thocht the tynis[8];
Thy name but[9] blame, and royal fame diuine is;
Thow port at schort of our comfort and reid,
Till[10] bring all thing till glaiding efter deid,
All wicht but sicht of thy greit micht ay crynis[11],
O schene I mene, nane may sustene thy feid[12].

Haill rois maist chois till clois thy fois greit micht,
Haill stone quhilk schone vpon the throne of licht,
Vertew, quhais trew sweit dew ouirthrew al vice,
Was ay ilk day gar say the way of licht ;
Amend, offend, and send our end ay richt.
Thow stant, ordant as sanct, of grant[13] maist wise,
Till be supplie, and the hie gre[14] of price.
Delite the tite[15] me quite of site[16] to dicht,
For I apply schortlie to thy deuise.

---

[1] grave.　　[2] condign.　　[3] without whom.　　[4] bring the poor to great prosperity.　　[5] without a peer.　　[6] before thy glory.　　[7] avails.
[8] loses.　　[9] without.　　[10] to.　　[11] diminishes.　　[12] hatred.
[13] giving.　　[14] degree.　　[15] quickly.　　[16] shame.

THE GHOST OF CREUSA.

[From *The Aeneid*.]

How Eneas socht his spous, all the cost,
And how to him apperis hir grete gost.

To Priamus palice eftir socht I than,
An syne onto the temple fast I ran :
Quhar, at the porchis or closter of Juno,
Than all bot waist, thocht it was girth[1], stude **tho**
Phenix and dour Vlixes, wardanes tway,
For to observe and keip the spreith[2] or pray:
Thiddir in ane heip was gaderit precius geir,
Riches of Troy, and wther jewellis seir
Reft from all partis ; and, of templis brynt,
Of massy gold the veschale war furth hynt
From the goddis, and goldin tabillis all,
With precius vestmentis of spuilȝe triumphall :
The ȝing childring[3], and frayit matrounis eik,
Stude all on raw, with mony peteous screik
About the tresour quhymperand woundir sair.
And I also my self so bald wox thair,
That I durst schaw my voce in the dirk nycht,
And cleip and cry fast throw the stretis on hycht
Full dolorouslie, Creusa ! Creusa !
Agane, feil sise[4], in vane I callit swa[5],
Throw howsis and the citie quhar I ȝoid,
But[6] outhir rest or resoun, as I war woid[7] ;
Quhill that the figour of Creusa and gost,
Of far mair statur than air quhen scho was lost,
Before me, catife, hir seikand, apperit thair.
Abaisit I wolx, and widdersyns[8] start my hair,
Speik mycht I nocht, the voce in my hals[9] sa stak.
Than sche, belife, on this wise to me spak,

[1] though it was a sanctuary.   [2] booty.   [3] young children.
[4] many times.   [5] so.   [6] without.   [7] mad.   [8] in extraordinary
fashion.   [9] neck.

With sic wourdis my thochtis to assuage ;
O my suete spous, into sa furious raige
Quhat helpis thus thi selfin to turment ?
This chance is nocht, but goddis willis went[1];
Nor it is nocht [a] lefull thing, quod sche,
Fra hyne Creuse thou turs[2] away with the,
Nor the hie governour of the hevin abufe is
Will suffir it so to be ; bot the behufis
From thens to wend full far into exile,
And our the braid see saile full mony a myle,
Or thou cum to the land Hesperia,
Quhar, with soft cours, Tybris of Lidia
Rynnis throw the riche feildis of peple stout.
Thair is grete substaunce ordanit the, but dowt,
Thair sall thou haue ane realme, thair sall thou ryng[3],
And wed to spous the dochtir of a kyng.
Thy weping and thi teris do away,
Quhilk thou makis for thi luifit Crewsay :
For I, the nece of mychty Dardanus,
And guide dochtir vnto the blissit Venus,
Of Mirmidonis the realme sall neuir behald,
Nor ʒit the land of Dolopes so bald,
Nor go to serve na matroun Gregioun ;
Bot the grete moder of goddis ilk one
In thir cuntreis withhaldis me for evir.
Adew, fair weile, for ay we man dissevir !
Thou be guide frend, luif wele, and keip fra skaith
Our a ʒong sone, is comoun till ws baith.
Quhen this was spokin, away fra me she glaid,
Left me weping and feil wordis wald haue said :
For sche sa lichtlie wanyst in the air,
That with myne armes thrise I pressit thair
About the hals hir for to haue bilappit,
And thryse all wais my handis togiddir clappit ;
The figour fled as lycht wynd, or son beyme,
Or mast liklie a waverand sweving or dreyme.

---

[1] the way of the gods' will.   [2] draw.   [3] reign.

DIDO'S HUNTING.

[From *The Aeneid*.]

Quhou that the Quene to hunteyn raid at morow,
And of the first day of hyr joy and sorow.

Furth of the see, with this, the dawing[1] springis.
As Phebus rais, fast to the ȝettis[2] thringis
The chois galandis, and huntmen thaim besyde,
With ralis and with nettis strang and wyde,
And hunting speris stif with hedis braid;
From Massylyne horsmen thik thiddir raid,
With rynning hundis, a full hugë sort.
Noblis of Cartage, hovand[3] at the port,
The quene awatis that lang in chalmer dwellis:
Hir fers steid stude stamping, reddy ellis,
Rungeand the fomy goldin bitt jingling;
Of goldin pall wrocht his riche harnissing;
And scho, at last, of palice ischit out,
With huge menȝe walking hir about,
Lappit in ane brusit[4] mantill of Sydony,
With gold and perle the bordour all bewry,
Hingand by hir syde the cais with arrowis ground;
Hir brycht tressis envolupit war and wound
Intill a kuafe of fyne gold wyrin[5] threid;
The goldin buttoun claspit hir purpour weid.
And furth scho passit with all hir company:
The Troiane peple forgadderit, by and by
Joly and glaid the fresche Ascanius ȝing.
Bot first of all, most gudlie, hym self thar king,
Enee gan entir in falloschip, but dout,
And vnto thaim adionyt his large rowt.
Lyk quhen Apollo list depart or ga
Furth of his wintring realm of Lisia,

[1] dawn. [2] gates. [3] waiting. [4] embroidered. [5] made of wire.

And leif the flude Exanthus for a quhile,
To vesy [1] Delos his moderis land and ile,
Renewand ringis and dancis, mony a rowt ;
Mixt togiddir, his altaris standing abowt,
The peple of Crete, and thaim of Driopes,
And eik the payntit folkis Agathirces,
Schowtand on ther gise with clamour and vocis hie ;
Apon thi top, mont Cynthus, walkis he,
His wavand haris, sum tyme, doing down thring [2]
With a soft garland of lawrere sweit smelling,
And wmquhile thaim gan balmyng and anoynt,
And into gold addres, at full gude poynt [3] ;
His grundin dartis clattering by his syde.
Als fresch, als lusty did Eneas ryde ;
With als gret bewtie in his lordlie face.

SLEEP.

[From *The Aeneid.*]

Quhat sorow dreis [4] queyne Dido all the nycht,
And quhow Mercuir bad Enee tak the flycht.

The nycht follows, and euery wery wicht
Throw out the erd has caucht anone richt
The sound plesand slepe thame likit best ;
Woddis and rageand seis war at rest ;
And the sternis thar myd cours rollis down ;
All feyldis still, but othir noyis or sown ;
And bestis and birdis of diuers culloris seir [5],
And quhatsumevir in the braid lochis weir,
Or amang buskis harsk leyndis [6] ondir the spray,
Throw nichtis silence slepit quhar thai lay,
Mesing [7] ther besy thocht and curis smart,
All irksum laubour for3et and out of hart.
Bot the onrestles fey [8] spreit did nocht so
Of this wnhappy Phenician Dido :

---

[1] to visit.   [2] making his hair hang thickly down.   [3] in good order.
[4] suffers.   [5] several.   [6] dwells among rough bushcs.   [7] diminishing.
[8] fated.

For neuir mair may scho sleip a wynk,
Nor nychtis rest in ene nor breist lat synk:
The hevy thochtis multiplyis euir onane[1];
Strang luif begynis to rage and ryse agane,
And felloun stormis of ire gan hir to schaik:
Thus fynaly scho out bradis [2], alaik!
Rolling allane sere thingis in hir thocht.

SPRING.

[From the *Prologue to the Aeneid*, Bk. v.]

Glad is the ground of the tender florist grene,
Birdis the bewis and thir schawis[3] schene,
The wery hunter to fynd his happy pray,
The falconer the riche riveir our to flene,
The clerk reiosis his buikis our to seyne,
The luiffar to behald his lady gay,
Ʒoung folk thaim schurtis[4] with gam, solace, and play;
Quhat maist delytis or likis every wycht,
Therto steris thar curage day or nycht.

Knychtis delytis to assay sterand[5] stedis,
Wantoun gallandis to traill in sumptuus wedis;
Ladeis desyris to behald and be sene;
Quha wald be thrifty courteouris sais few credis;
Sum plesance takis in romanis that he redis,
And sum has lust to that was never sene:
How mony hedis als feil consatis[6] bene;
Tua appetitis vneith accordis with vther;
This likis the, perchance, and nocht thi brodir.

Plesance and joy rycht halesum and perfyte is,
So that the wys therof in prouerb writis,
Ane blyth spreit makis greyn and flurist age.
Myn author eik in Bucolikis[7] enditis,
The ʒoung infant first with lauchter delytis

---

[1] one another. [2] starts. [3] thickets. [4] amuse. [5] restive.
[6] so many fancies. [7] See Virgil, Ecl. 4.

To knaw his modir, quhen he is litil page ;
Quha lauchis nocht, quod he, in his barnage,
Genyus, the God, delitith nocht their table,
Nor Juno thaim to keip in bed is able.

THE TRIBES OF THE DEAD.

[From *The Aeneid.*]

During this tyme Eneas gan aduert,
Within a vaill fer thens closit apert,
Quhair stude a wod with sowchand[1] bewis schene,
The flude Lethe flowand throw the fair grene ;
About the quhilk peple vnnomerable,
And silly saulis, fleis fast, but fabill,
Quhill all the feildis of thar dyn resoundis :
Lyke as in medowis and fresche fluris boundis,
The byssy beis in schene symmeris tyde,
On diuers colorit flouris scalit wyde,
Flokkis about the blomyt lillyis quhyte,
And vthir fragrant blosumys redemyte[2].

THE DESTINY OF ROME.

[From *The Aeneid.*]

Anchises gyffis Eneas gud teiching,
To gyde the peple ondir his gouerning.

The peple of vdyr realmis, son, sayd he,
Bene moyr expert in craftis, and moir sle[3]
To forge and carve lyflyk staturis of bras,
Be countinance as the spreit tharin was ;
I traist, forsuith heyreftyr mony ane
Sall hew quyk facis furth of marbyll stane ;

---

[1] rustling.   [2] adorned.   [3] sly, clever.

Sum wtheris better can thair causis pleid ;
Sum bene mair crafty in ane wthir steid,
With rewlis and with mesouris by and by
For til excers the art of geometry ;
And sum moir subtel to discrive and prent
The sternis movingis and the hevynis went[1] :
Bot thow, Romane, remember, as lord and syre,
To rewle the pepill vndir thyne impyre ;
Thir sall thi craftis be at[2] weil may seme,
The paix to modyfy and eik manteme,
To pardoun all cumis ȝoldin and recreant,
And prowd rabellis in batale for to dant.

[1] path.   [2] that.

STEPHEN HAWES.

[Of Stephen Hawes little is known beyond the facts that he was a native of Suffolk, that he was educated at Oxford, had travelled in France, and was Groom of the Privy Chamber to Henry VII. We can gather also that he was alive in January 1520-21, and that he was dead in 1530. He was the author of several minor poems which are treasured by collectors, but are of no literary value. It is a proof of the carelessness of those who have dealt with Hawes, that they have assigned to him *The Temple of Glasse*, though Hawes has himself expressly stated (*Pastime of Pleasure*, canto xiv.) that Lydgate was the author. Hawes' great work is *The Pastime of Pleasure, or the Historie of Graunde Amoure and La Belle Pucel*, written in or about 1506, and first printed in 1509. It is an allegorical poem describing the education and history of one Grande Amoure, who learns in the Tower of Doctrine and in the Tower of Chivalry those accomplishments which are necessary to constitute a perfect knight worthy of a perfect love—La Belle Pucel. His career through the world is then delineated—his combats with monsters, his strange adventures, his marriage, his death, his fame. The poem is dedicated, with an elaborate apology for its deficiencies, to Henry VII, and terminates with another apology 'unto all Poets' on the same grounds.]

Hawes belongs to the Provençal School. His model and master was, as he is constantly reiterating, Lydgate, though he was well acquainted with the works of Chaucer, whose comic vein he occasionally affects, with the verses of Gower, and with the narrative poetry of France and Italy. His poem is elaborately allegorical, though the allegory is not alway easy to follow in detail, and is obviously much impeded with extraneous matter. The style has little of the fluency of Lydgate, and none of his vigour; the picturesqueness and brilliance which are characteristic of Chaucer are not less characteristic of Chaucer's Scotch disciples who were Hawes' contemporaries. The narrative, though by no means lacking incident, and by no means unenlivened with beauties both of sentiment and expression, too often stagnates in

prolix discussions, and wants as a rule life and variety. The com-
position is often loose and feeble, the vocabulary is singularly
limited, and bad taste is conspicuous in every canto. But Hawes,
with all his faults, is a true poet. He has a sweet simplicity, a
pensive gentle air, a subdued cheerfulness about him which have
a strange charm at this distance of dissimilar time. Though the
hand of the artist is not firm, and the colouring sometimes too
sober, his pictures are very graphic. Take one out of many :—

> ' The way was troublous and ey nothyng playne,
> Tyll at the last I came into a dale,
> Beholdyng Phoebus declinying lowe and pale.
> With my greyhoundes, in the fayre twylight
> I sate me downe.'

His verse is sometimes harsh, but it often breathes a plaintive
music, and has a weirdly beautiful rhythm ' which falls on the
ear like the echo of a vanished world,' and seems to transport us
back to the dim cloister of some old mediaeval abbey. One
such stanza we give :—

> ' O mortall folke you may beholde and see
> Howe I lye here, sometime a mighty knight,
> The end of joye and all prosperite
> Is death at last, thorough his course and mighte,
> After the daye there cometh the darke nighte,
> *For though the daye be never so long,*
> *At last the belle ringeth to evensong.'*

That couplet alone should suffice for immortality. We may claim
also for this neglected poet complete originality at an age when
English poetry at least had degenerated into mere translations,
into feeble narratives, or into sickly imitations of Chaucer.

But there are two other interesting points connected with *The
Pastime of Pleasure.* It marks with singular precision a great
epoch in our literature. It is the last expiring echo of Medi-
aevalism ; it is the first articulate prophecy of the Renaissance.
It is the link between *The Canterbury Tales* and *The Faery Queen.*
Hawes is in poetry what Philippe de Commines is in prose :
he belongs to the old world and he breathes its atmosphere—he
belongs also to the new, for its first rays are falling on him. He
connects the two. The weeds of a time sad and sombre indeed
hang about him but Hope is the refrain of his song.

> 'Drive despaire away,
> And live in hopë which shall do you good.
> Joy cometh after when the payne is past,
> Be ye pacient and sober in mode:
> To wepe and waile, all is for you in waste.
> Was never payne, but it had joy at last
> In the fayre morrowe.'

The dawn had broken, the morning he felt was near. Again, *The Pastime of Pleasure* was the precursor of *The Faery Queen.* The two poems are similar in allegorical purpose, similar in the development of their allegory. Some of the incidents, though not identical, are of the same character, and if it would be going too far to say that Spenser was a disciple of Hawes, it would not be going too far to say that Spenser had been a careful student of *The Pastime of Pleasure,* had been indebted to it for many a useful hint, many a slight preliminary sketch, many a pleasing effect of rhythm and cadence. We have dealt with some minuteness on Hawes, because of the injustice which all his critics have so inexplicably done him. 'He is,' says Scott, 'a bad imitator of Lydgate, ten times more tedious than his original.' 'Even his name may be omitted,' adds Campbell, 'without any treason to the cause of taste.' Our extracts are, we may add, selected from *The Pastime of Pleasure* : his minor poems are best forgotten.

J. Churton Collins.

DIALOGUE BETWEEN GRAUNDE AMOURE AND LA PUCEL.

[From Cantos xviii. and xix.]

Amoure.

O swete lady, the good perfect starre
Of my true hart, take ye nowe pitie,
Thinke on my paine, whiche am tofore you here,
With your swete eyes beholde you and se,
Howe thought and wo, by great extremitie
Hath chaunged my hue into pale and wanne.
It was not so when I to loue began.

Pucel.

So me thinke, it dothe right well appeare
By your coloure, that loue hath done you wo,—
Your heuy countenaunce, and your doleful cheare,—
Hath loue suche might, for to aray you so
In so short space? I maruell muche also
That you woulde loue me, so sure in certayne
Before ye knew that I woulde loue agayne.

Amoure.

My good deare hart, it is no maruaile why;
Your beauty cleare and louely lokes swete,
My hart did perce with loue so sodainely,
At the firste time, that I did you mete
In the olde temple, when I did you grete.
O lady deare, that pers'd me to the root;
O floure of comfort, all my heale and boote[1].

Pucel.

Your wo and paine, and all your languishyng
Continually, ye shall not spende in vayne,
Sithe I am cause of your great mournyng.
Nothinge exile you shall I by disdaine,
Your hart and mine shall neuer part in twaine,

[1] For these two lines the Ed. of 1555 reads :—

Your beaute my herte so surely assayde
That syth that tyme it hath to you obayde.

Thoughe at the first I wouldne not condescende,
It was for feare ye did some yll entende.

Amoure.

With thought of yll my minde was neuer mixt
To you, madame, but always cleare and pure
Bothe daye and nyght, vpon you whole perfixt
Put I my minde, yet durst nothing discure
Howe for your sake I did such wo endure,
Till nowe this houre with dredfull hart so faint,
To you, swete hart, I haue made my complaint.

Pucel.

I demed oft you loued me before ;
By your demenoure I did it espye,
And in my minde I judged euermore
That at the last ye woulde full secretely
Tell me your minde, of loue right gentilly :
All ye haue done so my mercy to craue
In all worship, you shall my true loue haue.

Amoure.

O gemme of vertue, and lady excellent
Aboue all other in beauteous goodlines,
O eyen bright as starre refulgent,
O profounde cause of all my sickenes,
Nowe all my joye and all my gladnes,
Wouldne God that we were joyned in one
In mariage, before this daye were gone.

 AMOURE LAMENTS THE ABSENCE OF LA BELLE PUCEL.

[From Canto xx.]

Then agayne I went to the tower melodious
Of good dame Musicke, my leaue for to take ;
And priuely with these wordes dolorous
I saied ; O tower, thou maiest well aslake
Suche melody nowe ; in the more to make
The gemme is gone of all famous port
That was chefe cause of the great comfort.

N 2

Whilome thou was the faire tower of light,
But nowe thou art replete with darkenes,
She is nowe gone, that shone in the so bright
Thow wast sometime the tower of gladnes,
Now maist thou be the tower of heauines,
For the chefe is gone of all thy melody,
Whose beauty cleare made most swete armony.

The faire carbuncle, so full of clearenes,
That in the truely did most purely shine,
The pearle of pitie, replete with swetenes,
The gentle gillofloure, the goodly columbine,
The redolent plante of the dulcet vyne,
The dede aromatike may no more encense,
For she is so farre out of thy presence.

Ah, ah ! truely, in the time so past
Mine errande was, the often for to se ;
Nowe for to enter I may be agast
When thou art hence, the starre of beauty,
For all my delite was to beholde the :
Ah Tower, Tower ! all my ioye is gone ;
In me to enter comfort there is none.

So then inwardly my selfe bewaylyng
In the tower I went, into the habitacle
Of dame Musicke, where she was singyng
The ballades swete, in her fayre tabernacle ;
Alas, thought I, this is no spectacle
To fede mine eyen, whiche are nowe all blynde,
She is not here, that I was wont to finde.

Then of dame Musicke, with all lowlines,
I did take my leaue, withouten tariyng ;
She thanked me with all her mekenes.
And all alone, forthe I went musyng :
Ah, ah, quoth I, my loue and likyng
Is none faire hence, on whom my whole delite
Daiely was set vpon her to haue sight.

Farewell, swete harte, farewell, farewel, farewel,
Adieu, adieu, I wouldne I were you by ;
God geue me grace with you sone to dwell
Like as I did for to se you dayly ;
Your lowly cheare and gentle company
Reioysed my hart with fode most delicate,
Mine eyen to se you were insaciate.

THE CHARACTER OF A TRUE KNIGHT.

[From Canto xxviii.]

For knyghthode is not in the feates of warre
As for to fight in quarrell ryght or wrong,
But in a cause which trouthe can not defarre.
He ought himselfe for to make sure and strong
Justice to kepe, myxt with mercy among,
And no quarell a knyght ought to take
But for a trouthe, or for a womman's sake.

For first good hope his legge harneyes shoulde be,
His habergion, of perfect ryghteousnes
Gyrde fast wyth the girdle of chastitie.
His riche placarde shoulde be good busines
Brodred with almes so full of larges ;
The helmet, mekenes, and the shelde, good fayeth,
His swerde God's word, as Saynt Paule sayeth.

Also true wydowes, he ought to restore
Unto their ryght, for to attayne their dower ;
And to vpholde, and maytayne euermore
The wealth of maydens, wyth his myhty power,
And to his souerayne at euery maner hower
To be ready, true, and eke obeysaunt,
In stable loue fyxte, and not variaunt.

DESCRIPTION OF LA BELLE PUCEL.

[From Canto xxx.]

I sawe to me appeare
The flower of comfort, the starre of vertue cleare,
Whose beauty bryght into my hart did passe,
Like as fayre Phebus dothe shyne in the glasse.

So was my harte by the stroke of loue
With sorowe persed and with mortall payne,
That vnneth I myght from the place remoue
Where as I stode, I was so take certayne.
Yet vp I loked to se her agayne,
And at aduenture, with a sory mode
Up then I went, where as her person stode.

And first of all, my harte gan to learne
Right well to regester in remembraunce
Howe that her beauty I might then decerne
From toppe to tooe endued with pleasaunce,
Whiche I shall shewe withouten variaunce ;
Her shining heere so properly she dresses
Aloft her forheade with fayre golden tresses.

Her forheade stepe, with fayre browes ybent,
Her eyen gray, her nose straight and fayre.
In her white chekes the faire blonde it went
As among the wite the redde to repayre ;
Her mouthe right small, her breathe swete of **ayre ;**
Her lippes soft and ruddy as a rose ;
No hart alive but it woulde him appose.

With a little pitte in her well fauoured **chynne,**
Her necke long, as white as any lillye,
With vaynes blewe in which the bloude ranne **in,**
Her pappes rounde, and therto right pretye ;
Her armes slender, and of goodly bodye,
Her fingers small and therto right long,
White as the milke, with blewe vaynes among.

Her fete proper, she gartred well her hose :
I neuer sawe so fayre a creature ;
Nothing she lacketh, as I do suppose,
That is longyng to faire dame Nature.
Yet more ouer her countenaunce so pure,
So swete, so louely, woulde any hart enspire
With feruent loue to attayne his desire.

But what for her maners passeth all,
She is bothe gentle, good, and vertuous.
Alas, what fortune did me to her call
Without that she be to me pitifull?
With her so fettred, in paynes dolorous.
Alas, shall pitie be from her exiled,
Whiche all vertus hath so vndefiled?

JOHN SKELTON.

[THE date of Skelton's birth is not known; it probably took place some-
where about 1460. He began his career as a sober scholar; he ended it as
a ribald priest. In his first capacity he was tutor to Prince Henry (after-
wards Henry VIII), the Laureate of three Universities, and the friend of
Caxton and Erasmus, who has described him as *litterarum Anglicarum
lumen et decus*. In his second capacity he was rector of Diss in Norfolk
and a hanger-on about the Court of Henry VIII. He died at Westminster,
where he had taken sanctuary to escape the wrath of Wolsey, in 1529.
Some of his poems are said to have been printed in London in 1512;
a completer collection of them appeared in 1568. but it was not until Dyce's
admirable collection in 1843 that they were published in their integrity.]

Skelton's claims to notice lie not so much in the intrinsic ex-
cellence of his work as in the complete originality of his style, in
the variety of his powers, in the peculiar character of his satire,
and in the ductility of his expression when ductility of expression
was unique. His writings, which are somewhat voluminous, may
be divided into two great classes — those which are written in
his own peculiar measure, and which are all more or less of the
same character, and those which are written in other measures and
in a different tone. To this latter class belong his serious poems,
and his serious poems are now deservedly forgotten. Two of them,
however, *The Bowge of Court*, a sort of allegorical satire on the
court of Henry VIII, and the morality of *Magnificence*, which gives
him a creditable place among the fathers of our drama, contain
some vigorous and picturesque passages which have not been
thrown away on his successors. As a lyrical poet Skelton also
deserves mention. His ballads are easy and natural, and though
pitched as a rule in the lowest key, evince touches of real poetical
feeling. When in the other poems his capricious muse breaks out
into lyrical singing, as she sometimes does, the note is clear, the
music wild and airy. *The Garlande of Laurell* for example con-
tains amid all its absurdities some really exquisite fragments.

But it is as the author of *The Boke of Colin Clout, Why come ye nat to Court, Ware the Hawke, The Boke of Philipp Sparowe,* and *The Tunnyng of Elinore Rummyng,* that Skelton is chiefly interesting. These poems are all written in that headlong voluble breathless doggrel which, rattling and clashing on through quick-recurring rhymes, through centos of French and Latin, and through every extravagant caprice of expression, has taken from the name of its author the title of Skeltonical verse. The three first poems are satires. *Colin Clout* is a general attack on the ignorance and sensuality of the clergy. The second is a fierce invective against Cardinal Wolsey, and the third is directed against a brother clergyman who was, it appears, in the habit of flying his hawks in Skelton's church. These three poems are all in the same strain, as in the same measure—grotesque, rough, intemperate, but though gibbering and scurrilous, often caustic and pithy, and sometimes rising to a moral earnestness which contrasts strangely with their uncouth and ludicrous apparel.

> ' Though my rime be ragged,
> Tatter'd and jagged,
> Rudely raine-beaten,
> Rusty and moth-eaten ;
> If ye take wel therewith,
> It hath in it some pith.'

And the attentive student of Skelton will soon discover this. Indeed he reminds us more of Rabelais than any author in our language. In *The Boke of Philipp Sparowe* he pours out a long lament for the death of a favourite sparrow which belonged to a fair lay nun. This poem was probably suggested by Catullus' Dirge on a similar occasion. In Skelton, however, the whole tone is burlesque and extravagant, though the poem is now and then relieved by pretty fancies and by graceful touches of a sort of humorous pathos. In *The Tunnyng of Elinore Rummynge* his powers of pure description and his skill in the lower walks of comedy are seen in their highest perfection. In this sordid and disgusting delineation of humble life he may fairly challenge the supremacy of Swift and Hogarth. But Skelton is, with all his faults, one of the most versatile and one of the most essentially original of all our poets. He touches Swift on one side, and he touches Sackville on the other.

J. CHURTON COLLINS.

A Lullabye.

With Lullay, lullay, lyke a chylde
  Thou slepyst to long, thou art begylde.

My darlyng dere, my daysy floure,
  Let me, quod he, ly in your lap.
Ly styll, quod she, my paramoure,
  Ly styll hardely, and take a nap.
  Hys hed was hevy, such was his hap,
All drowsy, dremyng, dround in slepe,
That of hys love he toke no kepe.
                With Hey, lullay, &c.

With ba, ba, ba, and bas, bas, bas,
  She cheryshed hym both cheke and chyn,
That he wyst neuer where he was:
  He had forgotten all dedely syn.
  He wantyd wyt her love to wyn,
He trusted her payment, and lost all hys pray[1]:
She left hym slepyng, and stale away,
              Wyth Hey, lullay, &c.

The ryvers rowth[2], the waters wan ;
  She sparyd not to wete her fete ;
She wadyd over she found a man
  That halsyd[3] her hartely, and kyst her swete.
  Thus after her cold she cought a hete.
My lafe, she sayd, rowtyth[4] in hys bed:
I wys he hath a hevy hed,
              Wyth Hey, lullay, &c.

What dremyst thou, drunchard, drowsy pate !
  Thy lust[5] and lykyng is from thé gone :
Thou blynkerd blowboll[6], thou wakyst to late ;
  Behold thou lyeste, luggard, alone !
  Well may thou sygh, well may thou grone,
To dele wyth her so cowardly :
I wys, powle hachet, she bleryd thyne I[7].

[1] *Or* pay (?)   [2] rough.   [3] embraced.   [4] snoreth
     [5] pleasure.   [6] drunkard.   [7] deceived you.

PICTURE OF RIOT.

[From *The Bowge of Courte*[1].]

Wyth that came Ryott, russhynge all at once,
A rusty gallande, to-ragged and to-rente :
And on the borde he whyrled a payre of bones ;
Quater treye dews he clatered as he wente :
Now have at all, by Sainte Thomas of Kente !
And ever he threwe and kyst[2] I wote nere what,
His here[3] was growen thorowe oute his hat.

Thenne I behelde how he dysgysed was :
His hede was hevy for watchynge over nyghte,
His eyen blereed, his face shone lyke a glas,
His gowne so shorte that it ne cover myghte
His rumpe, he wente so all for somer lyghte,
His hose was garded[4] wyth a lyste of grene,
Yet al the knee they were broken I wene.

His cote was checked with patches red and blewe,
Of Kyrkeby Kendall was his shorte demye[5],
And ay he sange, ' In fayth, decon thow crewe'
His elbowe bare, he ware his gere so nye[6] :
His nose a droppynge, his lyppes were full drye,
And by his syde his whynarde[7] and his pouche
The devyll myghte daunce therein for ony crowche[8].

TO MAYSTRESS MARGARET HUSSEY.

[From *The Garlande of Laurell.*]

Mirry Margaret,
As mydsomer flowre ;
Jentill as fawcoun
Or hawke of the towere :

[1] i. e. *The Rewards of a Court. Bowge* is properly ' allowance of meat and
drink' (Fr. *bouche*). [2] cast. [3] hair. [4] trimmed. [5] waist-
coat, or jacket. [6] so short (?). [7] dagger. [8] without meeting
with any *cross*, i. e. piece of money so marked.

With solace and gladnes,
Moche mirthe and no madness,
All good and no badness,
  So joyously,
  So maydenly,
  So womanly,
  Her demenyng
  In every thynge,
  Far, far passynge
  That I can endyght,
  Or suffyce to wryghte,
  Of mirry Margarete,
  As mydsomer flowre,
  Jentyll as fawcoun
  Or hawke of the towre :
  As pacient and as styll,
  And as full of good wyll
  As faire Isaphill ;
  Colyaunder,
  Swete pomaunder,
  Goode Cassaunder ;
  Stedfast of thought,
  Wele made, wele wrought ;
  Far may be sought,
  Erst that ye can fynde
  So corteise, so kynde,
  As mirry Margaret,
  This mydsomer floure,
  Jentyll as fawcoun
  Or hawke of the towre.

From Colyn Cloute.

  I Colyn Clout
As I go about
And wandryng as I walke
I heare the people talke ;
Men say for syluer and golde
Miters are bought and sold ;

There shall no clergy appose
A myter nor a crosse
But a full purse.

   A straw for Goddes curse !
What are they the worse ?
For a sinnoniake,
Is but a hermoniake [1],
And no more ye make
Of symony men say
But a childes play.

   Over this, the forsayd raye
Report how the pope maye
A holy anker [2] call
Out of the stony wall,
And hym a bysshopp make
If he on him dare take
To kepe so hard a rule,
To ryde vpon a mule
Wyth golde all betrapped,
In purple and paule belapped.
Some hatted and some capped,

   Rychely be wrapped,
God wot to theyt great paynes,
In rochettes of fine raynes [3];
Whyte as morowes mylke,
Their tabertes of fine silke,
Their stirops of mixt golde begared [4],
Their may no cost be spared.
Their moyles [5] golde doth eate,
Theyr neighbours dye for meat.

   What care they though Gill sweat,
Or Jacke of the Noke ?
The pore people they yoke
With sommons and citacions
And excommunications

---

[1] A word unexplained by Dyce. Mr. Skeat suggests that harmoniac =
promoter of harmony; a man who makes things pleasant all round.
[2] anchorite.   [3] linen made at Rennes in Brittany.   [4] adorned
[5] mules.

Aboute churches and market;
The bysshop on his carpet
At home full soft doth syt,
This is a feareful fyt,
To heare the people iangle !
How warely they wrangle,
Alas why do ye not handle,
And them all mangle?
Full falsly on you they lye
And shamefully you ascry[1],
And say as untruly,
As the butterfly
A man might say in mocke
Ware[2] the wethercocke
Of the steple of Poules[3],
And thus they hurt their soules
In sclaunderyng you for truth,
Alas it is great ruthe !
Some say ye sit in trones
Like prynces *aquilonis*[3],
And shryne your rotten bones
With pearles and precious stones,
But now the commons grones
And the people mones
For preestes[4] and for lones
Lent and neuer payde,
But from day to day delaid,
The commune welth decayd.
Men say ye are tunge tayde[5],
And therof speake nothing
But dissimuling and glosing.
Wherfore men be supposing
That ye geue shrewd[6] counsel
Against the commune wel,
By pollyng[7] and pillage
In cities and village,

---

[1] call out against.　　　[2] were.　　　[3] Like so many Lucifers.
[4] advances.　　　[5] tied.　　[6] evil.　　　[7] plundering.

By taxyng and tollage,
Ye have monks to have the culerage
For coueryng of an old cottage,
That committed is a collage,
In the charter of dottage,
Tenure *par service de sottage,*
And not *par service de socage,*
After old segnyours
And the learning of Litleton tenours,
Ye haue so ouerthwarted
That good lawes are subuerted,
And good reason peruerted.

SIR DAVID LYNDESAY.

[Born circ. 1490, died 1558.]

Dunbar's attitude toward the change of religion, in his time impending, is that of a wholly unconscious precursor ; he is a minor Chaucer, who would have had less sympathy with men like Wyclyffe than his master had. Sir David Lyndesay was a 'spirit of another sort'—a child of the new age, when the trumpets of the Reformation had summoned the strong minds of the time to take their sides for or against the old order. Indefinitely less of a poet,—hardly a poet at all,—he was yet a literary power filling a place and discharging a function of his own ; a trenchant satirist, almost a dramatist ; a political and moral pamphleteer, whose versified pamphlets are always sustained at a high level by vigour and courage, and occasionally illumined by gleams of imagination.

Lyndesay's life is part of the history of his time. The following dates are its mere landmarks. He was born at The Mount in Fifeshire about the year 1490, the junior by ten years of Luther and Sir Thomas More, the senior by fifteen of Knox. He was a student of St. Andrews in 1508, and passed from the University to the service of the court. In 1513 he was present with James IV at Linlithgow when a supposed apparition came to warn the monarch against his fatal expedition. Subsequently he was gentleman-usher to the young prince—a fact to which he alludes in one of those appeals for promotion, which recall the similar petitions of Dunbar :—

> 'When thou was young, I bore thee in mine arm,
> Full tenderly till thou begowth to gang.'

In 1530 he was knighted and made Lyon King of Arms, or chief court herald, in which capacity he served in several foreign embassies. In 1535 his *Thrie Estates* was acted at Cupar Fife, the court and company sitting nine hours to listen to it. 1536 must have been the date of the *King's Flyting*, one of the

most audacious compositions in the language. Next year the king's wife, Magdalene, died before her coronation, and Lyndesay wrote the *Deploratioun*, which may be compared, though unfavourably, with Chaucer's *Lament for the Duchess*. The metre is the rhyme royal, and the 147th line,

> 'Twynkling lyke sterris in ane frostie nycht,'

is transcribed verbatim from the Prologue to the Canterbury Tales. In 1542 the poet witnessed at Falkland the death of the king (James V), who had been his consistent patron. In 1547, after the assassination of Beaton, he was present with the garrison in the castle of St. Andrews, and was among the most urgent of those there assembled in persuading Knox to assume the direction of affairs. In 1555 we hear of his presiding over a meeting of heralds to pronounce on some point of their pseudo-science. In 1558 he died at his family seat, having mingled in all the great movements of his age.

Lyndesay's verse, on which his reputation as a writer depends, is all connected with the contemporary state of his country. To the lightest as well as the gravest—ranging from tedious allegory to lively ridicule—he has attached political and social applications. More than half his works are allegories. In the earliest, and as regards imaginative decoration the richest, *The Dreme*, he is led through a series of dissolving views of the past ages of the world, a journey to Hades, and a flight beyond the stars to an interview with 'Sir Commonweal,' who joins with him in lamentation over a realm misgoverned by an 'ouir young king' and dissolute priests. In the same strain he harps in his *Complaynt*, in the direct attack on ecclesiastical corruption put into the mouth of a dying parrot, under the title of *The Testament of the Papyngo*, and in *The Tragedy of the Cardinal*, the last of which passes on the moral of the Fall of Princes from Lydgate to Sackville. In all of these, and elsewhere, he preaches, with less consistency, the old sermon of Wyclyffe against the corruptions of wealth, and upholds, for the admiration of his readers, the poverty of the Apostolic age. In *Kitteis Confession* (c. 1541) he crosses the line drawn by Dunbar, and commits himself to a direct attack on one of the still established institutions of the Church, glancing incidentally at her foreign ceremonial—

> 'And mekle Latin he did mummil,
> I hard na thing but hummil bummil'—

and referring, as professed reformers in most ages have been wont to do, to the better practice of the 'gude kirk primitive.' In the *Complaynt of Bagsche,* an old dog who has to give place to a new favourite, we have a reflection on the fickleness of court favour; in *The Jousting of Watson and Barbour* a satire on the medical profession; in the attack on *Syde Taillis* a rough exposure of the affected fashions of the day. In his *Squire Meldrum,* the most pleasing and lively of his narrative pieces, Lyndesay appears as a late metrical romancer, taking as the basis of his story the career and exploits of a contemporary Scotch laird. *The Satyre of the Thrie Estates,* a well-sustained invective against the follies and vices of the time, the first approach to a regular dramatic composition in Scotland, and the most considerable of our Moralities, abounds in exhibitions of the author's unrestrained Rabelaisian humour. It is impossible to read three pages without laughing, but there are many pages which it would be impossible to read at all to any modern audience. In his latest work, the *Dialog concerning the Monarchie* (c. 1553) Lyndesay reverts to the allegorical manner of his *Dreme,* and represents himself in converse with an old man, Experience, on 'the miserable estate of the world.' After a polemical defence of the use of his native tongue (v. inf.), the poem glides into a somewhat tiresome metrical history of the ancient kingdoms of the earth; it ends with an attack on that of the Pope as Antichrist, and a prophecy of the millennium, which he anticipates in the year 2000 A.D. In the Prologue to this—his most elaborate composition—the author speaks modestly of his own artistic skill. He has never slept on Parnassus, nor kept company with the Muses, nor drunk of Helicon: his inspiration is drawn from Calvary; and he prays that the miracle of Cana may be renewed in converting the water of his instruction into wine. This candid self-criticism is on the whole correct. Lyndesay was rather a man of action bent on popularising his keen convictions than a professional writer. The bias of his mind and the temper of his time were alike unfavourable to finished works of art. His superabundant energy and ready humour made him a power, but he had no inclination to philosophise in solitude or to refine at leisure. His life was spent amid stormy politics, and we need not wonder that a pressure of affairs similar to that which for a space held even the genius of Milton in abeyance, should have marred the literary productions of a man who had more talent than genius, and who wrote 'currente calamo' on such various themes with an almost fatal fluency. His greatest admirers have confessed that 'he has written so many verses that they cannot always be expected to reach a very high standard.' Passages in *The Dreme*, *Squire Meldrum*, and *The Monarchie*, may for grace of description be set beside any corresponding to them in the works of his predecessors ; but his writings are in the main more distinguished for trenchant sense, vivacity, courage, and observing power than by high imagination. He himself speaks of his 'raggit rural verse,' and he willingly passes from more delicate fancies to discourse on the grave matters with the rehearsal of which he desires rather to edify than to delight his readers. His style is generally incisive, and though frequently disfigured by 'aureate' terms, leaves us little room to doubt of the author's meaning. Unlike Dunbar, Lyndesay may almost be said to have been born a Protestant ; but he never ventured beyond the range of the leading Reformers of his age. He is a Calvinist, more tolerant of sins of blood than errors of brain, rejoicing like Tertullian over the agonies of the damned. His mission was to amuse and arouse the people of his time, to affront them with a reflection of their vices, and to set to rough music the thunder and the whirlwind of sixteenth-century iconoclasm.

J. Nichol.

From the Prologue to 'The Dreme.'

Efter that I the lang wynteris nycht
    Had lyne walking[1], in to my bed, allone,
Throuch hevy thocht, that no way sleip[2] I mycht,
    Rememberyng of divers thyngis gone :
    So, up I rose, and clethit me anone ;
Be this, fair Tytane with his lemis[3] lycht
Ouer all the land had spred his baner brycht.

With cloke and hude I dressit me belyve[4],
    With dowbyll schone, and myttanis on my handis ;
Howbeit the air was rycht penetrative,
    Yit fure I furth, lansing ouirhorte[5] the landis,
    Toward the see, to schorte[6] me on the sandis ;
Because unblomit was baith bank and braye,
And so, as I was passing be the waye,

I met dame Flora, in dule weid dissagysit[7],
    Quhilk into May wes dulce, and delectabyll ;
With stalwart stormis, hir sweitnes wes supprisit ;
    Hir hevynlie hewis war turnit into sabyll,
    Quhilkis umquhile war to luffaris[8] amiabyll.
Fled frome the froste, the tender flouris I saw,
Under dame Naturis mantyll, lurking law[9].

    *   *   *   *   *   *

Pensyve in hart, passing full soberlie
    Unto the see, ordward I fure anone ;
The see was furth, the sand wes smooth and drye ;
    Then up and doune I musit myne allone,
    Tyll that I spyit ane lyttill cave of stone,
Heych in ane craig : upwart I did approche.
But tarying, and clam up in the roche :

[1] waking.   [2] Observe the use of *ei* for several southern vowel-sounds.
[3] rays.   [4] at once.   [5] athwart.   [6] amuse.   [7] disguised.
[8] lovers.   [9] low.

And purposit, for passing of the tyme,
 Me to defend from ociositie
With pen and paper to register in ryme
 Sum mery mater of Antiquitie :
 Bot Idelnes, ground of iniquitie,
Scho maid so dull my spreitis, me within,
That I wyste nocht at quhat end to begin.

But satt styll in that cove, quhare I mycht see
 The wolteryng of the waliis [1] up and down ;
And this fals Warldis instabylytie
 Unto that see makkand [2] comparisoun,
 And of this Warldis wracheit variatioun
To thame that fixis all thair hole intent,
Consideryng quho most had suld most repent.

So, with my hude my hede I happit warme,
 And in my cloke I fauldit boith my feit ;
I thocht my corps with cauld suld tak no harme,
 My mittanis held my handis weill in heit ;
 The skowland craig me coverit frome the sleit :
Thare styll I satt, my bonis for to rest,
Tyll Morpheus, with sleip, my spreit opprest.

So throw the bousteous [3] blastis of Eolus,
 And throw my walkyng on the nycht before,
And throw the seyis movyng marvellous
 Be Neptunus, with mony route and rore,
 Constrainit I was to sleip, withouttin more :
And quhat I dremit, in conclusion
I sall you tell, ane marvellous Visioun.

[1] waves.   [2] Northern participial form.   [3] boisterous.

FROM 'THE TESTAMENT AND COMPLAYNT OF THE PAPINGO.'

Kyng James the First, the patroun of prudence,
  Gem of ingyne, and peirll of polycie,
Well of Justice, and flude of eloquence,
  Quhose vertew doith transcende my fantasie
  For tyll discryve ; yit quhen he stude most hie
Be fals exhorbitant conspiratioun
That prudent Prince was pieteouslie put down.

Als, James the Secunde, roye of gret renoun,
  Beand in his superexcelland glore,
Throuch reakless schuttyng of one gret cannoun
  The dolent deith, allace ! did hym devore.
  One thyng thare bene, of quhilk I marvell more,
That Fortune had at hym sic mortall feid[1]
Throuch fyftie thousand, to waill[2] him by the heid.

My hart is peirst with panes, for to pance[3],
  Or wrytt, that courtis variatioun
Of James the Third, quhen he had governance,
  The dolour, dreid, and desolatioun,
  The change of court and conspiratioun ;
And quhon that Cochrane, with his companye,
That tyme in courte clam so presumpteouslye.

 * * * * * *

Allace ! quhare bene that rycht redoutit roye,
  That potent prince, gentyll King James the Feird[4] ?
I pray to Christe his saule for to convoye :
  Ane greater nobyll rang nocht in to the eird.
  O Atropus ! warye[5] we maye thy weird ;
For he wes myrrour of humylitie,
Lode sterne and lampe of liberalytie.

And of his court, throuch Europe sprang the fame,
  Of lustie Lordis and lufesum Ladyis ying,
Tryumphand tornayis, justyng, and kychtly game,
  With all pastyme, accordyng for ane kyng :
  He wes the glore of princelie governyng,

[1] feud. [2] choose. [3] think. [4] fourth. [5] curse.

Quhilk, throuch the ardent lufe he had to France,
Agane Ingland did move his ordinance.

Of Floddoun Feilde the rewyne to revolve,
 Or that most dolent daye for tyll deplore,
I nyll, for dreid that dolour yow dissolve,
 Schaw how that prince, in his tryumphand glore,
 Distroyit was, quhat nedeith proces more ?
Nocht be the vertew of Inglis ordinance
Bot, be his awin wylfull mysgovernance.

FROM 'ANE SATYRE OF THE THREI ESTAITIS.'

Veritie.

For our Christ's saik, I am richt weill content
To suffer all thing that sall pleis his grace,
 Howbeit, ye put ane thousand till torment,
Ten hundreth thowsand sall ryse into thair place.

[Veritie sits down on hir knies and sayis:]

Yet up, thow slepis all too lang, O Lord,
 And mak sum ressonabill reformatioun,
On thame that dois tramp down thy gracious word,
 And hes ane deidlie indignatioun,
 At them, quha maks maist trew narratioun :
Suffer me not, Lord, mair to be molest,
 Gude Lord, I mak the supplicatioun,
With thy unfriends let me nocht be supprest.

*　　*　　*　　*　　*　　*

Pardoner.

My patent pardouns, ye may se,
Cum fra the Cane of Tartarei,
 Weill seald with oster schellis ;
Thocht ye have na contritioun,
Ye sall have full remissioun,
 With help of buiks and bellis.
Heir is ane relict, lang and braid,
Of Fine Macoult the richt chaft blaid[1],
 With teith and al togidder :

---

[1] jaw-bone.

Of Colling's cow, heir is ane horne,
For eating of Mackonnal's corne
    Was slain into Baquhidder.
Heir is ane coird, baith great and lang,
Quhilk hangit Johne the Armistrang :
    Of gude hemp soft and sound :
Gude, halie peopill, I stand for'd,
Quha ever beis hangit with this cord
    Neids never to be dround.
The culum [1] of Sanct Bryd's kow,
The gruntill [2] of Sanct Antonis sow,
    Quhilk buir his haly bell ;
Quha ever he be heiris this bell clinck,
Gif me ane dacat for till drink,
    He sall never gang to hell.

*   *   *   *   *   *

Pauper.

Marie ! I lent my gossop my mear to fetch hame coills,
And he hir drounit into the Querrell hollis ;
And I ran to the Consistorie, for to pleinze [3],
And 'thair I happinit amang ane greidie meinze [4].
Thay gave me first ane thing thay call *Citandum*,
Within aucht dayis, I gat bot *Lybellandum*,
Within ane moneth, I gat *ad Opponendum*
In half ane yeir I gat *Interloquendum*,
And syne, I gat, how call ye it ? *ad Replicandum.*
Bot, I could never ane word yit understand him ;
And than, thay gart me cast out many plackis,
And gart me pay for four-and-twentie actis :
Bot, or thay came half gait to *Concludendum*
The Feind ane plack was left for to defend him.
Thus, thay post-ponit me twa yeir, with thair traine,
Syne, *Hodie ad octo*, bad me cum againe,
And than, thir ruiks, thay roupit [5] wonder fast,
For sentence silver, thay cryit at the last.
Of *Pronunciandum* they maid me wonder faine ;
Bot I got never my gude gray meir againe.

[1] tail.   [2] snout.   [3] complain.   [4] crew.   [5] croaked.

From 'The Monarchie.'

Christ, efter his glorious Ascentioun,
  Tyll his Disciplis send the Holy Spreit,
In toungis of fyre, to that intentioun,
  Thay, beand of all languages repleit,
  Throuch all the warld, with wordis fair and sweit,
Tyll every man the faith thay suld furth schaw
In thare owin leid[1], delyverand thame the Law.

Tharefore I thynk one gret dirisioun,
  To heir thir Nunnis and Systeris nycht and day
Syngand and sayand Psalmes and Orisoun,
  Nocht understandyng quhat thay syng nor say.
  Bot lyke one Stirlyng or ane Papingay,
Quhilk leirnit ar to speik be lang usage:
Thame I compair to byrdis in ane cage.

Rycht so childreyng and ladyis of honouris
  Prayis in Latyne, to thame ane uncuth[2] leid,
Mumland thair Matynis, Evinsang, and thair Houris,
  Thare Pater Noster, Ave, and thare Creid.
  It wer als plesand to thare spreit, in deid,
God have mercy on me, for to say thus,
As to say, *Miserere mei Deus*.

Sanct Jerome in his propir toung Romane
  The Law of God he trewlie did translait,
Out of Hebrew and Greik, in Latyne plane,
  Quhilk hes bene hid from us lang tyme, God wait,
  Onto this tyme: bot, efter myne consait,
Had Sanct Jerome bene borne in tyll Argyle
In to Yrische toung his bukis had done compyle.

Prudent Sanct Paull doith mak narratioun
  Twycheyng the divers leid of every land,
Sayand, there bene more edificatioun
  In fyve wordis that folk doith understand,
  Nor to pronounce of wordis ten thousand
In strange langage, sine wait not quhat it menis:
I thynk sic pattryng is not worth twa prenis[3].

     *   *   *   *   *   *

[1] language.   [2] unknown.   [3] pins.

The Hope of Immortality.

All creature that ever God creat,
  As wryttis Paull, thay wys to se that day
Quhen the childryng of God, predestinat,
  Sall do appeir in thare new fresche array ;
  Quhen corruptioun beis clengit clene away,
And changeit beis thair mortall qualitie
In the gret glore of immortalitie.

And, moreattour, all dede thyngis corporall,
  Vnder the concave of the Hevin impyre,
That now to laubour subject ar, and thrall,
  Sone, mone, and sterris, erth, walter, air, and fyre,
  In one maneir thay have ane hote desyre,
Wissing that day, that thay may be at rest,
As Erasmus exponis manifest.

We sé the gret Globe of the Firmament
  Continuallie in moveyng marvellous ;
The sevin Planetis, contrary thare intent,
  Are reft about, with course contrarious ;
  The wynd, and see, with stormys furious,
The trublit air, with frostis, snaw and rane,
Unto that day thay travell evir in pane.

And all the Angellis of the Ordouris Nyne,
  Haveand compassioun of our misereis,
Thay wys efter that day, and to that fyne [1],
  To sé us freed frome our infirmeteis,
  And clengit [2] frome thir gret calamiteis
And trublous lyfe, quhilk never sall have **end**
On to that day, I mak it to thee kend [3].

[1] end.   [2] cleaned.   [3] known.

ENGLISH BALLADS.

In treating of the Ballads, or old popular poetry of England, it is impossible to follow the plan generally adopted in this collection. We cannot arrange them by date of composition, for, while the plots and situations are often of immemorial age, the language is sometimes that of the last century. They are therefore inserted here, as they were first committed to the press and sold as broad-sheets not much later than the period at which we have arrived. About the authors of the ballads, and their historical date, we know nothing. Like the *Volks-lieder* of other European countries, the popular poems of England were composed by the people for the people. Again, the English ballads, and those of the Lowland Scotch, deal with topics common to the peasant singers of Denmark, France, Greece, Italy, and the Slavonic countries. The wide distribution of these topics is, like the distribution of *märchen* or popular tales, a mark of great antiquity. We cannot say when they originated, or where, or how; we only know that, in one shape or other, the themes of romantic ballads are very ancient. There are certain incidents, like that of the return of the dead mother to her oppressed children; like the sudden recovery of a fickle bridegroom's heart by the patient affection of his first love; like the adventure of May Colvin with a lover who has slain seven women, and tries to slay her; like the story of the bride who pretends to be dead that she may escape from a detested marriage, which are in all European countries the theme of popular song. Again, the pastimes and labours of the husbandmen and shepherd were, long ago, a kind of natural opera. Each task had its old song,—ploughing, harvest, seed-time, marriage, burial, had appropriate ballads or dirges. Aubrey, the antiquary, mentions ' a song sung in the ox-house, when they *wassel* the oxen.' A similar chant survives in Berry. Further, each of the rural dance-tunes had its ballad-accompaniment, and the dance was sometimes a rude dramatic representation of the action described in the poem. Many of the surviving

volks-lieder are echoes from the music of this idyllic world of
dance and song from the pleasant England in which

> ' When Tom came home from labour,
>   And Cis from milking rose,
> Merrily went the tabor,
>   And merrily went their toes.'

Other European ballads are echoes from the same stage of
social life, but they are clearer, sweeter, more full and unbroken
in tone than the lays of rural England. Our ballads speak of
adventures known to Romaic, Danish, and Italian peasants ; but
in listening to them we hear the drawl of the dull rustic, and
catch the snivelling drone of the provincial moralist. Unlike
the Provençal, or Romaic, or Lowland Scotch ballads, the English
remains are too often flat, garrulous, spiritless, and didactic. They
lack the picturesqueness, the simplicity, the felicitous choice of
expression, the fire, the speed of the best European *volks-lieder*.
The probable reason of this flatness and languor will be stated
presently ; in the meantime we must note that the ballads of the
Lowland Scotch, recovered from oral tradition, have the fire which
we miss in English popular poems. It is for this reason that
many of our selected ballads are chosen from the northern Border.
The poets were none the less English in blood and language.

Before attempting to assign the causes of the poverty of English
ballads, it may be as well to prove the fact. The death of Douglas
in the English ballad of Chevy Chase is a passage that has won
the praise of Addison. It runs thus :—

> ' With that there came an arrow keene
>   Out of an English bow,
> Which struck Erle Douglas on the breast,
>   A deepe and deadlye blow;
>
> Who never said more words than these,
>   " Fight on, my merrymen all !
> For why, my life is at an end,
>   Lord Pearcy sees my fall." '

In the Scotcn ballad this event is prepared for by a dream
which visits Douglas, a dream singularly impressive and romantic.

> ' But I hae dreamed a dreary dream,
>   Beyond the Isle of Sky;
> I saw a dead man win a fight,
>   But I think that man was I.'

This supernatural effect is repeated at the moment of Douglas's fall, and thus a new charm is won for the poem, which is missed in *Chevy Chase.* The supernatural is almost invariably treated in a gross and flat style by the English balladist. He never thrills the reader with that shudder of awe which is caused by *Clerk Saunders,* the *Wife of Usher's Well,* the *Demon Lover,* and *Sir Roland.* To give another example: the story of the *Dead Man's Ride* is common in European popular poetry. The German popular version has been lost in the fame of Bürger's *Lenore.* Everywhere the ballad tells how a dead lover (in Greece it is a dead brother), is roused from the sleep of death by the grief of a mistress or a mother, how the dead man carries his bride, or his sister, behind him on the saddle in a swift night ride, while the birds in the roadside cry, 'who is the fair girl that rides with the corpse?' 'who is the lover, perfumed with the incense of the dead?' The Romaic version is perhaps the most moving of all. The dead brother gallops with the living sister to the house of the bereaved mother; she hears his knock, and comes to the door, thinking that he is Charon, the emissary of death—Charon, who need not visit her, for she has already given him all her children but one daughter, and she is in a distant land,

Ἀν ἦσα Χαρός διάβαινε, καὶ ἄλλα παιδιὰ δὲν ἔχω;

Thus she speaks; and even as she speaks, she recognises the ghost of her son, and dies of terror in the presence of the living and the dead. In England this ballad becomes *The Suffolk Miracle* (Child, *English and Scotch Ballads,* vol. i. p. 217); 'a relation of a young man, who, two months after his death, appeared to his sweetheart, and carried her on horse-back behind him for forty miles in two hours, and was never seen after but in her grave.' The ballad tells us how the young people loved each other, and how the father of the girl disapproved of the engagement :—

> 'Forty miles distant was she sent
> Unto his brother, with intent
> That she should there so long remain,
> Till she had changed her mind again.'

The lover dies of grief, and his ghost pays a morning visit to the house where the lady is living,

> 'Which, when her uncle understood,
> He hoped it would be for her good;'

and gave his consent to the homeward ride, which the spectre accomplished at the creditable pace of twenty miles an hour. It would be easy, but it is perhaps superfluous, to go on multiplying examples of the poetic flatness of the English ballad. The enthusiasm of the specialist and the collector may be fired by the combat between Robin Hood and 'the bloody Butcher,' but who can call this sort of thing—poetry?

> 'Robin he marcht in the greene forest,
>   Under the greenwood spray,
> And there he was ware of a proud bucher,
>   Came driving flesh that way;
>
> The Bucher he had a cut-tailed dogg,' &c.

If this be not enough, consider the exquisite final stanza of *The Ladye's Fall* :—

> 'Take heed you dainty damsells all,
>   Of flattering words beware;
> And to the honour of your name,
>   Have you a specyal care!'

As a general rule the Lowland Scotch ballads have escaped the didactic drivel and the long-drawn whine of the English examples. It is true that in one of them we learn, from a marvellously prosaic bard, how

> 'John Thomson fought against the Turks,'

and how 'this young chieftain' (namely Thomson) 'sat alone. But this weakness is rare enough in the poetry of the Northern Border. Even in a comparatively modern ballad, composed on a murder committed at Warristoun, near Edinburgh in 1600, there are picturesque touches. The lady of Warristoun had procured the death of her cruel husband. In the ballad she exclaims :—

> 'Warristoun, Warristoun!
>   I wish that ye may sink for sin,
> I was but fifteen years auld,
>   When first I entered your gates within.

To any one who knew the gloomy house of Warristoun, hanging over the deep black pool below, this verse must have seemed charged with the sentiment of *The Fall of the House of Usher*. The ballad is a fine example of the working of popular fancy on a historical datum.

Popular poetry has often been compared to the wild rose, the wild stock out of which the richer garden roses are grown. If the wild stock be so poor and feeble in England, how comes it, we may ask, that English cultivated poetry is so rich in colour and perfume? In simpler language, if the people is so devoid of poetry, how has the race come to produce so many great poets and the noblest poetic literature of the modern world, while artistic poets are rare indeed among races which have great wealth of popular song? This is not the place to attempt a full answer to the question ; we can only defend the natural imagination of the English people by saying that we do not really possess its unsophisticated productions. The English ballads are not, or are very rarely, pure *volks-lieder.* The vast majority of them have not been collected from oral tradition, like the ballads of the Scotch Border, of Italy, and of Greece. As soon as printing was firmly established in England, the traditional songs were distributed in cheap broad-sheets. The people 'love a ballad but even too well ; if it be doleful matter, merrily set down, or a very pleasant thing indeed, and sung lamentably.' Pedlars like Shakspeare's Autolycus 'had songs for man or woman of all sizes.' These songs may originally have been true *volks-lieder*—many of them, indeed, can have been nothing else. In passing, however, through the hands of the printers and poor scholars who prepared them for the press, they became dull, long-drawn, and didactic. The loyalty, good-humour, and love of the free air and the green-wood remain, but the clerks have spoiled the praise of 'Robin Hood, the good outlaw.' The ballads wandered about the land, corrupted from the simplicity that pleased the untaught, into harmony with the roughest educated taste. By Addison's time these broad-sheet ballads had been pasted on the walls of chambers in country houses. In the country, says *The Spectator* (No. 85, June 7, 1711), 'I cannot, for my Heart, leave a Room before I have thoroughly studied the Walls of it, and examined the several printed Papers which are usually pasted upon them.' And on a wall, Addison says, he found 'the old Ballad of *The two Children in the Wood*, which is one of the darling songs of the common People.' Most of our English ballads are gathered from old broad-sheets and ancient MS. collections. To say that is to say that they are dashed with the humblest literary common-place, that they do not come straight from the heart and lips of a singing people, like the modern Greeks or Italians. They have acquired, in the hands of half-educated printers and editors, a tone which is not the tone of the people. They are almost as bald, often, as Dr. Johnson declared them to be—as bald as Johnson's parody :—

> ' I put my hat upon my head, and went into the Strand,
> And there I saw another man, with his hat in his hand.'

The history of English ballad-collecting may be summed up very briefly. We know from Sir Philip Sidney's *Defence of Poesie*, and from many passages in the Elizabethan drama, that ballads were both sung by 'blind crowders,' like the minstrels on the modern Greek frontier, and distributed by pedlars. Addison not only studied English *volks-lieder*, but also those of France and Italy. He tells us that Lord Dorset 'had a numerous collection of old English Ballads, and took a particular pleasure in the reading of them.' Mr. Dryden was of the same humour, so was Pepys of the famous diary. ' The little conceited wits of the age' laughed at Addison, but Dryden ventured to publish some ballads in *Miscellany Poems* (1684-1708). A *Collection of Old Ballads* (since reprinted) was put out in 1723. Ramsay's *Evergreen*, containing many popular songs, appeared in 1724. The great event in the history of the taste for ballads was the publication of Percy's *Reliques of Ancient Poetry*, in 1765. Percy, as is well known, altered, softened, and diluted the old copies which he found in a folio MS. that came into his possession. A correct text from the folio, with excessively copious notes and *prolegomena*, was published by Messrs. Furnivall and Hales (London, 1867-68, 3 vols.). Other noteworthy collections are those of Herd (1769), Ritson, Buchan, Motherwell, Kinloch, Jamieson (1806), and above all, *The Border Minstrelsy* of Scott. Perhaps the best modern collection, the most scholarly, and the least overladen with notes, is that of Professor F. J. Child (*English and Scotch Ballads*, Boston, U.S. 1864). *The Ballad Book* of Mr. W. Allingham (London, 1864) is the companion of every true ballad lover.

The poetic character and quality of the ballads will be best learned from these poems themselves. They have the imaginative daring of early and simple minds ; they often deal with great tragic situations, with deep and universal passions. They are most poetical when the ardour, the anguish, the love, the remorse of some passionate mind becomes for once articulate, as in the cry of *Waly, waly*, the regret of *Edom o' Gordon*, the mysterious wail of *The Wife o' Usher's Well*, or the monotonous chant of *The Lyke-wake Dirge*.

In selecting Ballads for a purely poetical collection, it is neces-
sary to choose, not those which the historian, the antiquary,
the student of early society might prefer, but those which have
most poetical power and charm, and are least embellished by
modern editors. We may, for the purposes of this work, divide
Ballads into five classes—the Historical, or Mythico-historical,
to represent which we pick out *Sir Patrick Spens*, and *Edom
o' Gordon*. In each of these poems the popular fancy works on
true historical data. The second class is the Romantic, and here
Glasgerion, *The Douglas Tragedy*, *The Twa Corbies*, and *Waly,
Waly* are chosen. As specimens of the popular treatment of
the Supernatural, we take *Clerk Saunders*, *The Wife of Usher's
Well*, and the fragment of a popular *Dirge*, like those which are
still sung by the women of Corsica and the Greek isles. Ballads
of the adventures of outlaws and wild marchmen will find their
representative in *Kinmont Willie*. As any selection, however
limited, is incomplete without fragments of the Robin Hood cycle,
we end with *Robin and the Widow's Three Sons*, and *Robin
Hood's Death and Burial*, while *The Bailiff's Daughter* illustrates
the more domestic ballads of the English people. These are
representatives of different classes of *volks-lieder*, but few poems
suffer so much in the process of selection. Too many of the
highest quality have to be omitted for want of space. And the
ballads are wronged too, when they are made to appear among
the more ornate and various measures of cultivated and artistic
poetry.

A. LANG.

HISTORICAL.

SIR PATRICK SPENS.

[This ballad is a confused echo of the Scotch expedition which should have brought the Maid of Norway to Scotland, about 1285. While *Dunfermline* is still spoken of as the favourite Royal residence, the Scotch nobles wear the *cork-heeled shoon* of a later century, a curious example of the medley common in traditional poetry.]

The king sits in Dunfermline town,
　　Drinking the blude-red wine ;
'O whare will I get a skeely skipper,
　　To sail this new ship of mine !'

O up and spake an eldern knight,
　　Sat at the king's right knee,—
'Sir Patrick Spens is the best sailor,
　　That ever sail'd the sea.'

Our king has written a braid letter,
　　And seal'd it with his hand,
And sent it to Sir Patrick Spens,
　　Was walking on the strand.

'To Noroway, to Noroway,
　　To Noroway o'er the faem ;
The king's daughter of Noroway,
　　'Tis thou maun bring her hame.'

The first word that Sir Patrick read,
　　Sae loud loud laughed he ;
The neist word that Sir Patrick read,
　　The tear blinded his e'e.

'O wha is this has done this deed,
　　And tauld the king o' me,
To send us out, at this time of the year,
　　To sail upon the sea?

'Be it wind, be it weet, be it hail, be it sleet[1],
   Our ship must sail the faem ;
The king's daughter of Noroway,
   'Tis we must fetch her hame.'

They hoysed their sails on Monenday morn,
   Wi' a' the speed they may ;
They hae landed in Noroway,
   Upon a Wodensday.

They hadna been a week, a week,
   In Noroway, but twae,
When that the lords o' Noroway
   Began aloud to say,—

'Ye Scottishmen spend a' our king's goud,
   And a' our queenis fee.'
'Ye lie, ye lie, ye liars loud !
   Fu' loud I hear ye lie.

'For I brought as much white monie,
   As gane[2] my men and me,
And I brought a half-fou[3] o' gude red goud,
   Out o'er the sea wi' me.

'Make ready, make ready, my merrymen a' !
   Our gude ship sails the morn.'
'Now, ever alake, my master dear,
   I fear a deadly storm !

'I saw the new moon, late yestreen,
   Wi' the auld moon in her arm ;
And, if we gang to sea, master,
   I fear we 'll come to harm.'

They hadna sailed a league, a league,
   A league but barely three,
When the lift grew dark, and the wind blew loud,
   And gurly grew the sea.

---

[1] A line adapted in *Kinmont Willie*, as the formulae of the Iliad recurs in the Odyssey.   [2] suffice.   [3] the eighth part of a peck.

The ankers brak, and the topmasts lap,
    It was sic a deadly storm;
And the waves cam o'er the broken ship,
    Till a' her sides were torn.

'O where will I get a gude sailor,
    To take my helm in hand,
Till I get up to the tall top-mast,
    To see if I can spy land?'

'O here am I, a sailor gude,
    To take the helm in hand,
Till you go up to the tall top-mast;
    But I fear you'll ne'er spy land.'

He hadna gane a step, a step,
    A step but barely ane,
When a bout flew out of our goodly ship,
    And the salt sea it came in.

'Gae, fetch a web o' the silken claith,
    Another o' the twine,
And wap them into our ship's side,
    And let na the sea come in.'

They fetched a web o' the silken claith,
    Another of the twine,
And they wapped them round that gude ship's side,
    But still the sea came in.

O laith, laith, were our gude Scots lords
    To weet their cork-heel'd shoon!
But lang or a' the play was play'd,
    They wat their hats aboon.

And mony was the feather-bed,
    That flattered on the faem;
And mony was the gude lord's son,
    That never mair cam hame.

The ladyes wrang their fingers white,
   The maidens tore their hair,
A' for the sake of their true loves ;
   For them they 'll see na mair.

O lang, lang, may the ladyes sit,
   Wi' their fans into their hand,
Before they see Sir Patrick Spens
   Come sailing to the strand !

And lang, lang, may the maidens sit,
   Wi' their goud kaims in their hair,
A' waiting for their ain dear loves !
   For them they 'll see na mair.

O forty miles off Aberdeen,
   'Tis fifty fathoms deep,
And there lies gude Sir Patrick Spens,
   Wi' the Scots lords at his feet.

EDOM O' GORDON.

[Popular version of the story of the burning of the House of Towey, a hold of the Forbes's, by the Gordons, in 1571. There is one English version, named *Captain Car*.]

It fell about the Martinmas,
   When the wind blew shrill and cauld,
Said Edom o' Gordon to his men,
   'We maun draw to a hauld.

'And whatna hauld sall we draw to,
   My merry men and me ?
We will gae to the house of the Rodes,
   To see that fair ladye.'

The lady stood on her castle wa',
　Beheld baith dale and down ;
There she was aware of a host of men
　Came riding towards the town.

'O see ye not, my merry men a',
　O see ye not what I see?
Methinks I see a host of men ;
　I marvel who they be.'

She ween'd it had been her lovely lord,
　As he cam' riding hame ;
It was the traitor, Edom o' Gordon,
　Wha reck'd noi sin nor shame.

She had na sooner buskit hersell,
　And putten on her gown,
Till Edom o' Gordon an' his men
　Were round about the town[1].

They had nae sooner supper set,
　Nae sooner said the grace,
But Edom o' Gordon an' his men
　Were lighted about the place.

The lady ran up to her tower-head,
　As fast as she could hie,
To see if by her fair speeches
　She could wi' him agree.

'Come doun to me, ye lady gay,
　Come doun, come doun to me ;
This night sall ye lig within mine arms,
　To-morrow my bride sall be.'

'I winna come down, ye fause Gordon,
　I winna come down to thee ;
I winna forsake my ain dear lord,—
　And he is na far frae me.'

---

[1] *Town* is used in Scotland for any country house or farm-buildings.

'Gie owre your house, ye lady fair,
  Gie owre your house to me;
Or I sall burn yoursell therein,
  But an your babies three.'

'I winna gie owre, ye fause Gordon,
  To nae sic traitor as thee;
And if ye burn my ain dear babes,
  My lord sall mak' ye dree.

'Now reach my pistol, Glaud, my man,
  And charge ye weel my gun;
For, but an I pierce that bluidy butcher,
  My babes, we been undone!'

She stood upon her castle wa',
  And let twa bullets flee:
She miss'd that bluidy butcher's heart,
  And only razed his knee.

'Set fire to the house!' quo' fause Gordon,
  Wud wi' dule and ire:
'Faus ladye, ye sall rue that shot
  As ye burn in the fire!'

'Wae worth, wae worth ye, Jock, my man!
  I paid ye weel your fee;
Why pu' ye out the grund-wa' stane,
  Lets in the reek to me?

'And e'en wae worth ye, Jock, my man!
  I paid ye weel your hire;
Why pu' ye out the grund-wa' stane,
  To me lets in the fire?'

'Ye paid me weel my hire, ladye,
  Ye paid me weel my fee:
But now I'm Edom o' Gordon's man,—
  Maun either do or dee.'

O then bespake her little son,
    Sat on the nurse's knee :
Says, 'O mither dear, gie owre this house,
    For the reek it smothers me.'

'I wad gie a' my goud, my bairn,
    Sae wad I a' my fee,
For ae blast o' the western wind,
    To blaw the reek frae thee.'

O then bespake the daughter dear,—
    She was baith jimp and sma':
'O row' me in a pair o' sheets,
    A tow me owre the wa'!'

They row'd her in a pair o' sheets,
    And tow'd her owre the wa';
But on the point o' Gordon's spear
    She gat a deadly fa'.

O bonnie, bonnie was her mouth,
    And cherry were her cheeks,
And clear, clear was her yellow hair,
    Whereon her red blood dreeps.

Then wi' his spear he turn'd her owre;
    O gin her face was wan!
He said, 'Ye are the first that e'er
    I wish'd alive again.'

He cam and lookit again at her;
    O gin her skin was white !
'I might hae spared that bonnie face
    To hae been some man's delight.'

'Busk and boun, my merry men a',
    For ill dooms I do guess ;—
I cannot look on that bonnie face
    As it lies on the grass.'

‘Wha looks to freits, my master dear,
  Its freits will follow them ;
Let it ne’er be said that Edom o’ Gordon
  Was daunted by a dame.’

But when the ladye saw the fire
  Come flaming o’er her head,
She wept, and kiss’d her children twain,
  Says, ‘ Bairns, we been but dead.’

The Gordon then his bugle blew,
  And said, ‘Awa’, awa’ !
This house o’ the Rodes is a’ in a flame ;
  I hauld it time to ga’.’

And this way lookit her ain dear lord,
  As he came owre the lea ;
He saw his castle a’ in a lowe,
  Sae far as he could see.

‘Put on, put on, my wighty men,
  As fast as ye can dri’e !
For he that ’s hindmost o’ the thrang
  Sall ne’er get good o’ me.’

Then some they rade, and some they ran,
  Out-owre the grass and bent ;
But ere the foremost could win up,
  Baith lady and babes were brent.

And after the Gordon he is gane,
  Sae fast as he might dri’e ;
And soon i’ the Gordon’s foul heart’s blude
  He ’s wroken his fair ladye.

ROMANTIC.

GLASGERION.

[Glasgerion, or Kurion the Pale, was a Celtic minstrel, whom Chaucer places in the company of such bards as 'blind Thamyris and blind Mae-onides.' This ballad exists in the Scotch version of *Glenkindie* (Jamieson, i. 93). It is here printed from Percy's *Reliques*, Bohn's Ed.]

Glasgerion was a kings owne sonne,
  And a harper he was goode ;
He harped in the kings chambere,
  Where cuppe and caudle stoode,

And soe did hee in the queens chambere,
  Till ladies waxed glad,
And then bespake the kinges daughter,
  And these wordes thus shee sayd :

'Strike on, strike on, Glasgerion,
  Of thy striking doe not blinne ;
Theres never a stroke comes oer thy harpe,
  But it glads my hart withinne.'

'Faire might he fall,' quoth hee,
  'Who taught you nowe to speake !
I have loved you, ladye, seven longe yeere,
  My minde I neere durst breake.'

'But come to my bower, my Glasgerion,
  When all men are att rest :
As I am a ladie true of my promise,
  Thou shalt bee a welcome guest.'

Home then came Glasgerion,
  A glad man, lord ! was hee :
'And, come thou hither, Jacke my boy,
  Come hither unto mee.

'For the kinges daughter of Normandye
  Hath granted mee my boone;
And att her chambere must I bee
  Beffore the cocke have crowen.'

'O master, master,' then quoth hee,
  'Lay your head downe on this stone;
For I will waken you, master deere,
  Afore it be time to gone.'

But up then rose that lither ladd,
  And hose and shoone did on;
A coller he cast upon his necke,
  He seemed a gentleman.

And when he came to the ladyes chamber,
  He thrild upon a pinn:
The lady was true of her promise,
  And rose and lett him inn.

He did not take the lady gaye
  To boulster nor to bed:
Nor thoughe hee had his wicked wille,
  A single word he sed.

He did not kisse that ladyes mouthe,
  Nor when he came, nor yode:
And sore that ladye did mistrust,
  He was of some churls bloud.

But home then came that lither ladd,
  And did off his hose and shoone;
And cast the coller from off his necke:
  He was but a churles sonne.

'Awake, awake, my deere master,
  The cock hath well-nigh crowen;
Awake, awake, my master deere,
  I hold it time to be gone

'For I have saddled your horse, mastèr,
 Well bridled I have your steede,
And I have served you a good breakfast,
 For thereof ye have need.'

Up then rose good Glasgerion,
 And did on hose and shoone,
And cast a coller about his necke:
 For he was a kinge his sonne.

And when he came to the ladyes chambere,
 He thrilled upon the pinne;
The lady was more than true of promise,
 And rose and let him inn.

'O whether have you left with me
 Your bracelet or your glove?
Or are you returned back againe
 To know more of my love?'

Glasgerion swore a full great othe,
 By oake, and ashe, and thorne;
'Ladye, I was never in your chambere,
 Sith the time that I was borne.'

'O then it was your lither foot-page,
 He hath beguiled mee:'
Then shee pulled forth a little pen-knìffe,
 That hanged by her knee.

Sayes, 'There shall never noe churlès blood
 Within my bodye spring:
No churlès blood shall eer defile
 The daughter of a kinge.'

Home then went Glasgerion,
 And woe, good lord! was hee:
Sayes, 'Come thou hither, Jacke my boy,
 Come hither unto mee.

'If I had killed a man to-night,
   Jacke, I would tell it thee :
But if I have not killed a man to-night,
   Jacke, thou hast killed three.'

And he puld out his bright browne sword,
   And dryed it on his sleeve,
And he smote off that lither ladds head,
   Who did his ladye grieve.

He sett the swords poynt till his brest,
   The pummil until a stone :
Throw the falsenesse of that lither ladd,
   These three lives were all gone.

THE DOUGLAS TRAGEDY.

[This ballad exists in Denmark, and in other European countries. The
Scotch have localised it, and point out Blackhouse, on the w.ld Douglas
Burn, a tributary of the Yarrow, as the scene of the tragedy.]

'Rise up, rise up, now, Lord Douglas,' she says,
   'And put on your armour so bright ;
Let it never be said, that a daughter of thine
   Was married to a lord under night.

'Rise up, rise up, my seven bold sons,
   And put on your armour so bright,
And take better care of your youngest sister,
   For your eldest's awa the last night.'

He's mounted her on a milk-white steed,
   And himself on a dapple grey,
With a bugelet horn hung down by his side,
   And lightly they rode away.

Lord William lookit o'er is left shoulder,
   To see what he could see,
And there he spy'd her seven brethren bold,
   Come riding over the lee.

'Light down, light down, Lady Marg'ret,' he said,
  And hold my steed in your hand,
Until that against your seven brothers bold,
  And your father, I mak a stand.'

She held his steed in her milk-white hand,
  And never shed one tear,
Until that she saw her seven brethren fa',
  And her father hard fighting, who loved her so dear.

'O hold your hand, Lord William !' she said,
  'For your strokes they are wond'rous sair ;
True lovers I can get many a ane,
  But a father I can never get mair '

O she's ta'en out her handkerchief,
  It was o' the holland sae fine,
And aye she dighted her father's bloody wounds,
  That were redder than the wine.

'O chuse, O chuse, Lady Marg'ret,' he said,
  'O whether will ye gang or bide ?'
'I'll gang, I'll gang, Lord William,' she said,
  'For ye have left me no other guide.'

He's lifted her on a milk-white steed,
  And himself on a dapple grey,
With a bugelet horn hung down by his side,
  And slowly they baith rade away.

O they rade on, and on they rade,
  And a' by the light of the moon,
Until they came to yon wan water,
  And there they lighted down.

They lighted down to tak a drink
  Of the spring that ran sae clear ;
And down the stream ran his gude heart's blood,
  And sair she gan to fear.

'Hold up, hold up, Lord William,' she says,
  'For I fear that you are slain!'
''Tis naething but the shadow of my scarlet cloak,
  That shines in the water sae plain.'

O they rade on, and on they rade,
  And a' by the light of the moon,
Until they cam' to his mother's ha' door,
  And there they lighted down.

'Get up, get up, lady mother,' he says,
  'Get up, and let me in!—
Get up, get up, lady mother,' he says,
  'For this night my fair ladye I've win.

'O mak my bed, lady mother,' he says,
  'O mak it braid and deep!
And lay Lady Marg'ret close at my back,
  And the sounder I will sleep.'

Lord William was dead lang ere midnight,
  Lady Marg'ret lang ere day—
And all true lovers that go thegither,
  May they have mair luck than they!

Lord William was buried in St. Mary's kirk,
  Lady Margaret in Mary's quire;
Out o' the lady's grave grew a bonny red rose,
  And out o' the knight's a brier.

And they twa met, and they twa plat,
  And fain they wad be near;
And a' the warld might ken right weel,
  They were twa lovers dear.

But bye and rade the Black Douglas,
  And wow but he was rough!
For he pull'd up the bonny brier,
  And flang'd in St. Mary's loch.

THE TWA CORBIES [1].

[An English version makes the lady faithful,—

'She lifted up his bloody head,
  And kissed his wounds that were so red;
  She buried him before the prime,
  She was dead herself ere evensong time.']

As I was walking all alane,
I heard twa corbies making a mane;
The tane unto the t'other say,
'Where sall we gang and dine to-day?'

'In behint yon auld fail dyke,
I wot there lies a new-slain knight;
And nae body kens that he lies there,
But his hawk, his hound, and lady fair.

'His hound is to the hunting gane,
His hawk to fetch the wild-fowl hame,
His lady's ta'en another mate,
So we may make our dinner sweet.

'Ye'll sit on his white hause bane,
And I'll pike out his bonny blue een:
Wi' ae lock o' his gowden hair,
We'll theek [2] our nest when it grows bare.

'Mony a one for him makes mane,
But nane sall ken whare he is gane;
O'er his white banes, when they are bare,
The wind sall blaw for evermair.'

       [1] crows.   [2] thatch.

WALY, WALY.

[This fragment, variously corrupted, is often printed as part of a rather dull ballad, concerned with events in the history of Lord James Douglas, of the Laird of Blackwood, and of the lady who utters the beautiful lament here printed.]

O waly, waly, up the bank,
    O waly, waly, doun the brae,
And waly, waly, yon burn-side,
    Where I and my love were wont to gae !
I lean'd my back unto an aik,
    I thocht it was a trustie tree,
But first it bow'd and syne it brak',—
    Sae my true love did lichtlie me.

O waly, waly, but love be bonnie
    A little time while it is new !
But when it 's auld it waxeth cauld,
    And fadeth awa' like the morning dew.
O wherefore should I busk my heid,
    Or wherefore should I kame my hair ?
For my true love has me forsook,
    And says he 'll never lo'e me mair.

Noo Arthur's Seat sall be my bed,
    The sheets sall ne'er be press'd by me ;
Saint Anton's well sall be my drink ;
    Since my true love's forsaken me.
Martinmas wind, when wilt thou blaw,
    And shake the green leaves off the tree ?
O gentle death, when wilt thou come ?
    For of my life I am wearie.

'Tis not the frost that freezes fell,
    Nor blawing snaw's inclemencie,
'Tis not sic cauld that makes me cry ;
    But my love's heart grown cauld to me.

When we cam' in by Glasgow toun,
  We were a comely sicht to see ;
My love was clad in the black velvet,
  An' I mysel' in cramasie.

But had I wist before I kiss'd
  That love had been so ill to win,
I'd lock'd my heart in a case o' goud,
  And pinn'd it wi' a siller pin.
Oh, oh! if my young babe were born,
  And set upon the nurse's knee ;
And I mysel' were dead and gane,
  And the green grass growing over me !

SUPERNATURAL.

Clerk Saunders.

Clerk Saunders and may Margaret
  Walked ower yon garden green ;
And sad and heavy was the love
  That fell thir twa between.

'A bed, a bed,' Clerk Saunders said,
  'A bed for you and me !'
'Fye na, fye na,' said may Margaret,
  'Till anes we married be.

'For in may come my seven bauld brothers,
  'Wi' torches burning bright ;
They'll say—"We hae but ae sister,
  And behold she's wi' a knight !"'

'Then I'll take the sword frae my scabbard,
  And slowly lift the pin ;
And you may swear, and safe your aith,
  Ye never let Clerk Saunders in.

'And take a napkin in your hand,
  And tie up baith your bonny een ;
And you may swear, and safe your aith,
  Ye saw me na since late yestreen.'

It was about the midnight hour,
  When they asleep were laid,
When in and came her seven brothers,
  Wi' torches burning red.

When in and came her seven brothers,
  Wi' torches shining bright ;
They said, 'We hae but ae sister,
  And behold her lying with a knight !'

Then out and spake the first o' them,
  'I bear the sword shall gar him die !'
And out and spake the second o' them,
  'His father has nae mair than he !'

And out and spake the third o' them,
  'I wot that they are lovers dear !'
And out and spake the fourth o' them,
  'They hae been in love this mony a year !'

Then out and spake the fifth o' them,
  'It were great sin true love to twain !'
And out and spake the sixth o' them,
  'It were shame to slay a sleeping man !'

Then up and gat the seventh o' them,
  And never a word spake he ;
But he has striped his bright brown brand
  Out through Clerk Saunders' fair bodye.

Clerk Saunders he started, and Margaret she turned
  Into his arms as asleep she lay ;
And sad and silent was the night
  That was atween thir twae.

And they lay still and sleeped sound,
    Until the day began to daw ;
And kindly to him she did say,
    ' It is time, true love, you were awa'.'

But he lay still, and sleeped sound,
    Albeit the sun began to sheen ;
She looked atween her and the wa',
    And dull and drowsie were his een.

Then in and came her father dear,
    Said—' Let a' your mourning be :
I 'll carry the dead corpse to the clay,
    And I 'll come back and comfort thee.'

' Comfort weel your seven sons ;
    For comforted will I never be :
I ween 'twas neither knave nor loon
    Was in the bower last night wi' me.'

The clinking bell gaed through the town,
    To carry the dead corse to the clay ;
And Clerk Saunders stood at may Margaret's window,
    I wot, an hour before the day.

' Are ye sleeping, Margaret ?' he says,
    Or are ye waking presentlie ?
Give me my faith and troth again,
    I wot, true love, I gied to thee.'

' Your faith and troth ye sall never get,
    Nor our true love sall never twin,
Until ye come within my bower,
    And kiss me cheik and chin.'

' My mouth it is full cold, Margaret,
    It has the smell, now, of the ground ;
And if I kiss thy comely mouth,
    Thy days of life will not be lang[1].

     [1] *Al.* Thy days will soon be at an end.

'O, cocks are crowing a merry midnight,
　I wot the wild fowls are boding day;
Give me my faith and troth again,
　And let me fare me on my way.'

'Thy faith and troth thou sall na get,
　And our true love shall never twin,
Until ye tell what comes of women,
　　I wot, who die in strong traivelling?'

'Their beds are made in the heavens high,
　Down at the foot of our good lord's knee,
Weel set about wi' gillyflowers:
　I wot sweet company for to see.

'O cocks are crowing a merry midnight,
　I wot the wild fowl are boding day;
The psalms of heaven will soon be sung,
　And I, ere now, will be missed away.'

Then she has ta'en a crystal wand,
　And she has stroken her troth thereon;
She has given it him out at the shot-window,
　Wi' mony a sad sigh, and heavy groan.

'I thank ye, Marg'ret; I thank ye, Marg'ret;
　And aye I thank ye heartilie;
Gin ever the dead come for the quick,
　Be sure, Marg'ret, I'll come for thee.'

It's hosen and shoon, and gown alone,
　She climbed the wall, and followed him,
Until she came to the green forest,
　And there she lost the sight o' him.

'Is there ony room at your head, Saunders?
　Is there ony room at your feet?
Or ony room at your side, Saunders,
　Where fain, fain, I wad sleep?'

'There's nae room at my head, Marg'ret,
   There's nae room at my feet ;
My bed it is full lowly now :
   Amang the hungry worms I sleep.

'Cauld mould is my covering now,
   But and my winding-sheet ;
The dew it falls nae sooner down,
   Than my resting-place is weet.

'But plait a wand o' bonnie birk,
   And lay it on my breast ;
And shed a tear upon my grave,
   And wish my saul gude rest.

'And fair Marg'ret, and rare Marg'ret,
   And Marg'ret o' veritie,
Gin ere ye love another man,
   Ne'er love him as ye did me.'

Then up and crew the milk-white cock,
   And up and crew the gray ;
Her lover vanish'd in the air,
   And she gaed weeping away.

The Wife of Usher's Well.

[Sometimes printed as part of *The Three Clerks o' Owsenford.*]

There lived a wife at Usher's Well,
   And a wealthy wife was she ;
She had three stout and stalwart sons,
   And sent them o'er the sea.

They hadna been a week from her,
   A week but barely ane,
When word came to the carline wife,
   That her three sons were gane.

They hadna been a week from her,
    A week but barely three,
Whan word came to the carline wife,
    That her sons she'd never see.

'I wish the wind may never cease,
    Nor fishes[1] in the flood,
Till my three sons come hame to me,
    In earthly flesh and blood!'

It fell about the Martinmas,
    When nights are lang and mirk,
The carline wife's three sons came hame,
    And their hats were o' the birk.

It neither grew in syke nor ditch,
    Nor yet in ony sheugh[2];
But at the gates o' Paradise,
    That birk grew fair eneugh.

    *   *   *   *   ●

'Blow up the fire, my maidens!
    Bring water from the well!
For a' my house shall feast this night,
    Since my three sons are well.'

And she has made to them a bed,
    She's made it large and wide;
And she's ta'en her mantle her about,
    Sat down at the bed-side.

    *   *   *   *   ●

Up then crew the red red cock,
    And up and crew the gray;
The eldest to the youngest said,
    ''Tis time we were away.'

The cock he hadna craw'd but once,
    And clapp'd his wings at a',
When the youngest to the eldest said,
    'Brother, we must awa.

---

[1] *Al.* 'Nor fish be' (? 'Nor freshets ').   [2] trench.

'The cock doth craw, the day doth daw,
  The channerin' worm doth chide ;
Gin we be mist out o' our place,
  A sair pain we maun bide.

'Fare ye weel, my mother dear !
  Fareweel to barn and byre !
And fare ye weel, the bonny lass,
  That kindles my mother's fire.'

       *   *   *   *   *

A LYKE-WAKE DIRGE.

[Contains popular beliefs common to Asiatic and European races, as to
the trials of the Dead.]

This ae nighte, this ae nighte,
  Every night and alle,
Fire and sleet, and candle lighte,
  And Christe receive thy saule.

When thou from hence away are paste,
  Every night and alle ;
To Whinny-muir thou comest at laste ;
  And Christe receive thye saule.

If ever thou gavest hosen and shoon,
  Every night and alle ;
Sit thee down, and put them on ;
  And Christe receive thye saule.

If hosen and shoon thou ne'er gavest nane,
  Every night and alle :
The whinnes shall pricke thee to the bare bane ;
  And Christe receive thye saule.

From Whinny-muir when thou mayst passe,
  Every night and alle ;
To Brigg o' Dread thou comest at laste ;
  And Christe receive thye saule.

       *   *   *   *   *

From Brigg o' Dread when thou mayst passe,
    Every night and alle ;
To Purgatory fire thou comest at laste ;
    And Christe receive thye saule.

If ever thou gavest meat or drink,
    Every night and alle ;
The fire shall never make thee shrinke ;
    And Christe receive thye saule.

If meate or drinke thou never gavest nane,
    Every night and alle ;
The fire will burn thee to the bare bane ;
    And Christe receive thy saule.

This ae nighte, this ae nighte,
    Every nighte and alle ;
Fire and sleet, and candle lighte,
    And Christe receive thye saule.

A SONG OF THE SCOTCH MARCHES.

KINMONT WILLIE.

[The events here reported occurred in 1596. The ballad is the best example of those which treat of rescues, and lawless exploits in the debate-able land.]

O have ye na heard o' the fause Sakelde ?
    O have ye na heard o' the keen Lord Scroop ?
How they hae ta'en bauld Kinmont Willie,
    On Hairibee to hang him up ?

Had Willie had but twenty men,
    But twenty men as stout as he,
Fause Sakelde had never the Kinmont ta'en,
    Wi' eight score in his cumpanie.

They band his legs beneath the steed,
    They tied his hands behind his back ;
They guarded him, fivesome on each side,
    And they brought him ower the Liddel-rack.

They led him thro' the Liddel-rack,
    And also thro' the Carlisle sands
They brought him to Carlisle castell,
    To be at my Lord Scroop's commands.

' My hands are tied, but my tongue is free,
    And whae will dare this deed avow ?
Or answer by the border law ?
    Or answer to the bauld Buccleuch !'

' Now haud thy tongue, thou rank reiver !
    There 's never a Scot shall set ye free :
Before ye cross my castle yate,
    I trow ye shall take farewell o' me.'

' Fear na ye that, my lord,' quo' Willie :
    ' By the faith o' my body, Lord Scroop,' he said,
' I never yet lodged in a hostelrie,
    But I paid my lawing before I gaed.'

Now word is gane to the bauld Keeper,
    In Branksome Ha', where that he lay,
That Lord Scroop has ta'en the Kinmont Willie,
    Between the hours of night and day.

He has ta'en the table wi' his hand,
    He garr'd the red wine spring on hie—
' Now Christ's curse on my head,' he said,
    ' But avenged of Lord Scroop I 'll be !

' O is my basnet[1] a widow's curch[2] ?
    Or my lance a wand of the willow tree ?
Or my arm a ladye's lilye hand,
    That an English lord should lightly me !

---

[1] helmet.   [2] coif.

'And have they ta'en him, Kinmont Willie,
　Against the truce of border tide?
And forgotten that the bauld Buccleuch
　Is Keeper here on the Scottish side?

'And have they e'en ta'en him, Kinmont Willie,
　Withouten either dread or fear?
And forgotten that the bauld Buccleuch
　Can back a steed, or shake a spear?

'O were there war between the lands,
　As well I wot that there is none,
I would slight Carlisle castell high,
　Tho' it were builded of marble stone.

'I would set that castell in a low[1],
　And sloken it with English blood!
There's nevir a man in Cumberland,
　Should ken where Carlisle castell stood.

'But since nae war's between the lands,
　And there is peace, and peace should be;
I'll neither harm English lad nor lass,
　And yet the Kinmont freed shall be!'

He has call'd him forty marchmen bauld,
　I trow they were of his ain name,
Except Sir Gilbert Elliot call'd,
　The laird of Stobs, I mean the same.

He has call'd him forty marchmen bauld,
　Were kinsmen to the bauld Buccleuch;
With spur on heel, and splent on spauld[2],
　And gleuves of green, and feathers blue.

There were five and five before them a',
　Wi' hunting horns and bugles bright;
And five and five came wi' Buccleuch,
　Like warden's men, arrayed for fight:

---

[1] flame.　　　　　[2] armour on shoulder.

And five and five, like a mason gang,
   That carried the ladders lang and hie;
And five and five, like broken men;
   And so they reached the Woodhouselee.

And as we cross'd the Bateable Land,
   When to the English side we held,
The first o' men that we met wi',
   Whae sould it be but fause Sakelde?

'Where be ye gaun, ye hunters keen?'
   Quo' fause Sakelde; 'come tell to me!'
'We go to hunt an English stag,
   Has trespassed on the Scots countrie.'

'Where be ye gaun, ye marshal men?'
   Quo' fause Sakelde; 'come tell me true!'
'We go to catch a rank reiver,
   Has broken faith wi' the bauld Buccleuch.'

'Where are ye gaun, ye mason lads,
   Wi' a' your ladders, lang and hie?'
'We gang to herry a corbie's nest,
   That wons not far frae Woodhouselee.'

'Where be ye gaun, ye broken men?'
   Quo' fause Sakelde; 'come tell to me!'
Now Dickie of Dryhope led that band,
   And the never a word o' lear had he.

'Why trespass ye on the English side?
   Row-footed outlaws, stand!' quo' he;
The never a word had Dickie to say,
   Sae he thrust the lance through his fause bodie.

Then on we held for Carlisle toun,
   And at Staneshaw-bank the Eden we cross'd;
The water was great and meikle of spait,
   But the nevir a horse nor man we lost.

And when we reached the Staneshaw-bank,
    The wind was rising loud and hie;
And there the. laird garr'd leave our steeds,
    For fear that they should stamp and nie.

And when we left the Staneshaw-bank,
    The wind began full loud to blaw,
But 'twas wind and weet, and fire and sleet,
    When we came beneath the castle wa'.

We crept on knees, and held our breath,
    Till we placed the ladders against the wa';
And sae ready was Buccleuch himsell
    To mount the first, before us a'.

He has ta'en the watchman by the throat,
    He flung him down upon the lead—
'Had there not been peace between our land,
    'Upon the other side thou hadst gaed!—

'Now sound out, trumpets!' quo' Buccleuch;
    'Let's waken Lord Scroop, right merrilie!'
Then loud the warden's trumpet blew—
    '*O wha dare meddle wi' me?*'

Then speedilie to work we gaed,
    And raised the slogan ane and a',
And cut a hole thro' a sheet of lead,
    And so we wan to the castle ha'.

They thought King James and a' his men
    Had won the house wi' bow and spear;
It was but twenty Scots and ten,
    That put a thousand in sic a stear!

Wi' coulters, and wi' fore-hammers,
    We garr'd the bars bang merrilie,
Untill we cam to the inner prison,
    Where Willie o' Kinmont he did lie.

And when we cam to the lower prison,
  Where Willie o' Kinmont he did lie—
'O sleep ye, wake ye, Kinmont Willie,
  Upon the morn that thou's to die?'

'O I sleep saft, and I wake aft;
  Its lang since sleeping was fleyed frae me!
Gie my service back to my wife and bairns,
  And a' gude fellows that spier for me.'

Then Red Rowan has hente him up,
  The starkest man in Teviotdale—
'Abide, abide now, Red Rowan,
  Till of my Lord Scroope I take farewell.

'Farewell, farewell, my gude Lord Scroope!
  My gude Lord Scroope, farewell!' he cried—
'I'll pay you for my lodging maill[1],
  When first we meet on the border side.'

Then shoulder high, with shout and cry,
  We bore him down the ladder lang;
At every stride Red Rowan made,
  I wot the Kinmont's airns played clang!

'O mony a time,' quo' Kinmont Willie,
  I have ridden horse baith wild and wood;
But a rougher beast than Red Rowan,
  I ween my legs have ne'er bestrode.

'O mony a time,' quo' Kinmont Willie,
  'I've pricked a horse out oure the furs[2];
But since the day I backed a steed,
  I never wore sic cumbrous spurs!'

We scarce had won the Staneshaw-bank,
  When a' the Carlisle bells were rung,
And a thousand men, in horse and foot,
  Cam wi' the keen Lord Scroope along.

---

[1] rent.   [2] furrows.

Buccleuch has turned to Eden water,
    Even where it flowed frae bank to brim,
And he has plunged in wi' a' his band,
    And safely swam them thro' the stream.

He turned him on the other side,
    And at Lord Scroope his glove flung he—
'If ye like na my visit in merry England,
    In fair Scotland come visit me!'

All sore astonished stood Lord Scroope,
    He stood as still as rock of stane;
He scarcely dared to trew his eyes,
    When thro' the water they had gane.

'He is either himself a devil frae hell,
    Or else his mother a witch maun be;
I wad na ha ridden that wan water,
    For a' the gowd in Christentie.'

ROBIN HOOD BALLADS.

Robin Hood rescuing the Widow's Three Sons.

There are twelve months in all the year,
    As I hear many say,
But the merriest month in all the year
    Is the merry month of May.

Now Robin Hood is to Nottingham gone,
    With a link a down, and a day,
And there he met a silly old woman,
    Was weeping on the way.

'What news? what news? thou silly old woman,
    What news hast thou for me?'
Said she, 'There's my three sons in Nottingham town
    To-day condemned to die.'

'O, have they parishes burnt?' he said,
  'Or have they ministers slain?
Or have they robbed any virgin?
  Or other men's wives have ta'en?'

'They have no parishes burnt, good sir,
  Nor yet have ministers slain,
Nor have they robbed any virgin,
  Nor other men's wives have ta'en.'

'O, what have they done?' said Robin Hood,
  'I pray thee tell to me.'
'It's for slaying of the king's fallow deer,
  Bearing their long bows with thee.'

'Dost thou not mind, old woman,' he said,
  'How thou madest me sup and dine?
By the truth of my body,' quoth bold Robin Hood,
  'You could not tell it in better time.'

Now Robin Hood is to Nottingham gone,
  With a link a down, and a day,
And there he met with a silly old palmer,
  Was walking along the highway.

'What news? what news? thou silly old man,
  What news, I do thee pray?'
Said he, 'Three squires in Nottingham town
  Are condemn'd to die this day.'

'Come change thy apparel with me, old man,
  Come change thy apparel for mine;
Here is ten shillings in good silver,
  Go drink it in beer or wine.'

'O, thine apparel is good,' he said
  'And mine is ragged and torn;
Wherever you go, wherever you ride,
  Laugh not an old man to scorn.'

'Come change thy apparel with me, old churl,
    Come change thy apparel with mine;
Here is a piece of good broad gold,
    Go feast thy brethren with wine.'

Then he put on the old man's hat,
    It stood full high on the crown:
'The first bold bargain that I come at,
    It shall make thee come down.'

Then he put on the old man's cloak,
    Was patch'd black, blue, and red;
He thought it no shame, all the day long,
    To wear the bags of bread.

Then he put on the old man's breeks,
    Was patch'd from leg to side:
'By the truth of my body,' bold Robin can say,
    'This man loved little pride.'

Then he put on the old man's hose,
    Were patch'd from knee to wrist:
'By the truth of my body,' said bold Robin Hood,
    'I'd laugh if I had any list.'

Then he put on the old man's shoes,
    Were patch'd both beneath and aboon;
Then Robin Hood swore a solemn oath,
    'It's good habit that makes a man.'

Now Robin Hood is to Nottingham gone,
    Wi'h a link a down and a down,
And there he met with the proud sheriff,
    Was walking along the town.

'Save you, save you, sheriff!' he said;
    'Now heaven you save and see!
And what will you give to a silly old man
    To-day will your hangman be?'

'Some suits, some suits,' the sheriff he said,
  'Some suits I 'll give to thee;
Some suits, some suits, and pence thirteen,
  To-day 's a hangman's fee.'

Then Robin he turns him round about,
  And jumps from stock to stone :
'By the truth of my body,' the sheriff he said,
  'That 's well jumpt, thou nimble old man.'

'I was ne'er a hangman in all my life,
  Nor yet intends to trade;
But curst be he,' said bold Robin,
  'That first a hangman was made!

'I 've a bag for meal, and a bag for malt,
  And a bag for barley and corn;
A bag for bread, and a bag for beef,
  And a bag for my little small horn.

'I have a horn in my pockèt,
  I got it from Robin Hood,
And still when I set it to my mouth,
  For thee it blows little good.'

'O, wind thy horn, thou proud fellòw!
  Of thee I have no doubt.
I wish that thou give such a blast,
  Till both thy eyes fall out.'

The first loud blast that he did blow,
  He blew both loud and shrill;
A hundred and fifty of Robin Hood's men
  Came riding over the hill.

The next loud blast that he did give,
  He blew both loud and amain,
And quickly sixty of Robin Hood's men
  Came shining over the plain.

'O, who are these,' the sheriff he said,
  'Come tripping over the lee?'
'They're my attendants,' brave Robin did say;
  'They'll pay a visit to thee.'

They took the gallows from the slack,
  They set it in the glen,
They hanged the proud sheriff on that,
  Released their own three men.

Robin Hood's Death and Burial.

[The close of this ballad singularly resembles a Romaic song on the death of a famous klepht, or brigand, in Fauriel's collection.]

When Robin Hood and Little John,
    Down a down, a down, a down,
  Went o'er yon bank of broom,
Said Robin Hood to Little John,
  'We have shot for many a pound:
    Hey down, a down, a down.

'But I am not able to shoot one shot more,
  My arrows will not flee;
But I have a cousin lives down below,
  Please God, she will bleed me.'

Now Robin is to fair Kirkley gone,
  As fast as he can win;
But before he came there, as we do hear,
  He was taken very ill.

And when that he came to fair Kirkley-hall,
  He knock'd all at the ring,
But none was so ready as his cousin herself
  For to let bold Robin in.

'Will you please to sit down, cousin Robin,' she said,
  'And drink some beer with me?
'No, I will neither eat nor drink
  Till I am blooded by thee.'

'Well, I have a room, cousin Robin,' she said,
  'Which you did never see,
And if you please to walk therein,
  You blooded by me shall be.'

She took him by the lily-white hand,
  And led him to a private room,
And there she blooded bold Robin Hood,
  Whilst one drop of blood would run.

She blooded him in the vein of the arm,
  And locked him up in the room ;
There did he bleed all the live-long day,
  Until the next day at noon.

He then bethought him of a casement door,
  Thinking for to be gone ;
He was so weak he could not leap,
  Nor he could not get down.

He then bethought him of his bugle-horn,
  Which hung low down to his knee ;
He set his horn ùnto his mouth,
  And blew out weak blasts three.

Then Little John, when hearing him,
  As he sat under the tree,
'I fear my master is near dead,
  He blows so wearily.'

Then Little John to fair Kirkley is gone,
  As fast as he can dri'e ;
But when he came to Kirkley-hall,
  He broke locks two or three :

Until he came bold Robin to,
  Then he fell on his knee :
'A boon, a boon,' cries Little John,
  'Master, I beg of thee.'

'What is that boon,' quoth Robin Hood,
  'Little John, thou begs of me?'
'It is to burn fair Kirkley-hall,
  And all their nunnery.'

'Now nay, now nay,' quoth Robin Hood,
  'That boon I'll not grant thee;
I never hurt woman in all my life,
  Nor man in woman's company.

'I never hurt fair maid in all my time,
  Nor at my end shall it be;
But give me my bent bow in my hand,
  And a broad arrow I'll let flee;
And where this arrow is taken up,
  There shall my grave digg'd be.

'Lay me a green sod under my head,
  And another at my feet;
And lay my bent bow by my side,
  Which was my music sweet;
And make my grave of gravel and green,
  Which is most right and meet.

'Let me have length and breadth enough,
  With a green sod under my head;
That they may say, when I am dead,
  Here lies bold Robin Hood.'

These words they readily promis'd him,
  Which did bold Robin please;
And there they buried bold Robin Hood,
  Near to the fair Kirklèys.

DOMESTIC.

THE BAILIFF'S DAUGHTER OF ISLINGTON.

There was a youthe, and a well-beloved youthe,
　And he was a squires son;
He loved the bayliffes daughter deare,
　That lived in Islington.

Yet she was coye, and would not believe
　That he did love her soe,
Noe nor at any time would she
　Any countenance to him showe.

But when his friendes did understand
　His fond and foolish minde,
They sent him up to faire London,
　An apprentice for to binde.

And when he had been seven long yeares,
　And never his love could see, —
'Many a teare have I shed for her sake,
　When she little thought of mee.'

Then all the maids of Islington
　Went forth to sport and playe,
All but the bayliffes daughter deare;
　She secretly stole awaye.

She pulled off her gowne of greene,
　And put on ragged attire,
And to faire London she would go
　Her true love to enquire.

As as she went along the high road,
　The weather being hot and drye,
She sat her downe upon a green bank,
　And her true love came riding bye.

She started up, with a colour soe redd,
   Catching hold of his bridle-reine ;
'One penny, one penny, kind sir,' she sayd,
   'Will ease me of much paine.'

'Before I give you one penny, sweet-heart,
   Praye tell me where you were borne.'
'At Islington, kind sir,' sayd shee,
   'Where I have had many a scorne.'

'I prythee, sweet-heart, then tell to mee,
   O tell me, whether you knowe
The bayliffes daughter of Islington.'
   'She is dead, sir, long agoe.'

'If she be dead, then take my horse,
   My saddle and bridle also ;
For I will into some farr countrye,
   Where noe man shall me knowe.'

'O staye, O staye, thou goodlye youthe,
   She standeth by thy side ;
She is here alive, she is not dead,
   And readye to be thy bride.'

'O farewell griefe, and welcome joye,
   Ten thousand times therefore ;
For nowe I have founde mine owne true love,
   Whom I thought I should never see more.'

SIR THOMAS WYATT.

[THOMAS WYATT, the eldest son of Sir Henry Wyatt, a baronet of ancient family, was born at Allington Castle, in Kent, in 1503. In the Court of Henry VIII he soon became a conspicuous figure, famous for his wit, his learning, his poetical talents, his linguistic attainments, his skill in athletic exercises, his fascinating manners and his handsome person. From a courtier he developed into a statesman and a diplomatist, and in the duties incident to statesmanship and diplomacy most of his life was passed. He died at Sherborne, while on his road to Falmouth, and was buried there October 11th, 1542. His poems were first printed in *Tottel's Miscellany* in 1557.]

Wyatt and Surrey are usually classed together—*par nobile fratrum*—the Dioscuri of the Dawn. They inaugurated that important period in our literature known as the Era of Italian Influence, or that of the Company of Courtly Makers—the period which immediately preceded and ushered in the age of Spenser and Shakespeare. With some of the characteristics of expiring mediævalism still lingering about them, the prevailing spirit of their poetry is the spirit of the Renaissance,—not its colour, not its exuberance, not its intoxication ; but its classicism, its harmony, and its appreciation of form. With the writings of Virgil, Martial and Seneca, in ancient, and with the writings of Petrarch and his school in modern times, they were evidently familiar, and they have as evidently made them their models. The influence of that school is indeed manifest in almost everything these poets have left us, sometimes directly in translations, in professed imitation, in turns of expression, still oftener indirectly in tone, form and style : but they owed more to the Italy of the fourteenth than to the Italy of the first century. To Wyatt and Surrey our debt is a great one. They introduced and naturalised the Sonnet, both the Sonnet of the true Petrarchian type and the Sonnet which was afterwards carried to such perfection in the hands of Shakespeare and Daniel. In Surrey we find the first germ of the Bucolic Eclogue. In Wyatt we have our first classical satirist. Of our lyrical poetry they were the founders. Their tone, their style, their rhythm, their measures, were at once adopted by a school of disciples, and have ever since maintained their popularity among poets. In their lyrics indeed is to be found the seed of everything that is most charming in the form of Jonson and Herrick, of Waller and Suckling, of Cowley and Prior. They gave us—but this is the glory of Surrey alone—the first specimens of blank verse that our language can boast. They were the creators of that majestic measure the heroic quatrain. They enriched diction with fulness and involution. They were the first of our poets who had learned the great secret of transfusing the spirit of one language into that of another, who had the good taste to select the best models and the good sense to adhere to them. They gave the deathblow to that rudeness, that grotesqueness, that prolixity, that diffuseness, that pedantry, which had deformed with fatal persistency the poetry of mediævalism, and while they purified our language from the Gallicisms of Chaucer and his followers, they fixed the permanent standard of our versification. To them we are indebted for the great reform which substituted a metrical for a rhythmical structure. Their services to our literature may at once be realised by comparing their work with that of their immediate predecessors, and by observing its influence on the writers in the four Miscellanies which appeared between 1557 and the publication of *England's Helicon* in 1600. Indeed these interesting men stand in much the same relation to the poetical literature of England as Boscan and Garcilaso de la Vega stand to the poetical literature of Castile.

It is unfortunately not possible to decide how far these two poets acted and re-acted on each other. We are however inclined to think that Wyatt was the master-spirit, and that Surrey has been enabled to throw him so completely and so unfairly into the shade, mainly because he had his friend's patterns to work upon. Wyatt was his senior by at least fourteen years, and Wyatt's poems, if we except at least the Satires and the Penitential Psalms, were in all probability early works.

The poems of Wyatt consist of Sonnets, Lyrics in all varieties of measure, Rondeaux, Epigrams, Satires, and a poetical paraphrase of the Penitential Psalms. His genius is essentially imitative. His Sonnets are either direct translations or servile imitations of Petrarch's. Of his lyrics some are borrowed from the Spanish, some from the French, some from the Italian ; all, with the exception of half a dozen perhaps, are more or less modelled on writings in those languages. What we call his Epigrams are for the most part versions from the Strambotti of Serafino d' Aquila. One of his Satires is an abridged imitation of the Tenth Satire of Alamanni, the other two were respectively suggested by Horace and Persius. Even in his version of the Penitential Psalms he was careful to follow in the footsteps of Dante and Alamanni. The dignity and gravity which characterise the structure of some of his lyric periods appear to have been caught from the poets of Castile. His general tone is sombre, sententious and serious, and he is too often reflecting when he ought to be feeling. The greater part of his poetry is wasted in describing with weary minuteness transports of slighted and requited affection, but his true place is among observant men of the world, scholars and moralists. His versification is often harsh and uncouth, except in some of his lyrics, which are occasionally very musical, and in his Satires, which are uniformly terse and smooth. He is inferior to Surrey in diction, in taste, in originality, and in poetical feeling ; but it may be doubted whether the more delicate genius of the younger poet would have been able to achieve so complete a triumph over the mechanism of expression had he not been preceded by his robuster brother.

J. CHURTON COLLINS.

[The lover having dreamed enjoying of his love, complaineth that the
dream is not either longer or truer.]

Unstable dream, according to the place,
Be steadfast once, or else at least be true :
By tasted sweetness make me not to rue
The sudden loss of thy false feigned grace.
By good respect, in such a dangerous case,
Thou broughtest not her into these tossing seas ;
But madest my sprite to live, my care to encrease,
My body in tempest her delight to embrace.
The body dead, the spirit had his desire ;
Painless was the one, the other in delight.
Why then, alas, did it not keep it right,
But thus return to leap into the fire ;
   And when it was at wish, could not remain ?
   Such mocks of dreams do turn to deadly pain.

[The lover beseecheth his mistress not to forget his stedfast faith
and true intent.]

Forget not yet the tried intent
Of such a truth as I have meant ;
My great travail so gladly spent,
   Forget not yet !

Forget not yet when first began
The weary life ye know, since whan
The suit, the service none tell can ;
   Forget not yet !

Forget not yet the great assays,
The cruel wrong, the scornful ways,
The painful patience in delays,
   Forget not yet !

Forget not ! oh ! forget not this,
How long ago hath been, and is
The mind that never meant amiss.
      Forget not yet !

Forget not then thine own approved,
The which so long hath thee so loved,
Whose steadfast faith yet never moved :
      Forget not yet !

[The lover complaineth of the unkindness of his love.]

My lute, awake ! perform the last
Labour that thou and I shall waste ;
And end that I have now begun :
And when this song is sung and past,
My lute ! be still, for I have done.

As to be heard where ear is none ;
As lead to grave in marble stone,
My song may pierce her heart as soon ;
Should we then sing, or sigh, or moan ?
No, no, my lute ! for I have done.

The rock doth not so cruelly,
Repulse the waves continually,
As she my suit and affection :
So that I am past remedy ;
Whereby my lute and I have done.

Proud of the spoil that thou hast got
Of simple hearts thorough Love's shot,
By whom, unkind, thou hast them won ;
Think not he hath his bow forgot,
Although my lute and I have done.

Vengeance shall fall on thy disdain,
That makest but game of earnest pain ;
Trow not alone under the sun
Unquit to cause thy lovers plain,
Although my lute and I have done.

May chance thee lie withered and old
In winter nights, that are so cold,
Plaining in vain unto the moon ;
Thy wishes then dare not be told :
Care then who list, for I have done.

And then may chance thee to repent
The time that thou hast lost and spent,
To cause thy lovers sigh and swoon :
Then shalt thou know beauty but lent,
And wish and want, as I have done.

Now cease, my lute ! This is the last
Labour that thou and I shall waste ;
And ended is that we begun :
Now is thy song both sung and past ;
My lute, be still, for I have done.

On his Return from Spain.

Tagus farewell ! that westward with thy streams
Turns up the grains of gold already tried ;
For I with spur and sail go seek the Thames
Gainward the sun that showeth her wealthy pride.
And to the town that Brutus sought by dreams,
Like bended moon that leans her lusty side ;
My king, my country alone for whom I live,
Of mighty Love the winds for this me give [1]!

From the second Satire.

My Poins, I cannot frame my tongue to feign,
To cloak the truth for praise without desert
Of them that list all vices to retain.
I cannot honour them that set their part

[1] *Al.* My king, my country, I seek, for whom I live;
O mighty Jove, the winds for this me give!

With Venus, and Bacchus, all their life long,
Nor hold my peace of them although I smart.
I cannot crouch nor truckle to such a wrong,
To worship them like God on earth alone
That are as wolves these sely lambs among.
I cannot with my words complain and moan,
And suffer nought ; nor smart without complaint,
Nor turn the word that from my mouth has gone.
I cannot speak and look like as a saint,
Use wiles for wit and make deceit a pleasure,
Call craft counsel, for lucre still to paint ;
I cannot wrest the law to fill the coffer,
With innocent blood to feed myself fat
And do most hurt where that most help I offer.
I am not he that can allow the state
Of high Caesar, and damn Cato to die,
That by his death did scape out of the gate
From Caesar's hands, if Livy doth not lie,
And would not live where Liberty was lost;
So did his heart the common wealth apply.
I am not he, such eloquence to boast
To make the crow in singing as the swan ;
Nor call the lion of coward beasts the most,
That cannot take a mouse as the cat can :
And he that dieth for hunger of the gold,
Call him Alexander, and say that Pan
Passeth Apollo in music manifold,
Praise Sir Topas for a noble tale
And scorn the story that the Knight told ;
Praise him for counsel that is drunk of ale ;
Grin when he laughs, that beareth all the sway ;
Frown when he frowns, and groan when he is pale
On other's lust to hang both night and day.
None of these points could ever frame in me ;
My wit is nought, I cannot learn the way.

THE EARL OF SURREY.

[HENRY HOWARD was the eldest son of Thomas Earl of Surrey, by his second wife, the Lady Elizabeth Stafford, daughter of Edward Stafford, Duke of Buckingham. The date and place of his birth are alike unknown. It probably occurred in 1517. He became Earl of Surrey on the accession of his father to the dukedom of Norfolk in 1524. The incidents of his early life are buried in obscurity; the incidents of his later life rest on evidence rarely trustworthy and frequently apocryphal. He was beheaded on Tower Hill January 21, 1547, nominally on a charge of high treason, really in consequence of having fallen a victim to a Court intrigue, the particulars of which it is now impossible to unravel. With regard to the chronology of his various poems we have nothing to guide us. Though they were extensively circulated in manuscript during his lifetime, they were not printed till June 1557, when they made their appearance, together with Wyatt's poems and several fugitive pieces by other authors, in *Tottel's Miscellany*.]

The works of Surrey, though not so numerous as those of his friend Wyatt, are of a very varied character. They consist of sonnets, of miscellaneous poems in different measures, of lyrics, of elegies, of translations, of Scriptural paraphrases, of two long versions from Virgil. The distinctive feature of Surrey's genius is its ductility; its characteristic qualities are grace, vivacity, pathos, picturesqueness. He had the temperament of a true poet, refinement, sensibility, a keen eye for the beauties of nature, a quick and lively imagination, great natural powers of expression. His tone is pure and lofty, and his whole writings breathe that chivalrous spirit which still lingered among the satellites of the eighth Henry. His diction is chaste and perspicuous, and though it bears all the marks of careful elaboration it has no trace of stiffness or pedantry. His verse is so smooth, and at times so delicately musical, that Warton questioned whether in these qualities at least our versification has advanced since Surrey tuned it for the first time. Without the learning of Wyatt, his literary skill is far greater. His taste is exquisite. His love poetry, which is distinguished by touches of genuine feeling, is modelled for the most part on the Sonnetti and Ballati of Petrarch, though it has little of Petrarch's frigid puerility and none of his metaphysical extravagance. The Laura of Surrey is the fair Geraldine. We may perhaps suspect the existence of some less shadowy object. As a lyrical poet, when he permits himself to follow his own bent he is easy and graceful. His elegiac verses and his epitaph on Clere have been deservedly praised for their pathos, dignity, and terseness, and his translation from Martial makes us regret that he has not left us more in the same vein. His versions from Virgil we are not inclined to rank so highly as Warton does, but they are interesting as being the first *English* versions from the poets of antiquity worthy of the name, and as furnishing us with the earliest specimens of that verse which was to become the omnipotent instrument of Shakespeare and Milton. As a sonneteer he follows closely in the footsteps of Petrarch, though he is not, like Wyatt, a servile copyist, and he is entitled to the high praise of being not only the first who introduced the sonnet into our language, but of having made that difficult form of composition the obedient interpreter of a poet's feelings and of a poet's fancies. His most unsuccessful pieces are his Scriptural paraphrases and the poems written in Alexandrines, though one of these, *The Complaint of a Dying Lover*, is valuable as being, next to Henryson's *Robine and Makyne*, the first pastoral poem in British literature.

J. CHURTON COLLINS.

Description of Spring,

[Wherein each thing renews, save only the lover.]

The soote season, that bud and bloom forth brings,
With green hath clad the hill, and eke the vale.
The nightingale with feathers new she sings ;
The turtle to her make[1] hath told her tale.
Summer is come, for every spray now springs,
The hart hath hung his old head on the pale ;
The buck in brake his winter coat he slings ;
The fishes flete with new repaired scale ;
The adder all her slough away she slings ;
The swift swallow pursueth the flies smale ;
The busy bee her honey now she mings[2] ;
Winter is worn that was the flowers' bale.
　　And thus I see among these pleasant things
　　Each care decays, and yet my sorrow springs!

A Complaint by Night of the Lover not beloved.

Alas ! so all things now do hold their peace !
Heaven and earth disturbed in no thing ;
The beasts, the air, the birds their song do cease ;
The nightës car the stars about doth bring.
Calm is the sea ; the waves work less and less :
So am not I, whom love, alas ! doth wring,
Bringing before my face the great increase
Of my desires, whereat I weep and sing,
In joy and woe, as in a doubtful ease.
For my sweet thoughts sometime do pleasure bring ;
But by and by, the cause of my disease
Gives me a pang, that inwardly doth sting.
　　When that I think what grief it is again,
　　To live and lack the thing should rid my pain.

---

[1] mate.　　　　　　[2] mingles.

[Prisoned in Windsor, he recounteth his pleasure there passed.]

So cruel prison how could betide, alas,
As proud Windsor? where I in lust and joy,
With a King's son, my childish years did pass,
In greater feast than Priam's sons of Troy.
Where each sweet place returns a taste full sour,
The large green courts, where we were wont to hove[1],
With eyes cast up into the maiden's tower,
And easy sighs, such as folk draw in love.
The stately seats, the ladies bright of hue,
The dances short, long tales of great delight;
With words and looks, that tigers could but rue;
When each of us did plead the other's right.
The palme-play[2] where, despoiled for the game,
With dazed eyes oft we by gleams of love
Have missed the ball, and got sight of our dame,
To bait her eyes, which kept the leads above.
The gravelled ground, with sleeves tied on the helm,
On foaming horse, with swords and friendly hearts;
With cheer, as though one should another whelm,
When we have fought, and chased oft with darts;
With silver drops the mead yet spread for ruth,
In active games of nimbleness and strength,
Where we did strain, trained with swarms of youth,
Our tender limbs, that yet shot up in length.
The secret groves, which o´t we made resound
Of pleasant plaint, and of our ladies' praise;
Recording oft what grace each one had found,
What hope of speed, what dread of long delays.
The wild forest, the clothed holts with green;
With reins availed, and swift ybreathed horse,
With cry of hounds, and merry blasts between,
When we did chase the fearful hart of force.
The void walls eke, that harboured us each night:
Wherewith, alas! reviveth in my breast
The sweet accord, such sleeps as yet delight;
The pleasant dreams, the quiet bed of rest;—

[1] hover.   [2] tennis.

The secret thoughts, imparted with such trust ;
The wanton talk, the divers change of play ;
The friendship sworn, each promise kept so just,
Wherewith we passed the winter night away.
And with this thought the blood forsakes the face ;
The tears berain my cheeks of deadly hue :
The which, as soon as sobbing sighs, alas !
Upsupped have, thus I my plaint renew :
'O place of bliss, renewer of my woes !
Give me account, where is my noble fere[1],
Whom in thy walls thou dost each night enclose,
To other lief[2], but unto me most dear.'
Echo, alas ! that doth my sorrow rue
Returns thereat a hollow sound of plaint.
Thus I alone, where all my freedom grew,
In prison pine, with bondage and restraint ;
And with remembrance of the greater grief,
To banish the less, I find my chief relief.

THE MEANS TO ATTAIN HAPPY LIFE.

[Translated from Martial.]

Martial, the things that do attain
  The happy life be these, I find ;
The riches left, not got with pain ,
  The fruitful ground, the quiet mind.

The equal friend, no grudge, no strife,
  No charge of rule nor governance ;
Without disease, the healthful life ;
  The household of continuance.

The mean[3] diet, no delicate fare ;
  True wisdom joined with simpleness ;
The night discharged of all care,
  Where wine the wit may not oppress.

The faithful wife, without debate ;
  Such sleeps as may beguile the night ;
Contented with thine own estate,
  Ne wish for death, ne fear his might.

[1] companion.   [2] dear.   [3] moderate.

S 2

A Praise of his Love.

[Wherein he reproveth them that compare their ladies with his.]

Give place, ye lovers, here before
That spent your boasts and brags in vain ;
My lady's beauty passeth more
The best of yours, I dare well sayen,
Than doth the sun the candle light
Or brightest day the darkest night.

And thereto hath a troth as just
As had Penelope the fair ;
For what she saith, ye may it trust,
As it by writing sealed were :
And virtues hath she many moe
Than I with pen have skill to show.

I could rehearse, if that I would,
The whole effect of Nature's plaint,
When she had lost the perfect mould,
The like to whom she could not paint :
With wringing hands, how she did cry,
And what she said, I know it, I.

I know she swore with raging mind,
Her kingdom only set apart,
There was no loss by law of kind
That could have gone so near her heart ;
And this was chiefly all her pain ;
'She could not make the like again.'

Sith Nature thus gave her the praise,
To be the chiefest work she wrought ;
In faith, methinks ! some better ways
On your behalf might well be sought,
Than to compare, as ye have done,
To match the candle with the sun.

AN EPITAPH ON CLERE, SURREY'S FAITHFUL FRIEND AND FOLLOWER.

Norfolk sprung thee, Lambeth holds thee dead;
Clere, of the Count of Cleremont, thou hight;
Within the womb of Ormond's race thou bred,
And saw'st thy cousin[1] crowned in thy sight.
Sheltou for love, Surrey for lord thou chase[2],
(Aye me! whilst life did last that league was tender)
Tracing whose steps thou sawest Kelsal blaze,
Landrecy burnt, and battered Boulogne render.
At Montreuil gates, hopeless of all recure,
Thine Earl, half dead, gave in thy hand his will;
Which cause did thee this pining death procure,
Ere summers four times seven thou couldst fulfill.
   Ah! Clere! if love had booted, care, or cost,
   Heaven had not won, nor earth so timely lost.

ON THE DEATH OF SIR THOMAS WYATT.

Wyatt resteth here that quick could never rest:
   Whose heavenly gifts increased by disdain,
And virtue sank the deeper in his breast;
   Such profit he by envy could obtain.

A head where wisdom mysteries did frame,
   Whose hammers beat still in that lively brain,
As on a stithe where that some work of fame
   Was daily wrought, to turn to Britain's gain.

A visage stern and mild: where both did grow
   Vice to contemn, in virtue to rejoice;
Amid great storms whom grace assured so
   To live upright, and smile at fortune's choice.

A hand that taught what might be said in rhyme;
   That reft Chaucer the glory of his wit;
A mark, the which (unperfected for time)
   Some may approach, but never none shall hit.

---

[1] Thomas Clere was first cousin of Anne Boleyn.   [2] Didst choose.

A tongue that served in foreign realms his king;
   Whose courteous talk to virtue did inflame
Each noble heart : a worthy guide to bring
   Our English youth by travail unto fame.

An eye whose judgment none affect could blind,
   Friends to allure and foes to reconcile,
Whose piercing look did represent a mind
   With virtue fraught reposed void of guile.

A heart where dread was never so imprest
   To hide the thought that might the truth advance ;
In neither fortune loft[1], nor yet represt,
   To swell in wealth, or yield unto mischance.

A valiant corpse, where force and beauty met,
   Happy alas, too happy but for foes,
Lived, and ran the race that nature set ;
   Of manhood's shape where she the mould did lose.

But to the heavens that simple soul is fled,
   Which left, with such as covet Christ to know,
Witness of faith that never could be dead ;
   Sent for our health, but not received so.

Thus for our guilt this jewel have we lost ;
The earth his bones, the heavens possess his ghost.

          [1] exalted.

GEORGE GASCOIGNE.

[GEORGE GASCOIGNE was born circ. 1536; died 1577. The dates of his poems are:—

1572. *A hundred Sundry Flowers bound up in one small Posy.*
1575. *The Posies corrected, perfected, and augmented by the Author.*
  ,,   *The Glass of Government.*
1576. *The Steel Glass, with the Complaint of Philomene.*
1587. *The Pleasantest Works of George Gascoigne, newly compiled into one volume.*]

Amongst the poets that immediately preceded the great Eliza-
bethan Period, which may be said to begin with the publication
of *The Shepherd's Calendar* in 1580, Gascoigne occupied, and
occupies, a notable place. Bolton indeed, in his *Hypercritica*,
speaks slightingly of him : 'Among the lesser late poets George
Gascoigne's Works may be endured'; but for the most part he is
mentioned with high respect and praise. Raleigh commends *The
Steel Glass* in what are his earliest known verses. Puttenham
distinguishes him for 'a good metre and for a plentiful vein.'
Webbe calls him 'a witty gentleman, and the very chief of our late
rimers'; 'gifts of wit,' he says, 'and natural promptness appear in
him abundantly.' Amongst other eulogists may be named Nash,
Gabriel Harvey, Whetstone.

He was a man of family and position, well known to and
amongst the 'Inns of Court men,' who, in the Elizabethan age,
as in that of Queen Anne, passed for the arch wits and critics as
well as the first gentlemen of the day ; and when campaigning in
the Low Countries he met with adventures which added to his per-
sonal prestige. Thus he was a conspicuous figure in the society
of his time, and for this reason, if for nothing else, his verses
would win esteem and circulation.

Gascoigne, then, is interesting as a poet who was popular during
Shakspere's boyhood and Spenser's adolescence. But he is yet
more important as one who did real service in the way of extend-
ing and improving the form of literature—as a pioneer of the

Elizabethan Period. ' Whoever,' says Nash, ' my private opinion condemns as faulty, Master Gascoigne is not to be abridged of his deserved esteem, who first beat the path to that perfection which our best poets have aspired to since his departure ; whereto he did ascend by comparing the Italian with the English, as Tully did *Græca cum Latinis.*' He is the author of our earliest extant comedy in prose—possibly the earliest written—*The Supposes,* a translation of Ariosto's *Suppositi,* and in part the author of one of our earliest tragedies, of *Jocasta*—a paraphrase rather than a translation of the *Phoïnissai* of Euripides ; he is one of our earliest writers of formal satire and of blank verse, and in his ' Certain Notes of Instruction concerning the making of verse or rime in English written at the request of Master Edouardo Donati,' one of the earliest essayists, if not the earliest, on English metres.

Happily, we can add, his works have not only these historical claims on our attention ; they have intrinsic merits. His lyrics are occasionally characterised by a certain lightness and grace, which give and will give them a permanent life. Singing of all a lover's moods and experiences —how he passions, laments, complains, recants, is refused, is encouraged—he is never a mere mimic of his Italian masters, or, though somewhat monotonous, wanting in vigour and sincerity. His style is clear and unaffected. The crude taste of his age is often enough apparent ; and in this respect his ' poor rude lines,' if we ' compare them with the bettering of the times,' may sometimes make but no great show ; but here too he rises above his fellows, who are often simply grotesque when they mean to be fervent, and are dull when they are not grotesque. He writes in various metres with various facility and skill. Of blank verse his mastery is imperfect ; he is like a child learning to walk, whose progress is from chair to chair : he lacks freedom and fluency. The metre of his *Complaint of Philomene* is ill chosen for its purpose. It is a jig, not a movement of ' even step and musing gait.' Much of his work is autobiographical. We can trace him ' from gay to grave,' perhaps we may add ' from lively to severe ' ; for in his later years, by a reaction that is common enough, it would seem he took a somewhat morbid view of the life he was leaving, under-prizing it, after the manner of zealots, even as in his youth he had prized it too highly.

JOHN W. HALES.

The Arraignment of a Lover.

At Beauty's bar as I did stand,
When false Suspect accused me,
George (quoth the Judge), hold up thy hand,
Thou art arraigned of flattery :
Tell therefore how thou wilt be tried :
Whose judgement here wilt thou abide ?

My Lord (quoth I) this Lady here,
Whom I esteem above the rest,
Doth know my guilt if any were :
Wherefore her doom shall please me best.
Let her be Judge and Juror both,
To try me guiltless by mine oath.

Quoth Beauty, no, it fitteth not,
A prince herself to judge the cause :
Will is our Justice well you wot,
Appointed to discuss our laws :
If you will guiltless seem to go,
God and your country quit you so.

Then Craft the crier call'd a quest,
Of whom was Falsehood foremost fere,
A pack of pickthanks were the rest,
Which came false witness for to bear,
The jury such, the judge unjust,
Sentence was said I should be trussed.

Jealous the jailer bound me fast,
To hear the verdict of the bill,
George (quoth the Judge) now thou art cast,
Thou must go hence to Heavy Hill,
And there be hanged all but the head,
God rest thy soul when thou art dead.

Down fell I then upon my knee,
All flat before Dame Beauty's face,
And cried Good Lady pardon me,
Which here appeal unto your grace,
You know if I have been untrue,
It was in too much praising you.

And though this Judge do make such haste,
To shed with shame my guiltless blood :
Yet let your pity first be placed,
To save the man that meant you good,
So shall you show yourself a Queen,
And I may be your servant seen.

(Quoth Beauty) well : because I guess,
What thou dost mean henceforth to be,
Although thy faults deserve no less,
Than Justice here hath judged thee,
Wilt thou be bound to stint all strife
And be true prisoner all thy life ?

Yea madam (quoth I) that I shall,
Lo Faith and Truth my sureties :
Why then (quoth she) come when I call,
I ask no better warrantise.
Thus am I Beauty's bounden thrall,
At her command when she doth call.

A Strange Passion of a Lover.

Amid my bale I bathe in bliss,
I swim in Heaven, I sink in hell :
I find amends for every miss,
And yet my moan no tongue can tell.
I live and love (what would you more ?)
As never lover lived before.

I laugh sometimes with little lust,
So jest I oft and feel no joy ;
Mine eye is builded all on trust,
And yet mistrust breeds mine annoy.

I live and lack, I lack and have ;
I have and miss the thing I crave.

These things seem strange, yet are they true.
Believe me, sweet, my state is such,
One pleasure which I would eschew,
Both slakes my grief and breeds my grutch.
So doth one pain which I would shun,
Renew my joys where grief begun.

Then like the lark that passed the night,
In heavy sleep with cares oppressed ;
Yet when she spies the pleasant light,
She sends sweet notes from out her breast.
So sing I now because I think
How joys approach, when sorrows shrink.

And as fair Philomene again
Can watch and sing when other sleep ;
And taketh pleasure in her pain,
To wray the woe that makes her weep.
So sing I now for to bewray
The loathsome life I lead alway.

The which to thee dear wench I write,
That know'st my mirth but not my moan :
I pray God grant thee deep delight,
To live in joys when I am gone.
I cannot live ; it will not be :
I die to think to part from thee.

PIERS PLOUGHMAN.

[From *The Steel Glass*.]

Behold him, priests, and though he stink of sweat,
Disdain him not : for shall I tell you what ?
Such climb to heaven before the shaven crowns :
But how ? forsooth with true humility.
Not that they hoard their grain when it is cheap,
Nor that they kill the calf to have the milk,

Nor that they set debate between their lords,
By earing up the balks that part their bounds :
Nor for because they can both crouch and creep
(The guileful'st men that ever God yet made)
When as they mean most mischief and deceit,
Nor that they can cry out on landlords loud,
And say they rack their rents an ace too high,
When they themselves do sell their landlord's lamb
For greater price than ewe was wont be worth.
(I see you Piers, my glass was lately scoured.)
But for they feed with fruits of their great pains
Both king and knight and priests in cloister pent :
Therefore I say that sooner some of them
Shall scale the walls which lead us up to heaven,
Than cornfed beasts, whose belly is their God,
Although they preach of more perfection.

Epilogus.

Alas, (my lord), my haste was all too hot,
I shut my glass before you gazed your fill,
And at a glimpse my seely self have spied,
A stranger troop than any yet were seen :
Behold, my lord, what monsters muster here,
With angels face, and harmful hellish hearts,
With smiling looks and deep deceitful thoughts,
With tender skins, and stony cruel minds,
With stealing steps, yet forward feet to fraud.
Behold, behold, they never stand content,
With God, with kind, with any help of Art,
But curl their locks with bodkins and with braids,
But dye their hair with sundry subtle sleights,
But paint and slick till fairest face be foul,
But bumbast, bolster, frizzle and perfume :
They marr with musk the balm which nature made,
And dig for death in delicatest dishes.
The younger sort come piping on apace,
In whistles made of fine enticing wood,

Till they have caught the birds for whom they brided,
And on their backs they bear both land and fee,
Castles and towers, revenues and receipts,
Lordships and manors, fines, yea farms and all.
What should these be? (speak you my lovely lord)
They be not men: for why they have no beards.
They be no boys which wear such sidelong gowns.
They be no Gods, for all their gallant gloss.
They be no devils (I trow) which seem so saintish.
What be they? women? masking in men's weeds?
With dutchkin doublets, and with jerkins jagged?
With Spanish spangs and ruffs set out of France,
With high copt hats and feathers flaunt a flaunt?
They be so sure even *woe* to *Men* in deed.
Nay then, my lord, let shut the glass apace,
High time it were for my poor Muse to wink,
Since all the hands, all paper, pen and ink,
Which ever yet this wretched world possest,
Cannot describe this sex in colours due.
No, No, my lord, we gazed have enough,
(And I too much; God pardon me therefore),
Better look off than look an ace too far:
And better mum than meddle overmuch,
But if my glass do like my lovely lord,
We will espy some sunny summers day,
To look again and see some seemly sights.
Meanwhile my muse right humbly doth beseech,
That my good lord accept this vent'rous verse
Until my brains may better stuff devise.

THOMAS SACKVILLE.

[THOMAS SACKVILLE was born in 1536 at Buckhurst in Sussex, where his family had been settled since the Conquest. After some time spent at Oxford and Cambridge, he entered parliament (1557–58), and in the beginning of Elizabeth's reign he became known as a poetical writer. Between 1557 and 1563 he took part in *The Tragedy of Gorboduc*, and also planned a work called *The Mirror of Magistrates*, a series of poetical examples, showing 'with how grievous plagues vices are punished in Great Princes and Magistrates, and how frail and unstable worldly prosperity is found, where fortune seemeth most highly to favour.' He wrote the *Induction*, a preface, and the Story of Henry Stafford, Duke of Buckingham. But he soon threw himself into the risks of public life. On the whole he was successful. In 1567 he was created Lord Buckhurst. He experienced the fitful temper of the Queen in various public employments. He sat on several of the great state trials of the time—those of the Duke of Norfolk, Mary Queen of Scots, the Earl of Essex. In 1599 he was made Lord High Treasurer. James I created him Earl of Dorset in 1604. In 1608 he died, 'while sitting at the council table at Whitehall.']

The scanty remains of Sackville's poetry are chiefly interesting because they show a strong sense of the defects of the existing poetical standard, and a craving after something better. They show an effort after a larger and bolder creation of imagery; as where the poet, copying Dante, imagines himself guided by the Genius of Sorrow through the regions of the great Dead, there to hear from their own mouths the sad vicissitudes of their various stories. There is a greater restraint and severity than had yet been seen in the choice of language and ornament, though stiffness and awkwardness of phrase, and the still imperfect sense of poetical fitness and grace, show that the writer could not yet reach in execution what he aimed at in idea. And there is visible both in the structure of the seven-line stanzas, and in the flow of the verses themselves, a feeling for rhythmic stateliness and majesty corresponding to his solemn theme. In their cadences, as well as in the allegorical figures and pathetic moralising of Sackville's verses, we see a faint anticipation of Spenser, who inscribed one of the prefatory Sonnets of the *Faery Queene* to one who may have been one of his masters in his art.

R. W. CHURCH.

FROM 'THE INDUCTION.'

[Sorrow guides the poet to the realms of the dead.]

Then looking upward to the heaven's leams,
With nighted stars thick powder'd every where,
Which erst so glisten'd with the golden streams,
That cheerful Phoebus spread from down his sphere,
Beholding dark oppressing day so near,
The sudden sight reduced to my mind,
The sundry changes that in earth we find.

That musing on this worldly wealth in thought,
Which comes, and goes, more faster than we see
The flickering flame that with the fire is wrought,
My busy mind presented unto me
Such fall of peers as in the realms had be,
That oft I wish'd some would their woes descrive,
To warn the rest whom fortune left alive.

And straight forth stalking with redoubled pace,
For that I saw the night draw on so fast,
In black all clad, there fell before my face
A piteous wight, whom woe had all forewaste :
Forth from her eyen the crystal tears out brast :
And sighing sore her hands she wrung and fold,
Tare all her hair, that ruth was to behold.

  * * * * * *

I stood aghast, beholding all her plight,
'Tween dread and dolour, so distrain'd in heart,
That, while my hairs upstarted with the sight,
The tears outstream'd for sorrow of her smart :
But, when I saw no end that could apart
The deadly dewle which she so sore did make,
With doleful voice then thus to her I spake :

  * * * * * *

'O Sorrow, alas, sith Sorrow is thy name,
And that to thee this drear doth well pertain,
In vain it were to seek to cease the same :
But, as a man himself with sorrow slain,
So I, alas, do comfort thee in pain,

That here in sorrow art foresunk so deep,
That at thy sight I can but sigh and weep.'
    *   *   *   *   *   *
For forth she paced in her fearful tale :
'Come, come,' quoth she, 'and see what I shall show,
Come, hear the plaining and the bitter bale
Of worthy men by Fortune overthrow :
Come thou and see them rueing all in row,
They were but shades that erst in mind thou roll'd :
Come, come with me, thine eyes shall them behold'
    *   *   *   *   *   *
Flat down I fell, and with all reverence
Adored her, perceiving now that she,
A goddess, sent by godly providence,
In earthly shape thus show'd herself to me,
To wail and rue this world's uncertainty :
And, while I honour'd thus her godhead's might,
With plaining voice these words to me she shright.

'I shall thee guide first to the grisly lake,
And thence unto the blissful place of rest,
Where thou shalt see, and hear, the plaint they make
That whilom here bare swing among the best :
This shalt thou see : but great is the unrest
That thou must bide, before thou canst attain
Unto the dreadful place where these remain.'
    *   *   *   *   *   *
Thence come we to the horrour and the hell,
The large great kingdoms, and the dreadful reign
Of Pluto in his throne where he did dwell,
The wide waste places, and the hugy plain,
The wailings, shrieks, and sundry sorts of pain,
The sighs, the sobs, the deep and deadly groan :
Earth, air, and all, resounding plaint and moan.

Here pul'd the babes, and here the maids unwed
With folded hands their sorry chance bewail'd,
Here wept the guiltless slain, and lovers dead,
That slew themselves when nothing else avail'd :
A thousand sorts of sorrows here, that wail'd

With sighs, and tears, sobs, shrieks, and all yfear,
That, oh, alas, it was a hell to hear.

*   *   *   *   *   *

Lo here, quoth Sorrow, princes of renown,
That whilom sat on top of fortune's wheel,
Now laid full low, like wretches whirled down,
Ev'n with one frown, that stay'd but with a smile:
And now behold the thing that thou, ere while,
Saw only in thought : and what thou now shalt hear,
Recount the same to kesar, king and peer.'

*   *   *   *   *   *

COMPLAINT OF THE DUKE OF BUCKINGHAM.

So long as fortune would permit the same,
I liv'd in rule and riches with the best :
And pass'd my time in honour and in fame,
That of mishap no fear was in my breast:
But false fortune, when I suspected least,
Did turn the wheel, and with a doleful fall
Hath me bereft of honour, life, and all.

Lo, what avails in riches floods that flows?
Though she so smil'd, as all the world were his:
Even kings and kesars biden fortune's throws,
And simple sort must bear it as it is.
Take heed by me that biith'd in baleful bliss:
My rule, my riches, royal blood and all,
When fortune frown'd, the feller made my fall.

For hard mishaps, that happens unto such
Whose wretched state erst never fell no change,
Agrieve them not in any part so much
As their distress, to whom it is so strange
That all their lives, nay, passed pleasures range,
Their sudden woe, that aye wield wealth at will,
Algates their hearts more piercingly must thrill.

For of my birth, my blood was of the best,
First born an earl, then duke by due descent :
To swing the sway in court among the rest,
Dame Fortune me her rule most largely lent,
And kind with courage so my corpse had blent,
That lo, on whom but me did she most smile ?
And whom but me, lo, did she most beguile ?

Now hast thou heard the whole of my unhap,
My chance, my change, the cause of all my care :
In wealth and woe, how fortune did me wrap,
With world at will, to win me to her snare :
Bid kings, bid kesars, bid all states beware,
And tell them this from me that tried it true :
Who reckless rules, right soon may hap to rue.

SLEEP.

By him lay heavy Sleep, the cousin of Death,
Flat on the ground, and still as any stone,
A very corpse, save yielding forth a breath :
Small keep took he, whom Fortune frowned on,
Or whom she lifted up into the throne
Of high renown : but as a living death,
So, dead alive, of life he drew the breath.

The body's rest, the quiet of the heart,
The travail's ease, the still night's fear was he,
And of our life on earth the better part :
Reaver of sight, and yet in whom we see
Things oft that tide, and oft that never be :
Without respect, esteeming equally
King Croesus' pomp, and Irus' poverty.

EDMUND SPENSER.

[EDMUND SPENSER was born in London about 1552. He was educated at Merchant Taylors' School: his first poetical performances, translations from Petrarch and Du Bellay, published without his name in a miscellaneous collection, belong to the time of his leaving school in 1569. From that year to 1576 he was at Pembroke Hall, Cambridge. In 1579 he was in London, acquainted with Philip Sidney, and in Lord Leicester's household. In 1580 was published, but without his name, *The Shepheards Calender*; and in the autumn of that year he went to Ireland with Lord Grey of Wilton, as his private secretary. The remainder of his life, with the exception of short visits to England, was spent in Ireland, where he held various subordinate offices, and where he settled on a grant of forfeited land at Kilcolman in the county of Cork. In 1589 he accompanied Sir Walter Ralegh to London, and in 1590 published the first three books of *The Faerie Queene*. In 1591 he returned to Ireland, and a miscellaneous collection of compositions of earlier and later dates (*Complaints*) was published in London. In June 1594 he married, and the next year, 1595, he again visited London, and in Jan. 1595-6 published the second instalment of *The Faerie Queene* (iv-vi). With the same date, 1595, were published his *Colin Clouts Come Home again*, an account of his visit to the Court in 1589-90, and his *Amoretti Sonnets*, and an *Epithalamion*, relating to his courtship and marriage. At the end of 1598 his house was sacked and burnt by the Munster rebels, and he returned in great distress to London. He died at Westminster, Jan. 16, 1598-9, and was buried in the Abbey.]

Spenser was the first who in the literature of England since the Reformation made himself a name as a poet which could be compared with that of Chaucer, or of the famous Italians who then stood at the head of poetical composition. National energy had revived under the reign of Elizabeth, and with it had come a burst of poetical enthusiasm. Many persons tried their hand at poetry. Versification became a fashion. It was encouraged in the Court circles. The taste for poetry shows itself in a popular shape in ballads, and among scholars in translation; and amid a good deal of bad poetry there was some written which was genuine and beautiful, and which has survived to charm us still. The poetical spirit and feeling came out most naturally in short love poems, of which many of great grace and fire are preserved in the collections of the time ; the other form which it took at this time was the expression of the pathetic incidents and conditions of human greatness and fortune. Sir Philip Sidney, one of the most accomplished and most rising of the young men about the Court, encouraged an interest in poetry in his circle of friends, and some of them, Edward Dyer and Fulke Greville, have, like Sidney himself, left poems of merit. But while there was much poetical writing, and not a little poetical power even among men engaged in the business and wars of the time, such as Walter Ralegh, no successful attempt had been made to produce a great poetical work which might challenge comparison with the *Canterbury Tales* at home, or the *Orlando Furioso* abroad. Spenser was the first who had the ambition and also the power for such an enterprise. His earliest work, *The Shepherd's Calendar*, a series of what were called pastoral poems, after the fashion of the Italian models and some English imitators, partly original, partly translated or paraphrased, though very immature and very unequal in its composition, was at once felt to be something more considerable as a poetical achievement than anything which the sixteenth century had yet seen in England. The 'new poet' became almost a recognised title for the man who had shown, not merely by a few spirited fugitive stanzas, but in a sustained work, that he could write so sweetly and so well. The fame and the associations of *The Shepherd's Calendar* clung to him even to the end of his career. To the end he had a predilection for its pastoral colouring and scenery ; to the end he liked to give himself the rustic name by which he had represented himself in its dialogues, and called himself *Colin Clout*.

But *The Faery Queen* was something beyond the expectations raised by *The Shepherd's Calendar*. In its plan, its invention, and its execution, it took the world of its day by surprise. It opened a new road to English poetry, and new kingdoms to be won by it. The name of Spenser stands in point of time even before that of Shakespeare in the roll of modern English poets. A discoverer of something new to be done, he first did what all were trying to do, and broke down the difficulties of a great and magnificent art.

But the first are not always the greatest in poetry, any more than in painting, in music, in science, in geographical discovery : they lead the way and make it possible to greater men and greater things. Spenser delighted Shakespeare : he was the poetical master of Cowley and then of Milton, and, in a sense, of Dryden and even Pope. None but a man of strength, of originality, of rare sense of beauty and power of imagination and music, could have been this. But he was the great predecessor of yet greater successors. *The Faery Queen* is a noble and splendid work. When we think that it was the first of its kind, and that Spenser had no master of English, except in antiquity, to show him how to write, it is an astonishing one. But it has the imperfections and shortcomings of most original attempts to do what is new and hard, and what none have yet succeeded in ; and it has the imperfections which actually belonged to the genius, the mind and character of the writer.

The Faery Queen is, as every one knows, an allegorical poem ; and in this it differs from the Italian models then talked of and famous, from the works of Ariosto and Tasso, as well as from Chaucer. The idea and framework was taken from them ; the machinery, like theirs, was borrowed from the days, or rather the literature, of chivalry ; and like theirs, the story rolled on in stanzas, and Spenser invented for his purpose a new form of stanza, one of nine lines, instead of the eight-line one of the Italians. But, unlike them, Spenser avowedly designed to himself a moral purpose and meaning in his poem. It was not merely a brilliant and entertaining series of adventures, like the *Orlando*. It was not merely a poetical celebration of a great historical legend, a religious epic, like the *Gerusalemme*. It professed to be a veiled exposition of moral philosophy. It was planned, and all its imaginative wealth unfolded, in order to pourtray and recommend the virtues, and to exhibit philosophical speculations. It was intended to be a book, not for delight merely, but for instruction. Such a view of poetry was characteristically in harmony with the serious spirit of the time in England, which welcomed heartily all intellectual efforts, but which expected in them a purpose to do more than amuse, and had fashion on its side in putting the note of frivolity on what did not bear this purpose distinctly in view. Spenser thought it right to declare to his friends, and to set down in writing, the aim and intention of his poem. He described it as a work which 'is in heroical verse under the title of a *Faery Queen* to represent all the moral

virtues, assigning to every virtue a knight as the patron and de-
fender of the same, in whose actions and feats of arms and
chivalry the operations of that virtue, whereof he is the protector,
are to be expressed, and the vices and unruly appetites that
oppose themselves against the same, to be beaten down or over-
come.' And in a letter to Sir Walter Ralegh, written to give the
key to the poem, he says that the general end of his 'Allegory
or dark conceit,' and of all his book, is 'to fashion a gentleman
or noble person in virtuous and gentle discipline.' He indeed
sees this purpose and intention in the 'antique poets historical.'
Homer meant to represent 'a good governor and virtuous man'
in Agamemnon and Ulysses, Virgil meant the same in Aeneas,
Ariosto in Orlando. Tasso dissevered them, representing the
Ethical part of Moral Philosophy, or the virtues of a private man,
in Rinaldo; the other, 'named *Politicé*,' the public virtues of a
governor in Goffredo. In King Arthur, Spenser meant once more
to join both. 'By example of which excellent poets,' he says,
'I labour to pourtray in Arthur, before he was king, the image of
a brave knight, perfected in the XII *private* moral virtues, as
Aristotle hath devised; the which is the purpose of these first
twelve books; which if I find to be well accepted, I may be per-
haps encouraged to frame the other part of *politick* virtues in his
person, after that he came to be king.'

Of this large design of twenty-four books, each of twelve cantos,
little more than a fourth part was accomplished, or at any rate
has survived. The first three books were published in 1590;
three more, books iv, v, vi, were added to them in a second
edition in 1596. Two cantos, with a couple of stray stanzas,
were published after his death. The political part of the design
does not seem to have even come into sight of the poet.

The poem was designed in England, but it was mostly written
in Ireland, amid scenes of disorder and wretchedness, which sorely
tested not only the courage, but the justice, the wisdom, and the
humanity of the Englishmen who had any share in the govern-
ment of the most unfortunate of the Queen's dominions. It needed
indeed to be a knight as perfect in strength and goodness as the
ideal Arthur, to deal with the evils of Ireland. Spenser, as men
do in trying times, thought he saw the virtues partially realised in
the friends engaged in the difficult tasks round him: we, at our
point of view, are obliged to see how far the best and noblest of
them was from the poet's ideal. But the presence and actual

sight of all this energy, struggle, danger, courage, doubtless gave life to Spenser's conception of the life of warfare which he proposed to pourtray. It was before him on the spot ; and *The Faery Queen* is the reflection of it, tempered and sobered by the poet's purpose, to make it represent his conception of all that makes a man great and true in his resistance to the vices and evils of the world.

The Faery Queen purports to be a story, and the outline of the story, which was to bind it together, is given in the poet's explanatory letter to Sir Walter Ralegh, now prefixed to the poem. He imagines the Faery Queen, by whom he shadows forth Elizabeth, holding a great festival, on occasion of which twelve of her knights, each the example and champion of some particular virtue, undertake separate enterprises at her appointment and in her honour ; while Prince Arthur, in whom is represented the comprehensive Aristotelic virtue of magnificence, or greatness of soul, is to fall in with them one by one in his quest of his fated bride the Faery Queen, helping and saving them by the superior power of his virtue and his knightly skill. The adventures of the twelve knights were to furnish the ' Legends ' of the twelve books of the first portion of his design, the 'ethical' portion. He thought it inartificial for a poet to begin from the occasion and starting-point of these various adventures : 'A Poet,' he said, 'thrusteth himself into the middest, even when it most concerneth him, and there recoursing to the things forepast, and divining of things to come, maketh a pleasant analysis of all.' So he starts in the middle of one of the adventures, reserving his poetical account of the origin of them all, till he should have brought all his Knights back again to the Faery Queen's Court in the last book. The arrangement was an awkward one, and the Twelfth Book was never reached. Though we know the framework of the story, we do not know it from the poem itself. And as he went on with his work, the main story is soon lost in the separate ones, and the poem becomes a succession of adventures, stories, pictures, and allegories, with little attempt to keep them together.

In the First Book, the story and the allegory,—the dangers, the combats, the defeats, the final victory of the Red Cross Knight of Holiness, the champion of the Virgin Una with her milk-white lamb,—and that which all this shadowed, the struggle of true religion and godliness with its foes, its vicissitudes, and its triumph, both in the visible scene of the world's history, and in the heart of man, are both carried on clearly and consecutively. The Second Book, which takes the Knight of Temperance through his contest with violence, with the falsehood of extremes, with the madness of uncontrolled temper, with the temptations of Mammon, of riches and ambition, to the closing achievement, the conquest over all that Pleasure could present to allure and fascinate him, is straightforward and distinct in its construction. But after this the poet's hold over his story relaxes. The legend of Chastity in the next book presents the same idea as that of the second, but exhibited in the persons of the lady knight Britomart, and the virgin huntress Belphœbe, both of them in various aspects imaging the 'sacred saint' of the poet's worship. In the three later books, the legend of Justice is marked by its strong and definite representations of some great historical events of Spenser's age, the administration of Lord Grey of Wilton in Ireland, the blows dealt at the Spanish power in the Channel and in the Netherlands, the fate of Mary Queen of Scots. The legends of 'Friendship' and 'Courtesy' certainly exhibit examples of friendship and courtesy. But when we think of what friendship is, we wonder that Spenser has so little to say about it, and that his imagination found nothing more to work upon than the companionship in love or war, sometimes loyal, sometimes false, of men-at-arms : and so many other interests and incidents come in besides, that it seems rather arbitrary to assign the legends specially to these virtues. And then, with the exception of the fragment on 'Mutability,' which is part of a projected legend of 'Constancy,' the poem stops, and with it all our knowledge of the way in which it was to be carried forward.

The interest in *The Faery Queen* is twofold. There is the interest of the moral picture which it presents, and there is the interest of it as a work of poetical art.

The moral picture is of the ideal of noble manliness in Elizabeth's time. Besides the writers and the thinkers, the statesmen and the plotters, the traders and the commons, of that fruitful and vigorous age, there were the men of action : the men who fought in France and the Netherlands and Ireland, the men who created the English navy, and showed how it could be used : the men who tried for the north-west passage with Sir Humphrey Gilbert, and sailed round the world with Sir Francis Drake, and planted colonies in America with Sir Walter Ralegh : the men who chased the Armada to destruction, and dealt the return buffet to Spanish pride in the harbour of Cadiz; men who treated the sea as the rightful dominion of their mistress, and seeking adventures on it far and near, with or without her leave, reaped its rich harvests of plunder, from Spanish treasure ships and West Indian islands, or from the exposed towns and churches of the Spanish coast. They were at once men of daring enterprise and sometimes very rough execution; and yet men with all the cultivation and refinement of the time, courtiers, scholars, penmen, poets. These are the men whom Spenser had before his eyes in drawing his knights—their ideas of loyalty, of gallantry, of the worth and use of life,—their aims, their enthusiasm, their temptations, their foes, their defeats, their triumphs. In his tales of perpetual warfare, of perpetual resistance to evil, of the snares and desperate dangers through which they have to fight their way, there is a picture of the conditions which affect the whole life of man. The allegory may be applied, and was intended to be applied generally, to the difficulties which beset his course and the qualities necessary to overcome them. But it specially exhibits the ideals and standards and aspirations —the characteristic virtues and the characteristic imperfections, the simple loyalty and the frank selfishness, of the brilliant and high-tempered generation, who are represented by men like Philip Sidney and Walter Ralegh, and Howard of Effingham and Richard Grenville, or by families like those of Vere and Norreys and Carew.

As a work of art *The Faery Queen* at once astonishes us by the wonderful fertility and richness of the writer's invention and imagination, by the facility with which he finds or makes language for his needs, and above all, by the singular music and sweetness of his verse. The main theme seldom varies : it is a noble knight, fighting, overcoming, tempted, delivered ; or a beautiful lady, plotted against, distressed, in danger, rescued. The poet's affluence of fancy and speech gives a new turn and colour to each adventure. But besides that under these conditions there must be monotony, the poet's art, admirable as it is, gives room for objections. Spenser's style is an imitation of the antique ; and an imitation, however good, must want the master charm of naturalness, reality, simple truth. And in his system of work, with his brightness and quickness and fluency, he wanted self-restraint—the power of holding himself in, and of judging soundly of fitness and proportion. There was a looseness and carelessness, partly belonging to his age, partly his own. In the use of materials, nothing comes amiss to him. He had no scruple as a copyist. He took without ceremony any piece of old metal,—word, or story, or image—which came to his hand, and threw it into the melting-pot of his imagination, to come out fused with his own materials, often transformed, but often unchanged. The effect was sometimes happy, but not always so.

With respect to his diction, it must ever be remembered that the language was still in such an uncertain and unfixed state as naturally to invite attempts to extend its powers, and to enrich, supple, and colour it. Spenser avowedly set himself to do this. The editor of his first work, *The Shepherd's Calendar*, takes credit on his behalf for attempting 'to restore, as to their rightful heritage, such good and natural English words, as have been long time out of use, and almost clean disherited.' Spenser draws largely on Chaucer, both for his vocabulary and his grammar: and his authority and popularity have probably saved us a good many words which we could ill afford to lose. And some of his words we certainly have forgotten to our loss—such words as 'ingate' (like 'insight,') 'glooming,' 'fool-happy,' 'overgone,' and his many combinations with *en-* — 'empeopled,' 'engrieved,' 'enrace.' But it is not to enrich a language but to confuse and spoil it, when a writer forces on it words which are not in keeping with its existing usages and spirit, and much more when he arbitrarily deals with words to make them suit the necessities of metre and rime : and there is much of this in Spenser. He overdoes, especially in his earlier books, the old English expedient of alliteration, or 'hunting the letter,' as it was called, which properly belongs to a much earlier method of versification, and which the ear of his own generation had already learned to shrink from in excess. He not only revives old words, but he is licentious—as far as we are able to trace the usages of the time—in inventing new ones. He is unscrupulous in using inferior forms for better and more natural ones, not for the sake of the word, but for the convenience of the verse. The transfer of words—adjectives and verbs—from their strict use to a looser one,—the passage from an active to a neuter sense,—the investing a word with new associations,—the interchange of attributes between two objects, with the feelings or phrase which really belong to one reflected back upon the other —are, within limits, part of the recognised means by which language, and especially poetical language, extends its range. But Spenser was inclined to make all limits give way to his convenience, and the rapidity of his work. It is not only to us that his language is both strange and affectedly antique ; it looked the same to the men of his own time. It is a drawback to the value of Spenser as a monument of the English of his day, that it is often uncertain whether a form or a meaning of word may not be due simply to his own wayward and arbitrary use of it.

The Faery Queen has eclipsed all Spenser's other writings : but his other writings alone would be enough to place him, as his contemporaries placed him, at the head of all who had yet attempted English poetry. *The Shepherd's Calendar,* as has been said, with all its defects and affectations, showed force, skill, command of language and music as yet unknown. In it were shown the beginnings of two powers characteristic of Spenser : the power of telling a story, as in the fables of The Oak and Briar, and The Fox and Kid ; and the power of satire, a power which he used both there and afterwards in *Mother Hubberd's . Tale,* to lash the Church abuses of the time and the manners of the Court, and in using which he is in strong contrast, in his sobriety and self-restraint, to the coarse extravagance of such writing in his time. The Fox and Ape of *Mother Hubberd's Tale* is much nearer to the satire of Dryden and Pope, than it is to such writers as Donne and Hall. He did his necessary share of work in writing poems of salutation or congratulation for the great, or of lamentation for their misfortunes and sorrows. The *Prothalamion* celebrates the marriage of two ladies of the Worcester family ; and he bewailed the death of Sir Philip Sidney and the Earl of Leicester. Much of this poetry was conventional. But in it appear fine and beautiful passages. The *Prothalamion* has great sweetness and grace. The Dirges never fail to show his deep and characteristic feeling for the vicissitudes of our human state. Finally, his own love and courtship inspired a series of Sonnets, and a Wedding Hymn. The Sonnets on the whole are disappointing. There is warmth and sincerity in them ; but they want the individual stamp which makes such things precious. On the other hand, the Wedding Hymn, the *Epithalamion,* is one of the richest and most magnificent compositions of the kind in any language.

R. W. CHURCH.

Fable of the Oak and the Briar.

[From *The Shepheards Calender*, 1579-80. February.]

There grewe an aged Tree on the greene,
A goodly Oake sometime had it bene,
With armes full strong and largely displayd,
But of their leaves they were disarayde :
The bodie bigge, and mightely pight,
Throughly rooted, and of wonderous hight ;
Whilome had bene the King of the field,
And mochell mast to the husband did yielde,
And with his nuts larded many swine : ·
But now the gray mosse marred his rine ;
His bared boughes were beaten with stormes,
His toppe was bald, and wasted with wormes,
His honor decayed, his braunches sere.

Hard by his side grewe a bragging Brere,
Which proudly thrust into Thelement,
And seemed to threat the Firmament :
It was embellisht with blossomes fayre,
And thereto aye wonned to repayre
The shepheards daughters to gather flowres,
To peinct their girlonds with his colowres ;
And in his small bushes used to shrowde
The sweete Nightingale singing so lowde ;
Which made this foolish Brere wexe so bold,
That on a time he cast him to scold
And snebbe the good Oake, for he was old.

'Why standst there (quoth he) thou brutish blocke?
Nor for fruict nor for shadowe serves thy stocke ;
Seest how fresh my flowers bene spredde,
Dyed in Lilly white and Cremsin redde,
With Leaves engrained in lusty greene ;
Colours meete to clothe a mayden Queene ?
Thy wast bignes but combers the grownd,
And dirks the beauty of my blossomes rownd :
The mouldie mosse, which thee accloieth,

My Sinamon smell too much annoieth :
Wherefore soone I rede thee hence remove,
Least thou the price of my displeasure prove.'
So spake this bold brere with great disdaine :
Little him aunswered the Oake againe,
But yeelded, with shame and greefe adawed,
That of a weede he was overcrawed.

    Yt chaunced after upon a day,
The Hus-bandman selfe to come that way,
Of custome for to survewe his grownd,
And his trees of state in compasse rownd :
Him when the spitefull brere had espyed,
Causelesse complained, and lowdly cryed
Unto his lord, stirring up sterne strife.

    ' O, my liege Lord ! the God of my life !
Pleaseth you ponder your Suppliants plaint,
Caused of wrong and cruell constraint,
Which I your poore Vassall dayly endure ;
And, but your goodnes the same recure,
Am like for desperate doole to dye,
Through felonous force of mine enemie.'

    Greatly aghast with this piteous plea,
Him rested the goodman on the lea,
And badde the Brere in his plaint proceede.
With painted words tho gan this proude weede
(As most usen Ambitious folke :)
His colowred crime with craft to cloke.

    ' Ah, my soveraigne ! Lord of creatures all,
Thou placer of plants both humble and tall,
Was not I planted of thine owne hand,
To be the primrose of all thy land ;
With flowring blossomes to furnish the prime,
And scarlot berries in Sommer time ?
How falls it then that this faded Oake,
Whose bodie is sere, whose braunches broke,
Whose naked Armes stretch unto the fyre,
Unto such tyrannie doth aspire ;
Hindering with his shade my lovely light,
And robbing me of the swete sonnes sight ?

So beate his old boughes my tender side,
That oft the bloud springeth from woundes wyde;
Untimely my flowres forced to fall,
That bene the honor of your Coronall:
And oft he lets his cancker-wormes light
Upon my braunches, to worke me more spight;
And oft his hoarie locks downe doth cast,
Where-with my fresh flowretts bene defast:
For this, and many more such outrage,
Craving your goodlihead to aswage
The ranckorous rigour of his might,
Nought aske I, but onely to hold my right;
Submitting me to your good sufferance,
And praying to be garded from greevance.'
　To this the Oake cast him to replie
Well as he couth; but his enemie
Had kindled such coles of displeasure,
That the good man noulde stay his leasure,
But honve him hasted with furious heate,
Encreasing his wrath with many a threate;
His harmefull Hatchet he hent in hand,
(Alas! that it so ready should stand!)
And to the field alone he speedeth,
(Ay little helpe to harme there needeth!)
Anger nould let him speake to the tree,
Enaunter[1] his rage mought cooled bee;
But to the roote bent his sturdy stroake,
And made many wounds in the wast Oake.
The Axes edge did oft turne againe,
As halfe unwilling to cutte the graine;
Semed, the sencelesse yron dyd feare,
Or to wrong holy eld did forbeare;
For it had bene an auncient tree,
Sacred with many a mysteree,
And often crost with the priestes crewe[2],
And often halowed with holy-water dewe:
But sike fancies weren foolerie,
And broughten this Oake to this miserye;

　　　　[1] lest.　　　　　　　[2] holy vessel, cruise.

For nought mought they quitten him from decay,
For fiercely the good man at him did laye.
The blocke oft groned under the blow,
And sighed to see his neare overthrow.
In fine, the steele had pierced his pitth,
Tho downe to the earth he fell forthwith.
His wonderous weight made the ground to quake,
Thearth shronke under him, and seemed to shake :—
There lyeth the Oake, pitied of none !

Now stands the Brere like a lord alone,
Puffed up with pryde and vaine pleasaunce ;
But all this glee had no continuaunce :
For eftsones Winter gan to approche ;
The blustering Boreas did encroche,
And beate upon the solitarie Brere ;
For nowe no succoure was seene him nere.
Now gan he repent his pryde to late ;
For, naked left and disconsolate,
The byting frost nipt his stalke dead,
The watrie wette weighed downe his head,
And heaped snowe burdned him so sore,
That nowe upright he can stand no more ;
And, being downe, is trodde in the durt,
Of cattell, and brouzed, and sorely hurt.
Such was thend of this Ambitious brere,
For scorning Eld—

CHASE AFTER LOVE.

[March.]

Tho. It was upon a holiday,
  When shepheardes groomes han leave to playe,
    I cast to goe a shooting.
  Long wandring up and downe the land,
  With bowe and bolts in either hand,
    For birds in bushes tooting [1],
    At length within an Yvie todde [2],
    (There shrouded was the little God)
    I heard a busie bustling.

[1] looking about.   [2] a thick bush.

I bent my bolt against the bush,
Listening if any thing did rushe,
   But then heard no more rustling:
Tho, peeping close into the thicke,
Might see the moving of some quicke,
   Whose shape appeared not;
But were it faerie, feend, or snake,
My courage earnd[1] it to awake,
   And manfully thereat shotte.
With that sprong forth a naked swayne
With spotted winges, like Peacocks trayne,
   And laughing lope to a tree;
His gylden quiver at his backe,
And silver bowe, which was but slacke,
   Which lightly he bent at me:
That seeing, I levelde againe
And shott at him with might and maine,
   As thicke as it had hayled.
So long I shott, that al was spent;
Tho pumie stones I hastly hent
   And threwe; but nought availed:
He was so wimble and so wight,
From bough to bough he lepped light,
   And oft the pumies latched[2].
Therewith affrayd, I ranne away:
But he, that earst seemd but to playe,
   A shaft in earnest snatched,
And hit me running in the heele:
For then I little smart did feele,
   But soone it sore encreased;
And now it ranckleth more and more,
And inwardly it festreth sore,
   Ne wote I how to cease it.
Wil. Thomalin, I pittie thy plight,
  Perdie with Love thou diddest fight:
   I know him by a token;
For once I heard my father say,
How he him caught upon a day,
   (Whereof he will be wroken)

[1] yearned.   [2] caught.

Entangled in a fowling net,
Which he for carrion Crowes had set
   That in our Peere-tree haunted :
Tho sayd, he was a winged lad,
But bowe and shafts as then none had,
   Els had he sore be daunted.
But see, the Welkin thicks apace,
And stouping Phebus steepes his face :
   Yts time to hast us homeward.

DESCRIPTION OF MAYING.

[May.]

Palinode. Is not thilke the mery moneth of **May,**
When love-lads masken in fresh aray?
How falles it, then, we no merrier bene,
Ylike as others, girt in gawdy greene?
Our bloncket liveryes[1] bene all to sadde
For thilke same season, when all is ycladd
With pleasaunce : the grownd with grasse, the Woods
With greene leaves, the bushes with bloosming buds.
Yougthes folke now flocken in every where,
To gather May bus-kets and smelling brere :
And home they hasten the postes to dight,
And all the Kirke pillours eare day light,
With Hawthorne buds, and swete Eglantine,
And girlonds of roses, and Sopps in wine.
Such merimake holy Saints doth queme[2],
But we here sitten as drownd in a dreme.
  Piers. For Younkers, Palinode, such follies **fitte,**
But we tway bene men of elder witt.
  Pal. Sicker this morrowe, no lenger agoe,
I sawe a shole of shepeheardes outgoe
With singing, and shouting, and jolly chere :
Before them yode a lusty Tabrere,
That to the many a Horne-pype playd,
Whereto they dauncen, eche one with his mayd.

---

[1] gray coats.   [2] please.

To see those folkes make such jovysaunce,
Made my heart after the pype to daunce :
Tho to the greene Wood they speeden hem all,
To fetchen home May with their musicall :
And home they bringen in a royall throne,
Crowned as king : and his Queene attone
Was Lady Flora, on whom did attend
A fayre flocke of Faeries, and a fresh bend
Of lovely Nymphs. (O that I were there,
To helpen the Ladyes their Maybush beare !)
Ah ! Piers, bene not thy teeth on edge, to thinke
How great sport they gaynen with little swinck ?

THE COMPLAINT OF AGE.

[December.]

Whilome in youth, when flowrd my joyfull spring,
Like Swallow swift I wandred here and there ;
For heate of heedlesse lust me so did sting,
That I of doubted daunger had no feare :
   I went the wastefull woodes and forest wide,
   Withouten dreade of Wolves to bene espyed.

     *   *   *   *   *

How often have I scaled the craggie Oke,
All to dislodge the Raven of her nest ?
How have I wearied with many a stroke
The stately Walnut-tree, the while the rest
   Under the tree fell all for nuts at strife ?
   For ylike to me was libertee and lyfe.

     *   *   *   *   *

Tho gan my lovely Spring bid me farewel,
And Sommer season sped him to display
(For love then in the Lyons house did dwell)
The raging fyre that kindled at his ray.
   A comett stird up that unkindly heate,
   That reigned (as men sayd) in Venus seate.

Forth was I ledde, not as I wont afore,
When choise I had to choose my wandring waye,
But whether luck and loves unbridled lore
Woulde leade me forth on Fancies bitte to playe:
  The bush my bedde, the bramble was my bowre,
  The Woodes can witnesse many a wofull stowre.

Where I was wont to seeke the honey Bee,
Working her formall rowmes in wexen frame,
The grieslie Tode-stoole growne there mought I se,
And loathed Paddocks[1] lording on the same:
  And where the chaunting birds luld me asleepe,
  The ghastlie Owle her grievous ynne doth keepe.

Then as the springe gives place to elder time,
And bringeth forth the fruite of sommers pryde;
Also my age, now passed youngthly pryme,
To thinges of ryper season selfe applyed,
  And learnd of lighter timber cotes to frame,
  Such as might save my sheepe and me fro shame.

To make fine cages for the Nightingale,
And Baskets of bulrushes, was my wont:
Who to entrappe the fish in winding sale
Was better seene, or hurtful beastes to hont?
  I learned als the signes of heaven to ken,
  How Phœbe fayles, where Venus sittes, and when.

And tryed time yet taught me greater thinges;
The sodain rysing of the raging seas,
The soothe of byrdes by beating of their winges,
The power of herbs, both which can hurt and ease,
  And which be wont t' enrage the restlesse sheepe,
  And which be wont to worke eternall sleepe.

But, ah! unwise and witlesse Colin Cloute,
That kydst[2] the hidden kinds of many a wede,
Yet kydst not ene to cure thy sore hart-roote,
Whose ranckling wound as yet does rifelye bleede.
  Why livest thou stil, and yet hast thy deathes wound?
  Why dyest thou stil, and yet alive art founde?

[1] toads.　　　　　　　　　[2] knewest.

U 2

Thus is my sommer worne away and wasted,
Thus is my harvest hastened all to rathe ;
The eare that budded faire is burnt and blasted,
And all my hoped gaine is turnd to scathe :
　Of all the seede that in my youthe was sowne
　Was nought but brakes and brambles to be mowne.

My boughes with bloosmes that crowned were at firste,
And promised of timely fruite such store,
Are left both bare and barrein now at erst ;
The flattring fruite is fallen to grownd before.
　And rotted ere they were halfe mellow ripe ;
　My harvest, wast, my hope away dyd wipe.

The fragrant flowres, that in my garden grewe,
Bene withered, as they had bene gathered long ;
Theyr rootes bene dryed up for lacke of dewe,
Yet dewed with teares they han be ever among.
　Ah ! who has wrought my Rosalind this spight,
　To spil the flowres that should her girlond dight ?

And I, that whilome wont to frame my pype
Unto the shifting of the shepheards foote,
Sike follies nowe have gathered as too ripe,
And cast hem out as rotten and unsoote.
　The loser Lasse I cast to please no more ;
　One if I please, enough is me therefore.

And thus of all my harvest-hope I have
Nought reaped but a weedye crop of care ;
Which, when I thought have thresht in swelling sheave,
Cockel for corne, and chaffe for barley, bare :
　Soone as the chaffe should in the fan be fynd,
　All was blowne away of the wavering wynd.

So now my yeare drawes to his latter terme,
My spring is spent, my sommer burnt up quite ;
My harveste hasts to stirre up Winter sterne,
And bids him clayme with rigorous rage hys right :
　So nowe he stormes with many a sturdy stoure ;
　So now his blustring blast eche coste dooth scoure.

The carefull cold hath nypt my rugged rynde,
And in my face deepe furrowes eld hath pight :
My head besprent with hoary frost I fynd,
And by myne eie the Crow his clawe dooth wright :
  Delight is layd abedde ; and pleasure past ;
  No sonne now shines ; cloudes han all overcast.

Now leave, ye shepheards boyes, your merry glee ;
My Muse is hoarse and wearie of thys stounde :
Here will I hang my pype upon this tree :
Was never pype of reede did better sounde.
  Winter is come that blowes the bitter blaste,
  And after Winter dreerie death does hast.

Gather together ye my little flocke,
My little flock, that was to me so liefe ;
Let me, ah ! lette me in your foldes ye lock,
Ere the breme [1] Winter breede you greater griefe.
  Winter is come, that blowes the balefull breath,
  And after Winter commeth timely death.

Adieu, delightes, that lulled me asleepe ;
Adieu, my deare, whose love I bought so deare ;
Adieu, my little Lambes and loved sheepe ;
Adieu, ye Woodes, that oft my witnesse were :
  Adieu, good Hobbinoll, that was so true,
  Tell Rosalind, her Colin bids her adieu.

[From *The Faerie Queene*, Bk. i. 1589-90.]

THE RED CROSS KNIGHT AND UNA.

A gentle Knight was pricking on the plaine,
Ycladd in mightie armes and silver shielde,
Wherein old dints of deepe woundes did remaine,
The cruell markes of many a bloody fielde ;
Yet armes till that time did he never wield.
His angry steede did chide his foming bitt,
As much disdayning to the curbe to yield :
Full jolly knight he seemd, and faire did sitt,
As one for knightly giusts and fierce encounters fitt.

---

[1] sharp.

And on his brest a bloodie Crosse he bore,
The deare remembrance of his dying Lord,
For whose sweete sake that glorious badge he **wore,**
And dead, as living, ever him ador'd :
Upon his shield the like was also scor'd,
For soveraine hope which in his helpe he had.
Right faithfull true he was in deede and word,
But of his cheere did seeme too solemne sad ;
Yet nothing did he dread, but ever was ydrad.

Upon a great adventure he was bond,
That greatest Gloriana to him gave,
(That greatest Glorious Queene of Faery lond)
To winne him worshippe, and her grace to have,
Which of all earthly thinges he most did crave :
And ever as he rode his hart did earne
To prove his puissance in battell brave
Upon his foe, and his new force to learne,
Upon his foe, a Dragon horrible and stearne.

A lovely Ladie rode him faire beside,
Upon a lowly Asse more white then snow,
Yet she much whiter ; but the same did hide
Under a vele, that wimpled was full low ;
And over all a blacke stole shee did throw :
As one that inly mournd, so was she sad,
And heavie sate upon her palfrey slow ;
Seemed in heart some hidden care she had,
And by her, in a line, a milkewhite lambe she lad.

So pure and innocent, as that same lambe,
She was in life and every vertuous lore ;
And by descent from Royall lynage came
Of ancient Kinges and Queenes, that had of yore
Their scepters stretcht from East to Westerne shore,
And all the world in their subjection held ;
Till that infernall feend with foule uprore
Forwasted all their land, and them expeld ;
Whom to avenge she had this Knight from far compeld.

Behind her farre away a Dwarfe did lag,
That lasie seemd, in being ever last,
Or wearied with bearing of her bag
Of needments at his backe. Thus as they past,
The day with cloudes was suddeine overcast,
And angry Jove an hideous storme of raine
Did poure into his Lemans lap so fast,
That everie wight to shrowd it did constrain ;
And this faire couple eke to shroud themselves were fain.

Enforst to seeke some covert nigh at hand,
A shadie grove not farr away they spide,
That promist ayde the tempest to withstand ;
Whose loftie trees, yclad with sommers pride,
Did spred so broad, that heavens light did hide,
Not perceable with power of any starr :
And all within were pathes and alleies wide,
With footing worne, and leading inward farr.
Faire harbour that them seems, so in they entred ar.

And foorth they passe, with pleasure forward led,
Joying to heare the birdes sweete harmony,
Which, therein shrouded from the tempest dred,
Seemd in their song to scorne the cruell sky.
Much can they praise the trees so straight and hy,
The sayling Pine ; the Cedar proud and tall ;
The vine-propp Elme ; the Poplar never dry ;
The builder Oake, sole king of forests all ;
The Aspine good for staves ; the Cypresse funerall ;

The Laurell, meed of mightie Conquerours
And Poets sage ; the Firre that weepeth still :
The Willow, worne of forlorne Paramours ;
The Eugh, obedient to the benders will ;
The Birch for shaftes ; the Sallow for the mill ;
The Mirrhe sweete-bleeding in the bitter wound ;
The warlike Beech ; the Ash for nothing ill ;
The fruitfull Olive ; and the Platane round ;
The carver Holme ; the Maple seeldom inward sound.

Led with delight, they thus beguile the way,
Untill the blustring storme is overblowne ;
When, weening to returne whence they did stray,
They cannot finde that path, which first was showne,
But wander too and fro in waies unknowne,
Furthest from end then, when they neerest weene,
That makes them doubt their wits be not their owne :
So many pathes, so many turnings seene,
That which of them to take in diverse doubt they been.

The House of Pride.

High above all a cloth of State was spred,
And a rich throne, as bright as sunny day;
On which there sate, most brave embellished
With royall robes and gorgeous array,
A mayden Queene that shone as Titans ray,
In glistring gold and perelesse pretious stone ;
Yet her bright blazing beautie did assay
To dim the brightnesse of her glorious throne,
As envying her selfe, that too exceeding shone :

Exceeding shone, like Phœbus fayrest childe,
That did presume his fathers fyrie wayne,
And flaming mouthes of steedes, unwonted wilde,
Through highest heaven with weaker hand to rayne :
Proud of such glory and advancement vayne,
While flashing beames do daze his feeble eyen,
He leaves the welkin way most beaten playne,
And, rapt with whirling wheeles, inflames the skyen
With fire not made to burne, but fayrely for to shyne.

So proud she shyned in her princely state,
Looking to heaven, for earth she did disdayne,
And sitting high, for lowly she did hate :
Lo ! underneath her scornefull feete was layne
A dreadfull Dragon with an hideous trayne ;
And in her hand she held a mirrhour bright,
Wherein her face she often vewed fayne,
And in her selfe-lov'd semblance took delight ;
For she was wondrous faire, as any living wight.

Of griesly Pluto she the daughter was,
And sad Proserpina, the Queene of hell ;
Yet did she thinke her pearelesse worth to pas
That parentage, with pride so did she swell ;
And thundring Jove, that high in heaven doth dwell
And wield the world, she claymed for her syre,
Or if that any else did Jove excell ;
For to the highest she did still aspyre,
Or, if ought higher were than that, did it desyre.

And proud Lucifera men did her call,
That made her selfe a Queene, and crownd to be ;
Yet rightfull kingdome she had none at all,
Ne heritage of native soveraintie ;
But did usurpe with wrong and tyrannie
Upon the scepter which she now did hold :
Ne ruld her Realme with lawes, but pollicie,
And strong advizement of six wisards old,
That, with their counsels bad, her kingdome did uphold.

Soone as the Elfin knight in presence came,
And false Duessa, seeming Lady fayre,
A gentle Husher, Vanitie by name,
Made rowme, and passage for them did prepaire :
So goodly brought them to the lowest stayre
Of her high throne ; where they, on humble knee
Making obeysaunce, did the cause declare,
Why they were come her roiall state to see,
To prove the wide report of her great Majestee.

With loftie eyes, halfe loth to looke so lowe,
She thancked them in her disdainefull wise ;
Ne other grace vouchsafed them to showe
Of Princesse worthy ; scarse them bad arise.
Her Lordes and Ladies all this while devise
Themselves to setten forth to straungers sight :
Some frounce their curled heare in courtly guise ;
Some prancke their ruffes ; and others trimly dight
Their gay attyre ; each others greater pride does spight.

* * * * * *

Suddein upriseth from her stately place
The roiall Dame, and for her coche doth call :
All hurtlen forth ; and she, with princely pace,
As faire Aurora in her purple pall
Out of the East the dawning day doth call.
So forth she comes ; her brightnes brode doth blaze.
The heapes of people, thronging in the hall,
Doe ride each other upon her to gaze :
Her glorious glitterand light doth all mens eies amaze

So forth she comes, and to her coche does clyme,
Adorned all with gold and girlonds gay,
That seemd as fresh as Flora in her prime ;
And strove to match, in roiall rich array,
Great Junoes golden chayre ; the which, they say,
The gods stand gazing on, when she does ride
To Joves high hous through heavens bras-paved way,
Drawne of fayre Pecocks, that excell in pride,
And full of Argus eyes their tayles dispredden wide.

UNA'S MARRIAGE.

Then forth he called that his daughter fayre,
The fairest Un', his onely daughter deare,
His onely daughter and his only hayre ;
Who forth proceeding with sad sober cheare,
As bright as doth the morning starre appeare
Out of the East, with flaming lockes bedight,
To tell that dawning day is drawing neare,
And to the world does bring long-wished light :
So faire and fresh that Lady shewd herselfe in sight.

So faire and fresh, as freshest flowre in May ;
For she had layd her mournefull stole aside,
And widow-like sad wimple throwne away,
Wherewith her heavenly beautie she did hide,
Whiles on her wearie journey she did ride ;
And on her now a garment she did weare
All lilly white, withoutten spot or pride,
That seemd like silke and silver woven neare ;
But neither silke nor silver therein did appeare.

The blazing brightnesse of her beauties beame,
And glorious light of her sunshyny face,
To tell weie as to strive against the streame:
My ragged rimes are all too rude and bace
Her heavenly lineaments for to enchace.
Ne wonder ; for her own deare loved knight,
All were she daily with himselfe in place,
Did wonder much at her celestial sight :
Oft had he seene her faire, but never so faire dight.
* * * * * *

His owne two hands the holy knotts did knitt,
That none but death for ever can divide ;
His owne two hands, for such a turne most fitt,
The housling fire did kindle and provide,
And holy water thereon sprinckled wide ;
At which the bushy Teade[1] a groome did light,
And sacred lamp in secret chamber hide,
Where it should not be quenched day nor night,
For feare of evil fates, but burnen ever bright.

Then gan they sprinckle all the posts with wine,
And made great feast to solemnize that day :
They all perfumde with frankincense divine,
And precious odours fetcht from far away,
That all the house did sweat with great aray :
And all the while sweete Musicke did apply
Her curious skill the warbling notes to play,
To drive away the dull Melancholy ;
The whiles one sung a song of love and jollity.

During the which there was an heavenly noise
Heard sownd through all the Pallace pleasantly,
Like as it had bene many an Angels voice
Singing before th' eternall majesty,
In their trinall triplicities on hye :
Yett wist no creature whence that hevenly sweet
Proceeded, yet each one felt secretly
Himselfe thereby refte of his sences meet,
And ravished with rare impression in his sprite.

[1] torch.

Great joy was made that day of young and old,
And solemne feast proclaymd throughout the land,
That their exceeding merth may not be told :
Suffice it heare by signes to understand
The usuall joyes at knitting of loves band.
Thrise happy man the knight himselfe did hold,
Possessed of his Ladies hart and hand ;
And ever, when his eie did her behold,
His heart did seeme to melt in pleasures manifold.

Her joyous presence, and sweet company,
In full content he there did long enjoy ;
Ne wicked envy, ne vile gealosy,
His deare delights were hable to annoy ;
Yet, swimming in that sea of blisfull joy,
He nought forgott how he whilome had sworne,
In case he could that monstrous beast destroy,
Unto his Faery Queene backe to retourne ;
The which he shortly did, and Una left to mourne.

Now, strike your sailes, yee jolly Mariners,
For we be come unto a quiet rode,
Where we must land some of our passengers,
And light this weary vessell of her lode :
Here she a while may make her safe abode,
Till she repaired have her tackles spent,
And wants supplide ; And then againe abroad
On the long voiage whereto she is bent :
Well may she speede, and fairely finish her intent !

[From *The Faerie Queene*, Bk. ii.]

PHAEDRIA AND THE IDLE LAKE.

A harder lesson to learne Continence
In joyous pleasure then in grievous paine ;
For sweetnesse doth allure the weaker sence
So strongly, that uneathes it can refraine
From that which feeble nature covets faine :
But griefe and wrath, that be her enemies
And foes of life, she better can abstaine :
Yet vertue vauntes in both her victories,
And Guyon in them all shewes goodly maysteries.

Whom bold Cymochles traveiling to finde,
With cruell purpose bent to wreake on him
The wrath which Atin kindled in his mind,
Came to a river, by whose utmost brim
Wayting to passe, he saw whereas did swim
Along the shore, as swift as glaunce of eye,
A litle Gondelay, bedecked trim
With boughes and arbours woven cunningly,
That like a litle forrest seemed outwardly.

And therein sate a Lady fresh and fayre,
Making sweet solace to herselfe alone :
Sometimes she song as lowd as larke in ayre,
Sometimes she laught, as merry as Pope Jone ;
Yet was there not with her else any one,
That to her might move cause of meriment :
Matter of merth enough, though there were none,
She could devise ; and thousand waies invent
To feede her foolish humour and vaine jolliment.

Which when far off Cymochles heard and saw,
He lowdly cald to such as were abord
The little barke unto the shore to draw,
And him to ferry over that deepe ford.
The merry mariner unto his word
Soone hearkened, and her painted bote streightway
Turnd to the shore, where that same warlike Lord
She in receiv'd ; but Atin by no way
She would admit, albe the knight her much did pray.

Eftsoones her shallow ship away did slide,
More swift then swallow sheres the liquid skye,
Withouten oare or Pilot it to guide,
Or winged canvas with the wind to fly :
Onely she turnd a pin, and by and by
It cut away upon the yielding wave,
Ne cared she her course for to apply ;
For it was taught the way which she would have,
And both from rocks and flats it selfe could wisely save.

And all the way the wanton Damsell found
New merth her passenger to entertaine ;
For she in pleasaunt purpose did abound,
And greatly joyed merry tales to faine,
Of which a store-house did with her remaine :
Yet seemed, nothing well they her became ;
For all her wordes she drownd with laughter vaine,
And wanted grace in utt'ring of the same,
That turned all her pleasaunce to a scoffing game.

And other whiles vaine toyes she would devize,
As her fantasticke wit did most delight :
Sometimes her head she fondly would aguize
With gaudy girlonds, or fresh flowrets dight
About her necke, or rings of rushes plight :
Sometimes, to do him laugh, she would assay
To laugh at shaking of the leaves light
Or to behold the water worke and play
About her little frigot, therein making way.

Her light behaviour and loose dalliaunce
Gave wondrous great contentment to the knight,
That of his way he had no sovenaunce,
Nor care of vow'd revenge and cruell fight,
But to weake wench did yield his martiall might :
So easie was to quench his flamed minde
With one sweete drop of sensuall delight.
So easie is t'appease the stormy winde
Of malice in the calme of pleasaunt womankind.

Diverse discourses in their way they spent ;
Mongst which Cymochles of her questioned
Both what she was, and what that usage ment,
Which in her cott she daily practized ?
'Vaine man,' (saide she) 'that wouldest be reckoned
A straunger in thy home, and ignoraunt
Of Phaedria, (for so my name is red)
Of Phaedria, thine owne fellow servaunt ;
For thou to serve Acrasia thy selfe doest vaunt.

'In this wide Inland sea, that hight by name
The Idle lake, my wandring ship I row,
That knowes her port, and thither sayles by ayme,
Ne care, ne feare I how the wind do blow,
Or whether swift I wend, or whether slow :
Both slow and swift alike do serve my tourne ;
Ne swelling Neptune ne lowd thundring Jove
Can chaunge my cheare, or make me ever mourne .
My little boat can safely passe this perilous bourne.'

Whiles thus she talked, and whiles thus she toyd,
They were far past the passage which he spake,
And come unto an Island waste and voyd,
That floted in the midst of that great lake ;
There her small Gondelay her port did make,
And that gay payre, issewing on the shore,
Disburdned her. Their way they forward take
Into the land that lay them faire before,
Whose pleasaunce she him shewd, and plentifull great store.

It was a chosen plott of fertile land,
Emongst wide waves sett, like a litle nest,
As if it had by Natures cunning hand
Bene choycely picked out from all the rest,
And laid forth for ensample of the best :
No daintie flowre or herbe that growes on grownd,
No arborett with painted blossomes drest
And smelling sweete, but there it might be fownd
To bud out faire, and throwe her sweete smels al arownd.

No tree whose braunches did not bravely spring ;
No braunch whereon a fine bird did not sitt ;
No bird but did her shrill notes sweetely sing ;
No song but did containe a lovely ditt.
Trees, braunches, birds, and songs, were framed fitt
For to allure fraile mind to carelesse ease :
Carelesse the man soone woxe, and his weake witt
Was overcome of thing that did him please ;
So pleased did his wrathfull purpose faire appease.

Thus when shee had his eyes and sences fed
With false delights, and fild with pleasures vayn,
Into a shady dale she soft him led,
And layd him downe upon a grassy playn ;
And her sweete selfe without dread or disdayn
She sett beside, laying his head disarmd
In her loose lap, it softly to sustayn,
Where soone he slumbred fearing not be harmd :
The whiles with a love lay she thus him sweetly charmd.

'Behold, O man ! that toilesome paines doest take,
The flowrs, the fields, and all that pleasaunt growes,
How they them selves doe thine ensample make,
Whiles nothing envious nature them forth throwes
Out of her fruitfull lap ; how no man knowes,
They spring, they bud, they blossome fresh and faire,
And decke the world with their rich pompous showes ;
Yet no man for them taketh paines or care,
Yet no man to them can his carefull paines compare.

' The lilly, Lady of the flowring field,
The flowre-deluce, her lovely Paramoure,
Bid thee to them thy fruitlesse labors yield,
And soone leave off this toylsome weary stoure :
Loe, loe ! how brave she decks her bounteous boure,
With silkin curtens and gold coverletts,
Therein to shrowd her sumptuous Belamoure ;
Yet nether spinnes nor cards, ne cares nor fretts,
But to her mother Nature all her cares she letts.

'Why then doest thou, O man ! that of them all
Art Lord, and eke of nature Soveraine,
Wilfully make thyselfe a wretched thrall,
And waste thy joyous howres in needelesse paine,
Seeking for daunger and adventures vaine ?
What bootes it al to have, and nothing use ?
Who shall him rew that swimming in the maine
Will die for thrist, and water doth refuse ?
Refuse such fruitlesse toile, and present pleasures chuse.'

By this she had him lulled fast asleepe,
That of no worldly thing he care did take :
Then she with liquors strong his eies did steepe,
That nothing should him hastily awake.
So she him lefte, and did her selfe betake
Unto her boat again, with which she clefte
The slouthfull wave of that griesy lake :
Soone shee that Island far behind her lefte,
And now is come to that same place where first she wefte [1].

THE CAVE OF MAMMON.

As Pilot well expert in perilous wave,
That to a stedfast starre his course hath bent,
When foggy mistes or cloudy tempests have
The faithfull light of that faire lampe yblent,
And cover'd heaven with hideous dreriment,
Upon his card and compas firmes his eye,
The maysters of his long experiment,
And to them does the steddy helme apply,
Bidding his winged vessell fairely forward fly :

So Guyon having lost his trustie guyde,
Late left beyond that Ydle lake, proceedes
Yet on his way, of none accompanyde ;
And evermore himselfe with comfort feedes
Of his own vertues and praise-worthie deedes.
So, long he yode, yet no adventure found,
Which fame of her shrill trumpet worthy reedes ;
For still he traveild through wide wastfull ground,
That nought but desert wildernesse shewed all around.

At last he came unto a gloomy glade,
Cover'd with boughes and shrubs from heavens light,
Whereas he sitting found in secret shade
An uncouth, salvage, and uncivile wight,
Of griesly hew and fowle ill favour'd sight ;

[1] was wafted.

His face with smoke was tand, and eies were bleard,
His head and beard with sout were ill bedight,
His cole-blacke hands did seeme to have been seard
In smythes fire-spitting forge, and nayles like clawes appeard.

His yron cote, all overgrowne with rust,
Was underneath enveloped with gold ;
Whose glistring glosse, darkned with filthy dust,
Well yet appeared to have beene of old
A worke of rich entayle and curious mould,
Woven with antickes and wyld ymagery ;
And in his lap a masse of coyne he told,
And turned upside downe, to feede his eye
And covetous desire with his huge threasury.

And round about him lay on every side
Great heapes of gold that never could be spent ;
Of which some were rude owre, not purifide
Of Mulcibers devouring element ;
Some others were new driven, and distent
Into great Ingowes and to wedges square ;
Some in round plates withouten moniment ;
But most were stampt, and in their metal bare
The antique shapes of kings and kesars straunge and rare.

Soone as he Guyon saw, in great affright
And haste he rose for to remove aside
Those pretious hils from straungers envious sight,
And downe them poured through an hole full wide
Into the hollow earth, them there to hide.
But Guyon, lightly to him leaping, stayd
His hand that trembled as one terrifyde ;
And though himselfe were at the sight dismayd,
Yet him perforce restraynd, and to him doubtfull sayd :

'What art thou, man, (if man at all thou art)
That here in desert hast thine habitaunce,
And these rich hils of welth doest hide apart
From the worldes eye, and from her right usaunce ?'
Thereat, with staring eyes fixed askaunce,

In great disdaine he answerd: 'Hardy Elfe,
That darest view my direfull countenaunce,
I read thee rash and heedlesse of thy selfe,
To trouble my still seate, and heapes of pretious pelfe.

'God of the world and worldlings I me call,
Great Mammon, greatest god below the skye,
That of my plenty poure out unto all,
And unto none my graces do envye:
Riches, renowme, and principality,
Honour, estate, and all this worldes good,
For which men swinck and sweat incessantly,
Fro me do flow into an ample flood,
And in the hollow earth have their eternall brood.

'Wherefore, if me thou deigne to serve and sew[1],
At thy commaund lo! all these mountaines bee:
Or if to thy great mind, or greedy vew,
All these may not suffise, there shall to thee
Ten times so much be nombred francke and free.'
'Mammon,' (said he) 'thy godheads vaunt is vaine,
And idle offers of thy golden fee;
To them that covet such eye-glutting gaine
Proffer thy giftes, and fitter servaunts entertaine.

'Me ill besits, that in der-doing armes
And honours suit my vowed daies do spend,
Unto thy bounteous baytes and pleasing charmes,
With which weake men thou witchest, to attend;
Regard of worldly mucke doth fowly blend,
And low abase the high heroicke spright,
That joyes for crownes and kingdomes to contend:
Faire shields, gay steedes, bright armes be my delight;
Those be the riches fit for, an advent'rous knight.'

'Vaine glorious Elfe,' (saide he) 'doest not thou weet,
That money can thy wantes at will supply?
Sheilds, steeds, and armes, and all things for thee meet,
It can purvay in twinckling of an eye;
And crownes and kingdomes to thee multiply.

[1] follow.

X 2

Do not I kings create, and throw the crowne
Sometimes to him that low in dust doth ly,
And him that raignd into his rowme thrust downe,
And whom I lust do heape with glory and renowne?'

'All otherwise' (saide he) 'I riches read,
And deeme them roote of all disquietnesse;
First got with guile, and then preserv'd with dread,
And after spent with pride and lavishnesse,
Leaving behind them griefe and heavinesse:
Infinite mischiefes of them doe arize,
Strife and debate, bloodshed and bitternesse,
Outrageous wrong, and hellish covetize,
That noble heart as great dishonour doth despize.

'Ne thine be kingdomes, ne the scepters thine;
But realmes and rulers thou doest both confound,
And loyall truth to treason doest incline:
Witnesse the guiltlesse blood pourd oft on ground,
The crowned often slaine, the slayer cround;
The sacred Diademe in peeces rent,
And purple robe gored with many a wound,
Castles surprizd, great cities sackt and brent;
So mak'st thou kings, and gaynest wrongfull government.

'Long were to tell the troublous stormes that tosse
The private state, and make the life unsweet:
Who swelling sayles in Caspian sea doth crosse,
And in frayle wood on Adrian gulf doth fleet,
Doth not, I weene, so many evils meet.'
Then Mammon wexing wroth: 'And why then,' sayd,
'Are mortall men so fond and undiscreet
So evill thing to seeke unto their ayd,
And having not complaine, and having it upbrayd?'

'Indeede,' (quoth he) 'through fowle intemperaunce,
Frayle men are oft captiv'd to covetise;
But would they thinke with how small allowaunce
Untroubled Nature doth her selfe suffise,
Such superfluities they would despise,

Which with sad cares empeach our native joyes.
At the well-head the purest streames arise ;
But mucky filth his braunching armes annoyes,
And with uncomely weedes the gentle wave accloyes

'The antique world, in his first flowring youth,
Fownd no defect in his Creators grace ;
But with glad thankes, and unreproved truth,
The gifts of soveraine bounty did embrace :
Like Angels life was then mens happy cace ;
But later ages pride, like corn-fed steed,
Abusd her plenty and fat swolne encreace
To all licentious lust, and gan exceed
The measure of her meane and naturall first need.

'Then gan a cursed hand the quiet wombe
Of his great Grandmother with steele to wound,
And the hid treasures in her sacred tombe
With Sacriledge to dig. Therein he fownd
Fountaines of gold and silver to abownd,
Of which the matter of his huge desire
And pompous pride eftsoones he did compownd ;
Then avarice gan through his veines inspire
His greedy flames, and kindled life-devouring fire.'

'Sonne,' (said he then) 'lett be thy bitter scorne,
And leave the rudenesse of that antique age
To them that liv'd therin in state forlorne :
Thou, that doest live in later times, must wage
Thy workes for wealth, and life for gold engage.
If then thee list my offred grace to use,
Take what thou please of all this surplusage ;
If thee list not, leave have thou to refuse :
But refused doe not afterward accuse.'

'Me list not' (said the Elfin knight) 'receave
Thing offred, till I know it well be gott ;
Ne wote I but thou didst these goods bereave
From rightfull owner by unrighteous lott,
Or that bloodguiltinesse or guile them blott.'

'Perdy,' (quoth he) 'yet never eie did vew,
Ne tong did tell, ne hand these handled not ;
But safe I have them kept in secret mew
From hevens sight, and powre of al which them poursew.'

'What secret place' (quoth he) 'can safely hold
So huge a masse, and hide from heaven's eie ?
Or where hast thou thy wonne, that so much gold
Thou canst preserve from wrong and robbery ?'
'Come thou,' (quoth he) 'and see.' So by and by
Through that thick covert he him led, and fownd
A darkesome way, which no man could descry,
That deep descended through the hollow grownd,
And was with dread and horror compassed arownd.

At length they came into a larger space,
That stretcht itselfe into an ample playne ;
Through which a beaten broad high way did trace,
That streight did lead to Plutoes griesly rayne.
By that wayes side there sate internall Payne,
And fast beside him sat tumultuous Strife :
The one in hand an yron whip did strayne,
The other brandished a bloody knife ;
And both did gnash their teeth, and both did threten life.

On thother side in one consort there sate
Cruell Revenge, and rancorous Despight,
Disloyall Treason, and hart-burning Hate ;
But gnawing Gealosy, out of their sight
Sitting alone, his bitter lips did bight ;
And trembling Feare still to and fro did fly,
And found no place wher safe he shroud him might :
Lamenting Sorrow did in darknes lye,
And Shame his ugly face did hide from living eye.

And over them sad Horror with grim hew
Did alwaies sore, beating his yron wings ;
And after him Owles and Night-ravens flew,
The hatefull messengers of heavy things,
Of death and dolor telling sad tidings,

Whiles sad Celeno, sitting on a clifte,
A song of bale and bitter sorrow sings,
That hart of flint asonder could have rifte;
Which having ended after him she flyeth swifte.

All these before the gates of Pluto lay,
By whom they passing spake unto them nought;
But th' Elfin knight with wonder all the way
Did feed his eyes, and fild his inner thought.
At last him to a litle dore he brought,
That to the gate of Hell, which gaped wide,
Was next adjoyning, ne them parted ought:
Betwixt them both was but a little stride,
That did the house of Richesse from hell-mouth divide.

Before the dore sat selfe-consuming Care,
Day and night keeping wary watch and ward,
For feare least Force or Fraud should unaware
Breake in, and spoile the treasure there in gard:
Ne would he suffer Sleepe once thither-ward
Approch, albe his drowsy den were next;
For next to death is Sleepe to be compard;
Therefore his house is unto his annext:
Here Sleep, ther Richesse, and Hel-gate them both betwext.

So soon as Mammon there arrivd, the dore
To him did open and affoorded way:
Him followed eke Sir Guyon evermore,
Ne darkenesse him, ne daunger might dismay.
Soone as he entred was, the dore streight way
Did shutt, and from behind it forth there lept
An ugly feend, more fowle then dismall day,
The which with monstrous stalke behind him stept,
And ever as he went dew watch upon him kept.

Well hoped hee, ere long that hardy guest,
If ever covetous hand, or lustfull eye,
Or lips he layd on thing that likte him best,
Or ever sleepe his eie-strings did untye,
Should be his pray. And therefore still on hye

He over him did hold his cruell clawes,
Threatning with greedy gripe to doe him dye,
And rend in peeces with his ravenous pawes,
If ever he transgrest the fatall Stygian lawes.

That houses forme within was rude and strong,
Lyke an huge cave hewne out of rocky clifte,
From whose rough vaut the ragged breaches hong
Embost with massy gold of glorious guifte,
And with rich metall loaded every rifte,
That heavy ruine they did seeme to threatt;
And over them Arachne high did lifte
Her cunning web, and spred her subtile nett,
Enwrapped in fowle smoke and clouds more black than Jett.

Both roofe, and floore, and walls, were all of gold,
But overgrowne with dust and old decay,
And hid in darkenes, that none could behold
The hew thereof; for vew of cherefull day
Did never in that house it selfe display,
But a faint shadow of uncerten light:
Such as a lamp, whose life does fade away,
Or as the Moone, cloathed with clowdy night,
Does show to him that walkes in feare and sad affright.

In all that rowme was nothing to be seene
But huge great yron chests, and coffers strong,
All bard with double bends, that none could weene
Them to efforce by violence or wrong:
On every side they placed were along;
But all the grownd with sculs was scattered,
And dead mens bones, which round about were flong;
Whose lives, it seemed, whilome there were shed,
And their vile carcases now left unburied.

THE BOWER OF BLISS.

Thence passing forth, they shortly doe arryve
Whereas the Bowre of Blisse was situate ;
A place pickt out by choyce of best alyve,
That natures worke by art can imitate :
In which whatever in this worldly state
Is sweete and pleasing unto living sense,
Or that may dayntest fantasy aggrate [1],
Was poured forth with plentifull dispence
And made there to abound with lavish affluence.

Goodly it was enclosed rownd about,
As well their entred guestes to keep within,
As those unruly beasts to hold without ;
Yet was the fence thereof but weake and thin .
Nought feard theyr force that fortilage to win,
But wisedomes powre, and temperaunces might,
By which the mightiest things efforced bin :
And eke the gate was wrought of substaunce light,
Rather for pleasure then for battery or fight.

Yt framed was of precious yvory,
That seemd a worke of admirable witt ;
And therein all the famous history
Of Jason and Medea was ywritt ;
Her mighty charmes, her furious loving fitt ;
His goodly conquest of the golden fleece,
His falsed fayth, and love too lightly flitt ;
The wondred Argo, which in venturous peece
First through the Euxine seas bore all the flowr of Greece.

*   *   *   *   *   *

Eftsoones they heard a most melodious sound,
Of all that mote delight a daintie eare,
Such as attonce might not on living ground,
Save in this Paradise, be heard elsewhere :
Right hard it was for wight which did it heare,

[1] please.

To read what manner musicke that mote bee ;
For all that pleasing is to living eare
Was there consorted in one harmonee ;
Birdes, voices, instruments, windes, waters, all agree :

The joyous birdes, shrouded in chearefull shade
Their notes unto the voice attempred sweet ;
Th' Angelicall soft trembling voyces made
To th' instruments divine respondence meet ;
The silver sounding instruments did meet
With the base murmure of the waters fall ;
The waters fall with difference discreet,
Now soft, now loud, unto the wind did call ;
The gentle warbling wind low answered to all.

There, whence that Musick seemed heard to bee,
Was the faire Witch her selfe now solacing
With a new Lover, whom, through sorceree
And witchcraft, she from farre did thither bring :
There she had him now laid aslombering
In secret shade after long wanton joyes ;
Whilst round about them pleasauntly did sing
Many faire Ladies and lascivious boyes,
That ever mixt their song with light licentious toyes.

*   *   *   *   *   *

The whiles some one did chaunt this lovely lay :
Ah ! see, whoso fayre thing doest faine to see,
In springing flowre the image of thy day.
Ah ! see the Virgin Rose, how sweetly shee
Doth first peepe foorth with bashfull modestee,
That fairer seemes the lesse ye see her may.
Lo ! see soone after how more bold and free
Her bared bosome she doth broad display ;
Lo ! see soone after how she fades and falls away.

So passeth, in the passing of a day,
Of mortall life the leafe, the bud, the flowre ;
Ne more doth florish after first decay,
That earst was sought to deck both bed and bowre
Of many a lady', and many a Paramowre.

Gather therefore the Rose whilest yet is prime,
For soone comes age that will her pride deflowre;
Gather the Rose of love whilest yet is time,
Whilest loving thou mayst loved be with equall crime.

He ceast; and then gan all the quire of birdes
Their diverse notes t' attune unto his lay,
As in approvaunce of his pleasing wordes.
The constant payre heard all that he did say,
Yet swarved not, but kept their forward way
Through many covert groves and thickets close,
In which they creeping did at last display
That wanton Lady with her Lover lose,
Whose sleepie head she in her lap did soft dispose.

[From Book iv. 1595-6.]

GARDENS OF VENUS.

'Thus having past all perill, I was come
Within the compasse of that Islands space;
The which did seeme, unto my simple doome,
The onely pleasant and delightfull place
That ever troden was of footings trace:
For all that nature by her mother-wit
Could frame in earth, and forme of substance base,
Was there; and all that nature did omit,
Art, playing second natures part, supplyed it.

'No tree, that is of count, in greenewood growes,
From lowest Juniper to Ceder tall,
No flowre in field, that daintie odour throwes,
And deckes his branch with blossomes over all,
But there was planted, or grew naturall:
Nor sense of man so coy and curious nice,
But there mote find to please it selfe withall;
Nor hart could wish for any queint device,
But there it present was, and did fraile sense entice.

'In such luxurious plentie of all pleasure,
It seem'd a second paradise to ghesse,
So lavishly enricht with Natures threasure,
That if the happie soules, which doe possesse
Th' Elysian fields and live in lasting blesse,
Should happen this with living eye to see,
They soone would loath their lesser happinesse,
And wish to life return'd againe to bee,
That in this joyous place they mote have joyance free.

'Fresh shadowes, fit to shroud from sunny ray;
Faire lawnds, to take the sunne in season dew;
Sweet springs, in which a thousand Nymphs did play;
Soft rombling brookes, that gentle slomber drew;
High reared mounts, the lands about to view;
Low looking dales, disloignd from common gaze;
Delightfull bowres, to solace lovers trew;
False Labyrinthes, fond runners eyes to daze;
All which by nature made did nature selfe amaze.

'And all without were walkes and alleyes dight
With divers trees enrang'd in even rankes;
And here and there were pleasant arbors pight,
And shadie seates, and sundry flowring bankes,
To sit and rest the walkers wearie shankes:
And therein thousand payres of lovers walkt,
Praysing their god, and yeelding him great thankes,
Ne ever ought but of their true loves talkt,
Ne ever for rebuke or blame of any balkt.

'All these together by themselves did sport
Their spotlesse pleasures and sweet loves content.
But, farre away from these, another sort
Of lovers lincked in true harts consent,
Which loved not as these for like intent,
But on chast vertue grounded their desire,
Farre from all fraud or fayned blandishment;
Which, in their spirits kindling zealous fire,
Brave thoughts and noble deedes did evermore aspire.

'Such were great Hercules and Hyllus deare
Trew Jonathan and David trustie tryde
Stout Theseus and Pirithous his feare[1]
Pylades and Orestes by his syde ;
Myld Titus and Gesippus without pryde ;
Damon and Pythias, whom death could not sever :
All these, and all that ever had bene tyde
In bands of friendship, there did live for ever ;
Whose lives although decay'd, yet loves decayed never.

'Which when as I, that never tasted blis
Nor happie howre, beheld with gazefull eye,
I thought there was none other heaven then this;
And gan their endlesse happinesse envye,
That being free from feare and gealosye
Might frankely there their loves desire possesse ;
Whilest I, through paines and perlous jeopardie,
Was forst to seeke my lifes deare patronnesse :
Much dearer be the things which come through hard distresse.

'Yet all those sights, and all that else I saw,
Might not my steps withhold, but that forthright
Unto that purposd place I did me draw,
Where as my love was lodged day and night,
The temple of great Venus, that is hight
The Queene of beautie, and of love the mother,
There worshipped of every living wight ;
Whose goodly workmanship farre past all other
That ever were on earth, all were they set together.'

Wooing of Amoret.

'Into the inmost Temple thus I came,
Which fuming all with frankensence I found
And odours rising from the altars flame.
Upon an hundred marble pillors round
The roofe up high was reared from the ground,
All deckt with crownes, and chaynes, and girlands gay,
And thousand pretious gifts worth many a pound,
The which sad lovers for their vowes did pay ;
And all the ground was strow'd with flowres as fresh as May.

[1] companion.

'An hundred Altars round about were set,
All flaming with their sacrifices fire,
That with the steme thereof the Temple swet,
Which rould in clouds to heaven did aspire,
And in them bore true lovers vowes entire :
And eke an hundred brasen caudrons bright,
To bath in joy and amorous desire,
Every of which was to a damzell hight ;
For all the Priests were damzels in soft linnen dight.

'Right in the midst the Goddesse selfe did stand
Upon an altar of some costly masse,
Whose substance was uneath to understand :
For neither pretious stone, nor durefull brasse,
Nor shining gold, nor mouldring clay it was ;
But much more rare and pretious to esteeme,
Pure in aspect, and like to christall glasse,
Yet glasse was not, if one did rightly deeme ;
But, being faire and brickle, likest glasse did seeme.

*   *   *   *   *   *

'And all about her necke and shoulders flew
A flocke of litle loves, and sports, and joyes,
With nimble wings of gold and purple hew ;
Whose shapes seem'd not like to terrestriall boyes,
But like to Angels playing heavenly toyes,
The whilest their eldest brother was away,
Cupid their eldest brother ; he enjoyes
The wide kingdome of love with lordly sway,
And to his law compels all creatures to obay.

'And all about her altar scattered lay
Great sorts of lovers piteously complayning,
Some of their losse, some of their loves delay,
Some of their pride, some paragons disdayning,
Some fearing fraud, some fraudulently fayning,
As every one had cause of good or ill.
Amongst the rest some one, through Loves constrayning
Tormented sore. could not containe it still,
But thus brake forth, that all the temple it did fill.

'"Great Venus! Queene of beautie and of grace,
The joy of Gods and men, that under skie
Doest fayrest shine, and most adorne thy place;
That with thy smyling looke doest pacifie
The raging seas, and makst the stormes to flie;
Thee, goddesse, thee the winds, the clouds doe feare,
And, when thou spredst thy mantle forth on hie,
The waters play, and pleasant lands appeare,
And heavens laugh, and al the world shews joyous cheare.

*　　*　　*　　*　　*

'"So all the world by thee at first was made,
And dayly yet thou doest the same repayre;
Ne ought on earth that merry is and glad,
Ne ought on earth that lovely is and fayre,
But thou the same for pleasure didst prepayre;
Thou art the root of all that joyous is:
Great God of men and women, queene of th' ayre,
Mother of laughter, and welspring of blisse,
O graunt that of my love at last I may not misse!"

'So did he say: but I with murmure soft,
That none might heare the sorrow of my hart,
Yet inly groning deepe and sighing oft,
Besought her to graunt ease unto my smart,
'And to my wound her gratious help impart.
Whilest thus I spake, behold! with happy eye
I spyde where at the Idoles feet apart
A bevie of fayre damzels close did lye,
Wayting when as the Antheme should be sung on hye.

'The first of them did seeme of ryper yeares
And graver countenance then ail the rest:
Yet all the rest were eke her equall peares,
Yet unto her obayed all the best.
Her name was Womanhood; that she exprest
By her sad semblant and demeanure wyse:
For stedfast still her eyes did fixed rest,
Ne rov'd at random, after gazers guyse,
Whose luring baytes oftimes doe heedlesse harts entyse.

'And next to her sate goodly Shamefastnesse,
Ne ever durst her eyes from ground upreare,
Ne ever once did looke up from her desse [1],
As if some blame of evill she did feare,
That in her cheekes made roses oft appeare :
And her against sweet Cherefulnesse was placed,
Whose eyes, like twinkling stars in evening cleare,
Were deckt with smyles that all sad humors chaced,
And darted forth delights the which her goodly graced.

'And next to her sate sober Modestie,
Holding her hand upon her gentle hart ;
And her against sate comely Curtesie,
That unto every person knew her part ;
And her before was seated overthwart
Soft Silence, and submisse Obedience,
Both linckt together never to dispart ;
Both gifts of God, not gotten but from thence,
Both girlonds of his Saints against their foes offence.

'Thus sate they all around in seemely rate :
And in the midst of them a goodly mayd
Even in the lap of Womanhood there sate,
The which was all in lilly white arayd,
With silver streames amongst the linnen stray'd ;
Like to the Morne, when first her shyning face
Hath to the gloomy world itselfe bewray'd :
That same was fayrest Amoret in place,
Shyning with beauties light and heavenly vertues grace.

'Whom soone as I beheld, my hart gan throb
And wade in doubt what best were to be donne ;
For sacrilege me seem'd the Church to rob,
And folly seem'd to leave the thing undonne
Which with so strong attempt I had begonne.
Tho, shaking off all doubt and shamefast feare
Which Ladies love, I heard, had never wonne
Mongst men of worth, I to her stepped neare,
And by the lilly hand her labour'd up to reare.

[1] dais.

'Thereat that formost matrone me did blame,
And sharpe rebuke for being over bold ;
Saying, it was to Knight unseemely shame
Upon a recluse Virgin to lay hold,
That unto Venus services was sold.
To whom I thus : "Nay, but it fitteth best
For Cupids man with Venus mayd to hold,
For ill your goddesse services are drest
By virgins, and her sacrifices let to rest."

' With that my shield I forth to her did show,
Which all that while I closely had conceld ;
On which when Cupid, with his killing bow
And cruell shafts, emblazond she beheld,
At sight thereof she was with terror queld,
And said no more : but I, which all that while
The pledge of faith, her hand, engaged held,
Like warie Hynd within the weedie soyle,
For no intreatie would forgoe so glorious spoyle.

'And evermore upon the Goddesse face
Mine eye was fixt, for feare of her offence ;
Whom when I saw with amiable grace
To laugh at me, and favour my pretence,
I was emboldned with more confidence ;
And nought for nicenesse nor for envy sparing,
In presence of them all forth led her thence
All looking on, and like astonisht staring,
Yet to lay hand on her not one of all them daring.

'She often prayd, and often me besought,
Sometime with tender teares to let her goe,
Sometime with witching smyles ; but yet, for nought
That ever she to me could say or doe,
Could she her wished freedome fro me wooe :
But forth I led her through the Temple gate
By which I hardly past with much adoe :
But that same Ladie, which me friended late
In entrance, did me also friend in my retrate.

'No lesse did Daunger threaten me with dread,
Whenas he saw me, maugre all his powre,
That glorious spoyle of beautie with me lead,
Then Cerberus, when Orpheus did recoure
His Leman from the Stygian Princes boure;
But evermore my shield did me defend
Against the storme of every dreadfull stoure:
Thus safely with my love I thence did wend.'
So ended he his tale, where I this Canto end.

[From *The Faerie Queene*, Bk. vi.]

THE QUELLING OF THE BLATANT BEAST.

Through all estates he found that he had past,
In which he many massacres had left,
And to the Clergy now was come at last;
In which such spoile, such havocke, and such theft
He wrought, that thence all goodnesse he bereft,
That endlesse were to tell. The Elfin Knight,
Who now no place besides unsought had left,
At length into a Monastere did light,
Where he him found despoyling all with maine and might.

Into their cloysters now he broken had,
Through which the Monckes he chaced here and there,
And them pursu'd into their dortours[1] sad,
And searched all their cels and secrets neare:
In which what filth and ordure did appeare,
Were yrkesome to report; yet that foule Beast,
Nought sparing them, the more did tosse and teare,
And ransacke all their dennes from most to least,
Regarding nought religion, nor their holy heast.

From thence into the sacred Church he broke,
And robd the Chancell, and the deskes downe threw,
And Altars fouled, and blasphemy spoke,
And th' Images, for all their goodly hew,
Did cast to ground, whilest none was them to rew;

[1] dormitories.

So all confounded and disordered there :
But, seeing Calidore, away he flew,
Knowing his fatall hand by former feare ;
But he him fast pursuing soone approched neare.

Him in a narrow place he overtooke,
And fierce assailing forst him turne againe :
Sternely he turnd againe, when he him strooke
With his sharpe steele, and ran at him amaine
With open mouth, that seemed to containe
A full good pecke within the utmost brim,
All set with yron teeth in raunges twaine,
That terrifide his foes, and armed him,
Appearing like the mouth of Orcus griesly grim :

And therein were a thousand tongs empight
Of sundry kindes and sundry quality ;
Some were of dogs, that barked day and night ;
And some of cats, that wrawling still did cry ;
And some of Beares, that groynd continually ;
And some of Tygres, that did seeme to gren
And snar at all that ever passed by :
But most of them were tongues of mortall men,
Which spake reprochfully, not caring where nor when

And them amongst were mingled here and there
The tongues of Serpents, with three forked stings,
That spat out poyson, and gore-bloudy gere,
At all that came within his ravenings ;
And spake licentious words and hatefull things
Of good and bad alike, of low and hie,
Ne Kesars spared he a whit, nor Kings ;
But either blotted them with infamie,
Or bit them with his banefull teeth of injury.

*　　*　　*　　*　　*　　*

Full cruelly the Beast did rage and rore
To be downe held, and maystred so with might,
That he gan fret and fome out bloudy gore,
Striving in vaine to rere him selfe upright :
For still, the more he strove, the more the Knight

Did him suppresse, and forcibly subdew,
That made him almost mad for fell despight :
He grind, hee bit, he scratcht, he venim threw,
And fared like a feend right horrible in hew :

Or like the hell-borne Hydra, which they faine
That great Alcides whilome overthrew,
After that he had labourd long in vaine
To crop his thousand heads, the which still new
Forth budded, and in greater number grew.
Such was the fury of this hellish Beast,
Whilest Calidore him under him downe threw ;
Who nathemore his heavy load releast,
But aye, the more he rag'd, the more his powre increast.

Tho, when the Beast saw he mote nought availe
By force, he gan his hundred tongues apply,
And sharpely at him to revile and raile
With bitter termes of shamefull infamy ;
Oft interlacing many a forged lie,
Whose like he never once did speake, nor heare,
Nor ever thought thing so unworthily :
Yet did he nought, for all that, him forbeare,
But strained him so streightly that he chokt him neare.

At last, when as he found his force to shrincke
And rage to quaile, he tooke a muzzel strong
Of surest yron, made with many a lincke :
Therewith he mured up his mouth along,
And therein shut up his blasphemous tong,
For never more defaming gentle Knight,
Or unto lovely Lady doing wrong ;
And thereunto a great long chaine he tight,
With which he drew him forth, even in his own despight.

Like as whylome that strong Tirynthian swaine
Brought forth with him the dreadfull dog of hell,
Against his will fast bound in yron chaine,
And, roring horribly, did him compell
To see the hatefull sunne, that he might tell

To griesly Pluto what on earth was donne,
And to the other damned ghosts which dwell
For aye in darkenesse, which day-light doth shonne:
So led this Knight his captyve with like conquest wonne.

Yet greatly did the Beast repine at those
Straunge bands, whose like till then he never bore,
Ne ever any durst till then impose;
And chauffed inly, seeing now no more
Him liberty was left aloud to rore:
Yet durst he not draw backe, nor once withstand
The proved powre of noble Calidore,
But trembled underneath his mighty hand,
And like a fearefull dog him followed through the land

Him through all Faery land he follow's so,
As if he learned had obedience long,
That all the people, where so he did go,
Out of their townes did round about him throng,
To see him leade that Beast in bondage strong;
And seeing it much wondred at the sight:
And all such persons as he earst did wrong
Rejoyced much to see his captive plight,
And much admyr'd the Beast, but more admyr'd the Knight.

Thus was this Monster, by the maystring might
Of doughty Calidore, supprest and tamed,
That never more he mote endammadge wight
With his vile tongue, which many had defamed,
And many causelesse caused to be blamed.
So did he eeke long after this remaine,
Until that, (whether wicked fate so framed
Or fault of men,) he broke his yron chaine,
And got into the world at liberty againe.

    *   *   *   *   *   *

So now he raungeth through the world againe,
And rageth sore in each degree and state;
Ne any is that may him now restraine,
He growen is so great and strong of late,
Barking and biting all that him doe bate

Albe they worthy blame, or cleare of crime :
Ne spareth he most learned wits to rate,
Ne spareth he the gentle Poets rime ;
But rends without regard of person or of time.

Ne may this homely verse, of many meanest,
Hope to escape his venemous despite,
More then my former writs, all were they cleanest
From blamefull blot, and free from all that wite
With which some wicked tongues did it backebite,
And bring into a mighty Peres displeasure,
That never so deserved to endite.
Therefore do you, my rimes, keep better measure,
And seeke to please ; that now is counted wise mens threasure.

[From Bk. **vii.** (posthumous).]

CLAIMS OF MUTABILITY PLEADED BEFORE NATURE.

'Yet mauger Jove, and all his gods beside,
I do possesse the worlds most regiment ;
As if ye please it into parts divide,
And every parts inholders to convent,
Shall to your eyes appeare incontinent.
And, first, the Earth (great mother of us all)
That only seemes unmov'd and permanent,
And unto Mutabilitie not thrall,
Yet is she chang'd in part, and eeke in generall :

'For all that from her springs, and is ybredde,
How-ever faire it flourish for a time,
Yet see we soone decay ; and, being dead,
To turne againe unto their earthly slime :
Yet, out of their decay and mortall crime,
We daily see new creatures to arize,
And of their Winter spring another Prime,
Unlike in forme, and chang'd by strange disguise :
So turne they still about, and change in restlesse wise.

'As for her tenants, that is, man and beasts,
The beasts we daily see massacred dy
As thralls and vassals unto mens beheasts ;

And men themselves do change continually,
From youth to eld, from wealth to poverty,
From good to bad, from bad to worst of all :
Ne doe their bodies only flit and fly,
But eeke their minds (which they immortall call)
Still change and vary thought, as new occasions fall.'

*   *   *   *   *   *

[The Seasons and the Months pass by, and after them the Hours.]

And after these there came the Day and Night,
Riding together both with equall pase,
Th' one on a Palfrey blacke, the other white ;
But Night had covered her uncomely face
With a blacke veile, and held in hand a mace,
On top whereof the moon and stars were pight ;
And sleep and darknesse round about did trace :
But Day did beare upon his scepters hight
The goodly Sun encompast all with beames bright.

Then came the Howres, faire daughters of high Jove
And timely Night ; the which were all endewed
With wondrous beauty fit to kindle love ;
But they were virgins all, and love eschewed
That might forslack the charge to them foreshewed
By mighty Jove ; who did them porters make
Of heavens gate (whence all the gods issued)
Which they did daily watch, and nightly wake
By even turnes, ne ever did their charge forsake.

And after all came Life, and lastly Death ;
Death with most grim and griesly visage seene,
Yet is he nought but parting of the breath ;
Ne ought to see, but like a shade to weene,
Unbodied, unsoul'd, unheard, unseene :
But Life was like a faire young lusty boy,
Such as they faine Dan Cupid to have beene,
Full of delightfull health and lively joy,
Deckt all with flowres, and wings of gold fit to employ.

When these were past, thus gan the Titanesse :
' Lo ! mighty mother, now be judge, and say
Whether in all thy creatures more or lesse
CHANGE doth not raign and bear the greatest sway;
For who sees not that Time on all doth pray?
But Times do change and move continually:
So nothing heere long standeth in one stay:
Wherefore this lower world who can deny
But to be subject still to Mutability ?'

     *   *   *   *   *   *

' Then, since within this wide great Universe
Nothing doth firme and permanent appeare,
But all things tost and turned by transverse,
What then should let, but I aloft should reare
My Trophee, and from all the triumph beare ?
Now judge then, (O thou greatest goddesse trew)
According as thy selfe doest see and heare,
And unto me addoom that is my dew ;
That is, the rule of all, all being rul'd by you.'

So having ended, silence long ensewed ;
Ne Nature to or fro spake for a space,
But with firme eyes affixt the ground still viewed.
Meane-while all creatures, looking in her face,
Expecting th' end of this so doubtfull case,
Did hang in long suspence what would ensew,
To whether side should fall the soveraine place :
At length she, looking up with chearefull view,
The silence brake, and gave her doome in speeches few.

' I well consider all that ye have said,
And find that all things stedfastnesse do hate
And changed be ; yet, being rightly wayd,
They are not changed from their first estate ;
But by their change their being do dilate,
And turning to themselves at length againe,
Do worke their owne perfection so by fate :
Then over them Change doth not rule and raigne
But they raigne over Change, and do their states maintaine

‘ Cease therefore, daughter, further to aspire,
And thee content thus to be rul’d by mee,
For thy decay thou seekst by thy desire ;
But time shall come that all shall changed bee,
And from thenceforth none no more change shal see.’
So was the Titanesse put downe and whist,
And Jove confirm’d in his imperiall see.
Then was that whole assembly quite dismist,
And Natur’s selfe did vanish, whither no man wist.

[Fragment of the last Canto.]

When I bethinke me on that speech whyleare
Of Mutabilitie, and well it way !
Me seemes, that though she all unworthy were
Of the Heav’ns Rule : yet, very sooth to say,
In all things else she beares the greatest sway :
Which makes me loath this state of life so tickle,
And love of things so vaine to cast away ;
Whose flowring pride, so fading and so fickle,
Short Time shall soon cut down with his consuming sickle.

Then gin I thinke on that which Nature sayd,
Of that same time when no more Change shall be,
But stedfast rest of all things, firmely stayd
Upon the pillours of Eternity,
That is contrayr to Mutabilitie ;
For all that moveth doth in Change delight :
But thence-forth all shall rest eternally
With Him that is the God of Sabaoth hight :
O ! that great Sabaoth God, grant me that Sabaoths sight !

COMPLAINT OF THALIA (COMEDY).

[From *The Teares of the Muses* (1591).]

Where be the sweete delights of learnings treasure
That wont with Comick sock to beautefie
The painted Theaters, and fill with pleasure
The listners eyes and eares with melodie ;
In which I late was wont to raine as Queene,
And maske in mirth with Graces well beseene ?

O ! all is gone ; and all that goodly glee,
Which wont to be the glorie of gay wits,
Is layd abed, and no where now to see ;
And in her roome unseemly Sorrow sits,
With hollow browes and greisly countenaunce,
Marring my joyous gentle dalliaunce.

And him beside sits ugly Barbarisme,
And brutish Ignorance, ycrept of late
Out of dredd darknes of the deepe Abysme,
Where being bredd, he light and heaven does hate :
They in the mindes of men now tyrannize,
And the faire Scene with rudenes foule disguize.

All places they with follie have possest,
And with vaine toyes the vulgare entertaine ;
But me have banished, with all the rest
That whilome wont to wait upon my traine,
Fine Counterfesaunce, and unhurtfull Sport,
Delight, and Laughter, deckt in seemly sort.

All these, and all that els the Comick Stage
With seasoned wit and goodly pleasance graced,
By which mans life in his likest image
Was limned forth, are wholly now defaced ;
And those swete wits, which wont the like to frame,
Are now despizd, and made a laughing game.

And he, the man whom Nature selfe had made
To mock her selfe, and Truth to imitate,
With kindly counter under Mimick shade,
Our pleasant Willy, ah ! is dead of late :
With whom all joy and jolly meriment
Is also deaded, and in dolour drent.

In stead thereof scoffing Scurrilitie,
And scornfull Follie with Contempt is crept,
Rolling in rymes of shameles ribaudrie
Without regard, or due Decorum kept ;
Each idle wit at will presumes to make,
And doth the Learneds taske upon him take.

But that same gentle Spirit, from whose pen
Large streames of honnie and sweete Nectar flowe,
Scorning the boldnes of such base-borne men,
Which dare their follies forth so rashlie throwe,
Doth rather choose to sit in idle Cell,
Than so himselfe to mockerie to sell.

So am I made the servant of the manie,
And laughing stocke of all that list to scorne ;
Not honored nor cared for of anie,
But loath'd of losels as a thing forlorne :
Therefore I mourne and sorrow with the rest,
Untill my cause of sorrow be redrest.

SONNETS.

[1595.]

Lyke as a ship, that through the Ocean wyde,
By conduct of some star, doth make her way ;
Whenas a storme hath dimd her trusty guyde,
Out of her course doth wander far astray !
So I, whose star, that wont with her bright ray
Me to direct, with cloudes is over-cast,
Doe wander now, in darknesse and dismay,
Through hidden perils round about me plast ;

Yet hope I well that, when this storme is past,
My Helice, the lodestar of my lyfe,
Will shine again, and looke on me at last,
With lovely light to cleare my cloudy grief,
　　Till then I wander carefull, comfortlesse,
　　In secret sorow, and sad pensivenesse.

What guyle is this, that those her golden tresses
She doth attyre under a net of gold ;
And with sly skill so cunningly them dresses,
That which is gold, or heare, may scarse be told ?
Is it that mens frayle eyes, which gaze too bold,
She may entangle in that golden snare ;
And, being caught, may craftily enfold
Theyr weaker harts, which are not wel aware ?
Take heed, therefore, myne eyes, how ye doe stare
Henceforth too rashly on that guilefull net,
In which, if ever ye entrapped are,
Out of her bands ye by no meanes shall get.
　　Fondnesse it were for any, being free,
　　To covet fetters, though they golden bee !

Sweet Smile ! the daughter of the Queene of Love,
Expressing all thy mothers powrefull art,
With which she wants to temper angry Jove,
When all the gods he threats with thundring dart :
Sweet is thy vertue, as thy selfe sweet art.
For, when on me thou shinedst late in sadnesse,
A melting pleasance ran through every part,
And me revived with hart-robbing gladnesse.
Whylest rapt with joy resembling heavenly madnes,
My soule was ravisht quite as in a traunce ;
And feeling thence, no more her sorowes sadnesse,
Fed on the fulnesse of that chearefull glaunce,
　　More sweet than Nectar, or Ambrosiall meat,
　　Seemd every bit which thenceforth I did eat.

Joy of my life! full oft for loving you
I blesse my lot, that was so lucky placed:
But then the more your owne mishap I rew,
That are so much by so meane love embased.
For, had the equall hevens so much you graced
In this as in the rest, ye mote invent
Som hevenly wit, whose verse could have enchased
Your glorious name in golden moniment.
But since ye deignd so goodly to relent
To me your thrall, in whom is little worth;
That little, that I am, shall all be spent
In setting your immortall prayses forth:
  Whose lofty argument, uplifting me,
  Shall lift you up unto an high degree.

EPITHALAMION.

Ye learned sisters, which have oftentimes
Beene to me ayding, others to adorne,
Whom ye thought worthy of your gracefull rymes,
That even the greatest did not greatly scorne
To heare theyr names sung in your simple layes,
But joyed in theyr praise;
And when ye list your owne mishaps to mourne,
Which death, or love, or fortunes wreck did rayse,
Your string could soone to sadder tenor turne,
And teach the woods and waters to lament
Your dolefull dreriment:
Now lay those sorrowfull complaints aside;
And, having all your heads with girlands crownd,
Helpe me mine owne loves prayses to resound;
Ne let the same of any be envide:
So Orpheus did for his owne bride!
So   unto my selfe alone will sing;
The woods shall to me answer, and my Eccho ring.

Early, before the worlds light-giving lampe
His golden beame upon the hils doth spred,
Having disperst the nights unchearefull dampe,
Doe ye awake ; and, with fresh lusty-hed,
Go to the bowre of my beloved love,
My truest turtle dove ;
Bid her awake ; for Hymen is awake,
And long since ready forth his maske to move,
With his bright Tead that flames with many a flake,
And many a bachelor to waite on him,
In theyr fresh garments trim.
Bid her awake therefore, and soone her dight,
For lo ! the wished day is come at last,
That shall, for all the paynes and sorrowes past,
Pay to her usury of long delight :
And, whylest she doth her dight,
Doe ye to her of joy and solace sing,
That all the woods may answer, and your eccho ring.

Bring with you all the Nymphes that you can heare
Both of the rivers and the forrests greene,
And of the sea that neighbours to her neare :
Al with gay girlands goodly wel beseene.
And let them also with them bring in hand
Another gay girland,
For my fayre love, of lillyes and of roses,
Bound truelove wize, with a blew silke riband.
And let them make great store of bridale poses,
And let them eeke bring store of other flowers,
To deck the bridale bowers.
And let the ground whereas her foot shall tread,
For feare the stones her tender foot should wrong,
Be strewed with fragrant flowers all along,
And diapred lyke the discolored mead.
Which done, doe at her chamber dore awayt,
For she will waken strayt ;
The whiles doe ye this song unto her sing,
The woods· shall to you answer, and your Eccho ring.

*　　*　　*　　*　　*　　*　　*

Wake now, my love, awake! for it is time;
The Rosy Morne long since left Tithones bed,
All ready to her silver coche to clyme;
And Phœbus gins to shew his glorious hed.
Hark! how the cheerefull birds do chaunt theyr laies
And carroll of Loves praise.
The merry Larke hir mattins sings aloft;
The Thrush replyes; the Mavis descant playes;
The Ouzell shrills; the Ruddock warbles soft;
So goodly all agree, with sweet consent,
To this dayes merriment.
Ah! my deere love, why doe ye sleepe thus long,
When meeter were that ye should now awake,
T' awayt the comming of your joyous make,
And hearken to the birds love-learned song,
The deawy leaves among!
For they of joy and pleasance to you sing,
That all the woods them answer, and theyr eccho ring.

My love is now awake out of her dreames,
And her fayre eyes, like stars that dimmed were
With darksome cloud, now shew theyr goodly beams
More bright than Hesperus his head doth rere.
Come now, ye damzels, daughters of delight,
Helpe quickly her to dight:
But first come ye fayre houres, which were begot,
In Joves sweet paradice of Day and Night;
Which doe the seasons of the yeare allot,
And al, that ever in this world is fayre,
Doe make and still repayre:
And ye three handmayds of the Cyprian Queene,
The which doe still adorne her beauties pride,
Helpe to addorne my beautifullest bride:
And, as ye her array, still throw betweene
Some graces to be seene;
And, as ye use to Venus, to her sing,
The whiles the woods shal answer, and your eccho ring.

Now is my love all ready forth to come :
Let all the virgins therefore well awayt :
And ye fresh boyes, that tend upon her groome,
Prepare your selves ; for he is comming strayt.
Set all your things in seemely good aray,
Fit for so joyfull day :
The joyfulst day that ever sunne did see,
Faire Sun ! shew forth thy favourable ray,
And let thy lifull heat not fervent be,
For feare of burning her sunshyny face,
Her beauty to disgrace.
O fayrest Phœbus ! father of the Muse !
If ever I did honour thee aright,
Or sing the thing that mote thy mind delight,
Doe not thy servants simple boone refuse ;
But let this day, let this one day, be myne ;
Let all the rest be thine.
Then I thy soverayne prayses loud wil sing,
That all the woods shal answer, and theyr eccho ring.

*   *   *   *   *   *   *

Loe ! where she comes along with portly pace,
Lyke Phœbe, from her chamber of the East,
Arysing forth to run her mighty race,
Clad all in white, that seemes a virgin best.
So well it her beseemes, that ye would weene
Some angell she had beene.
Her long loose yellow locks lyke golden wyre,
Sprinckled with perle, and perling flowres atweene,
Doe lyke a golden mantle her attyre ;
And, being crowned with a girland greene,
Seeme lyke some mayden Queene.
Her modest eyes, abashed to behold
So many gazers as on her do stare,
Upon the lowly ground affixed are ;
Ne dare lift up her countenance too bold,
But blush to heare her prayses sung so loud,
So farre from being proud.

Nathlesse doe ye still loud her prayses sing,
That all the woods may answer, and your eccho ring.

* * * * * *

But if ye saw that which no eyes can see,
The inward beauty of her lively spright,
Garnisht with heavenly guifts of high degree,
Much more then would ye wonder at that sight,
And stand astonisht lyke to those which red
Medusaes mazeful hed.
There dwels sweet love, and constant chastity,
Unspotted fayth, and comely womanhood,
Regard of honour, and mild modesty ;
There vertue raynes as Queene in royal throne,
And giveth lawes alone,
The which the base affections doe obay,
And yeeld theyr services unto her will ;
Ne thought of thing uncomely ever may
Thereto approch to tempt her mind to ill.
Had ye once seene these her celestial threasures,
And unrevealed pleasures,
Then would ye wonder, and her prayses sing,
That al the woods should answer, and your echo ring

Open the temple gates unto my love,
Open them wide that she may enter in,
And all the postes adorne as doth behove,
And all the pillours deck with girlands trim,
For to receyve this Saynt with honour dew,
That commeth in to you.
With trembling steps, and humble reverence,
She commeth in, before th' Almighties view ;
Of her ye virgins learne obedience,
When so ye come into those holy places,
To humble your proud faces :
Bring her up to th' high altar, that she may
The sacred ceremonies there partake,
The which do endlesse matrimony make ;
And let the roring Organs loudly play

The praises of the Lord in lively notes ;
The whiles, with hollow throates,
The Choristers the joyous Antheme sing,
That al the woods may answere, and their eccho ring.

Behold, whiles she before the altar stands,
Hearing the holy priest that to her speakes,
And blesseth her with his two happy hands,
How the red roses flush up in her cheekes,
And the pure snow, with goodly vermill stayne
Like crimsin dyde in grayne :
That even th' Angels, which continually
About the sacred Altare doe remaine,
Forget their service and about her fly,
Ofte peeping in her face, that seems more fayre,
The more they on it stare.
But her sad eyes, still fastened on the ground,
Are governed with goodly modesty,
That suffers not one looke to glaunce awry,
Which may let in a little thought unsownd.
Why blush ye, love, to give to me your hand,
The pledge of all our band !
Sing, ye sweet Angels, Alleluya sing,
That all the woods may answere, and your eccho ring.

Now al is done : bring home the bride againe ;
Bring home the triumph of our victory :
Bring home with you the glory of her gaine
With joyance bring her and with jollity.
Never had man more joyfull day then this,
Whom heaven would heape with blis,
Make feast therefore now all this live-long day ;
This day for ever to me holy is.
Poure out the wine without restraint or stay,
Poure not by cups, but by the belly full,
Poure out to all that wull,
And sprinkle all the postes and wals with wine,
That they may sweat, and drunken be withall.
Crowne ye God Bacchus with a coronall,
And Hymen also crowne with wreathes of vine ;

And let the Graces daunce unto the rest,
For they can doo it best :
The whiles the maydens doe theyr carroll sing,
To which the woods shall answer, and theyr eccho ring.

Ring ye the bels, ye yong men of the towne,
And leave your wonted labors for this day :
This day is holy; doe ye write it downe,
That ye for ever it remember may.
This day the sunne is in his chiefest hight,
With Barnaby the bright,
From whence declining daily by degrees,
He somewhat loseth of his heat and light,
When once the Crab behind his back he sees.
But for this time it ill ordained was,
To chose the longest day in all the yeare,
And shortest night, when longest fitter weare :
Yet never day so long, but late would passe.
Ring ye the bels, to make it weare away,
And bonefiers make all day ;
And daunce about them, and about them sing,
That all the woods may answer, and your eccho ring.

Ah ! when will this long weary day have end,
And lende me leave to come unto my love ?
How slowly do the houres theyr numbers spend ?
How slowly does sad Time his feathers move ?
Hast thee, O fayrest Planet, to thy home,
Within the Westerne fome :
Thy tyred steedes long since have need of rest.
Long though it be, at last I see it gloome,
And the bright evening-star with golden creast
Appeare out of the East.
Fayre childe of beauty ! glorious lampe of love !
That all the host of heaven in rankes doost lead,
And guydest lovers through the nights sad dread,
How chearefully thou lookest from above,
And seemst to laugh atweene thy twinkling light,
As joying in the sight

Z 2

Of these glad many, which for joy doe sing,
That all the woods them answer, and their echo ring!

*   *   *   *   *   *

And ye high heavens, the temple of the gods,
In which a thousand torches flaming bright
Doe burne, that to us wretched earthly clods
In dreadful darknesse lend desired light ;
And all ye powers which in the same remayne,
More then we men can fayne !
Poure out your blessing on us plentiously,
And happy influence upon us raine,
That we may raise a large posterity,
Which from the earth, which they may long possesse
With lasting happinesse,
Up to your haughty pallaces may mount ;
And, for the guerdon of theyr glorious merit,
May heavenly tabernacles there inherit,
Of blessed Saints for to increase the count.
So let us rest, sweet love, in hope of this,
And cease till then our tymely joyes to sing :
The woods no more us answer, nor our eccho ring!

SIR PHILIP SIDNEY.

[PHILIP SIDNEY was the eldest son of the well-known Sir Henry Sidney, President of Wales and Lord Deputy of Ireland under Elizabeth, and through his mother, Lady Mary Dudley, grandson of the Duke of Northumberland executed in 1553, and nephew of Lord Leicester. He was born at Penshurst Nov. 29, 1554; he entered Shrewsbury School Oct. 17, 1564, on the same day as his friend and biographer Fulke Greville, afterwards Lord Brooke; and in 1568 he was sent to Christ Church, Oxford. From May 1572 to May 1575 Sidney was abroad, in France, Germany, and Italy; sheltered in Sir Francis Walsingham's house in Paris on the night of St. Bartholomew, and spending a considerable time at Frankfort with Hubert Languet the reformer, afterwards his constant correspondent. In 1575 he appeared at Elizabeth's Court, and took part in the Kenilworth progress. In 1577 he was sent as English ambassador to Rodolph II at Prague, returning the same year. He seems to have made acquaintance with Harvey and Spenser in 1578, and in 1580, while he was in retirement at Penshurst, after his letter of remonstrance to the Queen on the Anjou match, he and his sister, the well-known Countess of Pembroke, produced a joint poetical version of the Psalms, and the *Arcadia* was begun (published 1590). He returned to Court in the autumn of 1580, and the *Astrophel and Stella* sonnets (published 1591) probably date from the following year. *The Apologie for Poetrie* was written in or about 1581 (the first known edition is that of London 1595). Sidney was knighted in the same year. In 1583 he married Frances, daughter of Sir Francis Walsingham, and was for the second time a member of Parliament. In Nov. 1584 he was appointed governor of Flushing, and nearly two years later, on Sept. 22, 1586, received his fatal wound at the battle of Zutphen. A complete edition of Sidney's poems was published by the Rev. A. B. Grosart, London, 1877.]

The extraordinary effect produced by Sidney's personality upon English imagination has been in many respects very little weakened by time. His name is almost as suggestive now as it was to his own generation of a typical brilliancy and charm, clouded by premature death and scarcely to be matched again. This unique impression however with which the figure of 'Astrophel' is still charged, is to a large extent independent of the causes for it which influenced his contemporaries. We are for the most part moved by Sidney's life, by the romance of it or its political and historical interest. His youth, his love-story, his death,—these are what

affect us far more than his books; what he did and was, infinitely
beyond what he wrote.

> ' Death, courage, honour, make thy soul to live;
> Thy soul to live in heaven, thy name in tongues of men!'

His own time approached him somewhat differently. Browne's
praise of him, which puts the 'deep quintessence' of his wit in the
forefront of his merits, before it turns to dwell upon his 'honour,
virtue, valour, excellence,' represents the general Elizabethan
feeling about him better than the fine lines from Constable just
quoted. His literary influence, coming as he did in the early
Elizabethan days, while his great rivals to be were still for the
most part undiscovered, was no doubt heightened by his personal
story, but was at bottom a distinct and independent force. So
much is clear from that astonishing mass of elegiac prose and
verse heaped upon his grave, in itself a phenomenon in English
literary history; and as the Elizabethan time unfolds, the effect
of Sidney's writing and of his special qualities of thought and
style become more and more evident. Upon the generation which
grew up after him, and during the first half of the seventeenth
century, his influence remained undiminished. From Constable,
Ben Jonson, Browne, Wither, Crashaw, Waller, out of a much
wider circle, a string of passages could be quoted to prove the
extraordinary spell of Sidney as a poet, above all as the poet
of Stella, upon his successors. The mere name of Astrophel
seems to have thrilled the literary circle around him, and that
immediately following him, as no other name had power to thrill
them. A reputation so romantic, and so dependent on the
exceptional correspondence between Sidney's personality and
powers and the young, quick-witted, passionate, Elizabethan spirit
speaking through them, could scarcely hope to pass through
Puritanism and the eighteenth century unchallenged. Milton's
well-known protest against the use made by Charles I. on the
scaffold of 'that vain amatorious poem of Sir Philip Sidney's
Arcadia,' 'not to be read at any time without good caution,'
is significant of decline in one direction, while in another we are
brought up against some curious eighteenth-century judgments
which show not only the complete distaste of a classical age for
Sidney's literary performance, and the oblivion into which his best
work had fallen, but even impatience of his romantic personal
fame. 'When we come to enquire into the why and the wherefore
of this astonishing effect upon his contemporaries,' writes Horace

Walpole, who had never read a line of *Astrophel and Stella*, and had to be reminded by a friend of the existence of *The Apology for Poetry*, 'what do we find? Great valour? But it was an age of heroes! In full of all other talents, we have a tedious, lamentable, pedantic, pastoral romance which the patience of a young virgin in love cannot now wade through ; and some absurd attempts to fetter English verse in Roman chains.'

There could scarcely be a better specimen of the *jugement saugrenu*. Happily the antiquarian revival of the present century has so far affected Sidney among others, that such pure ignorance of his place in literary history is no longer possible. But it may well be questioned whether Sidney has yet regained that currency among us as a poet which he deserves. Thanks to the labour which has been spent upon him since 1800, his prose is better known and more truly classed than it used to be; but not even the best of his poems can be said to have recovered any real hold upon English feeling. The truth is, perhaps, that the general air of Sidney's verse, so to speak, does it injustice. Even the *Astrophel and Stella* sonnets have at first sight, as one turns over the pages, a barren, over-elaborate look, which is apt to lead to the classing of some of the most genuine and passionate of English poems with the undeniably dry and artificial verse of the *Arcadia*. Then again, his main subject is forbidding, his range is limited, and his note, to modern thinking, monotonous. We are some time in discovering in Sidney that sensitiveness to the great human problems, to the wider questions of life and thought in which the best English poetry is invariably steeped, and it is easy to put his work down as ranking with all the other second-rate love poetry of the time, neither much better nor worse than the verse of Constable or Thomas Watson. His own time, however, judged rightly in separating it widely from such performances. Sidney died at thirty-two, and his poetry is throughout the poetry of a young man, in love with art, with beauty, with ingenuity in all shapes, a courtier in the days when the court was a reality, a lover at a time when love was still bound to speak a conventional tongue and to express itself by certain outward conventional signs. The marring influence upon much of it of the theories of Gabriel Harvey's 'Areopagus' marks the difference in circumstance between himself and Spenser, his friend and temporary colleague in that whimsical scheme for bending English verse to classical shapes. In a few years Spenser was ridiculing the 'Areopagus,' and the 'passing singular odd' poems produced under its rules. Time sobered down the momentary extravagance, and the familiar ways of English verse reclaimed their master. Spenser's hexameters are mere literary curiosities, buried in the shadow of *The Fairy Queen.* Sidney's 'Roman feet' are one of the most prominent features of his best-known work, and were regarded as characteristic of him in days when the poems to Stella were forgotten. The freaks of the 'Areopagus' had no more real relation to his genius than they had to Spenser's ; but life left him no time to undo mistakes. Into what final mould his powers might have run is matter for speculation. The important point to notice is that death stepped in between him and that slow-coming maturity which belongs to all such rich and complex natures. His youth asserts itself in all he wrote. His best work is liable to youth's unripeness and inequality.

But the greatness of his gift is not to be doubted. As a series of sonnets the *Astrophel and Stella* poems are second only to Shakespeare's ; as a series of love-poems they are perhaps unsurpassed. Other writers are sweeter, more sonorous ; no other love-poet of the time is so real. The poems to Stella are steeped throughout in a certain keen and pungent individuality which leaves a haunting impression behind it. They represent, not a mere isolated mood, whether half-real like Daniel's passion for Delia, or wholly artificial like the mood of Thomas Watson's *Passions,* but a whole passage in a genuine life. Here is no question of the pastoral landscape with its conventional pair of figures. Sidney's every-day life as a courtier and politician, mingling with the pageantries and touching the great interests of his time, his personal character with its serious and Puritan bias, his hopes and fears for his own prospects and career,—these are the facts of solid and human reality which deepen and vary the music of his passion for Stella, like rocks in the current of a stream. Not that *Astrophel and Stella* is without its make-believes. It has its 'conceits,' its pieces of pure word-play, in the common Elizabethan manner. No writer in the full tide of literary fashion like Sidney could afford to neglect these. But it would be scarcely fanciful to say that even in the most clearly marked of what one may call his conceited sonnets, the true Sidneian note to a reader who has learnt to catch it is almost always discernible, a note of youth and eagerness easily felt but hard to be described.

As is well known, *Astrophel and Stella* contains the records of Sidney's love for Penelope Devereux, daughter of the first Earl

of Essex and sister to Elizabeth's favourite. They first met at Chartley in 1575, during the Kenilworth progress, when Sidney was twenty-one and Penelope a child of twelve, and in the years between 1576 and 1580 were commonly supposed to be destined for one another. Sidney however does not appear to have prosecuted his suit with much ardour—there are several allusions to this early blindness of his in *Astrophel and Stella*—and in 1580 his prospects had suddenly become so clouded by his own and Leicester's temporary disgrace, that it seems to have been thought prudent that Stella should look elsewhere. At any rate, when Sidney returned to court in the autumn of 1580, he found Penelope Devereux either married (there is a doubt about the date of the marriage) or pledged to Lord Rich. Disappointment and a sharp sense of injury, expressed with plain bitterness in one of his miscellaneous poems (see p. 362), shook his former liking into love, and during the following year, as far as dates can now be recovered, after Stella's marriage at any rate, as well as possibly before it, the *Astrophel and Stella* sonnets were written.

The chronology of these sonnets is now scarcely to be determined. They were not published till after Sidney's death, when they were either printed from completed MSS., in which the order had been slightly disarranged by Sidney himself, for the purpose of masking to some extent their autobiographical character, or were put together by his friends in carelessness or ignorance of the dates of many among them. The main thread however is still discernible, and a close sifting of the allusions to contemporary history in them, as well as a comparison of them with the correspondence between Languet and Sidney of 1580–81, might enable a more clear-headed editor than has yet arisen to handle Sidney, to explain much that is now obscure. There are three distinct stages in the series : the first representing a period of impetuous passion, when Sidney is wooing in hot eagerness, bending all the power of his genius to the glorification of Stella and the scorning of his supplanter Lord Rich, and yet dogged perpetually by returns upon himself, by outbursts of moral sensitiveness eminently characteristic ; the second a period of partial relenting **on** Stella's part and of joy on Sidney's :—

> ' Gone is the winter of my misery !
> My spring appears : O see what here doth grow,
> For Stella hath, with words where faith doth shine,
> Of her high heart given me the monarchy.'

And the third, a period of widening separation, when the lover, 'forced by Stella's laws of duty to depart,' sinks deeper and deeper into depression and discouragement. Joy, hope, delight, even tears, have forgotten him :—

> 'Only true sighs you do not go away:
> Thank may you have for such a thankful part;
> —Thankworthiest yet when you shall break my heart!'

Last of all, we may imagine, comes a sudden call to action, perhaps connected with the schemes of colonisation which we know to have been occupying his mind in 1582, and Sidney writes the 107th sonnet, the last but one in the series as printed, probably the true conclusion of the whole according to Sidney's plan.

> 'Sweet for a while give respite to my heart,
> Which pants as though it still should leap to thee,
> And on my thoughts give thy lieutenancy
> *To this great cause,* which needs both use and art.
> And as a queen who from her presence sends
> Whom she employs, dismiss from thee my wit,
> Till it have wrought what thy own will attends—
>
> O let not fools in me thy works reprove,
> And scorning say, 'See what it is to love!'

Scattered up and down these three divisions as the sonnets stand now, are sonnets which have no special fitness to one or other division, and others again that are clearly misplaced. Still, in the main, the story of the poems runs on unbroken, a living continuous whole growing step by step more real and more tragic. With very few exceptions, the *Astrophel and Stella* sonnets cannot be fairly judged apart from their context. Each sonnet depends upon those before and after it, and it is in the cumulative effect of the whole that Sidney's genius is most clearly felt. Other contemporary series of sonnets will bear unstringing without injury. A stray sonnet taken at random from *Delia* or Lodge's *Phillis* or from Drummond's love-sonnets will often compare favourably with one taken at random from *Astrophel and Stella.* But the weak sonnets in Sidney are like the weak places in some of Wordsworth's finest work, descents to commonplace which taken alone would be intolerable, but which in their proper context rather heighten than detract from the realistic and passionate effect of the whole. In order to preserve this general effect as much as possible, the plan of the present selection has been to take from each period a certain number of representative sonnets, which reproduce the original whole at least in outline, adding to these two specimens from the *Astrophel and Stella* songs, eleven in number, which were originally printed after the sonnets, but were interspersed among them in the *Arcadia* of 1598. The two sonnets beginning 'Thou blind man's mark, thou fool's self-chosen snare,' and 'Leave me, O Love which reachest but to dust,' which a recent editor has arbitrarily placed for the first time at the end of *Astrophel and Stella,* have been here carefully distinguished from that series. In some ways, in spite of their grand flow of verse and phrase, they are inferior to the majority of the *Astrophel and Stella* sonnets in workmanship, and also slightly different from them in plan. Sidney was probably not inclined to assign to them finally so conspicuous a place, and they were first published with other miscellaneous sonnets in the *Arcadia* of 1598. But that they were written towards the close of the Stella episode, perhaps about the time of the poet's marriage with Frances Walsingham, is certainly very likely, and their consonance with all that we know of that philosophical and high-minded Sidney in whom Elizabeth found an unwelcome counsellor, and Languet saw the hope of the Protestant cause in Europe, makes it justifiable to regard them as fit successors to any selection from *Astrophel and Stella,* and especially as closely connected with the 107th sonnet.

Of the rest of Sidney's poetry it is not necessary to say very much. The *Stella* poems brought him his contemporary fame, and upon them and the *Apology for Poetry* his claim to live in English letters must always rest. His other poems have the youthful faults which mar even *Astrophel and Stella,* only in far greater abundance. Mere 'thin diet of dainty words,' ingenuity unrelieved by a single touch of true feeling, the stock phrases and themes common to the hundred-and-one second-rate rhymers of the day, this is all that the voluminous verse of the *Arcadia,* with the exception of a few passages here and there, has to offer. The two songs quoted below from the 'Certain Sonnets—never before printed,' of 1595, belong to the great lyrical growth of the time, and are specimens of Sidney's freest and most spontaneous manner. One of them, the passionate dirge beginning 'Ring out ye bells, let mourning shews be spread,' has a swing and force which ought long ago to have rescued it from oblivion.

MARY A. WARD.

ASTROPHEL AND STELLA.

I.

Loving in truth, and fain in verse my love to show,
That she, dear she, might take some pleasure of my pain,—
Pleasure might cause her read, reading might make her know,
Knowledge might pity win, and pity grace obtain,—
I sought fit words to paint the blackest face of woe;
Studying inventions fine, her wits to entertain,
Oft turning others' leaves, to see if thence would flow
Some fresh and fruitful showers upon my sun-burn'd brain.
But words came halting forth, wanting Invention's stay;
Invention, Nature's child, fled step-dame Study's blows;
And others' feet still seem'd but strangers in my way.
Thus, great with child to speak, and helpless in my throes,
Biting my truant pen, beating myself for spite;
Fool, said my Muse to me, look in thy heart, and write.

5.

It is most true that eyes are form'd to serve
The inward light, and that the heavenly part
Ought to be King, from whose rules who do swerve,
Rebels to nature, strive for their own smart.
It is most true, what we call Cupid's dart
An image is, which for ourselves we carve,
And, fools, adore in temple of our heart,
Till that good god make church and churchmen starve:
True, that true beauty virtue is indeed,
Whereof this beauty can be but a shade,
Which, elements with mortal mixture breed:
True, that on earth we are but pilgrims made,
And should in soul up to our country move:
True, and yet true—that I must Stella love.

18.

With what sharp checks I in myself am shent
When into Reason's audit I do go,
And by just 'counts myself a bankrupt know
Of all those goods which heaven to me hath lent;
Unable quite to pay even Nature's rent,
Which unto it by birthright I do owe;
And, which is worse, no good excuse can show,
But that my wealth I have most idly spent!
My youth doth waste, my knowledge brings forth toys;
My wit doth strive those passions to defend,
Which, for reward, spoil it with vain annoys.
I see, my course to lose myself doth bend;
I see—and yet no greater sorrow take
Than that I lose no more for Stella's sake.

23.

The curious wits, seeing dull pensiveness
Bewray itself in my long-settled eyes,
Whence those same fumes of melancholy rise,
With idle pains and missing aim, do guess.
Some, that know how my spring I did address,
Deem that my Muse some fruit of knowledge plies;
Others, because the prince my service tries,
Think that I think State errors to redress:
But harder judges judge ambition's rage—
Scourge of itself, still climbing slippery place—
Holds my young brain captived in golden cage.
O fools, or over-wise: alas, the race
Of all my thoughts hath neither stop nor start
But only Stella's eyes and Stella's heart.

26.

Though dusty wits dare scorn Astrology,
And fools can think those lamps of purest light—
Whose numbers, ways, greatness, eternity,
Promising wonders, wonder do invite—
To have for no cause birthright in the sky
But for to spangle the black weeds of Night ;
Or for some brawl, which in that chamber high,
They should still dance to please a gazer's sight.
For me, I do Nature unidle know,
And know great causes great effects procure ;
And know those bodies high reign on the low.
And if these rules did fail, proof makes me sure,
Who oft foresee my after-following race,
By only those two stars in Stella's face.

30.

Whether the Turkish new moon minded be
To fill her horns this year on Christian coast ?
How Poland's king means without leave of host
To warm with ill-made fire cold Muscovy?
If French can yet three parts in one agree?
What now the Dutch in their full diets boast?
How Holland hearts, now so good towns be lost,
Trust in the shade of pleasant Orange-tree ?
How Ulster likes of that same golden bit
Wherewith my father once made it half tame?
If in the Scotch Court be no weltering yet?
These questions busy wits to me do frame :
I, cumbered with good manners, answer do,
But know not how ; for still I think of you.

31.

With how sad steps, O Moon, thou climb'st the skies!
How silently, and with how wan a face!
What, may it be that even in heavenly place
That busy archer his sharp arrows tries!
Sure, if that long-with-love-acquainted eyes
Can judge of love, thou feel'st a lover's case,
I read it in thy looks; thy languisht grace,
To me, that feel the like, thy state descries.
Then, even of fellowship, O Moon, tell me,
Is constant love deem'd there but want of wit?
Are beauties there as proud as here they be?
Do they above love to be lov'd, and yet
Those lovers scorn whom that love doth possess?
Do they call virtue there ungratefulness?

32.

Morpheus, the lively son of deadly Sleep,
Witness of life to them that living die,
A prophet oft, and oft an history,
A poet eke, as humours fly or creep;
Since thou in me so sure a power dost keep,
That never I with clos'd-up sense do lie,
But by thy work my Stella I descry,
Teaching blind eyes both how to smile and weep;
Vouchsafe, of all acquaintance, this to tell,
Whence hast thou ivory, rubies, pearl, and gold,
To show her skin, lips, teeth, and head so well?
Fool! answers he; no Indes such treasures hold;
But from thy heart, while my sire charmeth thee,
Sweet Stella's image I do steal to me.

33.

I might !—unhappy word—O me, I might,
And then would not, or could not, see my bliss ;
Till now wrapt in a most infernal night,
I find how heavenly day, wretch ! I did miss.
Heart, rend thyself, thou dost thyself but right ;
No lovely Paris made thy Helen his :
No force, no fraud robb'd thee of thy delight,
Nor Fortune of thy fortune author is ;
But to myself myself did give the blow,
While too much wit, forsooth, so troubled me,
That I respects for both our sakes must show :
And yet could not, by rising morn foresee
How fair a day was near : O punisht eyes,
That I had been more foolish, or more wise !

37.

This night, while sleep begins with heavy wings
To hatch mine eyes, and that unbitted thought
Doth fall to stray, and my chief powers are brought
To leave the sceptre of all subject things ;
The first that straight my fancy's error brings
Unto my mind is Stella's image, wrought
By Love's own self, but with so curious drought
That she, methinks, not only shines but sings.
I start, look, hark ; but what in closed-up sense
Was held, in opened sense it flies away,
Leaving me nought but wailing eloquence.
I, seeing better sights in sight's decay,
Call'd it anew, and wooèd Sleep again ;
But him, her host, that unkind guest had slain.

39.

Come, Sleep! O Sleep, the certain knot of peace,
The baiting-place of wit, the balm of woe,
The poor man's wealth, the prisoner's release,
Th' indifferent judge between the high and low;
With shield of proof shield me from out the press
Of those fierce darts Despair at me doth throw:
O make in me those civil wars to cease;
I will good tribute pay, if thou do so.
Take thou of me smooth pillows, sweetest bed,
A chamber deaf to noise and blind to light,
A rosy garland and a weary head:
And if these things, as being thine in right,
Move not thy heavy grace, thou shalt in me,
Livelier than elsewhere, Stella's image see.

48.

Soul's joy, bend not those morning stars from me,
Where Virtue is made strong by Beauty's might;
Where Love is chastness, Pain doth learn delight,
And Humbleness grows one with Majesty.
Whatever may ensue, O let me be
Co-partner of the riches of that sight;
Let not mine eyes be hell-driven from that light;
O look, O shine, O let me die, and see.
For though I oft myself of them bemoan
That through my heart their beamy darts be gone,
Whose cureless wounds even now most freshly bleed,
Yet since my death-wound is already got,
Dear killer, spare not thy sweet-cruel shot;
A kind of grace it is to slay with speed.

61.

Oft with true sighs, oft with uncallèd tears,
Now with slow words, now with dumb eloquence,
I Stella's eyes assayed, invade her ears ;
But this, at last, is her sweet-breath'd defence :
That who indeed in-felt affection bears,
So captives to his saint both soul and sense,
That, wholly hers, all selfness he forbears,
Then his desires he learns, his life's course thence.
Now, since her chaste mind hates this love in me,
With chastened mind I straight must show that she
Shall quickly me from what she hates remove.
O Doctor Cupid, thou for me reply ;
Driven else to grant, by angel's sophistry,
That I love not without I leave to love.

64.

No more, my dear, no more these counsels try ;
O give my passions leave to run their race ;
Let Fortune lay on me her worst disgrace ;
Let folk o'ercharged with brain against me cry ;
Let clouds bedim my face, break in mine eye ;
Let me no steps but of lost labour trace ;
Let all the earth with scorn recount my case,—
But do not will me from my love to fly.
I do not envy Aristotle's wit,
Nor do aspire to Caesar's bleeding fame ;
Nor aught do care though some above me sit ;
Nor hope nor wish another course to frame,
But that which once may win thy cruel heart :
Thou art my wit, and thou my virtue art.

66.

And do I see some cause a hope to feed,
Or doth the tedious burden of long woe
In weakened minds quick apprehending breed
Of every image which may comfort show?
I cannot brag of word, much less of deed,
Fortune wheels still with me in one sort slow ;
My wealth no more, and no whit less my need ;
Desire still on stilts of Fear doth go.
And yet amid all fears a hope there is,
Stolen to my heart since last fair night, nay day,
Stella's eyes sent to me the beams of bliss,
Looking on me while I look'd other way :
But when mine eyes back to their heaven did move,
They fled with blush which guilty seemed of love.

69.

O joy too high for my low style to show !
O bliss fit for a nobler state than me !
Envy, put out thine eyes, lest thou do see
What oceans of delight in me do flow !
My friend, that oft saw through all masks my woe,
Come, come, and let me pour myself on thee.
Gone is the Winter of my misery !
My Spring appears ; O see what here doth grow :
For Stella hath, with words where faith doth shine,
Of her high heart given me the monarchy :
I, I, O I, may say that she is mine !
And though she give but thus conditionly,
This realm of bliss while virtuous course I take,
No kings be crown'd but they some covenants make.

74.

I never drank of Aganippe well,
Nor ever did in shade of Tempe sit,
And Muses scorn with vulgar brains to dwell;
Poor layman I, for sacred rites unfit.
Some do I hear of poets' fury tell,
But, God wot, wot not what they mean by it;
And this I swear by blackest brook of hell,
I am no pick-purse of another's wit.
How falls it then, that with so smooth an ease
My thoughts I speak; and what I speak doth flow
In verse, and that my verse best wits doth please?
Guess we the cause! What, is it thus? Fie, no.
Or so? Much less. How then? Sure thus it is,
My lips are sweet, inspired with Stella's kiss.

84.

High way, since you my chief Parnassus be,
And that my Muse, to some ears not unsweet,
Tempers her words to trampling horses' feet
More oft than to a chamber-melody.
Now, blessèd you bear onward blessèd me
To her, where I my heart, safe-left, shall meet;
My Muse and I must you of duty greet
With thanks and wishes, wishing thankfully.
Be you still fair, honoured by public heed;
By no encroachment wrong'd, nor time forgot;
Nor blam'd for blood, nor sham'd for sinful deed;
And that you know I envy you no lot
Of highest wish, I wish you so much bliss,—
Hundreds of years you Stella's feet may kiss.

87.

When I was forced from Stella ever dear—
Stella, food of my thoughts, heart of my heart—
Stella, whose eyes make all my tempests clear—
By Stella's laws of duty to depart ;
Alas, I found that she with me did smart ;
I saw that tears did in her eyes appear ;
I saw that sighs her sweetest lips did part,
And her sad words my sadded sense did hear.
For me, I wept to see pearls scattered so ;
I sighed her sighs, and wailèd for her woe ;
Yet swam in joy, such love in her was seen.
Thus, while th' effect most bitter was to me,
And nothing then the cause more sweet could be,
I had been vexed, if vexed I had not been.

90.

Stella, think not that I by verse seek fame,
Who seek, who hope, who love, who live but thee ;
Thine eyes my pride, thy lips mine history :
If thou praise not, all other praise is shame.
Nor so ambitious am I, as to frame
A nest for my young praise in laurel tree :
In truth, I swear I wish not there should be
Graved in my epitaph a Poet's name.
Nor, if I would, could I just title make,
That any laud thereof to me should grow,
Without my plumes from others' wings I take :
For nothing from my wit or will doth flow,
Since all my words thy beauty doth endite,
And Love doth hold my hand, and makes me write.

92.

Be your words made, good Sir, of Indian ware,
That you allow me them by so small rate?
Or do you curted Spartans imitate?
Or do you mean my tender ears to spare,
That to my questions you so total are?
When I demand of Phoenix-Stella's state,
You say, forsooth, you left her well of late:
O God, think you that satisfies my care?
I would know whether she did sit or walk;
How clothed; how waited on; sighed she, or smiled;
Whereof,—with whom,—how often did she talk;
With what pastimes Time's journey she beguiled;
If her lips deigned to sweeten my poor name:
Say all; and all well said, still say the same.

92.

O fate, O fault, O curse, child of my bliss!
What sobs can give words grace my grief to show?
What ink is black enough to paint my woe?
Through me—wretch me—even Stella vexèd is.
Yet, truth—if caitif's breath may call thee—this
Witness with me, that my foul stumbling so,
From carelessness did in no manner grow;
But wit, confused with too much care, did miss.
And do I, then, myself this vain 'scuse give?
I have—live I, and know this—harmèd thee:
Though worlds 'quit me, shall I myself forgive?
Only with pains my pains thus easèd be,
That all thy hurts in my heart's wrack I read;
I cry thy sighs, my dear, thy tears I bleed.

107.

Stella, since thou so right a princess art
Of all the powers which life bestows on me,
That ere by them ought undertaken be,
They first resort unto that sovereign part ;
Sweet, for a while give respite to my heart,
Which pants as though it still should leap to thee :
And on my thoughts give thy lieutenancy
To this great cause, which needs both use and art.
And as a queen, who from her presence sends
Whom she employs, dismiss from thee my wit,
Till it have wrought what thy own will attends,
On servants' shame oft masters' blame doth sit :
O let not fools in me thy works reprove,
And scorning say, ' See what it is to love !'

SONGS FROM ASTROPHEL AND STELLA.

Seventh Song. Stella singing.

Whose senses in so ill consort their step-dame Nature lays,
That ravishing delight in them most sweet tunes do not raise ;
Or if they do delight therein, yet are so closed with wit,
As with sententious lips to set a title vain on it ;
O let them hear these sacred tunes, and learn in Wonder's
  schools,
To be, in things past bounds of wit, fools—if they be not fools !

Who have so leaden eyes, as not to see sweet Beauty's show,
Or, seeing, have so wooden wits, as not that worth to know,
Or, knowing, have so muddy minds, as not to be in love,
Or, loving, have so frothy thoughts, as eas'ly thence to move ;
O let them see these heavenly beams, and in fair letters read
A lesson fit, both sight and skill, love and firm love to breed.

Hear then, but then with wonder hear, see, but adoring, see,
No mortal gifts, no earthly fruits, now here descended be:
See, do you see this face? a face, nay, image of the skies,
Of which, the two life-giving lights are figured in her eyes:
Hear you this soul-invading voice, and count it but a voice?
The very essence of their tunes, when angels do rejoice!

Tenth Song.   Absence.

O dear life, when shall it be
That mine eyes thine eyes shall see,
And in them thy mind discover
Whether absence have had force
Thy remembrance to divorce
From the image of thy lover?

Or if I myself find not,
After parting, aught forgot,
Nor debarred from Beauty's treasure,
Let not tongue aspire to tell
In what high joys I shall dwell;
Only thought aims at the pleasure.

Thought, therefore, I will send thee
To take up the place for me:
Long I will not after tarry,
There, unseen, thou mayst be bold,
Those fair wonders to behold,
Which in them my hopes do carry.

Thought, see thou no place forbear,
Enter bravely everywhere,
Seize on all to her belonging;
But if thou wouldst guarded be,
Fearing her beams, take with thee
Strength of liking, rage of longing.

Think of that most grateful time
When my leaping heart will climb,

In my lips to have his biding,
There those roses for to kiss,
Which do breathe a sugared bliss,
Opening rubies, pearls dividing.

*　　*　　*　　*　　*

Think, think of those dallyings,
When with dove-like murmurings,
With glad moaning, passèd anguish,
We change eyes, and heart for heart,
Each to other do depart,
Joying till joy makes us languish.

O my thought, my thoughts surcease,
Thy delights my woes increase,
My life melts with too much thinking ;
Think no more, but die in me,
Till thou shalt revivèd be,
At her lips my nectar drinking.

[From the collection of Miscellaneous Poems first published in the *Arcadia*
of 1595, under the heading of *Certain Sonnets of Sir Philip Sidney never
before printed.*]

PHILOMELA.

The nightingale, as soon as April bringeth
　Unto her rested sense a perfect waking,
While late bare earth, proud of new clothing, springeth,
　Sings out her woes, a thorne her song-book making,
　And mournfully bewailing,
Her throat in tunes expresseth
What grief her breast oppresseth
　For Tereus' force on her chaste will prevailing.
O Philomela fair, O take some gladness,
That here is juster cause of plaintful sadness :
Thine earth now springs, mine fadeth ;
Thy thorn without, my thorn my heart invadeth.

A DIRGE.

Ring out your bells, let mourning shews be spread;
For Love is dead:
  All Love is dead, infected
With plague of deep disdain:
  Worth, as nought worth, rejected,
And Faith fair scorn doth gain.
   From so ungrateful fancy,
   From such a female frenzy,
   From them that use men thus,
   Good Lord, deliver us!

Weep, neighbours, weep; do you not hear it said
That Love is dead?
  His death-bed, peacock's folly;
His winding-sheet is shame;
  'His will, false-seeming wholly;
His sole executor, blame.
   From so ungrateful fancy,
   From such a female frenzy,
   From them that use men thus,
   Good Lord, deliver us!

Let dirge be sung, and trentals rightly read,
For Love is dead;
  Sir Wrong his tomb ordaineth
My mistress' marble heart;
  Which epitaph containeth,
'Her eyes were once his dart.'
   From so ungrateful fancy,
   From such a female frenzy,
   From them that use men thus,
   Good Lord, deliver us!

Alas, I lie: rage hath this error bred;
Love is not dead;

Love is not dead, but sleepeth
In her unmatchèd mind,
Where she his counsel keepeth,
Till due deserts she find.
Therefore from so vile fancy,
To call such wit a frenzy,
Who Love can temper thus,
Good Lord, deliver us !

I.

Thou blind man's mark, thou fool's self-chosen snare,
Fond fancy's scum, and dregs of scattered thought :
Band of all evils ; cradle of causeless care ;
Thou web of will, whose end is never wrought :
Desire ! Desire ! I have too dearly bought,
With price of mangled mind, thy worthless ware ;
Too long, too long, asleep thou hast me brought,
Who should my mind to higher things prepare.
But yet in vain thou hast my ruin sought ;
In vain thou mad'st me to vain things aspire ;
In vain thou kindlest all thy smoky fire ;
For Virtue hath this better lesson taught,—
Within myself to seek my only hire,
Desiring nought but how to kill Desire.

2.

Leave me, O Love, which reachest but to dust ;
And thou, my mind, aspire to higher things ;
Grow rich in that which never taketh rust ;
Whatever fades, but fading pleasure brings.
Draw in thy beams, and humble all thy might
To that sweet yoke where lasting freedoms be ;
Which breaks the clouds, and opens forth the light,
That doth both shine, and give us sight to see.

O take fast hold ; let that light be thy guide
In this small course which birth draws out to death,
And think how ill becometh him to slide,
Who seeketh heaven, and comes of heavenly breath.
Then farewell, world ; thy uttermost I see :
Eternal Love, maintain thy life in me !

FROM THE 'ARCADIA.'

Dorus to Pamela.

My sheep are thoughts, which I both guide and serve ;
Their pasture is fair hills of fruitless love,
On barren sweets they feed, and feeding starve.
I wail their lot, but will not other prove ;
My sheephook is wan hope, which all upholds ;
My weeds Desire, cut out in endless folds ;
  What wool my sheep shall bear, whilst thus they live,
  In you it is, you must the judgment give.

Night.

O Night, the ease of care, the pledge of pleasure,
Desire's best mean, harvest of hearts affected,
The seat of peace, the throne which is erected
Of human life to be the quiet measure ;
Be victor still of Phoebus' golden treasure,
Who hath our sight with too much sight infected ;
Whose light is cause we have our lives neglected,
Turning all Nature's course to self displeasure.
These stately stars in their now shining faces,
With sinless sleep, and silence wisdom's mother,
Witness his wrong which by thy help is easèd :
Thou art, therefore, of these our desert places
The sure refuge ; by thee and by no other
My soul is blest, sense joy'd, and fortune raisèd.

FULKE GREVILLE,

LORD BROOKE.

[FULKE GREVILLE, LORD BROOKE, born 1554, was the school-fellow and friend of Sidney. He held two important offices under Elizabeth's government, that of Secretary to the Principality of Wales (1583), and that of Treasurer of Marine Causes (1597). He seems to have spent the early years of James' reign in retirement, returning to Court about 1614, in which year he was made Chancellor of the Exchequer and Privy Councillor. In 1620 he was created Baron Brooke of Beauchamp's Court, and died in 1628 from the effects of a wound given him by a servant. The only works published in his lifetime were an elegiac poem on Sidney in *Phœnix Nest* (1593), a poem in Bodenham's *Belvedere* (1600), three poems in *England's Helicon*, and the Tragedy of *Mustapha* in 1609. An edition of his works, excluding the *Poems of Monarchy and Religion* (published 1670) appeared in 1633. In 1870 his complete works, prose and verse, were edited in the Fuller Worthies Library by the Rev. A. B. Grosart.]

The poems of Lord Brooke, written for the most part 'in his youth and familar exercise with Sir Philip Sidney,' according to the title page of the 1633 editions, have a real and permanent value, though they can never hope to appeal to any other than a limited and so to speak professional audience. They are the work of a man of great thinking power, and of singular nobility and upright-ness of character. The sheer power of mind shewn in these strange plays and treatises and so-called sonnets is undeniable. Every now and then it leads their author to a genuine success, to a fine chorus, a speech of weird and concentrated passion as impressive as a speech of Ford's, though even less human, a shorter poem of real and fanciful beauty. But generally we find this inborn power strug-gling with a medium of expression so cumbrous and intricate and stumbling, that neither thought nor fancy can find their way through it. Words are taxed beyond what they can bear ; all thoughts, whether great or trivial, are tortured into the same over-laboured dress ; there is no ease, no flow, no joy. More than this ; not only is the manner far removed from the true manner of poetry, but in large tracts of it the matter handled has nothing to do with poetry, 'The Declination of Monarchy,' 'Of Weak-minded Tyrants,' ' Of Laws,' 'Of Nobility,' 'Of Commerce,' 'Of Crown Revenue,'—these are not the subjects of the poet.   In the seventeenth century they were the subjects of the pamphleteer, and no one could have treated them in prose with greater ability and a more Miltonic swing and pregnancy of phrase than Lord Brooke.   Buried in pages of wearisome verse, his discussions of these and such-like topics, in spite of acuteness, in spite of a wide and modern political view, are intolerable as poetry and unreadable as political and philosophical argument.   His theory—as it was the theory of so many of his later contemporaries, of Sir John Davies, of Christopher Brooke, and Sir William Alexander—seems to have been that all subjects of serious human interest were equally within the sphere of poetry, or could be turned into poetry by a sort of *coup de main*.   On the other hand, he not only attempted to treat scientific matter poetically, but also to treat genuinely poetical matter, such as natural beauty or human passion, or religious emotion, scientifically, making analysis and comparison play the part of feeling, and preserving the same stiffness and pedantry of movement in the most passionate or graceful situations.   Yet at bottom Lord Brooke had many of the poet's gifts.   His worst things contain a scant measure of fine lines and passages, such as perhaps few other Elizabethan writers below the first circle could have written, expressed with admirable resonance and terseness.   At his best he rises very high, as we hope to show in the following extracts.   But of the exquisite Elizabethan fluency and archness, the transparent sweetness of Spenser, the spontaneity and brilliancy of Sidney, Lord Brooke had little or nothing.   His poetry bears witness in an extraordinary degree to the mental energy and acuteness of the time ; it is wholly lacking in the Elizabethan charm.   Sir William Davenant is reported to have said of him, that he had written good poetry in his youth and had then spoilt it by keeping it by him till old age.   Lord Brooke's own explanation of the peculiar quality of his work however goes deeper than this.   In the so-called Life of Sidney, after making a half apology for the romance and fancifulness of Sidney's *Arcadia*, and justifying the book as after all not lacking in 'images and examples (as directing threads) to guide every man through the confused Labyrinth of his own desires and life,' he continues : 'For my own part I found my creeping genius more fixed upon the images of life than the images of wit, and therefore chose not to write to them on whose foot the black ox had not already trod, as the proverb is, but to those only that are weatherbeaten in the sea of this world, such as having lost the sight of their gardens and groves, study to sail on a right course among rocks and quicksands.' Thus beside the young unpruned imagination of his friend, quenched before time had stolen from it a particle of its joyousness and luxuriance, he places his own elder and way-worn muse—the poetry of 'Life' beside the poetry of 'Wit.' Such a distinction breathes the spirit of a new world ; and in parting Lord Brooke from the writer of *Astrophel and Stella* places him mentally beside Milton and Bacon.

The folio edition of his works, of 1633, the materials for which had been revised and collected for publication by the author, contains three treatises, on ' Human Learning,' on 'Wars,' and 'An Inquisition upon Fame and Honour,' the tragedies of *Alaham* and *Mustapha*, and the hundred and ten sonnets of *Caelica*. The *Poems of Monarchy and Religion* were published later in 1670. *Mustapha* had also appeared earlier in 1609. To these Mr. Grosart, in a recent complete edition has added a few miscellaneous poems, the lament for Sidney, published in *The Phoenix' Nest* of 1593, two or three poems from *England's Helicon*, and a doubtful one from *The Paradise of Dainty Devices*. Of these we are not now concerned with the treatises. They were originally meant to serve as choruses between the acts of *Alaham* and *Mustapha*— a whimsical instance of the impracticability of Lord Brooke's genius—and, as we have already said, they are not without lines and passages of poetry. But in the main they are either matter for the biographer, or for the student of seventeenth-century speculation. The collection of shorter poems under the name of *Caelica* contains a number of love-poems, some perhaps genuine, others mocking and cynical, which, as in Habington's *Castara*, lead up to a concluding group of religious and philosophical pieces. With sonnets, properly so called, they have nothing more in com mon than the name. Some of them are undoubtedly echoes of *Astrophel and Stella*, harsh fantastic echoes which but rarely recall the music of the earlier strain. Sonnet 46, ' Patience, weak-fortun'd and weak-minded wit,' is an 'exercise' on the same theme as Sonnet 56 of *Astrophel and Stella*. The end of Sonnet 45 is a reminiscence of the tenth song in the same collection, and two better illustrations of poetical failure on the one hand, and such poetical success as the kind of theme admits of on the other, could scarcely be brought together than the thirteenth sonnet of *Caelica*, 'Cupid his boy's play many times forbidden,' as compared with the well-known 'His mother dear Cupid offended late' of *Astrophel and Stella*. This list might be largely extended with ever-increasing profit to Sidney's reputation. Still, when all deductions are made, *Caelica* brings its own peculiar reward to the reader. There are veins of poetry in it of a remote and fanciful kind, and what is not poetry will often affect us with the old-world charm, which is the true explanation of *Cultismo* wherever it appears in literary history, the charm of ingenuity as such, of mind-play pure and simple. To which may be added that among the religious poems of *Caelica* there is perhaps simpler and sincerer work than Lord Brooke produced anywhere else.

With regard to the poem-plays of *Alaham* and *Mustapha*, which may be compared with the much inferior 'Monarchical tragedies' of Sir William Alexander, nothing can be added to the well-known criticism of Charles Lamb, which describes them as 'political treatises, not plays,' in which 'all is made frozen and rigid with intellect,' or to Lord Brooke's own account of them as intended to illustrate the 'high ways of ambitious governours,' and the public and private ruin to which such ways tend. In spite of tragical situations, in spite of the injured youth of Mustapha, and the maiden heroism of Caelica, they are not tragical, and for all their high intellectual interest, they are very seldom poetical. In those rare instances however, where the poet succeeds in mastering and transforming the philosopher, there we have a very noble and perfect effect, such an effect as is reached in *The Chorus of Tartars* quoted below, where the plea of the world against the claims and promises of religion is put with a passion and directness which lifts it far above its surroundings.

The outer facts of Lord Brooke's prolonged literary career bring the world of Spenser and the world of Milton together in a striking way. He, with Spenser, Dyer, and Sidney, was a member of Harvey's 'Areopagus,' and there is other evidence of intercourse between him and Spenser. His friendship with Sidney is one of the classical stories in the history of English letters. On the other hand Davenant, the founder of the Restoration theatre, was the *protégé* of his old age, and he died the year before the composition of the *Ode on the Morning of Christ's Nativity.*

MARY A. WARD.

Chorus of Tartars.

[From the Tragedy of *Mustapha.*]

Vast Superstition ! Glorious style of weakness !
Sprung from the deep disquiet of man's passion,
To dissolution and despair of Nature :
Thy texts bring princes' titles into question :
Thy prophets set on work the sword of tyrants :
They manacle sweet Truth with their distinctions :
Let Virtue blood : teach Cruelty for God's sake ;
Fashioning one God ; yet Him of many fashions,
Like many-headed Error, in their passions.
Mankind ! Trust not these superstitious dreams,
Fear's idols, Pleasure's relics, Sorrow's pleasures :
They make the wilful hearts their holy temples,
The rebels unto government their martyrs.
No : Thou child of false miracles begotten !
False miracles, which are but ignorance of cause,
Lift up the hopes of thy abjected prophets :
Courage and Worth abjure thy painted heavens.
Sickness, thy blessings are ; Misery thy trial ;
Nothing, thy way unto eternal being ;
Death, to salvation ; and the grave to heaven.
So blest be they, so angel'd, so eterniz'd
That tie their senses to thy senseless glories,
And die, to cloy the after-age with stories.
Man should make much of Life, as Nature's table,
Wherein she writes the cypher of her glory.
Forsake not Nature, nor misunderstand her :
Her mysteries are read without Faith's eye-sight :
She speaketh in our flesh ; and from our senses
Delivers down her wisdoms to our reason.
If any man would break her laws to kill,
Nature doth for defence allow offences.

She neither taught the father to destroy :
Nor promis'd any man, by dying, joy.[1]

CHORUS OF PRIESTS.

[From *Mustapha.*]

Oh wearisome condition of Humanity !
Born under one law, to another bound,
Vainly begot and yet forbidden vanity,
Created sick, commanded to be sound :
What meaneth Nature by these diverse laws?
Passion and reason self-division cause.
Is it the mask or majesty of Power
To make offences that it may forgive?
Nature herself doth her own self deflower
To hate those errors she herself doth give.
For how should man think that he may not do
If Nature did not fail and punish too?
Tyrant to others, to herself unjust,
Only commands things difficult and hard ;
Forbids us all things which it knows we lust ;
Makes easy pains, impossible reward.
If Nature did not take delight in blood,
She would have made more easy ways to good.
We that are bound by vows and by promotion,
With pomp of holy sacrifice and rites,
To preach belief in God and stir devotion,
To preach of Heaven's wonders and delights,
Yet when each of us in his own heart looks
He finds the God there far unlike his books.

---

[1] These last four lines are in allusion to the plot of *Mustapha*, which turns upon the murder of the unresisting and innocent Mustapha by his father Solyman, in consequence of certain unjust suspicions.

Chorus of Good and Evil Spirits.

[From *Alaham.*]

Evil Spirits.

Why did you not defend that which was once your own?
Between us two, the odds of worth, by odds of power is known.
Besides map clearly out your infinite extent,
Even in the infancy of Time, when man was innocent[1];
Could this world then yield aught to envy or desire,
Where pride of courage made men fall, and baseness rais'd them
    higher?
Where they that would be great, to be so must be least,
And where to bear and suffer wrong, was Virtue's native crest.
Man's skin was then his silk; the world's wild fruit his food;
His wisdom, poor simplicity; his trophies inward good.
No majesty for power; nor glories for man's worth;
Nor any end, but—as the plants—to bring each other forth.
Temples and vessels fit for outward sacrifice,
As they came in, so they go out with that which you call vice.
The priesthood few and poor; no throne but open air;
For that which you call good, allows of nothing that is fair.
No Pyramids rais'd up above the force of thunder,
No Babel-walls by greatness built, for littleness a wonder,
No conquest testifying wit, with [dauntless] courage mixt;
As wheels whereon the world must run, and never can be fixt.
No arts or characters to read the great God in,
Nor stories of acts done; for these all entered with the sin.
A lazy calm, wherein each fool a pilot is!
The glory of the skilful shines, where men may go amiss.
Till we came in there was no trial of your might,
And since we were in men, yourselves presume of little right.
Then cease to blast the Earth with your abstracted dreams,
And strive no more to carry men against Affection's streams.

    *   *   *   *   *   *   *

Keep therefore where you are; descend not but ascend:
For, underneath the sun, be sure no brave state is your friend.

[1] i. e. 'consider the boundless power you enjoyed in the golden age.'

Good Spirits.

What have you won by this, but that curst under Sin,
You make and mar ; throw down and raise ; as ever to begin ;
Like meteors in the air, you blaze but to burn out ;
And change your shapes—like phantom'd clouds—to leave weak
    eyes in doubt.
Not Truth but truth-like grounds you work upon,
Varying in all but this, that you can never long be one :
Then play here with your art, false miracle devise ;
Deceive, and be deceivèd still, be foolish and seem wise ;
In Peace erect your thrones, your delicacy spread ;
The flowers of time corrupt, soon spring, and are as quickly
    dead.
Let War, which—tempest-like— all with itself o'erthrows,
Make of this diverse world a stage of blood-enamelled shows.
Successively both these yet this fate follow will,
That all their glories be no more than change from ill to ill.

SEED-TIME AND HARVEST.

[From *Caelica*, Sonnet XL.]

The nurse-life wheat within his green husk growing
Flatters our hopes and tickles our desire ;
Nature's true riches in sweet beauties shewing,
Which set all hearts with labour's love on fire.
No less fair is the wheat when golden ear,
Shews unto hope the joys of near enjoying :
Fair and sweet is the bud ; more sweet and fair
The rose, which proves that Time is not destroying.
Caelica, your youth, the morning of delight,
Enamel'd o'er with beauties white and red,
All sense and thoughts did to belief invite,
That love and glory there are brought to bed ;
    And your ripe years, Love, now they grow no higher,
    Turn all the spirits of man into desire [1].

[1] The reading of these last two lines is conjectural.

Elizabetha Regina.

[From *Caelica*, Sonnet LXXXII.]

Under a throne I saw a virgin sit,
The red and white rose quartered in her face,
Star of the North!—and for true guards to it,
Princes, church, states, all pointing out her grace.
The homage done her was not born of Wit;
Wisdom admir'd, Zeal took Ambition's place,
State in her eyes taught Order how to fit
And fix Confusion's unobserving race.
  Fortune can here claim nothing truly great,
  But that this princely creature is her seat.

Sonnet.

[From *Caelica*, Sonnet CX.]

Sion lies waste, and Thy Jerusalem,
O Lord, is fall'n to utter desolation;
Against Thy prophets and Thy holy men,
There sin hath wrought a fatal combination:
  Profan'd Thy name, Thy worship overthrown,
  And made Thee, living Lord, a God unknown.

Thy powerful laws, Thy wonders of creation,
Thy word incarnate, glorious heaven, dark hell,
Lie shadowed under man's degeneration;
Thy Christ still crucified for doing well;
  Impiety, O Lord, sits on Thy throne,
  Which makes Thee living Lord, a God unknown.

Man's superstition hath Thy truth entombed,
His atheism again her pomps defaceth;
That sensual, insatiable vast womb,
Of thy seen Church, Thy unseen Church disgraceth;
  There lives no truth, with them that seem Thine own,
  Which makes Thee, living Lord, a God unknown.

Yet unto Thee, Lord—mirror of transgression—
We who for earthly idols have forsaken,
Thy heavenly image—sinless, pure impression—
And so in nets of vanity lie taken,
　　All desolate implore that to Thine own,
　　Lord, Thou no longer live a God unknown.

Yea, Lord, let Israel's plagues not be eternal,
Nor sin for ever cloud Thy sacred mountains,
Nor with false flames spiritual but infernal,
Dry up Thy Mercy's ever springing fountains:
　　Rather, sweet Jesus, fill up time and come,
　　To yield to sin her everlasting doom.

An Elegy on Sir Philip Sidney[1].

Silence augmenteth grief, writing increaseth rage,
Staled are my thoughts, which loved and lost the wonder of
　　our age ;
Yet quickened now with fire, though dead with frost ere now,
Enraged I write, I know not what ; dead—quick—I know not how.

Hard-hearted minds relent and Rigour's tears abound,
And Envy strangely rues his end, in whom no fault she found.
Knowledge her light hath lost, Valour hath slain her knight,
Sidney is dead, dead is my friend, dead is the world's delight.

Place pensive wails his fall, whose presence was her pride,
Time crieth out, my ebb is come ; his life was my spring-tide !
Fame mourns in that she lost the ground of her reports,
Each living wight laments his lack, and all in sundry sorts.

He was (woe worth that word !) to each well-thinking mind
A spotless friend, a matchless man, whose virtue ever shined,
Declaring in his thoughts, his life and that he writ,
Highest conceits, longest foresights, and deepest works of wit.

*　　*　　*　　*　　*　　*　　*

[1] The authorship of this poem is by no means certain. Lamb however
believed it to be by Lord Brooke.

Farewell to you my hopes, my wonted waking dreams,
Farewell sometimes enjoyèd joy, eclipsèd are thy beams,
Farewell self-pleasing thoughts, which quietness brings forth,
And farewell friendship's sacred league, uniting minds of worth.

And farewell merry heart, the gift of guiltless minds,
And all sports, which for life's restore, variety assigns :
Let all that sweet is void ; in me no mirth may dwell ;
Philip the cause of all this woe, my life's content, farewell !

Now rhyme, the son of rage, which art no kin to skill,
And endless grief, which deads my life yet knows not how to kill,
Go, seek that hapless tomb, which if ye hap to find,
Salute the stones that keep the limbs, that held so good a mind

SIR EDWARD DYER.

[Born about 1550 at Sharpham near Glastonbury; educated at Balliol College, Oxford; ambassador to Denmark 1589; knighted 1596; died 1607.]

Sir Edward Dyer, 'for Elegy most sweete, solempne and of high conceit,' according to a contemporary judgment, makes the last in importance, though the first in date, of that trio of poet-friends celebrated in Sidney's well-known Pastoral:

> 'Join hearts and hands, so let it be:
> Make but one mind in bodies three.'

Very little authentic verse of his is now extant, nor is it probable that he produced much. On the other hand he has been freely credited with verses that do not belong to him, especially with certain poems that are now known to be by Lodge. Mr. Grosart has collected twelve pieces which may be attributed to him with a fair amount of certainty. Of these 'A Fancy' is interesting as having provoked a much better poem on the same model by Lord Brooke, and a later imitation by Robert Southwell. It is however too rambling and unequal for quotation. Dyer is now remembered by one poem only, the well-known 'My mind to me a kingdom is,' which though fluent and spirited verse, probably owes most of its reputation to the happiness of its opening. The little poem 'To Phillis the Fair Shepherdess' is in the lighter, less hackneyed Elizabethan vein, and makes a welcome interlude among the 'woeful ballads' which immediately surround it in *England's Helicon*, where it first appeared. Still, when all is said, Dyer, a man of action and affairs rather than of letters, is chiefly interesting for his connection with Sidney and Greville; and that stiff pathetic engraving of Sidney's funeral, which represents him as pall-bearer side by side with Lord Brooke, throws a light upon his memory that none of his poems have power to shed.

The last two extracts given below are taken from a book of which an apparently unique copy (dated 1588) is preserved in the Bodleian Library, under the title of *Sixe Idillia* (from Theocritus). Mr. Collier attributes this book to Dyer, on the ground of the initials E. D. given on the back of the title-page. This is weak evidence, but the fluency and sweetness of the translations make us loth to reject it.

MARY A. WARD.

My Mind to me a Kingdom is.

My mind to me a kingdom is,
   Such present joys therein I find,
That it excels all other bliss
   That earth affords or grows by kind :
Though much I want which most would have,
Yet still my mind forbids to crave.

No princely pomp, no wealthy store,
   No force to win the victory,
No wily wit to salve a sore,
   No shape to feed a loving eye ;
To none of these I yield as thrall :
For why? My mind doth serve for all.

I see how plenty [surfeits] oft,
   And hasty climbers soon do fall ;
I see that those which are aloft
   Mishap doth threaten most of all :
They get with toil, they keep with fear ;
Such cares my mind could never bear.

Content to live, this is my stay ;
   I seek no more than may suffice ;
I press to bear no haughty sway ;
   Look, what I lack my mind supplies :
Lo, thus I triumph like a king,
Content with that my mind doth bring.

Some have too much, yet still do crave ;
   I little have, and seek no more.
They are but poor, though much they have,
   And I am rich with little store ;
They poor, I rich ; they beg, I give ;
They lack, I leave ; they pine, I live.

I laugh not at another's loss ;
　I grudge not at another's pain ;
No worldly waves my mind can toss ;
　My state at one doth still remain :
I fear no foe, I fawn no friend ;
I loathe not life, nor dread my end.

Some weigh their pleasure by their lust,
　Their wisdom by their rage of will ;
Their treasure is their only trust ;
　A cloaked craft their store of skill :
But all the pleasure that I find
Is to maintain a quiet mind.

My wealth is health and perfect ease :
　My conscience clear my chief defence ;
I neither seek by bribes to please,
　Nor by deceit to breed offence :
Thus do I live ; thus will I die ;
Would all did so as well as I !

To Phillis the Fair Shepherdess.

My Phillis hath the morning Sun,
　At first to look upon her :
And Phillis hath morn-waking birds,
　Her rising still to honour.
My Phillis hath prime feathered flowers,
　That smile when she treads on them :
And Phillis hath a gallant flock
　That leaps since she doth own them.
But Phillis hath too hard a heart,
　Alas, that she should have it !
It yields no mercy to desert
　Nor grace to those that crave it.

Sweet Sun, when thou look'st on,
 Pray her regard my moan!
Sweet birds when you sing to her
 To yield some pity woo her!
Sweet flowers that she treads on,
 Tell her, her beauty dreads one.
And if in life her love she nill agree me,
Pray her before I die, she will come see me.

HELEN'S EPITHALAMION.

[From the *Sixe Idillia*.]

Like as the rising morning shows a grateful lightening,
When sacred night is past and winter now lets loose the spring,
So glittering Helen shined among the maids, lusty and tall.
As is the furrow in a field that far outstretcheth all,
Or in a garden is a Cypress tree, or in a trace
A steed of Thessaly, so she to Sparta was a grace.
No damsel with such works as she her baskets used to fill,
Nor in a diverse coloured web a woof of greater skill
Doth cut from off the loom : nor any hath such songs and lays
Unto her dainty harp, in Dian's and Minerva's praise,
As Helen hath, in whose bright eyes all Loves and Graces be.
O fair, O lovely maid, a matron now is made of thee ;
But we will every spring unto the leaves in meadows go
To gather garlands sweet, and there not with a little woe,
Will often think of thee, O Helen, as the sucking lambs
Desire the strouting bags and presence of their tender dams,
We all betimes for thee a wreath of Melitoe will knit,
And on a shady plane for thee will safely fasten it,
And all betimes for thee, under a shady plane below,
Out of a silver box the sweetest ointment will bestow ;
And letters shall be written in the bark that men may see
And read, Do humble reverence, for I am Helen's tree.

THE PRAYER OF THEOCRITUS FOR SYRACUSE.

(*Idyll* 16.)

O Jupiter, and thou Minerva fierce in fight,
And thou Proserpina, who with thy mother hast renown
By Lysimelia streams, in Ephyra that wealthy town,
Out of our island drive our enemies, our bitter fate,
Along the Sardine sea, that death of friends they may relate
Unto their children and their wives, and that the towns opprest
By enemies, of th' old inhabitants may be possest :
That they may till the fields, and sheep upon the downs may bleat
By thousands infinite and fat, and that the herd of neat
As to their stalls they go may press the lingering traveller.
Let grounds be broken up for seed, what time the grasshopper
Watching the shepherds by their flocks, in boughs close sing-
      ing lies,
And let the spiders spread their slender webs in armories,
So that of war the very name may not be heard again.
But let the Poets strive, King Hiero's glory for to strain
Beyond the Scythian sea, and far beyond those places where
Semiramis did build those stately walls and rule did bear.
'Mongst whom I will be one : for many other men beside
Jove's daughters love, whose study still shall be both far and wide,
Sicilian Arethusa with the people to advance
And warlike Hiero.   Ye Graces who keep resiance
In the Thessalian mount Orchomenus, to Thebes of old
So hateful, though of you beloved, to stay I will be bold
Where I am bid to come, and I with them will still remain,
That shall invite me to their house with all my Muses' train.
Nor you will I forsake : for what to men can lovely be
Without your company ?   The Graces always be with me.

HENRY CONSTABLE.

[Born about 1555: died before 1616. His *Diana* was first published in 1592. An edition by Mr. W. C. Hazlitt was published by Pickering in 1859.]

Almost nothing is known of the life of Henry Constable. He belonged to a Yorkshire family ; he was educated at Cambridge ; he was acquainted with the Earl of Essex, with Anthony Bacon, with the Earl of Shrewsbury and his wife, with the Countess of Pembroke and Lady Rich. His sonnets to the soul of Sir Philip Sidney seem to prove that he was honoured with the friendship of the auther of the *Defence of Poesie.* As 'a Catholic and an honest man,' as he calls himself, Constable could not escape suspicion in the suspicious England of his time. He passed much of his life in exile, wandering in France, Scotland, Italy, and Poland, and was acquainted with prisons and courts.

The slight but graceful genius of Constable is best defined by some of the epithets which his contemporary critics employed. They spoke of his 'pure, quick, and high delivery of conceit.' Ben Jonson alludes to his 'ambrosiac muse.' His secular poems are 'Certaine sweete sonnets in the praise of his mistress, Diana,' conceived in the style of Ronsard and the Italians. The verses of his later days, when he had learned, as he says, 'to live alone with God,' are also sonnets in honour of the saints, and chiefly of Mary Magdalene. They are ingenious, and sometimes too cleverly confuse the passions of divine and earthly love. In addition to the sonnets we have four pleasant lyrics which Constable contributed to *England's Helicon.* We select two of these pastorals, one being an idyllic dialogue between two shepherdesses ; the other, 'The Shepherd's Song of Venus and Adonis.' These things have at once the freshness of a young, and the trivial grace of a decadent literature, so curiously varied were the influences of the Renaissance in England. Shakespeare and Constable begin where Bion leaves off. Constable was neither more nor less than a fair example of a poet who followed rather than set the fashion. His sonnets were charged and overladen with ingenious conceits, but the freshness, the music, of his more free and flowing lyrics remain, and keep their charm.

A. LANG.

A Pastoral Song between Phillis and Amarillis, two Nymphs, each answering other line for line.

Phillis.

Fie on the sleights that men devise,
   Heigh ho silly sleights :
When simple maids they would entice,
   Maids are young men's chief delights.

Amarillis.

Nay, women they witch with their eyes,
   Eyes like beams of burning sun :
And men once caught, they soon despise ;
   So are shepherds oft undone.

Phillis.

If any young man win a maid,
   Happy man is he :
By trusting him she is betrayed ;
   Fie upon such treachery.

Amarillis.

If Maids win young men with their guiles,
   Heigh ho guileful grief ;
They deal like weeping crocodiles,
   That murder men without relief.

Phillis.

I know a simple country hind,
   Heigh ho silly swain :
To whom fair Daphne proved kind,
   Was he not kind to her again ?
He vowed by Pan with many an oath,
   Heigh ho shepherds God is he :
Yet since hath changed, and broke his troth,
   Troth-plight broke will plagued be.

Amarillis.

She hath deceived many a swain,
  Fie on false deceit :
And plighted troth to them in vain,
  There can be no grief more great.
Her measure was with measure paid,
  Heigh-ho, heigh-ho equal meed :
She was beguil'd that had betrayed,
  So shall all deceivers speed.

Phillis.

If every maid were like to me,
  Heigh-ho hard of heart :
Both love and lovers scorn'd should be,
  Scorners shall be sure of smart.

Amarillis.

If every maid were of my mind
  Heigh-ho, heigh-ho lovely sweet :
They to their lovers should prove kind,
  Kindness is for maidens meet.

Phillis.

Methinks, love is an idle toy,
  Heigh-ho busy pain :
Both wit and sense it doth annoy,
  Both sense and wit thereby we gain.

Amarillis.

Tush ! Phillis, cease, be not so coy,
  Heigh-ho, heigh-ho, coy disdain :
I know you love a shepherd's boy,
  Fie ! that maidens so should feign !

Phillis.

Well, Amarillis, now I yield,
  Shepherds, pipe aloud :
Love conquers both in town and field,
  Like a tyrant, fierce and proud.

The evening star is up, ye see;
  Vesper shines; we must away;
Would every lover might agree,
  So we end our roundelay.

THE SHEPHERD'S SONG OF VENUS AND ADONIS.

Venus fair did ride,
Silver doves they drew her,
By the pleasant launds,
Ere the sun did rise:
Vesta's beauty rich
Opened wide to view her,
Philomel records
  Pleasing harmonies.
Every bird of spring
Cheerfully did sing,
  Paphos' goddess they salute;
Now Love's Queen so fair
Had of mirth no care:
  For her son had made her mute.
In her breast so tender,
He a shaft did enter,
  When her eyes beheld a boy:
Adonis was he named,
By his mother shamed[1]:
  Yet he now is Venus' joy.

Him alone she met
  Ready bound for hunting;
Him she kindly greets,
  And his journey stays;
Him she seeks to kiss,
  No devises wanting;
Him her eyes still woo;
  Him her tongue still prays.
He with blushing red
Hangeth down the head,

---

[1] See the story of Myrrha in Ovid.

Not a kiss can he afford;
His face is turned away,
Silence said her nay,
    Still she woo'd him for a word.
'Speak,' she said, 'thou fairest;
    Beauty thou impairest,
See me, I am pale and wan:
    Lovers all adore me,
    I for love implore thee;'
—Crystal tears with that down ran.

Him herewith she forced
    To come sit down by her,
She his neck embraced,
    Gazing in his face:
He, like one transformed,
    Stirred no look to eye her;
Every herb did woo him,
    Growing in that place,
Each bird with a ditty
    Prayed him for pity
In behalf of Beauty's Queen:
    Water's gentle murmur
    Craved him to love her:
Yet no liking could be seen;
'Boy,' she said, 'look on me,
Still I gaze upon thee,
Speak, I pray thee, my delight.'
    Coldly he replied,
    And in brief denied
To bestow on her a sight.

'I am now too young
To be won by beauty,
Tender are my years
I am yet a bud.'
'Fair thou art,' she said,
'Then it is thy duty,
Wert thou but a blossom,
To effect my good.

Every beauteous flower
Boasteth in my power,
Birds and beasts my laws effect :
Myrrha thy fair mother,
Most of any other,
Did my lovely hests respect.
Be with me delighted,
Thou shalt be requited,
Every Nymph on thee shall tend :
All the Gods shall love thee,
Man shall not reprove thee :
Love himself shall be thy friend.'

'Wend thee from me, Venus,
   I am not disposed ;
Thou wring'st me too hard,
   Prithee let me go ;
Fie ! what a pain it is
Thus to be enclosed,
If love begin in labour,
It will end in woe.'
'Kiss me, I will leave.'
'Here a kiss receive.'
'A short kiss I do it find :
Wilt thou leave me so ?
Yet thou shalt not go ;
Breathe once more thy balmy wind.
It smelleth of the myrrh-tree,
That to the world did bring thee,
Never was perfume so sweet.'
When she had thus spoken,
She gave him a token,
And their naked bosoms meet.

'Now,' he said, 'let's go,
Hark, the hounds are crying,
Grisly Boar is up,
Huntsmen follow fast.'
At the name of Boar,
Venus seemed dying,

Deadly coloured pale,
Roses overcast.
'Speak,' said she, 'no more,
Of following the Boar,
Thou unfit for such a chase :
Course the fearful Hare,
Venison do not spare,
If thou wilt yield Venus grace.
Shun the Boar, I pray thee,
Else I still will stay thee.'
Herein he vowed to please her mind ;
Then her arms enlarged,
Loth she him discharged ;
Forth he went as swift as wind.

Thetis Phœbus' steeds
  In the West retained,
Hunting sport was past ;
  Love her love did seek :
Sight of him too soon,
Gentle Queen she gained,
On the ground he lay,
Blood hath left his cheek.
For an orped[1] swine
Smit him in the groin,
Deadly wound his death did bring :
Which when Venus found,
She fell in a swound,
And awaked, her hands did wring.
Nymphs and Satyrs skipping,
Came together tripping,
  Echo every cry expressed :
Venus by her power
Turn'd him to a flower,
Which she weareth in her crest.

[1] bristly

Sonnet prefixed to Sidney's Apology for Poetry, 1595.

Give pardon, blessed soul! to my bold cries,
If they, importune, interrupt thy song,
Which now with joyful notes thou sing'st among
The angel-quiristers of th' heavenly skies.
Give pardon eke, sweet soul! to my slow cries,
That since I saw thee now it is so long;
And yet the tears that unto thee belong,
To thee as yet they did not sacrifice;
I did not know that thou wert dead before,
I did not feel the grief I did sustain;
The greater stroke astonisheth the more,
Astonishment takes from us sense of pain:

> I stood amaz'd when others' tears begun,
> And now begin to weep when they have done.

THOMAS WATSON.

[THOMAS WATSON was born about 1557 in London; was educated at Oxford; became a student of law, and died in London, probably in 1592. His principal writings are—a translation into Latin of Sophocles' *Antigone*, 1581; *The Ἑκατομπαθία, or Passionate Centurie of Love*, 1582; *Amyntæ Gaudia* (in Latin), 1585; *Italian Madrigals Englished*, 1590; *The Teares of Fancy, or Love Disdained*, posthumously printed in 1593. Many of his poems were printed in the Miscellanies of the time.]

Thomas Watson is one of the best of the Elizabethan 'amorettists,' or writers of wholly artificial love-poetry, and his *Hecatompathia*, which Mr. Arber's reprint has put within the reach of every one, may be taken as a type and summary of the whole class. It consists of a hundred so-called sonnets or 'passions,' each of three six-lined stanzas, and each headed with a prose introduction describing the purport and often the literary origin of the poem. A series so furnished tells its own story; and we do not require to go back to Watson's epistle *To the frendly Reader* to appreciate his 'trauaile in penning these louepassions,' or to learn that his 'paines in suffering them' were 'but supposed.' Watson, in fact, was a purely literary poet. At Oxford, says Antony Wood, he spent his time 'not in logic and philosophy, as he ought to have done, but in the smooth and pleasant studies of poetry and romance.' To these studies, however, his devotion was serious; for he mastered four languages, so that he writes as familiarly of Sophocles and Apollonius Rhodius as of Ovid, of Petrarch and Ariosto as of Ronsard. He translated the *Antigone* into Latin, and it was one of his Latin poems that gave him the fancy name of Amyntas, under which the poets of the time ranked him with Colin Clout and with Astrophel. But the literature that he affected most was the love-poetry of the Italians— of Petrarch and his followers, of Seraphine and Fiorenzuola, and many others that are quite forgotten now. Sometimes translating, sometimes paraphrasing, sometimes combining them, he tells the story of his imaginary love, its doubts and fears and hopes, its torments and disappointment and final death, in that melodious Elizabethan English which not even monotony and make-believe can wholly deprive of charm. But still, Watson and his kindred poets have little more than an historical interest. They are but the posthumous children of the Courts of Love ; their occupation is to use the scholarship and the ingenuity of the Renascence to dress up the sentiment of the Middle Age—a sentiment no more real to them than it is to ourselves. They make no appeal to us ; their note has nothing of the note of passion and of truth that rings in the verse of Sidney and of Shakespeare.

EDITOR.

From the 'Hecatompathia.'

Passion II.

In this passion the Author describeth in how piteous a case the heart of
a lover is, being (as he feigneth here) separated from his own body,
and removed into a darksome and solitary wilderness of woes. The
conveyance of his invention is plain and pleasant enough of itself, and
therefore needeth the less annotation before it.

My heart is set him down twixt hope and fears
Upon the stony bank of high Desire,
To view his own made flood of blubbering tears,
Whose waves are bitter salt, and hot as fire :
  There blows no blast of wind but ghostly groans
  Nor waves make other noise than piteous moans.
As life were spent he waiteth Charon's boat,
And thinks he dwells on side of Stygian lake :
But black Despair sometimes with open throat,
Or spiteful Jealousy doth cause him quake,
  With howling shrieks on him they call and cry
  That he as yet shall neither live nor die :
Thus void of help he sits in heavy case,
And wanteth voice to make his just complaint.
No flower but Hyacinth in all the place,
No sun comes there, nor any heav'nly saint,
  But only she, which in himself remains,
  And joys her ease though he abound in pains.

Passion XL.

The sense contained in this Sonnet will seem strange to such as never have acquainted themselves with Love and his Laws, because of the contraieties mentioned therein. But to such, as Love at any time hath had under his banner, all and every part of it will appear to be a familiar truth. It is almost word for word taken out of Petrarch (where he beginneth,

> '*Pace non truouo, e non ho da far guerra;* *Parte prima*
> *E temo, espero, etc.?*') *Sonet.* 105.

All, except three verses, which this Author hath necessarily added, for perfecting the number, which he hath determined to use in every one of these his passions.

I joy not peace, where yet no war is found ;
I fear, and hope ; I burn, yet freeze withal ;
I mount to heav'n, yet lie but on the ground ;
I compass nought, and yet I compass all :
    I live her bond, which neither is my foe,
    Nor friend ; nor holds me fast, nor lets me go ;
Love will not that I live, nor lets me die ;
Nor locks me fast, nor suffers me to scape ;
I want both eyes and tongue, yet see and cry ;
I wish for death, yet after help I gape ;
    I hate myself, but love another wight ;
    And feed on grief, in lieu of sweet delight ;
At selfsame time I both lament and joy;
I still am pleas'd, and yet displeased still ;
Love sometimes seems a God, sometimes a Boy;
Sometimes I sink, sometimes I swim at will ;
    Twixt death and life, small difference I make ;
    All this dear Dame befalls me for thy sake.

Passion LXV.

In the first and second part of this passion, the Author proveth by exam-
ples, or rather by manner of argument, *A majori ad minus,* that he may
with good reason yield himself to the empery of Love, whom the gods
themselves obey; as Jupiter in heaven, Neptune in the seas, and Pluto
in hell. In the last staff he imitateth certain Italian verses of M. Giro-
lamo Parabosco; which are as followeth:—

> '*Occhi tuoi, anzi stelle alme, et fatali*   *Selua Seconda.*
> *Oue ha prescritto il ciel mio mal, mio ben:*
> *Mie lagrime, e sospir, mio riso, e canto;*
> *Mia speme, mio timor; mio foco e giaccio:*
> *Mia noia mio piacer; mia vita e morte.*'

Who knoweth not, how often Venus' son
Hath forced Jupiter to leave his seat?
Or else, how often Neptune he hath won
From seas to sands, to play some wanton feat ?
    Or, how he hath constrained the Lord of Styx
    To come on earth, to practise loving tricks ?
If heav'n, if seas, if hell must needs obey,
And all therein be subject unto Love ;
What shall it then avail, if I gainsay,
And to my double hurt his pow'r do prove?
    No, no, I yield myself, as is but meet :
    For hitherto with sour he yields me sweet.
From out my mistress' eyes, two lightsome stars,
He destinates estate of double kind,
My tears, my smiling cheer ; my peace, my wars ;
My sighs, my songs ; my fear, my hoping mind ;
    My fire, my frost ; my joy, my sorrow's gall ;
    My curse, my praise ; my death, but life with

JOHN LYLY.

[LITTLE is known of Lyly's life. He was born in Kent in 1554, studied at Magdalen College, Oxford, was patronised by Lord Burghley, and wrote plays for the Child players at the Chapel Royal,—the 'aery of children,' alluded to in Hamlet, 'little eyases, that cry out on the top of the question and are most tyrannically clapped for 't.' He died in 1606. His *Euphues* was published, first part in 1579, second part in 1580.]

The airy mirthful plays and pretty little songs of the 'witty, comical, facetiously quick and unparalleled John Lyly,' as his publisher described him, are a standing refutation of M. Taine's picture of England in the Elizabethan age as a sort of den of wild beasts. No Frenchman in any age was ever more light and gay than Queen Elizabeth's favourite writer of comedies, and the inventor or perfecter of a fashionable style of sentimental speech among her courtiers.

The epithet 'unparalleled' applied to Lyly was more exact than puffs generally are. Though he is said to have set a fashion of talk among the ladies of the Court and their admirers, he found no imitator in letters ; his peculiar style perished from literature with himself. Scott's Sir Percie Shafton is called a Euphuist, and is supposed to be an attempt at historical reproduction, but the caricature has hardly any point of likeness with the supposed original as we see it in the language which Lyly puts into the mouth of Euphues himself. Shafton is much more like Sidney's Rhombus or Shakespeare's Holofernes, a fantastic pedant at whom the real Euphuists would have mocked with as genuine contempt as plain people of the present time. The dainty courtier Boyet, in *Love's Labour's Lost*, who, according to the sarcastic Biron, 'picks up wit as pigeons pease,' is perhaps the nearest approach to a Euphuist such as was modelled upon Lyly that we have in literature. The essence of Lyly's Euphuism is its avoidance of

cumbrous and clumsy circumlocution ; his style is neat, precise,
quick, balanced ; full of puns and pretty conceits—

> ' Talking of stones, stars, plants, of fishes, flies,
> Playing with words and idle similes,'

as a satirist of the time describes it—but never verbose and heavy
as the Euphuists' style is sometimes represented.

Lyly wrote more comedies than any writer that preceded him,
but he had no influence that can be traced upon our literature.
We seem to find the key to their character in the fact that they
were written to be played by children and heard and seen by
ladies. Their pretty love-scenes, joyous pranks, and fantastically
worded moralisings, were too light and insubstantial as fare for
the common stage, and they were superseded as Court entertain-
ments after Elizabeth's death by masques in which ingenious
scenic effects were the chief attraction, and plays with an ampler
allowance of blood and muscle. Lyly's childlike comedies, with
their pigmy fun and pretty sentiment, were brushed aside by plays
that appealed more seriously to the senses and the imagination ;
but it seems almost a pity that the example of his neatness and
finish in construction did not take root. Perhaps the daintiness in
his manipulation of his materials would have been impossible if
the materials had been coarser or more solid.

Only one of Lyly's undoubted comedies, *The Woman in the
Moon*, was written in verse, and the verse differs little from his
prose. It shows the same neat, ingenious workmanship. The
reader is not conscious of any inward pressure of heightened
feeling upon Lyly's verse ; he probably chose this instrument in
preference to prose because it had become fashionable.

W. MINTO.

SAPPHO'S SONG.

[From *Sappho and Phao.*]

O cruel Love! on thee I lay
My curse, which shall strike blind the day;
Never may sleep with velvet hand
Charm thine eyes with sacred wand ;
Thy jailors still be hopes and fears ;
Thy prison-mates groans, sighs, and tears ;
Thy play to wear out weary times,
Fantastic passions, vows, and rhymes ;
Thy bread be frowns ; thy drink be gall ;
Such as when you Phao call
The bed thou liest on by despair ;
Thy sleep, fond dreams ; thy dreams, long care;
Hope (like thy fool) at thy bed's head,
Mock thee, till madness strikes thee dead,
As Phao, thou dost me, with thy proud eyes.
In thee poor Sappho lives, in thee she dies.

APELLES' SONG.

[From *Alexander and Campaspe.*]

Cupid and my Campaspe played
At cards for kisses—Cupid paid.
He stakes his quiver, bows and arrows,
His mother's doves and team of sparrows :
Loses them too ; then down he throws
The coral of his lip, the rose
Growing on's cheek (but none knows how);
With these the crystal of his brow,
And then the dimple of his chin—
All these did my Campaspe win.

At last he set her both his eyes.—
She won, and Cupid blind did rise.
O Love, has she done this to thee?
What shall, alas! become of me?

PAN'S SONG.

[From *Midas*.]

Pan's Syrinx was a girl indeed,
Though now she's turned into a reed.
From that dear reed Pan's pipe doth come,
A pipe that strikes Apollo dumb;
Nor flute, nor lute, nor gittern can
So chant it, as the pipe of Pan.
Cross-gartered swains, and dairy girls,
With faces smug and round as pearls,
When Pan's shrill pipe begins to play,
With dancing wear out night and day;
The bag-pipe drone his hum lays by
When Pan sounds up his minstrelsy.
His minstrelsy! O base! This quill
Which at my mouth with wind I fill
Puts me in mind though her I miss
That still my Syrinx' lips I kiss.

GEORGE PEELE.

[GEORGE PEELE was probably born in 1558. He was 'a most noted poet in the University' of Oxford, and taking up his residence in London became one of the band of Unive sity writers for the stage, with whom the 'player' Shakespeare's first efforts as a dramatist brought him into conflict. His first published play was a 'pastoral,' *The Arraignment of Paris*, which had been performed before Queen Elizabeth in 1584. It is supposed that he wrote more plays for the public stage than have been preserved. He also composed pageants for the great city festivals, making a precarious living by his wits. Occasional verses of Peele's appear in the poetic collections of the period. He died before 1598.]

Peele was one of the singers before the great Elizabethan sunrise, and his notes contain no anticipatory vibration of the burst of song that was to follow him. His University friends, even after Marlowe had made his voice heard, spoke of him as the Atlas of poetry, inferior to none, and in some respects superior to all; but this partial verdict can now be recorded only as an example of how contemporary criticism is sometimes mistaken. In reading his plays now one is more astonished that Greene and Nash should have considered him worthy to be named in the same breath with Marlowe, than that the theatrical managers of the time, so much to their indignation, should have rejected his plays in favour of the productions of non-academic workmen. Peele's blank verse, which was so much admired by his academic contemporaries, gives us a fair idea of the environment out of which Marlowe emerged, and increases our admiration of that mighty genius. It deserves the praise of 'smoothness' which it received from Campbell; it is graceful and elegant, but it has neither sinew nor majesty. I have quoted what seems to me to be the most favourable example of his use of this instrument, an address prefixed to one of his plays, *The Tale of Troy*, published in 1599, two years after the production of *Tamburlaine*. The inspiration of the subject seems to have contributed a fire and a freedom of movement which is generally lacking in Peele's blank verse. In using this form at all, Peele essayed an instrument which was beyond his powers and unsuited to his bent of feeling. His was an adroit, subtle, versatile mind, without massiveness or passionate intensity, and he is seen at his best in the expression of graceful and humorous fancies. He was not however a follower of Marlowe in the application of blank verse to tragic purposes. In the *Arraignment of Paris*, the prologue spoken by Ate is in that metre, and it is also adopted by Paris in his speech before the council of the Gods, and by Diana in her description of the nymph Eliza, a 'figure' of Queen Elizabeth. This seems to show that among the University poets, from whose circle Marlowe burst to reform the common stage, blank verse was considered the appropriate instrument for tragic and stately speeches. But it was not apparently till after the production of *Tamburlaine* that Peele wrote whole plays in blank verse. *David and Bethsabe* is the best of these, and is full of happy touches in the tender scenes, but the firmness of a masterly hand is wanting. The verse seldom moves far without having recourse to the crutch of weak and superfluous epithets. In the *Battle of Alcazar* Peele tried, perhaps at the instigation of his hard taskmasters the theatrical managers, to make up by sound and fury for his want of natural strength in the expression of passion, and thereby furnished Shakespeare with the model for some of the best-known extravagances of Pistol. Peele has also left us in *Sir Clyomon and Sir Clamydes* an example of the jigging measure of fourteen syllables, from which Marlowe aspired to redeem the stage. It cannot be said that Peele helped forward the great literary movement of his time ; he is perhaps the best illustration of the utmost that could be done by a cultured man of facile talent and poetic temperament before the advent of the great Elizabethans.

W. MINTO.

A FAREWELL TO SIR JOHN NORRIS AND SIR FRANCIS DRAKE.

Have done with care, my hearts ! aboard amain,
With stretching sails to plough the swelling waves ;
Bid England's shore and Albion's chalky cliffs
Farewell ; bid stately Troynovant adieu,
Where pleasant Thames from Isis silver head
Begins her quiet glide, and runs along
To that brave bridge, the bar that thwarts her course,
Near neighbour to the ancient stony tower,
The glorious hold that Julius Caesar built.
Change love for arms ; girt to your blades, my boys !
Your rests and muskets take, take helm and targe,
And let God Mars his consort make you mirth—
The roaring cannon, and the brazen trump,
The angry-sounding drum, the whistling fife,
The shrieks of men, the princely courser's neigh.
Now vail your bonnets to your friends at home ;
Bid all the lovely British dames adieu,
That under many a standard well-advanced
Have hid the sweet alarms and braves of love ;
Bid theatres and proud tragedians,
Bid Mahomet, Scipio, and mighty Tamburlaine,
King Charlemagne, Tom Stukely, and the rest,
Adieu. To arms, to arms, to glorious arms !
With noble Norris, and victorious Drake,
Under the sanguine cross, brave England's badge,
To propagate religious piety
And hew a passage with your conquering swords
By land and sea, wherever Phoebus' eye,
Th' eternal lamp of Heaven, lends us light ;
By golden Tagus, or the western Ind,
Or through the spacious bay of Portugal,
The wealthy ocean-main, the Tyrrhene sea,
From great Alcides' pillars branching forth,
Even to the gulf that leads to lofty Rome ;
There to deface the pride of Antichrist,
And pull his paper walls and popery down—
A famous enterprise for England's strength,

To steel your swords on Avarice' triple crown,
And cleanse Augeas' stalls in Italy.
To arms, my fellow-soldiers ! Sea and land
Lie open to the voyage you intend ;
And sea or land, bold Britons, far or near,
Whatever course your matchless virtue shapes,
Whether to Europe's bounds or Asian plains,
To Afric's shore, or rich America,
Down to the shades of deep Avernus' crags,
Sail on, pursue your honours to your graves.
Heaven is a sacred covering for your heads,
And every climate virtue's tabernacle.
To arms, to arms, to honourable arms !
Hoist sails, weigh anchors up, plough up the seas
With flying keels, plough up the land with swords.
In God's name venture on ; and let me say
To you, my mates, as Caesar said to his,
Striving with Neptune's hills ; 'You bear,' quoth he,
'Caesar and Caesar's fortune in your ships.'
You follow them, whose swords successful are ;
You follow Drake, by sea the scourge of Spain,
The dreadful dragon, terror to your foes,
Victorious in his return from Ind,
In all his high attempts unvanquished.
You follow noble Norris, whose renown,
Won in the fertile fields of Belgia,
Spreads by the gates of Europe to the courts
Of Christian kings and heathen potentates.
You fight for Christ, and England's peerless Queen,
Elizabeth, the wonder of the world,
Over whose throne the enemies of God
Have thundered erst their vain successless braves.
O ten times treble happy men, that fight
Under the cross of Christ and England's Queen,
And follow such as Drake and Norris are !
All honours do this cause accompany,
All glory on these endless honours waits.
These honours and this glory shall He send
Whose honour and whose glory you defend.

ROBERT GREENE.

[ROBERT GREENE was born at Norwich, probably in 1560. He was a graduate of St. John's College, Cambridge, in 1578, but took his degree of M A. five years later at Clare Hall. After this he travelled in Italy and Spain, and, returning to London, gained his living as a playwright and pamphleteer. He died in Dowgate, Sept. 3, 1592. His first work was the novel of *Mamillia*, 1580, which was followed by a rapid succession of tales, poems, plays, and pamphlets. His most remarkable lyrics appeared in *Menaphon*, 1587; *Never Too Late*, 1590; and *The Mourning Garment*, 1590.]

It has been well said that the lyrical brightness of Greene's smaller poems compared with the tame versification of his plays, is as surprising as 'when an indifferent walker proves a light and graceful runner.' Yet the reason is perhaps not very far to find ; personally a lover of riotous companions and outrageous surfeiting, this hopeless reprobate was imaginatively one of the purest of idyllic dreamers. There was an absolute chasm between the foulness of his life and the serenity of his intellect, and, at least until he became a repentant character, no literary theme interested him very much, unless it was interpenetrated with sentimental beauty. This element inspired what little was glowing and eloquent in his plays ; it tinctured the whole of his pastoral romances with a rosy Euphuism, and it turned the best of his lyrics to the pure fire and air of poetry. From his long sojourn in Italy and Spain he brought back a strong sense of the physical beauty of men and women, of fruits, flowers, and trees, of the coloured atmosphere and radiant compass of a southern heaven. All these things passed into his prose and into his verse, so that in many of the softer graces and innocent voluptuous indiscretions of the Elizabethan age he is as much a forerunner as Marlowe is in audacity of thought and the thunders of a massive line. For the outward part of his prose style he was obviously indebted to Lyly; for the inward character of his poetical matter less obviously, but more essentially, to Spenser, whose antiquated idioms, even, he affected to cherish. The publication of *Euphues* just preceded his apprenticeship in letters, and without question stimulated him to the production of his first work. He never reached the sententious force and persuasive morality of Lyly's extraordinary master-piece, but he made this form of literature acceptable to a less exacting taste. His own pastorals enjoyed a very wide success, and were imitated with more or less talent by Lodge, Dickenson, and other writers of less note. They were delicate blossoms of exotic growth, appealing wholly to a literary taste, and, being unable to hold their ground after the close of the sixteenth century, they were completely swept away by the tide of realistic pamphlets, coarse comedies, and sensational tragedies. It is impossible to regret this, because, although these tales of Arcadia and Silistria were full of sweetness and tender beauty, they were foreign to our native habit of mind, and their prevalence might have doomed us to some such tradition of artificial poetry as the example of Petrarch so long inflicted on Italian literature.

The lyrics of Greene show a sense of colour that recalls the masters of Italian painting in the century that preceded him, and it was certainly in the art of the south of Europe that he formed his favourite conception of the brown shepherd and rosy nymph reclining in a whispering boscage of green shadow, to whom appears in vision—

> 'the God that hateth sleep,
> Clad in armour all of fire,
> Hand in hand with Queen Desire.'

His employment of metre and rhythm were in unison with this golden style of imagery. His metres are very various, and are usually in direct analogy with the theme in hand. Doron glorifies Samela in a stanza that sounds like the tramp of a conquering army, while Menaphon laments the precarious and volatile nature of love in lines that rise and fall with the rush of a swallow's flight. Towards the end of his life Greene lost something of this metrical elasticity, and adopted for most of his ideas a sober six-line stanza; his only long poem, *A Maiden's Dream*, is written in rime-royal.

It is not easy to say much of the shorter pieces of Greene which is not also true of all the best verses of the early Elizabethan period. He is the type of that warm brood of poetic youth that still sings in chorus from the dells of *England's Helicon,* or the *Paradise of Princely Pleasures.* Life and the whole world of youthful pleasures attract him with their delight, and he hastens to clothe himself in a gay silken doublet, and to throw away his forefather's Puritan coat of hodden gray. But anything more specific and definite than this it would scarcely be safe to say. Greene has not Lodge's individuality of style, nor does he approach his finest flights, but he is more nearly allied to him than to any other of his contemporaries. It will probably seem to a careful reader that his ordinary level of writing was sustained at a higher point than Lodge's. In his rapid passages of octosyllabic verse Greene sometimes comes very close to Barnefield, and, through that mysterious and exquisite poet, to the juvenile manner of Shakespeare, with whom, as is well known, he cultivated a lively spirit of rivalry. But the most curious and notable thing, after all, about Greene's poetry is that, in all its sylvan sweetness, it should have proceeded from the lawless bully, whose ruffled hair and long red beard became a beacon and terror to all good citizens, till in the midst of his 'villainous cogging and foisting,' and all his rascally sleights, he was carried off in the thirty-second year of his life by a surfeit of Rhenish wine and pickled herrings. Upon the poor dishonoured head of this strange genius, the wretched woman who was with him when he died set a garland of bay-leaves, in a happy prescience of the tenderness with which posterity would pardon all his sins for the sake of his pure and beautiful verses.

EDMUND W. GOSSE.

Sephestia's Song to her Child.

Weep not, my wanton, smile upon my knee;
When thou art old there's grief enough for thee.
    Mother's wag, pretty boy,
    Father's sorrow, father's joy;
    When thy father first did see
    Such a boy by him and me,
    He was glad, I was woe,
    Fortune changèd made him so,
    When he left his pretty boy
    Last his sorrow, first his joy.

Weep not, my wanton, smile upon my knee,
When thou art old there's grief enough for thee.
    Streaming tears that never stint,
    Like pearl drops from a flint,
    Fell by course from his eyes,
    That one another's place supplies;
    Thus he grieved in every part,
    Tears of blood fell from his heart,
    When he left his pretty boy,
    Father's sorrow, father's joy.

Weep not, my wanton, smile upon my knee,
When thou art old there's grief enough for thee.
    The wanton smiled, father wept,
    Mother cried, baby leapt;
    More he crowed, more we cried,
    Nature could not sorrow hide:
    He must go, he must kiss
    Child and mother, baby bless,
    For he left his pretty boy,
    Father's sorrow, father's joy.
Weep not, my wanton, smile upon my knee,
When thou art old there's grief enough for thee.

SAMELA.

Like to Diana in her summer weed,
Girt with a crimson robe of brightest dye,
　　　　　　　Goes fair Samela ;
Whiter than be the flocks that straggling feed,
When washed by Arethusa faint they lie,
　　　　　　　Is fair Samela ;
As fair Aurora in her morning grey,
Decked with the ruddy g'ister of her love,
　　　　　　　Is fair Samela ;
Like lovely Thetis on a calmèd day,
When as her brightness Neptune's fancy move,
　　　　　　　Shines fair Samela ;
Her tresses gold, her eyes like glassy streams,
Her teeth are pearl, the breasts are ivory
　　　　　　　Of fair Samela ;
Her cheeks, like rose and lily yield forth gleams,
Her brow's bright arches framed of ebony ;
　　　　　　　Thus fair Samela
Passeth fair Venus in her bravest hue,
And Juno in the show of majesty,
　　　　　　　For she's Samela,
Pallas in wit ; all three, if you well view,
For beauty, wit, and matchless dignity
　　　　　　　Yield to Samela.

FAWNIA.

Ah, were she pitiful as she is fair,
　Or but as mild as she is seeming so,
Then were my hopes greater than my despair,
　Then all the world were heaven, nothing woe.
Ah, were her heart relenting as her hand,
　That seems to melt even with the mildest touch,
Then knew I where to seat me in a land,
　Under wide heavens, but yet [I know] not such.

So as she shows, she seems the budding rose,
　　Yet sweeter far than is an earthly flower,
Sovereign of beauty, like the spray she grows,
　　Compassed she is with thorns and cankered flower,
Yet were she willing to be plucked and worn,
She would be gathered, though she grew on thorn.

Ah, when she sings, all music else be still,
　　For none must be compared to her note ;
Ne'er breathed such glee from Philomela's bill,
　　Nor from the morning-singer's swelling throat.
Ah, when she riseth from her blissful bed,
　　She comforts all the world, as doth the sun,
And at her sight the night's foul vapour's fled ;
　　When she is set, the gladsome day is done.
O glorious sun, imagine me the west,
Shine in my arms, and set thou in my breast !

The Palmer's Ode in 'Never too Late.'

Old Menalcas, on a day,
As in field this shepherd lay,
Tuning of his oaten pipe,
Which he hit with many a stripe,
Said to Coridon that he
Once was young and full of glee.
'Blithe and wanton was I then :
Such desires follow men.
As I lay and kept my sheep,
Came the God that hateth sleep,
Clad in armour all of fire,
Hand in hand with queen Desire,
And with a dart that wounded nigh,
Pierced my heart as I did lie ;
That when I woke I 'gan swear
Phillis beauty's palm did bear.
Up I start, forth went I,
With her face to feed mine eye ;

There I saw Desire sit,
That my heart with love had hit,
Laying forth bright beauty's hooks
To entrap my gazing looks.
Love I did, and 'gan to woo,
Pray and sigh ; all would not do :
Women, when they take the toy,
Covet to be counted coy.
Coy she was, and I 'gan court ;
She thought love was but a sport ;
Profound hell was in my thought ;
Such a pain desire had wrought,
That I sued with sighs and tears ;
Still ingrate she stopped her ears,
Till my youth I had spent.
Last a passion of repent
Told me flat, that Desire
Was a brond of love's fire,
Which consumeth men in thrall,
Virtue, youth, wit, and all.
At this saw, back I start,
Beat Desire from my heart,
Shook off Love, and made an oath
To be enemy to both.
Old I was when thus I fled
Such fond toys as cloyed my head,
But this I learned at Virtue's gate,
The way to good is never late.'

SONG.

Sweet are the thoughts that savour of content ;
    The quiet mind is richer than a crown ;
Sweet are the nights in careless slumber spent ;
    The poor estate scorns fortune's angry frown :
Such sweet content, such minds, such sleep, such bliss,
Beggars enjoy, when princes oft do miss.

The homely house that harbours quiet rest ;
   The cottage that affords no pride nor care ;
The mean that 'grees with country music best ;
   The sweet consort of mirth and music's fare ;
Obscurèd life sets down a type of bliss :
A mind content both crown and kingdom is.

PHILOMELA'S ODE.

Sitting by a river's side,
Where a silent stream did glide,
Muse I did of many things,
That the mind in quiet brings.
I 'gan think how some men deem
Gold their god ; and some esteem
Honour is the chief content,
That to man in life is lent.
And some others do contend,
Quiet none, like to a friend.
Others hold, there is no wealth
Comparèd to a perfect health.
Some man's mind in quiet stands,
When he is lord of many lands :
But I did sigh, and said all this
Was but a shade of perfect bliss ;
And in my thoughts I did approve,
Nought so sweet as is true love.
Love 'twixt lovers passeth these,
When mouth kisseth and heart 'grees,
With folded arms and lips meeting,
Each soul another sweetly greeting ;
For by the breath the soul fleeteth,
And soul with soul in kissing meeteth.
If love be so sweet a thing,
That such happy bliss doth bring,
Happy is love's sugared thrall,
But unhappy maidens all,

Who esteem your virgin blisses,
Sweeter than a wife's sweet kisses.
No such quiet to the mind,
As true Love with kisses kind:
But if a kiss prove unchaste,
Then is true love quite disgraced.
Though love be sweet, learn this of me,
No sweet love but honesty.

ORPHEUS' SONG.

He that did sing the motions of the stars,
　Pale-coloured Phœbe's borrowing of her light,
Aspects of planets oft opposed in jars,
　Of Hesper, henchman to the day and night;
Sings now of love, as taught by proof to sing,
Women are false, and love a bitter thing.

I loved Eurydice, the brightest lass,
　More fond to like so fair a nymph as she;
In Thessaly so bright none ever was,
　But fair and constant hardly may agree:
False-hearted wife to him that loved thee well,
To leave thy love, and choose the prince of hell!

Theseus did help, and I in haste did hie
　To Pluto, for the lass I lovèd so:
The god made grant, and who so glad as I?
　I tuned my harp, and she and I 'gan go;
Glad that my love was left to me alone,
I lookèd back, Eurydice was gone:

She slipped aside, back to her latest love,
　Unkind, she wronged her first and truest feere!
Thus women's loves delight, as trial proves
　By false Eurydice I loved so dear,
To change and fleet, and every way to shrink,
To take in love, and lose it with a wink.

CHRISTOPHER MARLOWE.

[CHRISTOPHER MARLOWE was born at Canterbury in February, 1564, and educated at the King's School in his birth-place, and at Benet (Corpus Christi) College, Cambridge. He was killed in a tavern brawl, and was buried at Deptford, June 1, 1593. The dates and order of his works are somewhat uncertain Of his plays, the first, *Tamburlaine the Great*, a tragedy in two parts, must have been acted in public by 1587. It was followed by *The Tragical History of Dr Faustus*, *The Jew of Malta* (probably in 1589 or 1590), *The Massacre at Paris* (not earlier than the end of 1589), *Edward II*, and *The Tragedy of Queen Dido*, which was probably left unfinished at Marlowe's death, and completed by Nash. Another play, *Lust's Dominion*, was for some time wrongly attributed to Marlowe; but, in return for this injustice, the probability that he may have had at least a share in Shakespeare's 2 and 3 *Henry VI*, or in the plays on which those dramas were based, is now rather widely admitted. Of his poems, the translations of Ovid's *Amores* and the first book of Lucan's *Pharsalia* are of uncertain date. *The Passionate Shepherd to his Love* was first printed complete in *England's Helicon*, 1600, but is quoted in *The Jew of Malta*. *Hero and Leander* was left unfinished at Marlowe's death; Chapman completed it, dividing Marlowe's fragment into two parts, which now form the first two Sestiads of the poem.]

Marlowe has one claim on our affection which everyone is ready to acknowledge ; he died young. We think of him along with Chatterton and Burns, with Byron, Shelley, and Keats. And this is a fact of some importance for the estimate of his life and genius. His poetical career lasted only six or seven years, and he did not outlive his 'hot days, when the mad blood's stirring.' An old ballad tells us that he acted at the *Curtain* theatre in Shoreditch and 'brake his leg in one rude scene, When in his early age.' If there is any truth in the last statement, we may suppose that Marlowe give up acting and confined himself to authorship. He seems to have depended for his livelihood on his connection with the stage ; and probably, like many of his fellows and friends, he lived in a free and even reckless way. A more unusual characteristic of Marlowe's was his 'atheism.' No reliance can be placed on the details recorded on this subject ; but it was apparently only his death that prevented judicial proceedings being taken against him on account of his opinions. The note on which these proceedings would have been founded was the work of one Bame, who thought that 'all men in christianitei ought to endeavour that the mouth of so dangerous a member may be stopped,' and was hanged at Tyburn about eighteen months afterwards. But other testimony points in the same direction ; and a celebrated passage in Greene's *Groatsworth of Wit* would lead us to suppose that Marlowe was given to blatant profanities. Whatever his offences may have been—and there is nothing to make us think he was a bad-hearted man—he had no time to make men forget them. He was not thirty when he met his death.

The plan of the present volumes excludes selections from Marlowe's plays ; but as his purely poetical works give but a one-sided idea of his genius, and as his importance in the history of literature depends mainly on his dramatic writings, some general reference must be made to them. Even if they had no enduring merits of their own, their effect upon Shakespeare—an effect which, to say nothing of *Henry VI*, is most clearly visible in *Richard III*—and their influence on the drama would preserve them from neglect. The nature of this influence may be seen by a glance at Marlowe's first play. On the one hand it stands at the opposite pole to the classic form of the drama as it is found in Seneca, a form which had been adopted in *Gorboduc*, and which some of the more learned writers attempted to nationalise. There is no Chorus in *Tamburlaine* or in any of Marlowe's plays except *Dr. Faustus* ; and the action takes place on the stage instead of being merely reported. On the other hand, in this, the first play in blank verse which was publicly acted, he called the audience

> 'From jigging veins of rhyming mother-wits,
> And such conceits as clownage keeps in pay,'

and fixed the metre of his drama for ever as the metre of English tragedy. And, though neither here nor in *Dr. Faustus* could he yet afford to cast off all the conceits of clownage, he was in effect beginning to substitute works of art for the formless popular representations of the day. Doubtless it was only a beginning. The two parts of *Tamburlaine* are not great tragedies. They are full of mere horror and glare. Of the essence of drama, a sustained and developed action, there is as yet very little ; and what action there is proceeds almost entirely from the rising passion of a single character. Nor in the conception of this character has Marlowe quite freed himself from the defect of the popular plays, in which, naturally enough, personified virtues and vices often took the place of men. Still, if there is a touch of this defect in *Tamburlaine*, as in the *Jew of Malta*, it is no more than a touch. The ruling passion is conceived with an intensity, and portrayed with a sweep of imagination unknown before ; a requisite for the drama hardly less important than the faculty of construction is attained, and the way is opened for those creations which are lifted above the common and yet are living flesh and blood. It is the same with the language. For the buffoonery he partly displaced Marlowe substitutes a swelling diction, 'high astounding terms,' and some outrageous bombast, such as that which Shakespeare reproduced and put into the mouth of Pistol. But, laugh as we will, in this first of Marlowe's plays there is that incommunicable gift which means almost everything, *style* ; a manner perfectly individual, and yet, at its best, free from eccentricity. The 'mighty line' of which Jonson spoke, and a pleasure, equal to Milton's, in resounding proper names, meet us in the very first scene ; and in not a few passages passion, instead of vociferating, finds its natural expression, and we hear the fully-formed style, which in Marlowe's best writing is, to use his own words,

'Like his desire, lift upward and divine.'

'Lift upward' Marlowe's style was at first, and so it remained. It degenerates into violence, but never into softness. If it falters, the cause is not doubt or languor, but haste and want of care. It has the energy of youth ; and a living poet has described this among its other qualities when he speaks of Marlowe as singing

'With mouth of gold, and morning in his eyes.'

As a dramatic instrument it developed with his growth and acquired variety. The stately monotone of *Tamburlaine*, in which the pause falls almost regularly at the end of the lines, gives place in *Edward II* to rhythms less suited to pure poetry, but far more rapid and flexible. In *Dr. Faustus* the great address to Helen is as different in metrical effect as it is in spirit from the last scene, where the words seem, like Faustus' heart, to 'pant and quiver.' Even in the *Massacre at Paris*, the worst of his plays, the style becomes unmistakeable in such passages as this :

> ' Give me a look, that, when I bend the brows,
> Pale Death may walk in furrows of my face;
> A hand th₁t with a grasp may gripe the world;
> An ear to hear what my detractors say ;
> A royal seat, a sceptre, and a crown ;
> That those that dc behold them may become
> As men that stand and gaze against the sun.'

The expression ' lift upward' applies also, in a sense, to most of the chief characters in the plays. Whatever else they may lack, they know nothing of half-heartedness or irresolution. A volcanic self-assertion, a complete absorption in some one desire, is their characteristic. That in creating such characters Marlowe was working in dark places, and that he developes them with all his energy, is certain. But that in so doing he shows (to refer to a current notion of him) a ' hunger and thirst after unrighteousness,' a desire, that is, which never has produced or could produce true poetry, is an idea which Hazlitt could not have really intended to convey. Marlowe's works are tragedies. Their greatness lies not merely in the conception of an unhallowed lust, however gigantic, but in an insight into its tragic significance and tragic results ; and there is as little food for a hunger after unrighteousness (if there be such a thing) in the appalling final scene of *Dr. Faustus*, or, indeed, in the melancholy of Mephistopheles, so grandly touched by Marlowe, as in the catastrophe of *Richard III* or of Goethe's *Faust*. It is true, again, that in the later acts of the *Jew of Malta* Barabas has become a mere monster ; but for that very reason the character ceases to show Marlowe's peculiar genius, and Shakespeare himself has not portrayed the sensual lust after gold, and the touch of imagination which redeems it from insignificance, with such splendour as the opening speech of Marlowe's play. Whatever faults however the earlier plays have, it is clear, if *Edward II* be one of his latest works, that Marlowe was rapidly outgrowing them. For in that play, to say nothing of the two great scenes to which Lamb gave such high praise, the interest is no longer confined to a single character, and there is the most decided advance both in construction and in the dialogue.

Of the weightier qualities of Marlowe's genius the extracts from his purely poetical works give but little idea ; but just for that reason they testify to the variety of his powers. Everyone knows the verses ' Come live with me, and be my love,' with their pretty mixture of gold buckles and a belt of straw. This was a very

popular song ; Raleigh wrote an answer to it ; and its flowing
music has run in many a head beside Sir Hugh Evans's.   But the
shepherd would hardly be called ' passionate' outside the Arcadia
to which the lyric really belongs.   Of the beautiful fragment in
ottava rima nothing is known, except that it was first printed with
Marlowe's name in *England's Parnassus*, 1600.   The translations
of Lucan and Ovid (the former in blank verse) were perhaps early
studies.   It is curious that Marlowe should have set himself so
thankless a task as a version of Lucan which literally gives line
for line ; but the choice of the author is characteristic.   The
translation of Ovid's *Amores* was burnt on account of its indecency
in 1599, and it would have been no loss to the world if all the
copies had perished.   The interest of these translations is mainly
historical.   They testify to the passion for classical poetry, and in
particular to that special fondness for Ovid of which the literature
of the time affords many other proofs.   The study of Virgil and
Ovid was a far less mixed good for poetry than that of Seneca and
Plautus ; and it is perhaps worth noticing that Marlowe, who felt
the charm of classical amatory verse, and whose knowledge of
Virgil is shown in his *Queen Dido*, should have been the man
who, more than any other, secured the theatre from the dominion
of inferior classical dramas.

How fully he caught the inspiration, not indeed of the best
classical poetry, but of that world of beauty which ancient literature
seemed to disclose to the men of the Renascence, we can see
in many parts of his writings, in Faust's address to Helen, in
Gaveston's description of the sports at Court, in the opening of
Queen Dido ; but the fullest proof of it is the fragment of *Hero
and Leander*.   Beaumont wrote a *Salmacis and Hermaphroditus*,
Shakespeare a *Venus and Adonis*, but both found their true
vehicle in the drama.   Marlowe's poem not only stands far above
one of these tales, and perhaps above both, but it stands on a
level with his plays ; and it is hard to say what excellence he
might not have reached in the field of narrative verse.   The defect
of his fragment, the intrusion of ingenious reflections and of those
conceits with one of which our selection unhappily terminates, was
the fault of his time ; its merit is Marlowe's own.   It was suggested
indeed by the short poem of the Pseudo-Musaeus, an Alexandrian
grammarian who probably wrote about the end of the fifth century
after Christ, and appears to have been translated into English
shortly before 1589 ; but it is in essence original.   Written in the

so-called heroic verse, it bears no resemblance to any other poem in that metre composed before, nor, perhaps, is there any written since which decidedly recalls it, unless it be *Endymion.* 'Pagan' it is in a sense, with the Paganism of the Renascence : the more pagan the better, considering the subject. Nothing of the deeper thought of the time, no 'looking before and after,' no worship of a Gloriana or hostility to an Acrasia, interferes with its frank acceptance of sensuous beauty and joy. In this, in spite of much resemblance, it differs from *Endymion,* the spirit of which is not fruition but unsatisfied longing, and in which the vision of a vague and lovelier ideal is always turning the enjoyment of the moment into gloom. On the other hand, a further likeness to Keats may perhaps be traced in the pictorial quality of Marlowe's descriptions. His power does not lie in catching in the aspect of objects or scenes those deeper suggestions which appeal to an imagination stored with human experience as well as sensitive to colour and form ; for this power does not necessarily result in what we call pictorial writing ; but his soul seems to be in his eyes, and he renders the beauty which appeals directly to sense as vividly as he apprehends it. Nor is this the case with the description of objects alone. The same complete absorption of imagination in sense appears in Marlowe's account of the visit to Hero's tower. This passage is in a high degree voluptuous, but it is not prurient. For prurience is the sign of an unsatisfied imagination, which, being unable to present its object adequately, appeals to extraneous and unpoetic feelings. But Marlowe's imagination is completely satisfied ; and therefore, though he has not a high theme (for it is a mere sensuous joy that is described, and there is next to no real emotion in the matter), he is able to make fine poetry of it. Of the metrical qualities of the poem there can be but one opinion. Shakespeare himself, who quoted a line of it[1], never reached in his own narrative verse a music so spontaneous and rich, a music to which Marlowe might have applied his own words—

> 'That calls my soul from forth his living seat
> To move unto the measures of delight.'

---

[1]   'Dead shepherd, now I find thy saw of might :
     "Who ever loved that loved not at first sight?"'
As You Like It, iii. 5.

Marlowe had many of the makings of a great poet : a capacity for Titanic conceptions which might with time have become Olympian ; an imaginative vision which was already intense and must have deepened and widened ; the gift of style and of making words sing ; and a time to live in such as no other generation of English poets has known.   It is easy to reckon his failings.   His range of perception into life and character was contracted : of comic power he shows hardly a trace, and it is incredible that he should have written the Jack Cade scene of *Henry VI* ; no humour or tenderness relieves his pathos ; there is not any female character in his plays whom we remember with much interest ; and it is not clear that he could have produced songs of the first order.   But it is only Shakespeare who can do everything ; and Shakespeare did not die at twenty-nine.   That Marlowe must have stood nearer to him than any other dramatic poet of that time, or perhaps of any later time, is probably the verdict of nearly all students of the drama.   His immediate successors knew well what was lost in him ; and from the days of Peele, Jonson, Drayton, and Chapman, to our own, the poets have done more than common honour to his memory.

A. C. BRADLEY.

The Passionate Shepherd to his Love.

Come live with me, and be my love ;
And we will all the pleasures prove
That hills and valleys, dales and fields,
Woods or steepy mountain yields.

And we will sit upon the rocks,
Seeing the shepherds feed their flocks
By shallow rivers, to whose falls
Melodious birds sing madrigals.

And I will make thee beds of roses,
And a thousand fragrant posies ;
A cap of flowers, and a kirtle
Embroider'd all with leaves of myrtle ;

A gown made of the finest wool
Which from our pretty lambs we pull ;
Fair-linèd slippers for the cold,
With buckles of the purest gold ;

A belt of straw and ivy-buds,
With coral clasps and amber studs :
An if these pleasures may thee move,
Come live with me, and be my love.

The shepherd-swains shall dance and sing
For thy delight each May morning :
If these delights thy mind may move,
Then live with me, and be my love.

Fragment.

[From *England's Parnassus,* 1600.]

I walk'd along a stream, for pureness rare,
  Brighter than sun-shine ; for it did acquaint
The dullesi sight with all the glorious prey
  That in the pebble-pavèd channel lay.

No molten crystal, but a richer mine,
  Even Nature's rarest alchymy ran there,—
Diamonds resolv'd, and substance more divine,
  Through whose bright-gliding current might appear
A thousand naked nymphs, whose ivory shine,
  Enamelling the banks, made them more clear
Than ever was that glorious palace gate
Where the day-shining Sun in triumph sate.

Upon this brim the eglantine and rose,
  The tamarisk, olive, and the almond tree,
As kind companions, in one union grows,
  Folding their twining arms, as oft we see
Turtle-taught lovers either other close,
  Lending to dulness feeling sympathy;
And as a costly valance o'er a bed,
So did their garland-tops the brook o'erspread.

Their leaves, that differ'd both in shape and show,
  Though all were green, yet difference such in green,
Like to the checker'd bent of Iris' bow,
  Prided the running main, as it had been—

From the First Sestiad of 'Hero and Leander.'

On Hellespont, guilty of true love's blood,
In view and opposite two cities stood,
Sea-borderers, disjoin'd by Neptune's might;
The one Abydos, the other Sestos hight.
At Sestos Hero dwelt; Hero the fair,
Whom young Apollo courted for her hair,
And offer'd as a dower his burning throne,
Where she should sit, for men to gaze upon.
The outside of her garments were of lawn,
The lining purple silk, with gilt stars drawn;
Her wide sleeves green, and bordered with a grove,
Where Venus in her naked glory strov

To please the careless and disdainful eyes
Of proud Adonis, that before her lies ;
Her kirtle blue, whereon was many a stain,
Made with the blood of wretched lovers slain.
Upon her head she ware a myrtle wreath,
From whence her veil reach'd to the ground beneath :
Her veil was artificial flowers and leaves,
Whose workmanship both man and beast deceives :
Many would praise the sweet smell as she past,
When 'twas the odour which her breath forth cast ;
And there for honey bees have sought in vain,
And, beat from thence, have lighted there again.
About her neck hung chains of pebble-stone,
Which, lighten'd by her neck, like diamonds shone.
She ware no gloves ; for neither sun nor wind
Would burn or parch her hands, but, to her mind,
Or warm or cool them, for they took delight
To play upon those hands, they were so white.
Buskins of shells, all silver'd, usèd she,
And branch'd with blushing coral to the knee ;
Where sparrows perch'd, of hollow pearl and gold,
Such as the world would wonder to behold :
Those with sweet water oft her handmaid fills,
Which as she went, would cherup through their bills.
Some say, for her the fairest Cupid pin'd,
And, looking in her face, was strooken blind.
But this is true ; so like was one the other,
As he imagined Hero was his mother ;
And oftentimes into her bosom flew,
About her naked neck his bare arms threw,
And laid his childish head upon her breast,
And, with still panting rockt, there took his rest.

  * * * * * *

On this feast-day,—O cursèd day and hour !—
Went Hero thorough Sestos, from her tower
To Venus' temple, where unhappily,
As after chanc'd, they did each other spy.
So fair a church as this had Venus none :
The walls were of discolour'd jasper-stone,

Wherein was Proteus carved ; and over-head
A lively vine of green sea-agate spread,
Where by one hand light-headed Bacchus hung,
And with the other wine from grapes out-wrung.
Of crystal shining fair the pavement was ;
The town of Sestos call'd it Venus' glass :

* * * * * *

For know, that underneath this radiant flour
Was Danäe's statue in a brazen tower ;
Jove slyly stealing from his sister's bed,
To dally with Idalian Ganymed,
And for his love Europa bellowing loud,
And tumbling with the Rainbow in a cloud ;
Blood-quaffing Mars heaving the iron net
Which limping Vulcan and his Cyclops set ;
Love kindling fire, to burn such towns as Troy ;
Silvanus weeping for the lovely boy
That now is turn'd into a cypress-tree,
Under whose shade the wood-gods love to be.
And in the midst a silver altar stood :
There Hero, sacrificing turtle's blood,
Vail'd to the ground, veiling her eyelids close ;
And modestly they open'd as she rose :
Thence flew Love's arrow with the golden head ;
And thus Leander was enamourèd.
Stone-still he stood, and evermore he gaz'd,
Till with the fire, that from his countenance blaz'd,
Relenting Hero's gentle heart was strook :
Such force and virtue hath an amorous look.

It lies not in our power to love or hate,
For will in us is over-rul'd by fate.
When two are stript long e'er the course begin,
We wish that one should lose, the other win ;
And one especially do we affect
Of two gold ingots, like in each respect :
The reason no man knows ; let it suffice,
What we behold is censur'd by our eyes.
Where both deliberate, the love is slight :
Who ever lov'd, that lov'd not at first sight ?

He kneel'd ; but unto her devoutly pray'd :
Chaste Hero to herself thus softly said,
'Were I the saint he worships, I would hear him';
And, as she spake those words, came somewhat near him.
He started up ; she blush'd as one asham'd ;
Wherewith Leander much more was inflam'd.
He touch'd her hand ; in touching it she trembled :
Love deeply grounded, hardly is dissembled.
These lovers parled by the touch of hands :
True love is mute, and oft amazèd stands.
Thus while dumb signs their yielding hearts entangled,
The air with sparks of living fire was spangled ;
And night, deep-drench'd in misty Acheron,
Heav'd up her head, and half the world upon
Breath'd darkness forth (dark night is Cupid's day) :
And now begins Leander to display
Love's holy fire, with words, with sighs, and tears ;
Which, like sweet music, enter'd Hero's ears ;
And yet at every word she turn'd aside,
And always cut him off, as he replied.

    *   *   *   *   *   *

These arguments he us'd, and many more ;
Wherewith she yielded, that was won before.
Hero's looks yielded, but her words made war :
Women are won when they begin to jar.
Thus having swallow'd Cupid's golden hook,
The more she striv'd, the deeper was she strook :
Yet, evilly feigning anger, strove she still,
And would be thought to grant against her will.
So having paus'd awhile, at last she said,
'Who taught thee rhetoric to deceive a maid?
Ay me ! such words as these should I abhor,
And yet I like them for the orator.'
With that Leander stoop'd to have embrac'd her,
But from his spreading arms away she cast her,
And thus bespake him : 'Gentle youth, forbear
To touch the sacred garments which I wear.
Upon a rock, and underneath a hill,
Far from the town, (where all is whist and still,

Save that the sea, playing on yellow sand,
Sends forth a rattling murmur to the land,
Whose sound allures the golden Morpheus
In silence of. the night to visit us,)
My turret stands ; and there, God knows, I play
With Venus' swans and sparrows all the day.
A. dwarfish beldam bears me company,
That hops about the chamber where I lie,
And spends the night, that might be better spent,
In vain discourse and apish merriment :—
Come thither.' As she spake this, her tongue tripp'd,
Foɪ unawares, ' Come thither,' from her slipp'd ;
And suddenly her former colour chang'd,
And here and there her eyes through anger rang'd ;
And, like a planet moving several ways
At one self instant, she, poor soul, assays,
Loving, not to love at all, and every part
Strove to resist the motions of her heart :
And hands so pure, so innocent, nay, such
As might have made Heaven stoop to have a touch,
Did she.uphold to Venus, and again
Vow'd spotless chastity ; but all in vain ;
Cupid beats down her prayers with his wings ;
Her vows about the empty air he flings :
All deep enrag'd, his sinewy bow he bent,
And shot a shaft that burning from him went ;
Wherewith she strooken, look'd so dolefully,
As made love sigh to see his tyranny;
And, as she wept, her tears to pearl he turn'd,
And wound them on his arm, and for her mourn'd.

THOMAS LODGE.

[THOMAS LODGE was born in Lincolnshire about 1556, entered Trinity College, Oxford, in 1573, and died of the plague at Low Leyton, in Essex, in 1625. The most important of his numerous works are, *Scilla's Metamorphosis*, 1589; *Rosalynde Euphues' Golden Legacy*, 1590; *Phillis*, 1593; *A Fig for Momus*, 1595; *A Margarite of America*, 1596.]

Lodge was the least boisterous of the noisy group of learned wits who, with Greene and Marlowe at their head, invaded London from the universities during the close of Elizabeth's reign. He began to write as early as 1580, and was among the first who adopted the style invented by Lyly in his *Euphues*; but it was not until Greene had successfully composed several romances in this manner that Lodge came forward and surpassed both Greene and Lyly in his lovely fantastic pastoral of *Rosalynde*, composed under a tropical sky, as the author sailed with Captain Clarke between the Canaries and the Azores. During the next ten years Lodge was very prolific, closing this part of his career with the *Margarite of America*, an Arcadian romance, so named because the poet was in Patagonia when he wrote it. By this time, or soon after, all the young men of genius with whom he had associated were dead, and Lodge retired from literary life, and settled down as a physician. He lived on almost to the birth of Dryden; but his place as a poet is among the immediate followers of Spenser and precursors of Shakespeare.

In some respects Lodge is superior to most of the lyrical poets of his time. He is certainly the best of the Euphuists, and no one rivalled him in the creation of a dreamy scene, 'out of space, out of time,' where the loves and jousts of an ideal chivalry could be pleasantly tempered by the tending of sheep. His romances, with their frequent interludes of fine verse, are delightful reading, although the action flags, and there is simply no attempt at characterisation. A very courtly and knightly spirit of morality perfumes the stately sentences, laden with learned allusion and flowing imagery ; the lovers are devoted beyond belief, the knights are braver, the shepherds wiser, the nymphs more lovely and more flinty-hearted than tongue can tell ; the courteous amorous couples file down the long arcades of the enchanted forest, and find the madrigal that Rosader or the hapless Arsinous has fastened to the balsam-tree, or else they gather round the alabaster tomb of one who died for love, and read the sonnet that his own hand has engraved there. This languid elegant literature was of great service in refining both the language and the manners of the people. There was something false no doubt in the excessive delicacy of the sentiment, something trivial in the balanced rhythm and polish of the style ; but both were excessively pretty, and both made possible the pastoral and lyrical tenderness of the next half-century. Among all the Elizabethans, no one borrowed his inspiration more directly from the Italians than Lodge ; he was fortunately unaware of the existence of Marini, but the influence of Sannazaro and of the school of Tasso is strongly marked in his writings.

As a satirist Lodge is weak and tame ; as a dramatist he is wholly without skill ; as a writer of romances we have seen that he is charming, but thoroughly artificial. It is by his lyrical poetry that he preserves a living place in literature. His best odes and madrigals rank with the finest work of that rich age. In short pieces of an erotic or contemplative character he throws aside all his habitual languor, and surprises the reader, who has been toiling somewhat wearily through the forest of Arden, by the brilliance and rapidity of his verse, by the *élan* of his passion, and by the bright turn of his fancy. In his best songs Lodge shows a command over the more sumptuous and splendid parts of language, that reminds the reader of Marlowe's gift in tragedy ; and of all the Elizabethans Lodge is the one who most frequently recalls Shelley to mind. His passion in the *Rosalynde* has a little of the transcendental and ethereal character of the *Epipsychidion,* while now and again there are phrases so curiously like Shelley's own, that we are tempted to believe that the rare quartos of Lodge must have passed through the later poet's hands. One such example is the

> 'A Turtle sate upon a leafless tree,
> Mourning her absent fere,'

with its curious resemblance to

> 'A widow bird sate mourning for her love
> Upon a wintry bough.'

The sonnets of Lodge are gorgeous in language, but lax in construction ; he did not understand the art of concentrating and sustaining his fancy in a sonnet ; but the volume entitled *Phillis* contains many beautiful fragments and irregular pieces, tending more or less to the sonnet form.   His epics of *Scilla's Metamorphosis* and *Elstred* are rambling pieces in the six-line stanza, produced rather in consequence of the success of *Venus and Adonis* than out of any genuine desire to tell a classical story.   In each poem the action is neglected, and the tale, such as it is, is smothered under a shower of courtly, flowery fancies.   A poem 'in commendation of a solitary life,' is one of Lodge's most admirable pieces, but is too long to be given here, and does not lend itself to quotation.   He was a poet of fine genius, fervent, harmonious, and florid ; but he was too sympathetic or not strong enough to resist the current of contemporary taste, running swiftly towards conceit.

EDMUND W. GOSSE.

Rosalynd's Madrigal.

Love in my bosom, like a bee,
        Doth suck his sweet ;
Now with his wings he plays with me,
        Now with his feet.
    Within mine eyes he makes his nest,
    His bed amidst my tender breast ;
    My kisses are his daily feast,
    And yet he robs me of my rest :
        Ah ! wanton, will ye ?

And if I sleep, then percheth he
        With pretty flight,
And makes his pillow of my knee
        The livelong night.
    Strike I my lute, he tunes the string ;
    He music plays if so I sing ;
    He lends me every lovely thing,
    Yet cruel he my heart doth sting :
        Whist, wanton, will ye ?

Else I with roses every day
        Will whip you hence,
And bind you, when you long to play,
        For your offence ;
    I 'll shut my eyes to keep you in ;
    I 'll make you fast it for your sin ;
    I 'll count your power not worth a pin ;
    Alas ! what hereby shall I win,
        If he gainsay me ?

What if I beat the wanton boy
        With many a rod ?
He will repay me with annoy,
        Because a god.
    Then sit thou safely on my knee,
    And let thy bower my bosom be ;
    Lurk in mine eyes, I like of thee,
    O Cupid ! so thou pity me,
        Spare not, but play thee.

ROSADER'S DESCRIPTION OF ROSALYND.

Like to the clear in highest sphere,
  Where all imperial beauty shines,
Of selfsame colour is her hair,
  Whether unfolded or in twines ;
Her eyes are sapphires set in snow,
  Refining heaven by every wink ;
The gods do fear whenas they glow,
  And I do tremble when I think.

Her cheeks are like the blushing cloud
  That beautifies Aurora's face,
Or like the silver-crimson shroud
  That Phoebus' smiling looks doth grace ;
Her lips are like two budded roses,
  Whom ranks of lilies neighbour nigh,
Within whose bounds she balm encloses
  Apt to entice a deity.

Her neck like to a stately tower,
  Where Love himself emprisoned lies,
To watch for glances every hour,
  From her divine and sacred eyes ;
Her paps are centres of delight,
  Her paps are orbs of heavenly frame,
Where nature moulds the dew of light,
  To feed perfection with the same.

With orient pearl, with ruby red,
  With marble white, with sapphire blue,
Her body every way is fed,
  Yet soft to touch, and sweet in view ;
Nature herself her shape admires,
  The gods are wounded in her sight,
And Love forsakes his heavenly fires,
  And at her eyes his brand doth light.

Then muse not, Nymphs, though I bemoan
 The absence of fair Rosalynd ;
Since for her fair there 's fairer none,
 Nor for her virtues so divine.
   Heigh ho ! fair Rosalynd !
Heigh ho ! my heart, would God that she were mine !

THE HARMONY OF LOVE.

A very phoenix, in her radiant eyes
 I leave mine age, and get my life again ;
True Hesperus, I watch her fall and rise,
 And with my tears extinguish all my pain ;
My lips for shadows shield her springing roses,
 Mine eyes for watchmen guard her while she sleepeth,
My reasons serve to 'quite her faint supposes ;
 Her fancy, mine ; my faith her fancy keepeth ;
She flower, I branch ; her sweet my sour supporteth,
O happy Love, where such delights consorteth !

PHILLIS' SICKNESS.

How languisheth the primrose of Love's garden !
 How trill her tears the elixir of my senses !
Ambitious sickness, what doth thee so harden ?
 O spare, and plague thou me for her offences !
Ah ! roses ! love's fair roses ! do not languish !
 Blush through the milk-white veil that holds you covered ;
If heat or cold may mitigate your anguish,
 I 'll burn, I 'll freeze, but you shall be recovered.
Good God ! would Beauty mark, now she is crazed,
 How but one shower of sickness makes her tender,
Her judgments, then, to mark my woes amazed,
 To mercy should opinion's fort surrender ;
And I, oh ! would I might, or would she meant it !
Should harry love, who now in heart lament it.

LOVE'S WANTONNESS.

Love guides the roses of thy lips,
  And flies about them like a bee;
If I approach he forward skips,
  And if I kiss he stingeth me.

Love in thine eyes doth build his bower,
  And sleeps within their pretty shine,
And if I look the boy will lower,
  And from their orbs shoot shafts divine.

Love works thy heart within his fire,
  And in my tears doth firm the same,
And if I tempt it will retire,
  And of my plaints doth make a game.

Love, let me cull her choicest flowers,
  And pity me, and calm her eye,
Make soft her heart, dissolve her lowers,
  Then I will praise thy deity.

WILLIAM WARNER.

[WILLIAM WARNER was born in Oxfordshire about the middle of the sixteenth century, and died on the 9th of March, 1609, at Amwell. His chief work is *Albion's England*, 1586. It was at first prohibited, for reasons unknown, but afterwards became very popular. He perhaps translated the *Menaechmi* of Plautus 1595; and certainly wrote a prose collection of moralized stories, entitled *Syrinx*, 1597.]

Warner's chief and only poetical work is *Albion's England*, a curious medley of partly traditional history, with interludes of the *fabliau* kind. By some accident it has, since the author's death, secured an audience, not indeed wide, but much wider than that enjoyed by the work of contemporaries of far greater power. The pastoral episode of *Argentile and Curan* hit the taste of the eighteenth century, and Chalmers reprinted the whole poem in his *Poets*, very injudiciously following Ellis in dividing the fourteen-syllable lines into eights and sixes. In this form much of it irresistibly reminds the reader of Johnson's injurious parody of that metre : but in the original editions it appears to much greater advantage. The ascending and descending slope of the long lines is often managed with a good deal of art ; and as the following extract, giving the speeches of Harold and William before Hastings, will show, there is sometimes dignity in the sentiments and vigour in their expression. The author is too prone to adopt classical constructions, especially absolute cases, which often throw obscurity over his meaning. Warner is not, as he has been called, a ' good, honest, plain writer of moral rules and precepts'; nor is his work, as another authority asserts, ' written in Alexandrines.' But though he will not bear comparison with the better, even of the second-rate Elizabethans, such as Watson, Barnes, and Constable, much less with his fellow historians Drayton and Daniel, the singularity of the plan of his book, and some vigorous touches here and there, raise him above the mass.

There is, moreover, one thing in his work which is of considerable
literary interest.   Unlike almost all his contemporaries, he is
hardly at all ' Italianate.'   The Italian influence, which for a full
century coloured English poetry, is scarcely discernible in him,
and he is thus an interesting example of an English poet with
hardly any foreign strain in him except, as has been said, a certain
tinge of classical study.

                                                    G. SAINTSBURY.

Before the Battle of Hastings.

[From *Albion's England*, Bk. iv. Cap. 22.]

'See, valiant war-friends yonder be the first, the last, and all
The agents of our enemies : they henceforth cannot call
Supplies : for weeds at Normandy by this in porches grow :
Then conquer these would conquer you, and dread no further foe.
They are no stouter than the Brutes, whom we did hence exile :
Nor stronger than the sturdy Danes, our victory erewhile :
Nor Saxony could once contain, or scarce the world beside,
Our fathers who did sway by sword where listed them to bide.
Then do not ye degenerate, take courage by descent,
And by their burials, not abode, their force and flight prevent.
Ye have in hand your country's cause, a conquest they pretend,
Which (were ye not the same ye be) even cowards would defend.
I grant that part of us are fled, and linked to the foe,
And glad I am our army is of traitors cleared so,
Yea, pardon hath he to depart that stayeth malcontent :
I prize the mind above the man, like zeal hath like event.
Yet troth it is no well or ill this island ever had,
But through the well or ill support of subjects good or bad.
Not Caesar, Hengest, Swayn, or now (which ne'ertheless shall fail)
The Norman bastard (Albion true) did, could, or can prevail.
But to be self-false in this isle a self-foe ever is,
Yet wot I, never traitor did his treason's stipend miss.
Shrink who will shrink, let armour's weight press down the bur-
      dened earth,
My foes with wondering eyes shall see I over-prize my death.
But since ye all (for all, I hope, alike affected be,
Your wives, your children, lives and land, from servitude to free)
Are armed both in show and zeal, then gloriously contend
To win and wear the home-brought spoils of victory the end.
Let not the skinner's daughter's son possess what he pretends,
He lives to die a noble death that life for freedom spends.'
As Harold heartened thus his men, so did the Norman his ;
And looking wishly on the earth Duke William speaketh this :

'To live upon, or lie within, this is my ground or grave,
My loving soldiers, one of twain your duke resolves to have :
Nor be ye, Normans, now to seek in what you should be stout,
Ye come amidst the English pikes to hew your honours out.
Ye come to win the same by lance, that is your own by law ;
Ye come, I say, in righteous war revenging swords to draw.
Howbeit, of more hardy foes no passed fight hath sped ye,
Since Rollo to your now-abode with bands victorious led ye,
Or Turchus, son of Troylus, in Scythian Fazo bred ye.
Then worthy your progenitors ye seed of Priam's son,
Exploit this business : Rollons, do that which ye wish be done.
Three people have as many times got and foregone this shore,
It resteth now ye conquer it not to be conquered more :
For Norman and the Saxon blood conjoining, as it may,
From that consorted seed the crown shall never pass away.
Before us are our armed foes, behind us are the seas,
On either side the foe hath holds of succour and for ease ;
But that advantage shall return their disadvantage thus,
If ye observe no shore is left the which may shelter us.
And so hold out amidst the rough, whil'st they hale in for lee,
Whereas, whilst men securely sail not seldom shipwrecks be.
What should I cite your passed acts, or tediously incense
To present arms ? your faces show your hearts conceive offence,
Yea, even your courages divine a conquest not to fail ;
Hope, then, your duke doth prophesy, and in that hope prevail.
A people brave, a terrene Heaven, both objects worth your wars
Shall be the prizes of your prow's, and mount your fame to stars.
Let not a traitor's perjur'd son extrude us from our right,
He dies to live a famous life, that doth for conquest fight.'

WILLIAM SHAKESPEARE.

[WILLIAM SHAKESPEARE was born at Stratford on Avon in April 1564; there also he died, April 23rd (old style), 1616. The following are the titles of his poems, with the dates of publication: *Venus and Adonis*, 1593; *The Rape of Lucrece*, 1594; *The Passionate Pilgrim* (a miscellany which includes only a few pieces by Shakespeare), 1599; *The Phœnix and the Turtle* (printed with pieces on the same subject by other poets of the time, at the end of Robert Chester's *Love's Martyr, or Rosalin's Complaint*), 1601; *Sonnets*, 1609; *A Lover's Complaint* (in the same volume with the *Sonnets*), 1609.]

Shakespeare's genius was not one of those which ripen over-early. At thirty he was hardly past his years of apprenticeship as a dramatic craftsman; in comedy he was experimenting in various directions; in historical tragedy he submitted to the influence of his great fellow, Christopher Marlowe, who had risen to eminent stature while Shakespeare was still in his growing years; in pure tragedy he was feeling after a way of his own which should ennoble terror by its union with tenderness and beauty. It was at this time that his first essay as a non-dramatic poet was made. At what precise date the *Venus and Adonis* was written we cannot be certain; but no good reason appears for supposing that Shakespeare brought it up with him from Stratford, or indeed that it was written earlier than the year 1592. 'The first heir of my invention'—so its author describes the poem; but, in accordance with the feeling of his own day, he would naturally set aside his plays, none of which he had printed or thought of printing, as indeed mere *plays*—not *works*, not any part of literature proper,—while the *Venus and Adonis*, which was to give him rank among the poets of his time, he would regard as the first legitimate child of his imagination. Henry Wriothesley, the Earl of Southampton —young, clever, gallant, generous—had already honoured the rising dramatist with his notice, and to him Shakespeare dedicated 'his unpolished lines,' promising to take advantage of all idle hours until he have some ' graver labour' to present. The graver labour followed in 1594, and was offered to his patron with words of strong devotion. The two poems, the *Venus* and the *Lucrece*, may be looked on as companion pieces, belonging to the same period, presented to the same person, exhibiting the same characteristics of style.

Shakespeare's delight in beauty and his delight in wit, in the brightness and nimbleness of the play of mind, are manifest in all his earlier writings. Such delight was indeed part of the age as well as of the individual. The consciousness of new power proper to the Renaissance period, the bounding energy, the sense that all the human faculties were emancipated, resulted in great achievement, and no less in strange extravagance ; the lust of the eye was under slight restraint, and every clever fancy might caper as it pleased. In choosing the subject of his first poem, Shakespeare sought the most beautiful creatures which imagination had ever conceived for pasture of man's eye. What female figure so superb in loveliness as that of the queen of Love ? What mortal companion can she have comely to perfection save the boy Adonis ? But the common way of love, in which the man woos the woman, has been the theme of every poet ; how much more 'high fantastical' were the woman to woo the man, and spend all her wit, and all her ardour, and all her arts in striving to overcome his indifference ? Thus the subject of Venus enamoured, and the coldness of the boy Adonis, gave scope both to the poet's passion for beauty and his passion for ingenuity. Shakespeare attempts two things—first, to paint with brilliant words the chosen figures, and their encounterings ; secondly, to invent speeches for them in which the war of wit shall be maintained with glittering conceit, and high-wrought fantasy. The subject did not lay hold of him, compelling him to utterance ; rather he laboured hard to make the most of it, viewing it on this side and on that ; to use the word of his contemporaries, he ' subtilized' with it, until he could subtilize no farther. A couple of ice-houses these two poems of Shakespeare have been called by Hazlitt—'they are' he says, ' as hard, as glittering, and as cold.' Cold indeed they will seem to anyone who listens to hear in them the natural cry of human passion. But the paradox is true, that for a young poet of Elizabeth's age to be natural, direct, simple, would have been indeed unnatural. He was most happy when most fantastical ; he spun a shining web to catch conceits inevitably as a spider casts his thread ; the quick-building wit was itself warm while erecting its ice-houses.

As a narrative poem the *Lucrece* has this advantage over the *Venus and Adonis*, that it includes more of action, and that the theme is one which gives scope for deep and strenuous passion. For this reason the vice of style impresses us more here perhaps than in the earlier poem. The action is retarded by all manner of pretty ingenuities. Lucrece in her agony delivers *tirades* on Night, on Time, on Opportunity, as if they were theses for a degree in some academy of wit. Still the effect on a reader in the right mood is not that of frigid cleverness ; the faults are faults of youth ; the poet's pleasurable excitement can be perceived ; nay at times we feel the energetic fervour of his heart. Now and again the poetry surprises, not by singularity, but as Keats has said that poetry ought to surprise, by a fine excess ; sometimes a line is all gold seven times refined ; and there is throughout such evidence of a rich, abounding nature in the writer that we are happy with him even while we recognize the idle errors of his nonage. The first and most obvious excellence of the *Venus and Adonis*, Coleridge has said, and he might have extended the remark to the companion poem, ' is the perfect sweetness of the versification ; its adaptation to the subject ; and the power displayed in varying the march of the words without passing into a loftier and more majestic rhythm than was demanded by the thoughts, or permitted by the propriety of preserving a sense of melody predominant. The delight in richness and sweetness of sound, even to a faulty excess, if it be evidently original, and not the result of an easily imitable mechanism, I regard as a highly favourable promise in the compositions of a young man.' A highly favourable promise indeed ; but Shakespeare, as other young poets of original genius, was peculiarly susceptible to influences from the verse of contemporaries. It is easy to perceive that the author of *Venus and Adonis* had read with delight Lodge's *Glaucus and Silla*, and that in treating the more complex stanza of the *Lucrece* Shakespeare had gained something from *The Complaint of Rosamond* by Daniel, a poet possessing so much less than himself of the vital spirit of harmony. In both poems of Shakespeare his mind, it has been observed, hovers often within the limits of a single line ; there are also long cumulative passages of connected lines, each line an unit in the series ; the effect of such passages is rhetorical ; they tend toward a climax, after which the verse has to recommence from a new starting point.

Amid the tangle of amorous casuistry in the *Venus and Adonis* some relief is afforded by touches of delight in the rural landscape of England. When the poem was written Stratford was fresh in Shakespeare's memory ; its primrose banks, and 'blue-veined violets,' the bird 'tangled in a net,' the stallion, the hunted hare, the the red morn rain-betokening, the gentle lark which weary of rest

> 'From his moist cabinet mounts up on high,
> And wakes the morning, from whose silver breast
> The sun ariseth in his majesty.'

Both poems immediately became popular ; it was his sweetness of utterance which gave Shakespeare's first readers their chief delight ; he was to them 'honey-tongued Shakespeare,' 'mellifluous Shakespeare,' 'in whom the sweet wittie soul of Ovid lives' ; he was 'silver-tongued Melicert,' gifted with a 'honey-flowing vaine.' The time had not yet come to know him as the symphonist who could create the stormy harmonies of *Lear*, as the bitter trumpeter of doom announcing through *Timon* the fall of luxurious cities that wanton in unrighteousness.

In 1598 allusion was made by Francis Meres to Shakespeare's 'sugred sonnets among his private friends' ; next year two of the sugared sonnets—surreptitiously obtained, as we cannot but believe —appeared in *The Passionate Pilgrim*. It was not until ten years later that Thomas Thorpe published the collection of 154 Sonnets, and there is good reason for believing that their author did not sanction the publication. Thorpe dedicated his volume to 'The onlie Begetter of these ensuing Sonnets Mr. W. H.' wishing him 'all happiness and that eternity promised by our ever-living poet.' Who is this Mr. W. H., the inspirer of the sonnets ? And what is the purport of these poems ?

To the first question there is but one trustworthy answer—We do not know. Whether Mr. W. H. was William Herbert, Earl of Pembroke, or Henry Wriothesley, Earl of Southampton, or whether his name has wholly perished, though in Shakespeare's verse his fame endures, we cannot tell. We know him as '*Will*,' for Shakespeare plays with his christian name in the 135th and 143rd sonnets, and with '*Will*' we must remain contented. Patience perforce ! after all it is not essential to the understanding of the poems that we should solve Thorpe's riddle ; it is enough, if we believe that '*Will*' was no imaginary being, no abstraction of the brain, no allegorizing sonneteer's invention, but a creature of flesh and blood—a man, young, beautiful, wealthy, of high rank, full of charm and grace and condescension. To him the sonnets from 1 to 126 were addressed; they were written at intervals over a period of time certainly as long as three years (see sonnet 104), and probably longer; they are printed by Thorpe in their proper order, and form a series in which it is possible to find a few breaks, such as would naturally occur in poems connected with the real incidents of several years. The poem numbered 126, not a sonnet, consists of twelve lines in rhyming couplets; it forms an *Envoy* to the series of sonnets addressed to Shakespeare's friend, and it is complete; but Thorpe, not perceiving its special character, adds in the original edition marks intended to show that two lines are wanting. With 127 begins a new series, addressed to a woman. This woman Shakespeare loved with a kind of bitter love; he knew that her character was stained; he saw that she was the reverse of beautiful, according to common conceptions of beauty; still, to him she was beautiful. This pale-faced, dark-eyed woman drew to her the great poet with a singular fascination; he would linger by the virginal while she played, and watch her fingers as they moved over the keys; he would resolve no longer to remain in bondage to her strange power, and would return to beg for her renewal of regard. But dearer than this pale musician was the youth whom he worshipped with a fond idolatry. Their friendship was to be the honour, the comfort, the blessedness of Shakespeare's life. Alas, his dark enchantress has cast her eyes upon *Will*, and laid her snares for him! And so for the woman's sake the friendship of man and man is clouded, and the poor actor who had been lifted out of his sphere in a dream of new delight, sinks back and finds how hard the world goes with him, how sad a thing it is to be defrauded by those we hold most dear, how weak a thing his own heart is. He does not turn with fierce resentment against his friend; he only feels that it is very sad to be deserted; and with piteous casuistry he tries to argue against himself, to plead in his friend's defence, to find it natural that one so bright and young and engaging should turn away the head and pass him coldly by. But such estrangement did not last to the end. After a long absence the friends meet. *Will's* truer heart asserts itself; there are confessions and words of repentance on both sides; then follow forgiveness and reconciliation; once more heart and heart are united, —united now, after this bitter experience, never again to be tempted to disloyalty.

The story as here told in outline is plainly written in the two series of sonnets, which, though separate, are concerned with the same persons and refer to the same events. Let us look a little more closely at the first series. Shakespeare begins by urging upon his young friend the expediency of marriage; his father is dead; for his own sake, for his mother's sake, for his friend's sake, for the sake of the world, he should seek to renew his own life in that of a child who shall be heir to his beauty and his honour. His poet would fain make *Will* immortal in his verse, ay, and must not fail to do so, but why not defeat time by the worthier way of living offspring? Then Shakespeare turns (sonnet 26) from this pleading to dwell upon the beauty and the sweetness of his friend; all losses, needs, and griefs are cancelled by the joy of loving and being loved by a being so perfect. But presently the little rift within the lute is discovered; *Will* holds somewhat off from the low-born player, especially in public places. Is not this natural, and indeed inevitable? The player can at least look up and rejoice in his friend's happier fortune, his beauty, birth, wealth, wit. Then follows, during Shakespeare's absence, the more grievous wrong done to him by *Will*, and the lady of the virginal. Can Shakespeare forgive such a wrong? Even this he tries, but in vain; for are there not signs that *Will's* heart is really cold towards him? *Will* protests, and asserts his constancy; there is a leap-up of the flame of love once more. But time is passing, age is creeping nearer, the world seems more oppressed by ills, and what is there of solid and substantial good to set against all this? His friend's love; but what if his friend be himself infected with the general evil? What if he grow common? Public scandal is busy with his name. Were it not better to die than to live longer in a world where all tends daily from bad to worse? Moreover now the young aristocrat is lending a favourable ear to a rival poet, one possessed of art and learning to which Shakespeare is a stranger. Ah! it is best to say farewell at once, to wake rudely from the deceitful dream of joy! Let *Will* hate him—but hate him quick, that the bitterness of death may soon be past. Absence, and total silence follow. And then, when things seem most remediless, the old fibres of love begin to stir, the buried root to send forth a rod with blossoms. The two hearts never wholly estranged approach, draw yet closer, unite; all impediments to the marriage of true minds are put aside. The love that seemed ruined is built anew stronger than before. Now it is based not on beauty, not on considerations of interest, not on aught that time can destroy : now indeed Time is defeated ; not by offspring, not by verse, but by that which is alone free from time and fortune, by Love. Yet— thus the series closes—let us not be lifted up above measure ; however fair life and love may be, there is at last, for thee even as for me, the quietus of the grave.

Of the exquisite songs scattered through Shakespeare's plays it is almost an impertinence to speak. If they do not make their own way, like the notes in the wildwood, no words will open the dull ear to take them in. There is little song in the historical dramas ; how should there be much amid the debates of the council-chamber, the clash of swords, the tug of rival interests, the plotting of courtiers, the ambitious hypocrisies of priests ? To hear dainty snatches set to some clear-hearted tune—' Green Sleeves' perhaps or 'Light o' love'—we must haunt the palace of the enamoured Duke of Illyria, or wander under green boughs in Arden, or stray along the yellow sands of the enchanted island, or lurk behind the hedge while light-footed and light-fingered Autolycus sets the country air a-ringing with his sprightly tirra-lirra. In the tragedies Shakespeare has made use of song —his own or another's—always with deliberate forethought, always with the inevitable rightness of genius, to make the pity more rare and of a finer edge, to touch the skirts of darkness with a pathetic gleam, or to mingle some keen irony with the transitory triumph of life. We remember the wild and bitter gaiety, hiding so deep a sorrow, of Lear's poor boy quavering out weak notes across the tempest ; thought and affliction turned to prettiness in the distracted Ophelia's singing ; the rough ditty keeping time to strokes of the mattock as it tosses out the earth which is to lie on Ophelia's breast ; the high-pitched joviality of honest Iago—' And let me the canakin clink, clink' ; the volleying chorus, ' Cup us till the world go round,' shouted in Pompey's galley, while Menes stands by ready to fall to the triumvirs' throats ; the old song of willow sung by maid Barbara when Desdemona was a girl, and coming back to her on that night when a sad wife she goes bedward with eyes ripe for weeping, and with a heart still meek and innocent as the heart of a little child. But to hear songs, which 'dally with the innocence of love like the old age,' one should be silent.

EDWARD DOWDEN.

POEMS.

[From *Venus and Adonis.*]

O, what a sight it was, wistly to view
How she came stealing to the wayward boy!
To note the fighting conflict of her hue,
How white and red each other did destroy!
　But now her cheek was pale, and by and by
　It flash'd forth fire, as lightning from the sky.

Now was she just before him as he sat,
And like a lowly lover down she kneels ;
With one fair hand she heaveth up his hat,
Her other tender hand his fair cheek feels :
　His tenderer cheek receives her soft hand's print,
　As apt as new-fall'n snow takes any dint.

O, what a war of looks was then between them!
Her eyes petitioners to his eyes suing ;
His eyes saw her eyes as they had not seen them ;
Her eyes woo'd still, his eyes disdain'd the wooing :
　And all this dumb play had his acts made plain
　With tears, which, chorus-like, her eyes did rain.

Full gently now she takes him by the hand,
A lily prison'd in a gaol of snow,
Or ivory in an alabaster band ;
So white a friend engirts so white a foe :
　This beauteous combat, wilful and unwilling,
　Show'd like two silver doves that sit a-billing

　　　*　　　*　　　*　　　*　　　*　　　*

'Thou hadst been gone,' quoth she, 'sweet boy, ere this,
But that thou told'st me thou wouldst hunt the boar.
O, be advised ! thou know'st not what it is
With javelin's point a churlish swine to gore,
　Whose tushes never sheathed he whetteth still,
　Like to a mortal butcher bent to kill.

'On his bow-back he hath a battle set,
Of bristly pikes, that ever threat his foes;
His eyes, like glow-worms, shine when he doth fret;
His snout digs sepulchres where'er he goes;
　Being moved, he strikes whate'er is in his way,
　And whom he strikes his crooked tushes slay.

'His brawny sides, with hairy bristles arm'd,
Are better proof than thy spear's point can enter;
His short thick neck cannot be easily harm'd;
Being ireful, on the lion he will venture:
　The thorny brambles and embracing bushes,
　As fearful of him, part, through whom he rushes.

'Alas, he nought esteems that face of thine,
To which Love's eyes pay tributary gazes;
Nor thy soft hands, sweet lips and crystal eyne,
Whose full perfection all the world amazes;
　But having thee at vantage,—wondrous dread!
　Would root these beauties as he roots the mead.

'O, let him keep his loathsome cabin still;
Beauty hath nought to do with such foul fiends:
Come not within his danger by thy will;
They that thrive well take counsel of their friends.
　When thou didst name the boar, not to dissemble,
　I fear'd thy fortune, and my joints did tremble.'
　　*　　*　　*　　*　　*　　*
'But if thou needs wilt hunt, be ruled by me;
Uncouple at the timorous flying hare,
Or at the fox which lives by subtlety,
Or at the roe which no encounter dare:
　Pursue these fearful creatures o'er the downs,
　And on thy well-breathed horse keep with thy hounds.

'And when thou hast on foot the purblind hare,
Mark the poor wretch, to overshoot his troubles
How he outruns the wind and with what care
He cranks and crosses with a thousand doubles:
　The many musets through the which he goes
　Are like a labyrinth to amaze his foes.

'Sometime he runs among a flock of sheep,
To make the cunning hounds mistake their smell,
And sometime where earth-delving conies keep,
To stop the loud pursuers in their yell,
   And sometime sorteth with a herd of deer:
   Danger deviseth shifts; wit waits on fear:

'For there his smell with others being mingled,
The hot scent-snuffing hounds are driven to doubt,
Ceasing their clamorous cry till they have singled
With much ado the cold fault cleanly out;
   Then do they spend their mouths: Echo replies,
   As if another chase were in the skies.

'By this, poor Wat, far off upon a hill,
Stands on his hinder legs with listening ear,
To hearken if his foes pursue him still:
Anon their loud alarums he doth hear;
   And now his grief may be compared well
   To one sore sick that hears the passing-bell.

'Then shalt thou see the dew-bedabbled wretch
Turn, and return, indenting with the way;
Each envious brier his weary legs doth scratch,
Each shadow makes him stop, each murmur stay:
   For misery is trodden on by many,
   And being low never relieved by any.'

   *   *   *   *   *   *

With this, he breaketh from the sweet embrace,
Of those fair arms which bound him to her breast,
And homeward through the dark laund runs apace;
Leaves Love upon her back deeply distress'd.
   Look, how a bright star shooteth from the sky,
   So glides he in the night from Venus' eye;

Which after him she darts, as one on shore
Gazing upon a late-embarked friend,
Till the wild waves will have him seen no more,
Whose ridges with the meeting clouds contend:
   So did the merciless and pitchy night
   Fold in the object that did feed her sight.

Whereat amazed, as one that unaware
Hath dropp'd a precious jewel in the flood,
Or stonish'd as night-wanderers often are,
Their light blown out in some mistrustful wood,
   Even so confounded in the dark she lay,
   Having lost the fair discovery of her way.

And now she beats her heart, whereat it groans,
That all the neighbour caves, as seeming troubled,
Make verbal repetition of her moans ;
Passion on passion deeply is redoubled :
   'Ay me !' she cries, and twenty times 'Woe, woe !'
   And twenty echoes twenty times cry so.

   *   *   *   *   *   *

She looks upon his lips, and they are pale ;
She takes him by the hand, and that is cold ;
She whispers in his ears a heavy tale,
As if they heard the woeful words she told ;
   She lifts the coffer-lids that close his eyes,
   Where, lo, two lamps, burnt out, in darkness lies ;

Two glasses, where herself herself beheld,
A thousand times, and now no more reflect ;
Their virtue lost, wherein they late excell'd,
And every beauty robb'd of his effect :
   'Wonder of time,' quoth she, 'this is my spite,
   That, thou being dead, the day should yet be light.

'Since thou art dead, lo, here I prophesy :
Sorrow on love hereafter shall attend :
It shall be waited on with jealousy,
Find sweet beginning, but unsavoury end,
   Ne'er settled equally, but high or low,
   That all love's pleasure shall not match his woe.

'It shall be fickle, false and full of fraud,
Bud and be blasted in a breathing-while ;
The bottom poison, and the top o'erstraw'd
With sweets that shall the truest sight beguile :
   The strongest body shall it make most weak,
   Strike the wise dumb and teach the fool to speak.

'It shall be sparing and too full of riot,
Teaching decrepit age to tread the measures;
The staring ruffian shall it keep in quiet,
Pluck down the rich, enrich the poor with treasures;
    It shall be raging-mad and silly-mild,
    Make the young old, the old become a child.

'It shall suspect where is no cause of fear;
It shall not fear where it should most mistrust,
It shall be merciful and too severe,
And most deceiving when it seems most just;
    Perverse it shall be where it shows most toward,
    Put fear to valour, courage to the coward.

'It shall be cause of war and dire events,
And set dissension 'twixt the son and sire;
Subject and servile to all discontents,
As dry combustious matter is to fire:
    Sith in his prime Death doth my love destroy,
    They that love best their loves shall not enjoy.'

By this, the boy that by her side lay kill'd
Was melted like a vapour from her sight,
And in his blood that on the ground lay spill'd,
A purple flower sprung up, chequer'd with white,
    Resembling well his pale cheeks and the blood
    Which in round drops upon their whiteness stood.

[From *Lucrece.*]

By this, lamenting Philomel had ended
The well-tuned warble of her nightly sorrow,
And solemn night with slow sad gait descended
To ugly hell; when, lo, the blushing morrow
Lends light to all fair eyes that light will borrow:
    But cloudly Lucrece shames herself to see,
    And therefore still in night would cloister'd be.

Revealing day through every cranny spies,
And seems to point her out where she sits weeping;
To whom she sobbing speaks: 'O eye of eyes,
Why pry'st thou through my window? leave thy peeping:
Mock with thy tickling beams eyes that are sleeping:
  Brand not my forehead with thy piercing light,
  For day hath nought to do what's done by night.'

Thus cavils she with every thing she sees:
True grief is fond and testy as a child,
Who wayward once, his mood with nought agrees:
Old woes, not infant sorrows, bear them mild;
Continuance tames the one; the other wild,
  Like an unpractised swimmer plunging still,
  With too much labour drowns for want of skill.

So she, deep-drenched in a sea of care,
Holds disputation with each thing she views,
And to herself all sorrow doth compare;
No object but her passion's strength renews;
And as one shifts, another straight ensues:
  Sometime her grief is dumb and hath no words;
  Sometime 'tis mad and too much talk affords.

The little birds that tune their morning's joy
Make her moans mad with their sweet melody:
For mirth doth search the bottom of annoy;
Sad souls are slain in merry company;
Grief best is pleased with grief's society:
  True sorrow then is feelingly sufficed
  When with like semblance it is sympathised.

'Tis double death to drown in ken of shore;
He ten times pines that pines beholding food;
To see the salve doth make the wound ache more;
Great grief grieves most at that would do it good;
Deep woes roll forward like a gentle flood,
  Who, being stopp'd, the bounding banks o'erflows;
  Grief dallied with nor law nor limit knows.

'You mocking birds,' quoth she, 'your tunes entomb
Within your hollow-swelling feather'd breasts,
And in my hearing be you mute and dumb:
My restless discord loves no stops nor rests;
A woeful hostess brooks not merry guests:
  Relish your nimble notes to pleasing ears;
  Distress likes dumps when time is kept with tears.

'Come, Philomel, that sing'st of ravishment,
Make thy sad grove in my dishevell'd hair:
As the dank earth weeps at thy languishment,
So I at each sad strain will strain a tear,
And with deep groans the diapason bear;
  For burden-wise I 'll hum on Tarquin still,
  While thou on Tereus descant'st better skill.'

*　　*　　*　　*　　*　　*　　*

This plot of death when sadly she had laid,
And wiped the brinish pearl from her bright eyes,
With untuned tongue she hoarsely calls her maid,
Whose swift obedience to her mistress hies;
For fleet-wing'd duty with thought's feathers flies.
  Poor Lucrece' cheeks unto her maid seem so
  As winter meads when sun doth melt their snow.

Her mistress she doth give demure good-morrow,
With soft-slow tongue, true mark of modesty,
And sorts a sad look to her lady's sorrow,
For why her face wore sorrow's livery;
But durst not ask of her audaciously
  Why her two suns were cloud-eclipsed so,
  Nor why her fair cheeks over-wash'd with woe.

But as the earth doth weep, the sun being set,
Each flower moisten'd like a melting eye;
Even so the maid with swelling drops gan wet
Her circled eyne, enforced by sympathy
Of those fair suns set in her mistress' sky,
  Who in a salt-waved ocean quench their light,
  Which makes the maid weep like the dewy night.

A pretty while these pretty creatures stand,
Like ivory conduits coral cisterns filling ;
One justly weeps ; the other takes in hand
No cause, but company, of her drops spilling :
Their gentle sex to weep are often willing ;
   Grieving themselves to guess at others' smarts,
   And then they drown their eyes or break their hearts.

For men have marble, women waxen, minds,
And therefore are they form'd as marble will ;
The weak oppress'd, the impression of strange kinds
Is form'd in them by force, by fraud, or skill :
Then call them not the authors of their ill,
   No more than wax shall be accounted evil
   Wherein is stamp'd the semblance of a devil.

Their smoothness, like a goodly champaign plain,
Lays open all the little worms that creep ;
In men, as in a rough-grown grove, remain
Cave-keeping evils that obscurely sleep :
Through crystal walls each little mote will peep :
   Though men can cover crimes with bold stern looks,
   Poor women's faces are their own faults' books.

No man inveigh against the wither'd flower,
But chide rough winter that the flower hath kill'd :
Not that devour'd, but that which doth devour,
Is worthy blame. O, let it not be hild
Poor women's faults, that they are so fulfill'd
   With men's abuses : those proud lords, to blame,
   Make weak-made women tenants to their shame

Sonnets.

2.

When forty winters shall besiege thy brow,
And dig deep trenches in thy beauty's field,
Thy youth's proud livery, so gazed on now,
Will be a tatter'd weed, of small worth held :
Then being ask'd where all thy beauty lies,
Where all the treasure of thy lusty days,
To say, within thine own deep-sunken eyes,
Were an all-eating shame and thriftless praise.
How much more praise deserved thy beauty's use,
If thou couldst answer ' This fair child of mine
Shall sum my count and make my old excuse,'
Proving his beauty by succession thine !
   This were to be new made when thou art old,
   And see thy blood warm when thou feel'st it cold.

12.

When I do count the clock that tells the time,
And see the brave day sunk in hideous night ;
When I behold the violet past prime,
And sable curls all silver'd o'er with white ;
When lofty trees I see barren of leaves
Which erst from heat did canopy the herd,
And summer's green all girded up in sheaves
Borne on the bier with white and bristly beard,
Then of thy beauty do I question make,
That thou among the wastes of time must go,
Since sweets and beauties do themselves forsake
And die as fast as they see others grow ;
   And nothing 'gainst Time's scythe can make defence
   Save breed, to brave him when he takes thee hence.

18.

Shall I compare thee to a summer's day?
Thou art more lovely and more temperate:
Rough winds do shake the darling buds of May,
And summer's lease hath all too short a date:
Sometime too hot the eye of heaven shines,
And often is his gold complexion dimm'd;
And every fair from fair sometime declines,
By chance or nature's changing course untrimm'd;
But thy eternal summer shall not fade
Nor lose possession of that fair thou owest;
Nor shall Death brag thou wander'st in his shade,
When in eternal lines to time thou growest:
  So long as men can breathe or eyes can see,
  So long lives this and this gives life to thee.

23.

As an unperfect actor on the stage
Who with his fear is put besides his part,
Or some fierce thing replete with too much rage,
Whose strength's abundance weakens his own heart,
So I, for fear of trust, forget to say
The perfect ceremony of love's rite,
And in mine own love's strength seem to decay,
O'ercharged with burden of mine own love's might.
O, let my books be then the eloquence
And dumb presagers of my speaking breast,
Who plead for love and look for recompense
More than that tongue that more hath more express'd.
  O, learn to read what silent love hath writ:
  To hear with eyes belongs to love's fine wit.

29.

When, in disgrace with fortune and men's eyes,
I all alone beweep my outcast state
And trouble deaf heaven with my bootless cries
And look upon myself and curse my fate,
Wishing me like to one more rich in hope,
Featured like him, like him with friends possess'd,
Desiring this man's art and that man's scope,
With what I most enjoy contented least ;
Yet in these thoughts myself almost despising,
Haply I think on thee, and then my state,
Like to the lark at break of day arising
From sullen earth, sings hymns at heaven's gate ;
   For thy sweet love remember'd such wealth brings
   That then I scorn to change my state with kings.

30.

When to the sessions of sweet silent thought
I summon up remembrance of things past,
I sigh the lack of many a thing I sought,
And with old woes new wail my dear time's waste :
Then can I drown an eye, unused to flow,
For precious friends hid in death's dateless night,
And weep afresh love's long since cancell'd woe,
And moan the expense of many a vanish'd sight :
Then can I grieve at grievances forgone,
And heavily from woe to woe tell o'er
The sad account of fore-bemoaned moan,
Which I new pay as if not paid before.
   But if the while I think on thee, dear friend,
   All losses are restored and sorrows end.

32.

If thou survive my well-contented day,
When that churl Death my bones with dust shall cover,
And shalt by fortune once more re-survey
These poor rude lines of thy deceased lover,
Compare them with the bettering of the time,
And though they be outstripp'd by every pen,
Reserve them for my love, not for their rhyme,
Exceeded by the height of happier men.
O, then vouchsafe me but this loving thought:
'Had my friend's Muse grown with this growing age,
A dearer birth than this his love had brought,
To march in ranks of better equipage:
   But since he died and poets better prove,
    Theirs for their style I 'll read, his for his love.'

33.

Full many a glorious morning have I seen
Flatter the mountain-tops with sovereign eye,
Kissing with golden face the meadows green,
Gilding pale streams with heavenly alchemy;
Anon permit the basest clouds to ride
With ugly rack on his celestial face,
And from the forlorn world his visage hide,
Stealing unseen to west with this disgrace:
Even so my sun one early morn did shine
With all-triumphant splendour on my brow;
But out, alack! he was but one hour mine;
The region cloud hath mask'd him from me now.
   Yet him for this my love no whit disdaineth;
    Suns of the world may stain when heaven's sun staineth.

52.

So am I as the rich, whose blessed key
Can bring him to his sweet up-locked treasure,
The which he will not every hour survey,
For blunting the fine point of seldom pleasure.
Therefore are feasts so solemn and so rare,
Since, seldom coming, in the long year set,
Like stones of worth they thinly placed are,
Or captain jewels in the carcanet.
So is the time that keeps you as my chest,
Or as the wardrobe which the robe doth hide,
To make some special instant special blest,
By new unfolding his imprison'd pride.
    Blessed are you, whose worthiness gives scope,
    Being had, to triumph, being lack'd, to hope.

54.

O, how much more doth beauty beauteous seem
By that sweet ornament which truth doth give!
The rose looks fair, but fairer we it deem
For that sweet odour which doth in it live.
The canker-blooms have full as deep a dye
As the perfumed tincture of the roses,
Hang on such thorns and play as wantonly
When summer's breath their masked buds discloses:
But, for their virtue only is their show,
They live unwoo'd and unrespected fade,
Die to themselves.   Sweet roses do not so;
Of their sweet deaths are sweetest odours made:
    And so of you, beauteous and lovely youth,
    When that shall fade, my verse distills your truth.

66.

Tired with all these, for restful death I cry,
As, to behold desert a beggar born,
And needy nothing trimm'd in jollity,
And purest faith unhappily forsworn,
And gilded honour shamefully misplaced,
And maiden virtue rudely strumpeted,
And right perfection wrongfully disgraced,
And strength by limping sway disabled,
And art made tongue-tied by authority,
And folly doctor-like controlling skill,
And simple truth miscall'd simplicity,
And captive good attending captain ill:
   Tired with all these, from these would I be gone,
   Save that, to die, I leave my love alone.

70.

That thou art blamed shall not be thy defect,
For slander's mark was ever yet the fair;
The ornament of beauty is suspect,
A crow that flies in heaven's sweetest air.
So thou be good, slander doth but approve
Thy worth the greater, being woo'd of time;
For canker vice the sweetest buds doth love,
And thou present'st a pure unstained prime.
Thou hast pass'd by the ambush of young days,
Either not assail'd or victor being charged;
Yet this thy praise cannot be so thy praise,
To tie up envy evermore enlarged:
   If some suspect of ill mask'd not thy show,
   Then thou alone kingdoms of hearts shouldst owe.

73.

That time of year thou mayst in me behold
When yellow leaves, or none, or few, do hang
Upon those boughs which shake against the cold,
Bare ruin'd choirs, where late the sweet birds sang.
In me thou see'st the twilight of such day
As after sunset fadeth in the west,
Which by and by black night doth take away,
Death's second self, that seals up all in rest.
In me thou seest the glowing of such fire
That on the ashes of his youth doth lie,
As the death-bed whereon it must expire
Consumed with that which it was nourish'd by.
  This thou perceivest, which makes thy love more strong,
  To love that well which thou must leave ere long.

90.

Then hate me when thou wilt; if ever, now;
Now, while the world is bent my deeds to cross,
Join with the spite of fortune, make me bow,
And do not drop in for an after-loss:
Ah, do not, when my heart hath 'scaped this sorrow,
Come in the rearward of a conquer'd woe;
Give not a windy night a rainy morrow,
To linger out a purposed overthrow.
If thou wilt leave me, do not leave me last,
When other petty griefs have done their spite,
But in the onset come; so shall I taste
At first the very worst of fortune's might,
  And other strains of woe, which now seem woe,
  Compared with loss of thee will not seem so.

97.

How like a winter hath my absence been
From thee, the pleasure of the fleeting year!
What freezings have I felt, what dark days seen!
What old December's bareness every where!
And yet this time removed was summer's time,
The teeming autumn, big with rich increase,
Bearing the wanton burden of the prime,
Like widow'd wombs after their lords' decease:
Yet this abundant issue seem'd to me
But hope of orphans and unfather'd fruit;
For summer and his pleasures wait on thee,
And, thou away, the very birds are mute;
    Or, if they sing, 'tis with so dull a cheer
    That leaves look pale, dreading the winter's near.

98.

From you have I been absent in the spring,
When proud-pied April dress'd in all his trim
Hath put a spirit of youth in every thing,
That heavy Saturn laugh'd and leap'd with him.
Yet nor the lays of birds nor the sweet smell
Of different flowers in odour and in hue
Could make me any summer's story tell,
Or from their proud lap pluck them where they grew;
Nor did I wonder at the lily's white,
Nor praise the deep vermilion in the rose;
They were but sweet, but figures of delight,
Drawn after you, you pattern of all those.
    Yet seem'd it winter still, and, you away,
    As with your shadow I with these did play.

102.

My love is strengthen'd, though more weak in seeming ;
I love not less, though less the show appear :
That love is merchandized whose rich esteeming
The owner's tongue doth publish every where.
Our love was new and then but in the spring
When I was wont to greet it with my lays,
As Philomel in summer's front doth sing
And stops her pipe in growth of riper days :
Not that the summer is less pleasant now
Than when her mournful hymns did hush the night,
But that wild music burthens every bough
And sweets grown common lose their dear delight.
  Therefore like her I sometime hold my tongue,
  Because I would not dull you with my song.

104.

To me, fair friend, you never can be old,
For as you were when first your eye I eyed,
Such seems your beauty still. Three winters cold
Have from the forests shook three summers' pride,
Three beauteous springs to yellow autumn turn'd
In process of the seasons have I seen,
Three April perfumes in three hot Junes burn'd,
Since first I saw you fresh, which yet are green.
Ah ! yet doth beauty, like a dial-hand,
Steal from his figure and no pace perceived ;
So your sweet hue, which methinks still doth stand,
Hath motion and mine eye may be deceived :
  For fear of which, hear this, thou age unbred ;
  Ere you were born was beauty's summer dead.

106.

When in the chronicle of wasted time
I see descriptions of the fairest wights,
And beauty making beautiful old rhyme
In praise of ladies dead and lovely knights,
Then, in the blazon of sweet beauty's best,
Of hand, of foot, of lip, of eye, of brow,
I see their antique pen would have express'd
Even such a beauty as you master now.
So all their praises are but prophecies
Of this our time, all you prefiguring;
And, for they look'd but with divining eyes,
They had not skill enough your worth to sing:
  For we, which now behold these present days,
  Have eyes to wonder, but lack tongues to praise.

107.

Not mine own fears, nor the prophetic soul
Of the wide world dreaming on things to come,
Can yet the lease of my true love control,
Supposed as forfeit to a confined doom.
The mortal moon hath her eclipse endured
And the sad augurs mock their own presage;
Incertainties now crown themselves assured
And peace proclaims olives of endless age.
Now with the drops of this most balmy time
My love looks fresh, and Death to me subscribes,
Since, spite of him, I 'll live in this poor rhyme,
While he insults o'er dull and speechless tribes:
  And thou in this shalt find thy monument,
  When tyrants' crests and tombs of brass are spent.

110.

Alas, 'tis true I have gone here and there
And made myself a motley to the view,
Gored mine own thoughts, sold cheap what is most dear,
Made old offences of affections new ;
Most true it is that I have look'd on truth
Askance and strangely: but, by all above,
These blenches gave my heart another youth,
And worse essays proved thee my best of love.
Now all is done, have what shall have no end :
Mine appetite I never more will grind
On newer proof, to try an older friend,
A god in love, to whom I am confined.
    Then give me welcome, next my heaven the best,
    Even to thy pure and most most loving breast.

111.

O, for my sake do you with Fortune chide,
The guilty goddess of my harmful deeds,
That did not better for my life provide
Than public means which public manners breeds.
Thence comes it that my name receives a brand,
And almost thence my nature is subdued
To what it works in, like the dyer's hand:
Pity me then and wish I were renew'd ;
Whilst, like a willing patient, I will drink
Potions of eisel 'gainst my strong infection ;
No bitterness that I will bitter think,
Nor double penance, to correct correction.
    Pity me then, dear friend, and I assure ye
    Even that your pity is enough to cure me.

116.

Let me not to the marriage of true minds
Admit impediments.   Love is not love
Which alters when it alteration finds,
Or bends with the remover to remove:
O, no! it is an ever-fixed mark
That looks on tempests and is never shaken;
It is the star to every wandering bark,
Whose worth's unknown, although his height be taken.
Love's not Time's fool, though rosy lips and cheeks
Within his bending sickle's compass come;
Love alters not with his brief hours and weeks,
But bears it out even to the edge of doom.
  If this be error and upon me proved,
  I never writ, nor no man ever loved.

119.

What potions have I drunk of Siren tears,
Distill'd from limbecks foul as hell within,
Applying fears to hopes and hopes to fears,
Still losing when I saw myself to win!
What wretched errors hath my heart committed,
Whilst it hath thought itself so blessed never!
How have mine eyes out of their spheres been fitted
In the distraction of this madding fever!
O benefit of ill! now I find true
That better is by evil still made better;
And ruin'd love, when it is built anew,
Grows fairer than at first, more strong, far greater.
  So I return rebuked to my content
  And gain by ill thrice more than I have spent.

SONGS.

A MORNING SONG FOR IMOGEN.

[From *Cymbeline.*]

Hark, hark! the lark at heaven's gate sings,
 And Phoebus 'gins arise,
His steeds to water at those springs
 On chaliced flowers that lies;
And winking Mary-buds begin
 To ope their golden eyes:
With every thing that pretty is,
 My lady sweet, arise:
  Arise, arise.

SILVIA.

[From *The Two Gentlemen of Verona.*]

Who is Silvia? what is she,
 That all our swains commend her?
Holy, fair and wise is she;
 The heaven such grace did lend her,
That she might admired be.

Is she kind as she is fair?
 For beauty lives with kindness.
Love doth to her eyes repair,
 To help him of his blindness,
And, being help'd, inhabits there.

Then to Silvia let us sing,
 That Silvia is excelling;
She excels each mortal thing
 Upon the dull earth dwelling:
To her let us garlands bring.

Sigh no more, Ladies.

[From *Much Ado about Nothing.*]

Sigh no more, ladies, sigh no more,
  Men were deceivers ever,
One foot in sea and one on shore,
  To one thing constant never :
Then sigh not so, but let them go,
  And be you blithe and bonny,
Converting all your sounds of woe
  Into Hey nonny, nonny.

Sing no more ditties, sing no moe,
  Of dumps so dull and heavy ;
The fraud of men was ever so,
  Since summer first was leafy :
Then sigh not so, but let them go,
  And be you blithe and bonny,
Converting all your sounds of woe
  Into Hey nonny, nonny.

A Lover's Lament.

[From *Twelfth Night.*]

Come away, come away, death,
  And in sad cypress let me be laid ;
Fly away, fly away, breath ;
  I am slain by a fair cruel maid.
My shroud of white, stuck all with yew,
    O, prepare it !
My part of death, no one so true
    Did share it.

Not a flower, not a flower sweet,
　　On my black coffin let there be strown ;
Not a friend, not a friend greet
　　My poor corpse, where my bones shall be thrown .
A thousand thousand sighs to save,
　　　　Lay me, O, where
Sad true lover never find my grave,
　　　　To weep there !

ARIEL'S SONG.

[From *The Tempest.*]

Where the bee sucks, there suck I :
In a cowslip's bell I lie :
There I couch when owls do cry.
On the bat's back I do fly
After summer merrily.
Merrily, merrily, shall I live now
Under the blossom that hangs on the bough.

A SEA DIRGE.

[From *The Tempest.*]

Full fathom five thy father lies ;
　　Of his bones are coral made ;
Those are pearls that were his eyes :
　　Nothing of him that doth fade
But doth suffer a sea-change
Into something rich and strange.
Sea-nymphs hourly ring his knell :
　　　　　　　　Ding-dong.
Hark ! now I hear them,—Ding-dong, bell.

In the Greenwood.

[From *As You Like It.*]

Under the greenwood tree
Who loves to lie with me,
And turn his merry note
, Unto the sweet bird's throat,
Come hither, come hither, come hither:
Here shall he see
No enemy
Eut winter and rough weather.

Who doth ambition shun
And loves to live i' the sun,
Seeking the food he eats
And pleased with what he gets,
Come hither, come hither, come hither:
Here shall he see
No enemy
But winter and rough weather.

Winter.

[From *Love's Labour's Lost.*]

When icicles hang by the wall
 And Dick the shepherd blows his nail
And Tom bears logs into the hall
 And milk comes frozen home in pail,
When blood is nipp'd and ways be foul,
Then nightly sings the staring owl,
Tu-whit ;
Tu-who, a merry note,
While greasy Joan doth keel the pot.

When all aloud the wind doth blow
 And coughing drowns the parson's saw
And birds sit brooding in the snow
 And Marian's nose looks red and raw,

When roasted crabs hiss in the bowl,
Then nightly sings the staring owl,
　　　　　Tu-whit ;
Tu-who, a merry note,
While greasy Joan doth keel the pot.

SONG OF AUTOLYCUS.

[From *The Winter's Tale.*]

When daffodils begin to peer,
　With heigh ! the doxy over the dale,
Why, then comes in the sweet o' the year ;
　For the red blood reigns in the winter's pale.

The white sheet bleaching on the hedge,
　With heigh ! the sweet birds, O, how they sing !
Doth set my pugging tooth on edge ;
　For a quart of ale is a dish for a king.

The lark, that tirra-lyra chants,
　With heigh ! with heigh ! the thrush and the jay,
Are summer songs for me and my aunts,
　While we lie tumbling in the hay.

But shall I go mourn for that, my dear ?
　The pale moon shines by night :
And when I wander here and there,
　I then do most go right.

If tinkers may have leave to live,
　And bear the sow-skin budget,
Then my account I well may give,
　And in the stocks avouch it.

Jog on, jog on, the foot-path way,
　And merrily hent the stile-a :
A merry heart goes all the day,
　Your sad tires in a mile-a.

SAMUEL DANIEL.

[SAMUEL DANIEL was born near Taunton in 1562. He died at Becking-
ton in the county of his birth in 1619. His chief works were—*The Com-
plaint of Rosamond*, 1594; *Cleopatra*, 1594; *Epistles to Various Great Person-
ages*, 1601; *The Civil Wars*, 1604; *Philotas*, 1611; *Hymen's Triumph*, 1623;
A Defence of Rhyme, 1611.]

There are few poets, not of the first class, to whose merits
a stronger consensus of weighty opinion can be produced than that
which attests the value of Samuel Daniel's work. His contem-
poraries, while expressing some doubts as to his choice of subjects,
speak of him as 'well-languaged,' 'sharp-conceited,' and as a master
of pure English. The critics of the eighteenth century were sur-
prised to find in him so little that they could deem obsolete or in
bad taste. The more catholic censorship of Hazlitt, Lamb, and
Coleridge was delighted with his extraordinary felicity of expres-
sion, and the simple grace of his imagery and phrase. There can
be no doubt however that his choice of historical subjects for his
poetry was unfortunate for his fame. The sentence of Joubert is
not likely to be reversed : ' Il faut que son sujet offre au génie du
poëte une espèce de lieu fantastique qu'il puisse étendre et res-
serrer à volonté. Un lieu trop réel, une population trop historique
emprisonnent l'esprit et en gênent les mouvements.' This holds
true of all the Elizabethan historians ; and it holds truer perhaps
of Daniel than of Drayton. For the genius of the former had a
tender and delicate quality about it which was least of all applic-
able to such work, and seems to have lacked altogether the faculty
of narrative. Daniel's one qualification for the task was his power
of dignified moral reflection, in which, as the following extracts will
show, he has hardly a superior. This however, though an ad-
mirable adjunct to the other qualities required for the task, could
by no means compensate for their absence ; and the result is that
the *History of the Civil Wars* is with difficulty readable. *The
Complaint of Rosamond* is better.

It is however in the long poems only that the 'manner better suiting prose,' of which Daniel has been accused, appears. His minor work is in the main admirable, and displays incessantly the purity and felicity of language already noticed. His *Sonnet to Sleep* became a kind of model to younger writers, and imitations of it are to be found in the sonneteers of the time, sometimes with the opening epithet literally borrowed. The whole indeed of the *Sonnets to Delia* are excellent, and throughout Daniel's work single expressions and short passages of exquisite grace abound. The opening line, for instance, of the Address to Lady Anne Clifford,

> 'Upon the tender youth of those fair eyes,'

is perfect in its kind. So is the distich which begins one of the Sonnets :—

> 'The star of my mishap imposed this pain,
> To spend the April of my years in grief;'

and the invocation of Apollo :—

> 'O clear-eyed rector of the holy hill.'

It is in such things as these that the greater part of Daniel's charm consists, and they are scattered abundantly about his works. The rest of that charm lies in his combination of moral elevation with a certain picturesque peacefulness of spirit not often to be found in the perturbed race of bards. The *Epistle to the Countess of Cumberland* is unmatched before Wordsworth in the expression of this.

His two tragedies and his *Defence of Rhyme*, though neither of them falling strictly within our limits, are too important in connection with English poetry to be left unnoticed. *Cleopatra* and *Philotas* are noteworthy among the rare attempts to follow the example of Jodelle and Garnier in English. They contain much harmonious verse, and the choruses are often admirable of their kind. The *Defence of Rhyme*, directed against the mania which for a time infected Spenser and Sidney, which Webbe endeavoured to render methodic, and of which traces are to be found in Milton, is thoroughly sound in principle and conclusion, though that conclusion is supported by arguments which are as often bad as good.

G. SAINTSBURY.

SONNET LI. TO DELIA.

Care-charmer Sleep, son of the sable Night,
Brother to Death, in silent darkness born :
Relieve my languish and restore the light ;
With dark forgetting of my care, return,
And let the day be time enough to mourn
The shipwreck of my ill-adventured youth :
Let waking eyes suffice to wail their scorn
Without the torment of the night's untruth.
Cease dreams, the images of day desires,
To model forth the passions of the morrow ;
Never let rising sun approve you liars,
To add more grief to aggravate my sorrow.
    Still let me sleep, embracing clouds in vain,
    And never wake to feel the day's disdain.

THE DEATH OF TALBOT.

[From *History of the Civil War*, Bk. vi.]

So much true resolution wrought in those
Who had made covenant with death before,
That their small number (scorning so great foes)
Made France most happy, that there were no more,
And Fortune doubt to whom she might dispose
That weary day ; or unto whom restore
The glory of a conquest dearly bought,
Which scarce the conqueror could think well got.

For as with equal rage, and equal might,
Two adverse winds combat, with billows proud,
And neither yield (seas, skies maintain like fight,
Wave against wave oppos'd, and cloud to cloud) :
So war both sides with obstinate despite,
With like revenge ; and neither party bow'd :
Fronting each other with confounding blows,
No wound one sword unto the other owes.

Whilst Talbot (whose fresh ardour having got
A marvellous advantage of his years)
Carries his unfelt age as if forgot,
Whirling about where any need appears.
His hand, his eye, his wits all present wrought
The function of the glorious part he bears :
Now urging here, now cheering there, he flies ;
Unlocks the thickest troops where most force lies.

In midst of wrath, of wounds, of blood, and death
There is he most, where as he may do best ;
And there the closest ranks he severeth,
Drives back the stoutest powers that forward press'd,
There makes his sword his way.   There laboureth
The infatigable hand that never ceas'd ;
Scorning unto his mortal wounds to yield,
Till Death became best master of the field.

Then like a sturdy oak, that having long
Against the wars of fiercest winds made head,
When (with some forc'd tempestuous rage more **strong**
His down-borne top comes overmastered)
All the near bord'ring trees he stood among
Crushed with his weighty fall lie ruined :
So lay his spoils, all round about him slain,
T' adorn his death, that could not die in vain.

On th' other part, his most all-daring son
(Although the inexperience of his years
Made him less skill'd in what was to be done ;
And yet did carry him beyond all fears),
Flying into the main battalion
Near to the king, amidst the chiefest peers,
With thousand wounds became at length oppress'd,
As if he scorned to die but with the best

Who thus both having gained a glorious end,
Soon ended that great day ; that set so red,
As all the purple plains that wide extend
A sad tempestuous season witnessed.

So much ado had toiling France to rend
From us the right so long inherited ;
And so hard went we from what we possessed,
As with it went the blood we loved best.

Which blood not lost, but fast laid up with heed
In everlasting fame, is there held dear
To seal the memory of this day's deed;
Th' eternal evidence of what we were :
To which our fathers, we, and who succeed,
Do owe a sigh, for that it touched us near;
Nor must we sin so much as to neglect
The holy thought of such a dear respect.

To the Lady Margaret, Countess of Cumberland.

He that of such a height hath built his mind,
And rear'd the dwelling of his thoughts so strong,
As neither fear nor hope can shake the frame
Of his resolvèd powers ; nor all the wind
Of vanity or malice pierce to wrong
His settled peace, or to disturb the same,
What a fair seat hath he, from whence he may
The boundless wastes and wilds of man survey !

And with how free an eye doth he look down
Upon these lower regions of turmoil !
Where all the storms of passion mainly beat
On flesh and blood ; where honour, power, renown
Are only gay afflictions, golden toil ;
Where greatness stands upon as feeble feet
As frailty doth, and only great doth seem
To little minds, who do it so esteem.

He looks upon the mightiest monarch's wars
But only as on stately robberies ;
Where evermore the fortune that prevails
Must be the right : the ill-succeeding mars
The fairest and the best-faced enterprise.
Great pirate Pompey lesser pirates quails :

Justice, he sees, (as if seduced) still
Conspires with power, whose cause must not be ill.

He sees the face of right t' appear as manifold
As are the passions of uncertain man ;
Who puts it in all colours, all attires,
To serve his ends and make his courses hold.
He sees, that let deceit work what it can,
Plot and contrive base ways to high desires,
That the all-guiding Providence doth yet
All disappoint, and mocks this smoke of wit.

Nor is he mov'd with all the thunder cracks
Of tyrants' threats, or with the surly brow
Of Pow'r, that proudly sits on others' crimes,
Charg'd with more crying sins than those he checks.
The storms of sad confusion, that may grow
Up in the present for the coming times,
Appal not him, that hath no side at all
But of himself, and knows the worst can fall.

Although his heart (so near allied to earth)
Cannot but pity the perplexed state
Of troublous and distress'd mortality,
That thus make way unto the ugly birth
Of their own sorrows, and do still beget
Affliction upon imbecility ;
Yet seeing thus the course of things must run,
He looks thereon not strange, but as foredone.

And whilst distraught ambition compasses,
And is encompass'd ; whilst as craft deceives,
And is deceiv'd ; whilst man doth ransack man,
And builds on blood, and rises by distress ;
And th' inheritance of desolation leaves
To great-expecting hopes : he looks thereon
As from the shore of peace, with unwet eye,
And bears no venture in impiety.

From 'Hymen's Triumph.

Ah! I remember well (and how can I
But evermore remember well) when first
Our flame began, when scarce we knew what was
The flame we felt ; when as we sat and sighed
And looked upon each other, and conceived
Not what we ail'd,—yet something we did ail ;
And yet were well, and yet we were not well,
And what was our disease we could not tell.
Then would we kiss, then sigh, then look : and thus
In that first garden of our simpleness
We spent our childhood. But when years began
To reap the fruit of knowledge, ah, how then
Would she with graver looks, with sweet stern brow
Check my presumption and my forwardness ;
Yet still would give me flowers, still would me show
What she would have me, yet not have me know.

RICHARD BARNFIELD.

[Born at the Manor House of Norbury, Staffordshire, 1574. Died at Dorleston, or Darlaston, in the same county, 1627. His chief poems are—
The Affectionate Shepherd, 1594; *Cynthia, with certaine Sonnets and the Legende of Cassandra*, 1595; *The Encomion of Lady Pecunia*, 1598. Two poems from this latter source reappeared in *The Passionate Pilgrim*, 1599.]

Barnfield is a poet whose personality has only of late years emerged into something like distinctness, his best poems having till recently had the honour of bearing Shakespeare's name. The reprint of *The Affectionate Shepherd* by Mr. Halliwell in 1845, from the almost unique copy in Sion College Library, first made Barnfield known to modern readers ; about the same time doubts began to arise concerning the authorship of the poems in *The Passionate Pilgrim;* and lately, in 1876, Mr. Grosart was able to print for the Roxburghe Club the complete poems, together with a number of facts about Barnfield's family and a few about his life. Of the latter we only learn that he belonged to a good Staffordshire family; that he became a member of Brasenose College, Oxford, in 1589; that on leaving Oxford he passed several years in London, apparently as a member of that literary circle of which Lady Rich, Sidney's 'Stella,' was the centre ; and that after 1605 he disappeared, probably retiring like Shakespeare to his country home, but unlike him sending forth no poetic utterance into the world.

The oddity of Barnfield's principal performance, *The Affectionate Shepherd*, is best explained by the date of its composition. He was not twenty when he wrote it ; and we are thus more inclined to tolerate both the sentiment (it is an elaborate expansion of Virgil's second eclogue), and the boyishness and incongruities which mar the execution. It is strange enough that such a poem should be dedicated to a lady (Lady Rich); stranger still that it should open with what must have read like a caricature of that lady's own love-story ; strangest of all that Daphnis, after displaying all his Arcadian blandishments in vain through a hundred stanzas, should turn moralist and flood the obdurate Ganymede with 'lere I learned from a Beldame Trot'—didactic 'lere,' of which these lines are a fair example :—

> 'Be patient in extreame adversitie,
>   Man's chiefest credit growes by dooing well,
> Ee not high minded in prosperitie,
>   Falshood abhorre, no lying fable tell,
> Give not thyselfe to sloth, the sinke of shame,
> The moath of Time, the enemie to Fame!'

Yet the poem has qualities which mark it out from the mass of Elizabethan pastoral. It has fluency, music, colour. Barnfield combines in it a mastery of euphuistic antithesis with a real knowledge of the country and its sights and sounds ; its 'scarlet-dyed carnation bleeding yet,' its 'fine ruffe-footed Doves,' its 'curds and clowted creme,' the 'lyme-twigs and fine sparrow calles' for the birdcatcher, the 'springes in a frostie night' that take the woodcock. It is to be regretted that this eye for nature, this fine ear and honeyed tongue, were pressed into the service of a design too artificial and too alien from the common feeling of mankind.

There is nothing of this sort to say against the well-known Ode which we here quote, and which is indeed in no respect unworthy of the great name to which it was so long attributed. From its happy union of ethical matter and fanciful form, from its strongly personal note, it ranks among the most interesting of the productions of the lesser Elizabethans.

EDITOR.

SONNET.

[From *Cynthia, &c.*]

Beauty and Majesty are fallen at odds,
Th' one claims his cheek, the other claims his chin ;
Then Virtue comes and puts her title in :
Quoth she, I make him like th' immortal Gods.
Quoth Majesty, I own his looks, his brow ;
His lips, quoth Love, his eyes, his fair is mine ;
And yet, quoth Majesty, he is not thine,
I mix disdain with Love's congealed snow.
Ay, but, quoth Love, his locks are mine by right.
His stately gait is mine, quoth Majesty ;
And mine, quoth Virtue, is his Modesty.
Thus as they strive about the heavenly wight
    At last the other two to Virtue yield
    The lists of Love, fought in fair Beauty's field.

SONNET TO HIS FRIEND MAISTER R. L.[1]

[From *Poems in Divers Humors ;* also printed in *The Passionate Pilgrim.*]

If music and sweet poetry agree,
As they must needs, the sister and the brother,
Then must the love be great 'twixt thee and me,
Because thou lov'st the one, and I the other.
Dowland to thee is dear, whose heavenly touch
Upon the lute doth ravish human sense ;
Spenser to me, whose deep conceit is such
As, passing all conceit, needs no defence.
Thou lov'st to hear the sweet melodious sound
That Phoebus' lute, the queen of music, makes ;
And I in deep delight am chiefly drown'd
Whenas himself to singing he betakes.
    One god is god of both, as poets feign ;
    One knight loves both, and both in thee remain.

[1] Perhaps Richard Lynch, author of *Diella ; certaine sonnets* (1596).

An Ode.

[From the same.]

As it fell upon a day
In the merry month of May,
Sitting in a pleasant shade
Which a grove of myrtles made,
Beasts did leap, and birds did sing,
Trees did grow, and plants did spring;
Everything did banish moan,
Save the nightingale alone:
She, poor bird, as all forlorn,
Lean'd her breast up-till a thorn,
And there sung the dolefull'st ditty,
That to hear it was great pity:
'Fie, fie, fie,' now would she cry;
'Teru, teru!' by and by;
That to hear her so complain,
Scarce I could from tears refrain;
For her griefs, so lively shown,
Made me think upon mine own.
Ah, thought I, thou mourn'st in vain!
None takes pity on thy pain:
Senseless trees they cannot hear thee;
Ruthless beasts they will not cheer thee:
King Pandion he is dead;
All thy friends are lapp'd in lead;
All thy fellow birds do sing,
Careless of thy sorrowing.
[Even so, poor bird, like thee,
None alive will pity me.]
Whilst as fickle Fortune smiled,
Thou and I were both beguiled.
   Every one that flatters thee
Is no friend in misery.
Words are easy, like the wind;
Faithful friends are hard to find:

Every man will be thy friend
Whilst thou hast wherewith to spend ;
But if store of crowns be scant,
No man will supply thy want.
If that one be prodigal,
Bountiful they will him call,
And with such-like flattering,
' Pity but he were a king ; '
If he be addict to vice,
Quickly him they will entice ;
If to women he be bent,
They have at commandement :
But if Fortune once do frown,
Then farewell his great renown ;
They that fawn'd on him before
Use his company no more.
He that is thy friend indeed,
He will help thee in thy need :
If thou sorrow, he will weep ;
If thou wake, he cannot sleep ;
Thus of every grief in heart
He with thee doth bear a part.
These are certain signs to know
Faithful friend from flattering foe.

ROBERT SOUTHWELL.

[BORN at Horsham St. Faith's, Norfolk, about 1562; entered the Society of Jesus, 1578, at Rome; accompanied Father Garnet to England, was captured; and was executed at Tyburn, 1594-5. *St. Peter's Complaint, with other Poems*, was first published in 1595; *Maeoniae* in the same year; *Marie Magdalen's Funerall Teares*, 1609.]

Southwell's poems enjoyed a vast popularity in the last decade of the sixteenth and the beginning of the seventeenth century. *St. Peter's Complaint*, first printed in 1595, was again and again re-issued in that and the immediately following years. Both Hall and Marston refer to it in their Satires. 'Never,' says Bolton in his *Hypercritica*, 'must be forgotten *St. Peter's Complaint* and those other serious poems said to be father Southwell's; the English whereof, as it is most proper, so the sharpness and light of wit is very rare in them.'

No doubt this popularity was greatly due to the deep interest and pity excited by his misfortunes, encountered and borne with so rare a constancy. No Protestant could be so desperately bigoted as not to be touched by the sad yet noble story of what this young English gentleman dared and endured. Whatever may be thought of his cause, one can only admire the fearless devotion with which he gave himself up to it, reckless of danger, of torture, of death. 'Let antiquity,' says one whose office it then was to suppress so far as might be the efforts often at least miserably misguided, of the confederacy to which Southwell belonged, 'boast of its Roman heroes and the patience of captives in torments; our own age is not inferior to it, nor do the minds of the English cede to the Romans. There is at present confined one Southwell, a Jesuit, who, thirteen times most cruelly tortured, cannot be induced to confess anything, not even the colour of the horse whereon on a certain day he rode, lest from such indication his adversaries might conjecture in what house, or in company of what Catholics, he that day was.' He was only about twenty-four years of age—the exact year of his birth is not ascertained—when along with Garnet (afterwards associated with the

Gunpowder Plot, as was believed, and on evidence never yet successfully rebutted), he returned to England on his perilous mission. Some six years afterwards he fell into his enemies' hands. For three years he was closely confined in the Tower; and then came the ignominious end at Tyburn. Such a story could not but move men,—the story of a spirit so strong in its faith, zealous, inflexible.

Nor would those who were drawn to his writings by sympathy with his martyrdom fail to see in them the reflection of his lofty and devoted nature. Nearly all his poetry must have been written in the valley of the shadow of death, some of it in death's very presence. And throughout it we perceive the thoughts and beliefs that ever inspired and upheld him. Especially dear and welcome and present is the idea that ' Life is but loss.' Death is cruel, not for coming, but for delaying to come. This has often been said, but never with an intenser sincerity and conviction. ' This death,' he said just before 'the horses were started and the car removed from his feet' and he was hanged, 'although it may now seem base and ignominious, can to no rightly-thinking person appear doubtful but that it is beyond measure an eternal weight of glory to be wrought in us, who look not to the things which are visible, but to those which are unseen.' We may be sure these words were with him no vulgar commonplace.

And apart from their attraction as revealing the secret of his much-enduring spirit, his poems show a true poetic power. They show a rich and fertile fancy, with an abundant store of effective expression at its service. He inclines to sententiousness ; but his sentences are no mere prose edicts, as is so often the case with writers of that sort ; they are bright and coloured with the light and the hues of a vivid imagination. In imagery, indeed, he is singularly opulent. In this respect *St. Peter's Complaint* reminds one curiously of the almost exactly contemporary poem, Shakespeare's *Lucrece*. There is a like inexhaustibleness of illustrative resource. He delights to heap up metaphor on metaphor. Thus he describes Sleep as

> ' Death's ally, oblivion of tears,
>   Silence of passions, blame of angry sore,
> Suspense of loves, security of fears,
>   Wrath's lenity, heart's ease, storm's calmest shore;
> Senses' and souls' reprieval from all cumbers,
> Benumbing sense of ill with quiet slumbers.'

St. Peter's Complaint reminds one of *Lucrece* also in the minuteness of its narration, and in the unfailing abundance of thought and fancy with which every detail is treated. It is undoubtedly the work of a mind of no ordinary copiousness and force, often embarrassed by its own riches, and so expending them with a prodigal carelessness. Thus Southwell's defects spring not from poverty, but from imperfectly managed wealth ; or, to use a different image, the flowers are overcrowded in his garden, and the blaze of colour is excessive. Still, flowers they are. Like many another Elizabethan, he was wanting in art ; his genius ran riot.

JOHN W. HALES.

TIMES GO BY TURNS.

The lopped tree in time may grow again ;
Most naked plants renew both fruit and flower ;
The sorest wight may find release of pain,
The driest soil suck in some moist'ning shower ;
Times go by turns and chances change by course,
From foul to fair, from better hap to worse.

The sea of Fortune doth not ever flow,
She draws her favours to the lowest ebb ;
Her time hath equal times to come and go,
Her loom doth weave the fine and coarsest web ;
No joy so great but runneth to an end,
No hap so hard but may in fine amend.

Not always fall of leaf nor ever spring,
No endless night yet not eternal day ;
The saddest birds a season find to sing,
The roughest storm a calm may soon allay ;
Thus with succeeding turns God tempereth all,
That man may hope to rise yet fear to fall.

A chance may win that by mischance was lost ;
The well that holds no great, takes little fish ;
In some things all, in all things none are cross'd,
Few all they need, but none have all they wish ;
Unmeddled joys here to no man befall,
Who least hath some, who most hath never all.

LOSS IN DELAY.

Shun delays, they breed remorse ;
  Take thy time while time is lent thee ;
Creeping snails have weakest force,
  Fly their fault lest thou repent thee.
Good is best when soonest wrought,
Linger'd labours come to nought.

Hoist up sail while gale doth last,
   Tide and wind stay no man's pleasure ;
Seek not time when time is past,
   Sober speed is wisdom's leisure.
After-wits are dearly bought,
Let thy forewit guide thy thought.

Time wears all his locks before,
   Take thy hold on his forehead ;
When he flies he turns no more,
   And behind his scalp's naked.
Works adjourn'd have many stays,
Long demurs breed new delays.

Seek thy salve while sore is green,
   Fester'd wounds ask deeper lancing ;
After-cures are seldom seen,
   Often sought, scarce ever chancing.
Time and place give best advice,
Out of season, out of price.

Crush the serpent in the head,
   Break ill eggs ere they be hatch'd ;
Kill bad chickens in the tread,
   Fledged, they hardly can be catch'd.
In the rising stifle ill,
Lest it grow against thy will.

Drops do pierce the stubborn flint,
   Not by force but often falling ;
Custom kills with feeble dint,
   More by use than strength and vailing.
Single sands have little weight,
Many make a drawing freight.

Tender twigs are bent with ease,
   Aged trees do break with bending ;
Young desires make little prease[1],
   Growth doth make them past amending
Happy man, that soon doth knock
Babel's babes against the rock !

[1] press, crowd.

THE BURNING BABE.

As I in hoary winter's night stood shivering in the snow,
Surprised I was with sudden heat which made my heart to glow;
And lifting up a fearful eye to view what fire was near,
A pretty babe all burning bright did in the air appear,
Who scorched with exceeding heat such floods of tears did shed,
As though His floods should quench His flames with what His
        tears were fed;
Alas! quoth He, but newly born in fiery heats of fry,
Yet none approach to warm their hearts or feel my fire but I!
My faultless breast the furnace is, the fuel wounding thorns;
Love is the fire and sighs the smoke, the ashes shame and scorns;
The fuel Justice layeth on, and Mercy blows the coals;
The metal in this furnace wrought are men's defiled souls;
For which, as now on fire I am, to work them to their good,
So will I melt into a bath, to wash them in my blood:
With this He vanish'd out of sight, and swiftly shrunk away,
And straight I called unto mind that it was Christmas-day.

FROM 'ST. PETER'S COMPLAINT.'

Like solest swan, that swims in silent deep,
    And never sings but obsequies of death,
Sigh out thy plaints, and sole in secret weep,
    In suing pardon spend thy perjur'd breath;
Attire thy soul in sorrow's mourning weed,
And at thine eyes let guilty conscience bleed.

Still in the 'lembic of thy doleful breast
    Those bitter fruits that from thy sins do grow;
For fuel, self-accusing thoughts be best;
    Use fear as fire, the coals let penance blow;
And seek none other quintessence but tears,
That eyes may shed what enter'd at thine ears.

Come sorrowing tears, the offspring of my grief,
   Scant not your parent of a needful aid ;
In you I rest the hope of wish'd relief,
   By you my sinful debts must be defray'd :
Your power prevails, your sacrifice is grateful,
By love obtaining life to men most hateful.

Come good effect of ill-deserving cause,
   Ill gotten imps, yet virtuously brought forth ;
Self-blaming probates of infringed laws,
   Yet blamèd faults redeeming with your worth ;
The signs of shame in you each eye may read,
Yet, while you guilty prove, you pity plead.

O beams of mercy ! beat on sorrow's cloud,
   Pour suppling showers upon my parched ground ;
Bring forth the fruit to your due service vow'd,
   Let good desires with like deserts be crown'd :
Water young blooming virtue's tender flow'r,
Sin did all grace of riper growth devour.

Weep balm and myrrh, you sweet Arabian trees,
   With purest gums perfume and pearl your rine ;
Shed on your honey-drops, you busy bees,
   I, barren plant, must weep unpleasant brine :
Hornets I hive, salt drops their labour plies,
Suck'd out of sin, and shed by showering eyes.

If David, night by night, did bathe his bed,
   Esteeming longest days too short to moan ;
Tears inconsolable if Anna shed,
   Who in her son her solace had foregone ;
Then I to days and weeks, to months and years,
Do owe the hourly rent of stintless tears.

If love, if loss, if fault, if spotted fame,
   If danger, death, if wrath, or wreck of weal,
Entitle eyes true heirs to earned blame,
   That due remorse in such events conceal :
That want of tears might well enrol my name,
As chiefest saint in kalendar of shame.

RALEIGH.

[Born 1552, executed 1618. No early collected edition of his poems exists; such as were printed at all appeared for the most part in the Miscellanies of the time.]

Amongst all the restless, fervid, adventurous spirits of the Elizabethan age, perhaps there is none so conspicuous for those characteristics as Sir Walter Raleigh. A soldier from his youth; at an early period connected with the great maritime movements of his time ; ever the foremost hater and antagonist of Spain and all its works ; one of the first, if not the first, to fully conceive the idea of colonisation and to attempt to realise it, and at the same time taking an active—too active—part in the party intrigues and contentions of a court where the struggle for place and favour never ceased raging, yet amidst all his schemes and enterprises, noble and ignoble, finding leisure also for far other interests and pursuits ; capable of a keen enjoyment of poetry ; himself a poet of a true and genuine quality,—he is in a singular degree the representative of the vigorous versatility of the Elizabethan period.

His high imaginativeness is perceptible in the political conceptions and dreams which abounded in his busy brain. It can scarcely be doubted that, had his energies received a different direction, he would have won a distinguished place amongst the distinguished poets of his day. He whom Spenser styles 'the summer's nightingale' might have poured forth a full volume of song of rare strength and sweetness. But, as it was, he found little time for singing ; the wonder is he found any—that one so cumbered about much serving did not become altogether of the world worldly, that so occupied with actualities he still was visited even transiently by visions of divine things.

We are apt to pity his misfortunes ; and yet it may be they were the blessings of his chequered life. His disgraces and confinements in the Tower would after all seem to have been the times when his nobler self was asserted, and he communed with his own heart.

> 'Stone walls do not a prison make,
> Nor iron bars a cage.'

We have no pleasanter picture of him than that Spenser draws, when 'faultless' debarred from the presence of his 'Cynthia the Lady of the Sea,' he had withdrawn himself to his Irish estate and thence visited his neighbour the poet.

> ' He sitting me beside in that same shade,
> Provoked me to play some pleasant fit;
> And when he heard the music which I made,
> He found himself full greatly pleased at it.
>
> Yet æmuling my pipe, he took in hand
> My pipe, before that æmuled of many,
> And played thereon (for well that skill he conn'd),
> Himself as skilful in that art as any.
>
> He pip'd, I sang; and when he sang I pip'd;
> By change of turns each making other merry;
> Neither envying other, nor envied ;
> So piped we, until we both were weary.'

It is impossible not to connect two at least of his most famous pieces—*The Lie* and *The Pilgrimage*—with similar passages of his life, when, for one reason or another, he was 'under a cloud,' as he thought, but really in a clearer air.   His imprisonments were in fact his salvations.   Through the Traitor's Gate he passed to a tranquillity and thoughtfulness for which there seemed no opportunity outside.   In his cell in the White Tower his soul found and enjoyed a real freedom.

> ' Then, like a bird, it sits and sings,
> Then whets and claps its silver wings,
> And till prepared for longer flight,
> Waves in its plumes the various light.'

It is a significant tradition attached to several of his verses, that they were written the night before he was beheaded.   Of only one poem is it likely to be true ; in respect of several it can be certainly disproved ; but it illustrates the impression often produced by his poetry.   The sweet clear voice comes to us, as it were, through a barred and grated window ; and calls up the image of a solitary figure soothing and quieting itself with the thought, too often forgotten elsewhere and in other days, that there is a higher life than that of the courtier, a more splendid preferment than an earthly sovereign can give.

His poetic writings are but scanty in amount. One at least, his *Cinthia*, is lost ; part of a continuation of it, extant in a Hatfield MS., has been lately printed for the first time. His fame has been damaged by the unauthorised ascription to him of inferior and worthless pieces ; and, on the other hand, by taking away from him what he undoubtedly wrote. In respect of both rejection and appropriation, Dr. Hannah has performed for him a much-needed service in his excellent volume, ' The Poems of Sir Walter Raleig. collected and authenticated, with those of Sir Henry Wotton and other Courtly Poets from 1540 to 1650.'

JOHN W. HALES.

A Vision upon this Conceit of the Fairy Queen.

[Appended to Spenser's *Faery Queen*.]

Methought I saw the grave where Laura lay,
Within that temple where the vestal flame
Was wont to burn: and, passing by that way,
To see that buried dust of living fame,
Whose tomb fair Love and fairer Virtue kept,
All suddenly I saw the Fairy Queen;
At whose approach the soul of Petrarch wept,
And from thenceforth those graces were not seen,
For they this Queen attended; in whose stead
Oblivion laid him down on Laura's hearse.
Hereat the hardest stones were seen to bleed,
And groans of buried ghosts the heavens did pierce:
  Where Homer's spright did tremble all for grief,
  And cursed the access of that celestial thief.

Reply to Marlowe's 'The Passionate Shepherd to His Love[1].'

If all the world and love were young,
And truth in every shepherd's tongue,
These pretty pleasures might me move
To live with thee and be thy love.

But time drives flocks from field to fold,
When rivers rage and rocks grow cold;
And Philomel becometh dumb;
The rest complains of cares to come.

The flowers do fade, and wanton fields
To wayward winter reckoning yields:
A honey tongue, a heart of gall,
Is fancy's spring, but sorrow's fall.

[1] See p. 418.

Thy gowns, thy shoes, thy beds of roses,
Thy cap, thy kirtle, and thy posies,
Soon break, soon wither, soon forgotten,--
In folly ripe, in reason rotten.

Thy belt of straw and ivy buds,
Thy coral clasps and amber studs,—
All those in me no means can move
To come to thee and be thy love.

But could youth last, and love still breed;
Had joys no date, nor age no need;
Then those delights my mind might move
To live with thee and be thy love.

THE LIE.

Go, Soul, the body's guest,
　Upon a thankless arrant[1]:
Fear not to touch the best;
　The truth shall be thy warrant:
Go, since I needs must die,
And give the world the lie.

Say to the court, it glows
　And shines like rotten wood;
Say to the church, it shows
　What's good, and doth no good:
If court and church reply,
Then give them both the lie.

Tell potentates, they live
　Acting by others' action;
Not loved unless they give,
　Not strong but by a faction:
If potentates reply,
Give potentates the lie.

[1] errand.

Tell men of high condition,
  That manage the estate,
Their purpose is ambition,
  Their practice only hate:
And if they once reply,
Then give them all the lie.

Tell them that brave it most,
  They beg for more by spending,
Who, in their greatest cost,
  Seek nothing but commending:
And if they make reply,
Then give them all the lie.

Tell zeal it wants devotion;
  Tell love it is but lust;
Tell time it is but motion;
  Tell flesh it is but dust:
And wish them not reply,
For thou must give the lie.

Tell age it daily wasteth;
  Tell honour how it alters;
Tell beauty how she blasteth;
  Tell favour how it falters:
And as they shall reply,
Give every one the lie.

Tell wit how much it wrangles
  In tickle points of niceness;
Tell wisdom she entangles
  Herself in over-wiseness:
And when they do reply,
Straight give them both the lie.

Tell physic of her boldness;
  Tell skill it is pretension;
Tell charity of coldness;
  Tell law it is contention:
And as they do reply,
So give them still the lie.

Tell fortune of her blindness;
  Tell nature of decay;
Tell friendship of unkindness;
  Tell justice of delay:
And if they will reply,
Then give them all the lie.

Tell arts they have no soundness,
  But vary by esteeming;
Tell schools they want profoundness,
  And stand too much on seeming:
If arts and schools reply,
Give arts and schools the lie.

Tell faith it 's fled the city;
  Tell how the country erreth;
Tell manhood shakes off pity;
  Tell virtue least preferreth:
And if they do reply,
Spare not to give the lie.

So when thou hast, as I
  Commanded thee, done blabbing,—
Although to give the lie
  Deserves no less than stabbing,—
Stab at thee he that will,
No stab the soul can kill.

His Pilgrimage.

Give me my scallop-shell of quiet,
  My staff of faith to walk upon,
My scrip of joy, immortal diet,
  My bottle of salvation,
My gown of glory, hope's true gage;
And thus I'll take my pilgrimage.

Blood must be my body's balmer;
  No other balm will there be given;
Whilst my soul, like quiet palmer,
  Travelleth towards the land of heaven;

Over the silver mountains,
Where spring the nectar fountains:
    There will I kiss
    The bowl of bliss;
And drink mine everlasting fill
Upon every milken hill.
My soul will be a-dry before;
But after, it will thirst no more.

Then by that happy blissful day,
  More peaceful pilgrims I shall see,
That have cast off their rags of clay,
  And walk apparell'd fresh like me.
    I'll take them first
    To quench their thirst
  And taste of nectar suckets,
    At those clear wells
    Where sweetness dwells,
  Drawn up by saints in crystal buckets.

And when our bottles and all we
Are fill'd with immortality,
Then the blessed paths we'll travel,
Strow'd with rubies thick as gravel;
Ceilings of diamonds, sapphire floors,
High walls of coral and pearly bowers.
From thence to heaven's bribeless hall,
Where no corrupted voices brawl;
No conscience molten into gold,
No forg'd accuser bought or sold,
No cause deferr'd, no vain-spent journey,
For there Christ is the king's Attorney,
Who pleads for all without degrees,
And He hath angels, but no fees.
And when the grand twelve-million jury
Of our sins, with direful fury,
Against our souls black verdicts give,
Christ pleads His death, and then we live.

Be Thou my speaker, taintless pleader,
Unblotted lawyer, true proceeder!
Thou givest salvation even for alms;
Not with a bribed lawyer's palms.
And this is mine eternal plea
To Him that made heaven, earth, and sea,
That, since my flesh must die so soon,
And want a head to dine next noon,
Just at the stroke, when my veins start and spread,
Set on my soul an everlasting head!
Then am I ready, like a palmer fit,
To tread those blest paths which before I writ.

Of death and judgment, heaven and hell,
Who oft doth think, must needs die well.

Verses found in his Bible in the Gate-House at Westminster.

Even such is time, that takes in trust
Our youth, our joys, our all we have,
And pays us but with earth and dust;
Who, in the dark and silent grave,
When we have wandered all our ways,
Shuts up the story of our days;
But from this earth, this grave, this dust,
My God shall raise me up, I trust!

ELIZABETHAN MISCELLANIES.

THE Poetical Miscellanies are among the most characteristic productions of the age of Elizabeth, and no selection from the work of that age could be at all complete without a reference to them. Devised sometimes by an enterprising bookseller, sometimes by a literary editor like Clement Robinson or Francis Davison, they formed collections—*cancioneros* as it were—of the occasional verse of most of the poets of the day, and they thus preserve for us a mass of poems which, without such an opportunity for publication, the authors would infallibly have let die. Much of what is contained in the later miscellanies, especially in *England's Helicon*, was, it is true, reprinted from works already issued ; but much, on the other hand, was new. The value of the collections was at once recognised, and no work of any single author of the time had such success as fell to their lot ; for example, Tottell's Miscellany went through eight editions before 1587, and the *Paradyse of Dainty Devises* through nine between 1576 and 1606. They were not, however, books likely to survive the shocks of time ; and copies of these original editions are in almost all cases excessively rare. Fortunately most of the poems are now put beyond the risk of loss by the careful reprints of modern scholars, such as Sir Egerton Brydges, Mr. Park, Mr. Collier, and Mr. Arber.

The following is a list of the printed Miscellanies which are known to exist :—

(1) Tottell's Miscellany ; properly called *Songes and Sonettes, written by the ryght honorable Lorde Henry Haward, late Earle of Surrey, and other.* 1557.

This, which is of course not strictly Elizabethan, contains the first edition of Surrey's and Wyatt's poems ; poems by Nicholas Grimald, and about forty poems by uncertain authors, among whom are known to have been Thomas, Lord Vaux, Edward Somerset, and John Heywood.

(2) *The Paradyse of Daynty Devises, devised and written for the most part by M. Edwards, sometimes of her Majesties Chappel; the rest by sundry learned gentlemen, both of honoyr and woorshippe.* 1576.

In spite of its fantastic title the poems here contained are mostly didactic and religious. Among the writers may be named Richard Edwards (the M. or Mr. Edwards of the title-page), Lord Vaux, William Hunnis, and Jasper Heywood. The last-named contributes a poem, of too great length and too little strictly poetical merit to be here quoted, which reads like a curious anticipation of Polonius' advice to Laertes.

(3) *A Gorgious Gallery of Gallant Inventions.* Edited by T. Procter and (perhaps) O. Roydon. 1578.

An inferior collection.

(4) *A handefull of Pleasant Delites,* by Clement Robinson and divers other. 1584.

The title-page says the poems are 'newly devised to the newest tunes,' which suggests that many of these collections were primarily *song-books.*

(5) *Breton's Bower of Delites,* 1592.

Published supposititiously by one Richard Jones, and attributed to Nicholas Breton. It is really a Miscellany, and of the poems it contains only three or four are Breton's.

(6) *The Phœnix Nest,* edited by R. S. [? Richard Stapylton]. 1593.

Among the contributors are Edward Vere, Earl of Oxford, Sir W. Herbert, Lodge, Watson, and Peele.

(7) *The Arbor of Amorous Devises,* 1567.

The only known copy of this book has no title-page, but a sale catalogue of 1781, apparently describing a copy that cannot now be traced, quotes it as by Nicholas Breton. As such Mr. Grosart prints it in his collected edition of Breton's works. But, as the printer's prefatory letter declares, it is in fact a Miscellany, 'being many mens work excellent poets.' All the poems in the collection are anonymous; one of them is the lovely Lullaby we give on p. 500.

(8) *The Passionate Pilgrim,* 1599.

Contains writings of Shakespeare, Barnfield, Marlowe, Raleigh, and others.

(9) *England's Helicon*, 1600 ; edited by J. Bodenham.

This is the most celebrated and the richest of the whole class, and is in itself a compendium of all that is best or that at the time was famous among Elizabethan pastorals and love poems. Every living poet of eminence seems to have been drawn upon for a copy of verses, and much was added from the stores of those no longer living. Thus we have poems from Surrey, Spenser, Sidney, Lord Brooke, Greene, Lodge, Marlowe, and even from Shakespeare ; from Watson, Drayton, Browne; and much of what has since been rightly and wrongly attributed to Raleigh appears here under the title *Ignoto*. Some of the most celebrated poems, such as Sidney's 'Love is dead,' we give under their authors' names ; it is better in this place to quote only from those minor but still beautiful writers who are otherwise not represented in these volumes—such as Breton, the Shepherd Tonie (? Anthony Munday), and Bolton.

(10) *A Poetical Rapsody*, 1602.

The editor of this most interesting miscellany was **Francis Davison**, who with his brother Walter contributed many poems. The list of other writers includes Sidney, Raleigh, Sir John Davies, Watson, Sylvester, Charles Best, and many more, the editor pretending, after the fashion of those times, to throw the responsibility of inserting the works of such 'great and learned personages' upon the too presumptuous printer. It is interesting to note that Davison, writing in 1602, contrasts the poetry of twenty years before with 'the perfection which it has now attained'; a kind of boast which was commoner at the end of the seventeenth century than at the beginning. We may add that the 'Rapsody' passed through four editions in the reign of James I, and that in that of 1608 the poem of 'The Lie,' which we print under Raleigh's name, first appeared.

EDITOR.

[From *The Paradyse of Dainty Devises*, 1576.]

AMANTIUM IRAE.

In going to my naked bed, as one that would have slept,
I heard a wife sing to her child, that long before had wept:
She sighed sore and sang full sore, to bring the babe to rest,
That would not rest but cried still in sucking at her breast:
She was full weary of her watch, and grieved with her child,
She rocked it and rated it, until on her it smiled:
Then did she say now have I found the proverb true to prove
The falling out of faithful friends is the renewing of love.

    *   *   *   *   *   *   *

I marvel much, pardy, quoth she, for to behold the rout,
To see man, woman, boy and beast, to toss the world about:
Some kneel, some crouch, some beck, some check, and some
    can smoothly smile,
And some embrace others in arms, and there think many a wile:
Some stand aloof at cap and knee, some humble and some stout,
Yet are they never friends indeed, until they once fall out:
Thus ended she her song, and said before she did remove,
The falling out of faithful friends is the renewing of love.

R. Edwards.

[From *A Handefull of Pleasant Delites*, 1584.]

A PROPER SONNET.

(To any pleasant Tune.)

I smile to see how you devise
  New masking nets my eyes to blear;
Yourself you cannot so disguise,
  But as you are you must appear.

Your privy winks at board I see,
  And how you set your roving mind;
Yourself you cannot hide from me,
  Although I wink, I am not blind.

The secret sighs and feigned cheer
   That oft doth pain thy careful breast,
To me right plainly doth appear ;
   I see in whom thy heart doth rest.

And though thou mak'st a feigned vow
   That love no more thy heart should nip,
Yet think I know as well as thou
   The fickle helm doth guide the ship.

The salamander in the fire
   By course of wind doth bathe his limbs;
The floating fish tak'th his desire
   In running streams whereas he swims.

So thou in change dost take delight ;
   Full well I know thy slippery kind ;
In vain thou seem'st to dim my sight ;
   Thy rolling eyes bewray thy mind.

I see him smile that doth possess
   Thy love, which once I honoured most ·
If he be wise he may well guess
   Thy love, soon won, will soon be lost.

And sith thou can no more entice
   That he should still love thee alone,
Thy beauty now hath lost her price,
   I see thy savoury scent is gone.

Therefore leave off thy wonted play,
   But as thou art thou wilt appear ;
Unless thou canst devise a way
   To dark the sun that shines so clear.

And keep thy friend, that thou hast won ;
   In truth to him thy love supply ;
Lest he at length, as I have done,
   Take off thy bells, and let thee fly !

                          Anon.

[From *The Arbor of Amorous Devises*, 1597.]

A Sweet Lullaby.

Come little babe, come silly soul,
Thy father's shame, thy mother's grief,
Born as I doubt to all our dole,
And to thyself unhappy chief:
    Sing lullaby and lap it warm,
    Poor soul that thinks no creature harm.

Thou little think'st and less dost know
The cause of this thy mother's moan ;
Thou want'st the wit to wail her woe,
And I myself am all alone ;
    Why dost thou weep, why dost thou wail,
    And know'st not yet what thou dost ail?

Come little wretch, ah silly heart,
Mine only joy ; what can I more ?
If there be any wrong thy smart
That may the destinies implore ;
    'Twas I, I say, against my will ;
    I wail the time, but be thou still.

And dost thou smile ? oh, thy sweet face !
Would God himself he might thee see !
No doubt thou soon wouldst purchase grace,
I know right well, for thee and me.
    But come to mother, babe, and play ;
    For father false is fled away.

Sweet boy, if it by fortune chance
Thy father home again to send,
If death do strike me with his lance,
Yet mayst thou me to him commend ;
    If any ask thy mother's name,
    Tell how by love she purchased blame.

Then will his gentle heart soon yield ;
I know him of a noble mind ;
Although a lion in the field
A lamb in turn thou shalt him find ;
　　Ask blessing, babe ! be not afraid ;
　　His sugared words have me betrayed.

Then mayst thou joy and be right glad
Although in woe I seem to moan ;
Thy father is no rascal lad,
A noble youth of blood and bone ;
　　His glancing looks, if once he smile,
　　Right honest women may beguile.

Come little boy and rock asleep ;
Sing lullaby and be thou still ;
I that can do nought else but weep
Will sit by thee and wail my fill :
　　God bless my babe, and lullaby
　　From this thy father's quality !

　　　　　　　　　　　　Anon.

[From *England's Helicon*, 1600.]

A PALINODE.

As withereth the primrose by the river,
As fadeth summer's sun from gliding fountains,
As vanisheth the light-blown bubble ever,
As melteth snow upon the mossy mountains :
So melts, so vanisheth, so fades, so withers,
The rose, the shine, the bubble and the snow,
Of praise, pomp, glory, joy, which short life gathers,
Fair praise, vain pomp, sweet glory, brittle joy.
The withered primrose by the mourning river,
The faded summer's sun from weeping fountains,
The light-blown bubble, vanished for ever,
The molten snow upon the naked mountains,
　Are emblems that the treasures we uplay,
　Soon wither, vanish, fade, and melt away.

For as the snow, whose lawn did overspread
Th' ambitious hills, which giant-like did threat
To pierce the heaven with their aspiring head,
Naked and bare doth leave their craggy seat:
When as the bubble, which did empty fly,
The dalliance of the undiscerned wind,
On whose calm rolling waves it did rely,
Hath shipwreck made, where it did dalliance find:
And when the sunshine which dissolved the snow,
Coloured the bubble with a pleasant vary,
And made the rathe and timely primrose grow,
Swarth clouds withdraw, which longer time do tarry:
  O what is praise, pomp, glory, joy, but so
  As shine by fountains, bubbles, flowers or snow?

Edmund Bolton.

PHILLIDA AND CORYDON.

In the merry month of May,
In a morn by break of day,
Forth I walked by the wood-side,
When as May was in his pride:
There I spied all alone
Phillida and Corydon.
Much ado there was, God wot,
He would love and she would not.
She said never man was true,
He said, none was false to you.
He said, he had lov'd her long,
She said, Love should have no wrong.
Corydon would kiss her then,
She said, maids must kiss no men,
Till they did for good and all:
Then she made the shepherd call
All the heavens to witness truth:
Never lov'd a truer youth.
Thus with many a pretty oath,
Yea and nay, and faith and troth,

Such as silly shepherds use
When they will not Love abuse,
Love which had been long deluded,
Was with kisses sweet concluded,
And Phillida with garlands gay,
Was made the lady of the May.

Nicholas Breton.

To Colin Clout.

Beauty sat bathing by a spring,
  Where fairest shades did hide her,
The winds blew calm, the birds did sing,
  The cool streams ran beside her.
My wanton thoughts entic'd mine eye
  To see what was forbidden:
But better memory said, fie,
  So vain desire was chidden.
  Hey nonnie, nonnie, &c.

Into a slumber then I fell,
  When fond imagination
Seemed to see, but could not tell
  Her feature or her fashion.
But even as babes in dreams do smile,
  And sometimes fall a weeping,
So I awaked, as wise this while,
  As when I fell a sleeping.
  Hey nonnie, nonnie, &c.

Shepherd Tonie.

Phillida's Love-call to her Corydon, and his Replying.

Phil. Corydon, arise my Corydon,
            Titan shineth clear.
Cor. Who is it that calleth Corydon,
            Who is it that I hear?
Phil. Phillida thy true love calleth thee,
            Arise then, arise then;
              Arise and keep thy flock with me.

Cor.   Phillida, my true love, is it she?
        I come then, I come then,
           I come and keep my flock with thee.

Phil.   Here are cherries ripe my Corydon,
        Eat them for my sake.
Cor.   Here's my oaten pipe, my lovely one,
        Sport for thee to make.
Phil.   Here are threads, my true love, fine as silk,
        To knit thee, to knit thee
           A pair of stockings white as milk.
Cor.   Here are reeds, my true love, fine and neat,
        To make thee, to make thee
           A bonnet to withstand the heat.

Phil.   I will gather flowers my Corydon,
        To set in thy cap.
Cor.   I will gather pears, my lovely one,
        To put in thy lap.
Phil.   I will buy my true love garters gay,
        For Sundays, for Sundays,
           To wear about his legs so tall.
Cor.   I will buy my true love yellow say[1],
        For Sundays, for Sundays,
           To wear about her middle small.

Phil.   When my Corydon sits on a hill
        Making melody:
Cor.   When my lovely one goes to her wheel,
        Singing cheerily.
Phil.   Sure methinks my true love doth excel
        For sweetness, for sweetness,
           Our Pan that old Arcadian knight.
Cor.   And methinks my true love bears the bell
        For clearness, for clearness,
           Beyond the nymphs that be so bright.

Phil.   Had my Corydon, my Corydon,
        Been (alack) her[2] swain:

Thin serge: Fr. *saie.*   [2] The editions give 'my.'

Cor. Had my lovely one, my lovely one,
　　　　　Been in Ida plain :
Phil. Cynthia Endymion had refus'd,
　　　　　Preferring, preferring,
　　　　　　　My Corydon to play withal :
Cor. The queen of love had been excus'd
　　　　　Bequeathing, bequeathing,
　　　　　　　My Phillida the golden ball.

Phil. Yonder comes my mother, Corydon,
　　　　　Whither shall I fly?
Cor. Under yonder beech my lovely one,
　　　　　While she passeth by.
　　　　　Say to her thy true love was not here :
　　　　　Remember, remember,
　　　　　　　To-morrow is another day.
Cor. Doubt me not, my true love, do not fear :
　　　　　Farewell then, farewell then,
　　　　　　　Heaven keep our loves alway.
　　　　　　　　　　　　　Ignoto.

[From Davison's *Poetical Rapsody*, 1602.]

A FICTION : HOW CUPID MADE A NYMPH WOUND HERSELF WITH HIS ARROWS.

It chanc'd of late a shepherd's swain,
That went to seek a strayed sheep,
Within a thicket on the plain,
Espied a dainty Nymph asleep.

Her golden hair o'erspread her face,
Her careless arms abroad were cast,
Her quiver had her pillow's place,
Her breast lay bare to every blast.

The shepherd stood and gaz'd his fill ;
Nought durst he do, nought durst he say,
When chance, or else perhaps his will,
Did guide the God of Love that way.

The crafty boy that sees her sleep,
Whom if she wak'd, he durst not see,
Behind her closely seeks to creep,
Before her nap should ended be.

There come, he steals her shafts away,
And puts his own into their place ;
Nor dares he any longer stay,
But ere she wakes, hies thence apace.

Scarce was he gone when she awakes,
And spies the shepherd standing by ;
Her bended bow in haste she takes,
And at the simple swain let fly.

Forth flew the shaft and pierc'd his heart,
That to the ground he fell with pain ;
Yet up again forthwith he start,
And to the Nymph he ran amain.

Amaz'd to see so strange a sight,
She shot, and shot, but all in vain ;
The more his wounds, the more his might ;
Love yieldeth strength in midst of pain.

Her angry eyes are great with tears,
She blames her hands, she blames her skill ;
The bluntness of her shafts she fears,
And try them on herself she will.

Take heed, sweet Nymph, try not thy shaft,
Each littie touch will prick the heart ;
Alas ! thou knowest not Cupid's craft,
Revenge is joy, the end is smart.

Yet try she will, and prick some bare,
Her hands were glov'd, and next to hand
Was that fair breast, that breast so rare,
That made the shepherd senseless stand.

That breast she prick'd, and through that breast
Love finds an entry to her heart ;
At feeling of this new-come guest,
Lord, how the gentle Nymph doth start !

She runs not now, she shoots no more ;
Away she throws both shafts and bow ;
She seeks for that she shunn'd before,
She thinks the shepherd's haste too slow.

Though mountains meet not, lovers may ;
So others do, and so do they :
The God of Love sits on a tree,
And laughs that pleasant sight to see.

Anon., but attributed to ' A. W.'

A Sonnet of the Moon.

Look how the pale Queen of the silent night
Doth cause the ocean to attend upon her,
And he as long as she is in his sight,
With his full tide is ready her to honour :
But when the silver waggon of the Moon
Is mounted up so high he cannot follow,
The sea calls home his crystal waves to moan,
And with low ebb doth manifest his sorrow ;
So you, that are the sovereign of my heart,
Have all my joys attending on your will ;
My joys low-ebbing when you do depart,
When you return, their tide my heart doth fill ;
   So as you come, and as you do depart,
   Joys ebb and flow within my tender heart.

Charles Best.

Sonnet.

Were I as base as is the lowly plain,
And you, my love, as high as heaven above,
Yet should the thoughts of me your humble swain
Ascend to heaven in honour of my love.
Were I as high as heaven above the plain,
And you, my love, as humble and as low
As are the deepest bottoms of the main,
Wheresoe'er you were, with you my love should go.

Were you the earth, dear love, and I the skies,
My love should shine on you like to the sun,
And look upon you with ten thousand eyes,
Till heaven waxed blind, and till the world were done.
  Wheresoe'er I am, below, or else above you,
  Wheresoe'er you are, my heart shall truly love you.
                                            J. Sylvester.

A Hymn in praise of Neptune.

Of Neptune's empire let us sing,
At whose command the waves obey;
To whom the rivers tribute pay,
Down the high mountains sliding;
To whom the scaly nation yields
Homage for the crystal fields
        Wherein they dwell;
And every sea-god pays a gem
Yearly out of his wat'ry cell,
To deck great Neptune's diadem.

The Tritons dancing in a ring,
Before his palace gates do make
The water with their echoes quake,
Like the great thunder sounding:
The sea nymphs chant their accents shrill,
And the Syrens taught to kill
        With their sweet voice,
Make every echoing rock reply,
Unto their gentle murmuring noise,
The praise of Neptune's empery.
                                    T. Campion.

Of Corinna's Singing.

When to her lute Corinna sings,
Her voice revives the leaden strings,
And doth in highest notes appear
As any challenged echo clear.
But when she doth of mourning speak,
E'en with her sighs the strings do break.

And as her lute doth live and die,
Led by her passions, so must I :
For when of pleasure she doth sing,
My thoughts enjoy a sudden spring ;
But if she do of sorrow speak,
E'en from my heart the strings do break.

T. Campion.

MADRIGAL.

(In praise of Two.)

Faustina hath the fairest face,
And Phillida the better grace ;
   Both have mine eye enriched :
This sings full sweetly with her voice ;
Her fingers make so sweet a noise :
   Both have mine ear bewitched.
Ah me ! sith Fates have so provided,
My heart, alas ! must be divided.

MADRIGAL.

My Love in her attire doth show her wit,
It doth as well become her ;
For every season she hath dressings fit,
For winter, spring, and summer.
No beauty she doth miss
When all her robes are on ;
But Beauty's self she is
When all her robes are gone.

GEORGE CHAPMAN.

[BORN, probably, at Hitchin (1557? 1559?). 'Was sent (1574?) to the University, but whether first to this of Oxon or to that of Cambridge is to me unknown' (Antony Wood). Published *The Shadow of Night* (1594), *Ovid's Banquet of Sense* (1595), *De Guianâ, Carmen Epicum* (1596), *Hero and Leander* (1598), *Seven Books of Homer's Iliad* (1598), *Achilles' Shield* (1598), *Euthymiae Raptus, or The Tears of Peace, with Interlocutions* (1609), *Homer's Tenth Book of his Iliads* (1609), *Epicedium, or a Funeral Song*, in memory of Henry, Prince of Wales (1612), *Homer's Iliads in English* (1611, 1612), *First Twelve Books of the Odyssey* (1614), *Twenty-four Books of Homer's Odisses* (1614, 1615), *The Whole Works of Homer* (1616), *The Crowne of all Homer's Workes, Batrachomyomachia*, &c. (1624?). Chapman was also author of many plays. Died May 12, 1634.]

In spite of the force and originality of English dramatic poetry in the age of Shakespeare, the poetical character of the time had much in common with the Alexandrian epoch in Greek literary history. At Alexandria, when the creative genius of Greece was almost spent, literature became pedantic and obscure. Poets desired to show their learning, their knowledge of the details of mythology, their acquaintance with the more fantastic theories of contemporary science. The same faults mark the poetry of the Elizabethan age, and few writers were more culpably Alexandrian than George Chapman. The spirit of Callimachus or of Lycophron seems at times to have come upon him, as the *lutin* was supposed to whisper ideas extraordinarily good or evil, to Corneille. When under the influence of this possession, Chapman displayed the very qualities and unconsciously translated the language of Callimachus. He vowed that he detested popularity, and all that can please 'the commune reader.' He inveighed against the 'invidious detractor' who became a spectre that dogged him in every enterprise. He hid his meaning in a mist of verbiage, within a labyrinth ot conceits, and himself said, only too truly, about the 'sweet Leander' of Marlowe,

> 'I in floods of ink
> Must drown thy graces.'

It is scarcely necessary to justify these remarks by illustrations from Chapman's works. Every reader of the poems and the prefaces finds barbarism, churlish temper, and pedantry in profusion. In spite of unpopularity, Chapman 'rested as resolute as Seneca, satisfying himself if but a few, if one, or if none like' his verses.

Why then is Chapman, as it were· in his own despite, a poet still worthy of the regard of lovers of poetry? The answer is partly to be found in his courageous and ardent spirit, a spirit bitterly at odds with life, but still true to its own nobility, still capable, in happier moments, of divining life's real significance, and of asserting lofty truths in pregnant words. In his poems we find him moving from an exaggerated pessimism, a pessimism worthy of a Romanticist of 1830, to more dignified acquiescence in human destiny. *The Shadow of Night*, his earliest work, expresses, not without affectation and exaggeration, his blackest mood. Chaos seems better to him than creation, the undivided rest of the void is a happier thing than the crowded distractions of life. Night, which confuses all in shadow and rest, is his Goddess,

> 'That eagle-like doth with her starry wings,
> Beat in the fowls and beasts to Somnus' lodgings,
> And haughty Day to the infernal deep,
> Proclaiming silence, study, ease, and sleep.'

As for day,

> 'In hell thus let her sit, and never rise,
> Till morns leave blushing at her cruelties.'

In a work published almost immediately after *The Shadow of Night*, in *Ovid's Banquet of Sense*, Chapman 'consecrates his strange poems to those searching spirits whom learning hath made noble.' Nothing can well be more pedantic than the conception of the *Banquet of Sense*. Ovid watches Julia at her bath, and his gratification is described in a singular combination of poetical and psychological conceits. Yet in this poem, the redeeming qualities of Chapman and the soothing influence of that anodyne which most availed him in his contest with life, are already evident. *Learning* is already beginning to soothe his spirit with its spell. To *Learning*, as we shall see, he ascribed all the excellences which a modern critic assigns to culture. Learning, in a wide and non-natural sense, is his stay, support, and comfort. In the *Banquet of Sense*, too, he shows that patriotic pride in England, that enjoyment of her beauty, which dignify the *Carmen Epicum*, *de Guiana*, and appear strangely enough in the sequel of *Hero and Leander*. There are exquisite lines in the *Banquet of Sense*, like these, for example, which suggest one of Giorgione's glowing figures :—

> ' *She lay at length like an immortal soul,*
> *At endless rest in blest Elysium.*'

But Chapman's interest in natural science breaks in unseasonably—

> ' Betwixt mine eye and object, certain lines
> Move in the figure of a pyramis,
> Whose chapter in mine eyes gray apple shines,
> The base within my sacred object is ; '

—singular reflections of a lover by his lady's bower !

Chapman could not well have done a rasher thing than ' suppose himself executor to the unhappily deceased author of ' *Hero and Leander*. A poet naturally didactic, Chapman dwelt on the impropriety of Leander's conduct, and confronted him with the indignant goddess of Ceremony. In a passage which ought to interest modern investigators of Ceremonial Government, the poet makes ' all the hearts of deities ' hurry to Ceremony's feet :—

> ' She led Religion, all her body was
> Clear and transparent as the purest glass ;
> Devotion, Order, State, and Reverence,
> Her shadows were ; Society, Memory ;
> All which her sight made live, her absence die.'

The allegory is philosophical enough, but strangely out of place. The poem contains at least one image worthy of Marlowe—

> ' His most kind sister all his secrets knew,
> *And to her, singing like a shower, he flew.*'

This too, of Hero, might have been written by the master of verse :—

> ‘ Her fresh heat blood cast figures in her eyes,
> And she supposed she saw in Neptune’s skies
> How her star wander’d, washed in smarting brine,
> For her love’s sake, that with immortal wine
> Should be embathed, and swim in more heart’s-ease,
> Than there was water in the Sestian seas.’

It is in *The Tears of Peace* (1609), an allegory addressed to Chapman’s patron, the short-lived Henry, Prince of Wales, that the poet does his best to set forth his theory of life and morality. He ‘sat to it,’ he says, to his ‘criticism of life,’ and he was guided in his thoughts by his good genius, Homer. Inspired by Homer, he rises above himself, his peevishness, his controversies, his angry contempt of popular opinion, and he beholds the beauty of renunciation, and acquiesces in a lofty stoicism :—

> ‘ Free suffering for the truth makes sorrow sing,
> And mourning far more sweet than banquetting.’

He comforts himself with the belief that Learning, rightly under-derstood, is the remedy against discontent and restlessness :—

> ‘ For Learning’s truth makes all life’s vain war cease.’

It is Learning that

> ‘ Turns blood to soul, and makes both one calm man.’

By Learning man reaches a deep knowledge of himself, and of his relations to the world, and ‘ Learning the art is of good life’ :—

> *‘ Let all men judge, who is it can deny*
> *That the rich crown of old Humanity*
> *Is still your birthright? and was ne’er let down*
> *From heaven for rule of beasts’ lives, but your own?’*

These noble words still answer the feverish debates of the day, for, whatever our descent,

> ‘ Still, at the worst, we are the sons of men!’

In this persuasion, Chapman can consecrate his life to his work, can cast behind him fear and doubt,

> ‘ This glass of air, broken with less than breath,
> This slave bound face to face to death till death.’

His work was that which the spirit of Homer put upon him, in the green fields of Hitchin.

> 'There did shine,
> A beam of Homer's freër soul in mine,'

he says, and by virtue of that beam, and of his devotion to Homer, George Chapman still lives. When he had completed his translations he could say,

> 'The work that I was born to do, is done.'

Learning and work had been his staff through life, and had won him immortality. But for his *Homer*, Chapman would only be remembered by professional students. His occasional inspired lines would not win for him many readers. But his translations of the Iliad and Odyssey are masterpieces, and cannot die.

Chapman's theory of translation allowed him great latitude. He conceived it to be 'a pedantical and absurd affectation to turn his author word for word,' and maintained that a translator, allowing for the different genius of the Greek and English tongues, 'must adorn' his original 'with words, and such a style and form of oration, as are most apt for the language into which they are converted.' This is an unlucky theory, for Chapman's idea of 'the style and form of oration most apt for' English poetry was remote indeed from the simplicity of Homer. The more he admired Homer, the more Chapman felt bound to dress him up in the height of rhetorical conceit. He excused himself by the argument, that we have not the epics as Homer imagined them, that 'the books were not set together by Homer.' He probably imagined that, if Homer had had his own way with his own works, he would have produced something much more in the Chapman manner, and he kindly added, ever and anon, a turn which he fancied Homer would approve. The English reader must be on his guard against this custom of Chapman's, and must remember, too, that the translator's erudition was exceedingly fantastic. Thus Chapman derives the difficult word ἀλφηστὴς from the letter ἄλφα, the first in the Greek alphabet, and decides that the men whom Homer calls ἀλφησταὶ, are what modern slang calls 'A 1 men.' Again, he names the Phoenician who seduced the nurse of Eumaeus, 'a great-wench-net-layer,' a word derived by him from πολυπαίπαλος, thus, 'παλεύω, *pertraho in retia*, et παῖς, *puella*.' He is full of these strange philological theories, and he boldly

lets them loose in his translations. Chapman has another great
fault, allied indeed to a great excellence. In his speed, in the
rapidity of the movement of his lines, he is Homeric. The last
twelve books of the *Iliad* were struck out at a white heat, in fifteen
weeks. Chapman was carried away by the current of the Homeric
verse, and this is his great saving merit. Homer inspires him,
however uncouth his utterance, as Apollo inspired the Pythoness.
He 'speaks out loud and bold,' but not clear. In the heat of his
hurry, Chapman flies at any rhyme to end his line, and then his
rhyme has to be tagged on by the introduction of some utterly
un-Homeric mode of expression. Thus, in Chapman, the majestic
purity of Homer is tormented, the bright and equable speed of
the river of verse leaps brawling over rocks and down narrow
ravines. What can be more like Chapman, and less like Homer,
than these lines in the description of the storm,

> 'How all the tops he bottoms with the deeps,
> And in the bottoms all the tops he steeps'?

Here the Greek only says 'Zeus hath troubled the deep.' It is
thus that Chapman 'adorns his original.' Faults of this kind are
perhaps more frequent in the *Iliad* than in the *Odyssey*. Cole-
ridge's taste was in harmony with general opinion when he pre-
ferred the latter version, with its manageable metre, to the ruder
strain of the *Iliad*, of which the verse is capable of degenerating
into an amble, or dropping into a trot. The crudities, the in-
appropriate quaintnesses of Chapman's *Homer*, are visible enough,
when we read only a page or two, here and there, in the work.
Neither Homer, nor any version of Homer, should be studied
piece-meal. 'He must not be read,' as Chapman truly says, 'for
a few lines with leaves turned over capriciously in dismembered
fractions, but throughout ; the whole drift, weight, and height of
his works set before the apprehensive eyes of his judge.' Thus
read, the blots on Chapman's *Homer* almost disappear, and you
see 'the massive and majestic memorial, where for all the flaws
and roughnesses of the weather-beaten work the great workmen
of days unborn would gather to give honour to his name.'

A. LANG.

THE THAMES.

[From Ovid's *Banquet of Sense.*]

Forward and back and forward went he thus,
Like wanton Thamysis that hastes to greet
The brackish court of old Oceanus ;
And as by London's bosom she doth fleet,
　Casts herself proudly through the bridge's twists,
Where, as she takes again her crystal feet,
　She curls her silver hair like amourists,
Smooths her bright cheeks, adorns her brow with ships,
And, empress-like, along the coast she trips.

Till coming near the sea, she hears him roar,
Tumbling her churlish billows in her face,
Then, more dismay'd than insolent before,
Charged to rough battle for his smooth embrace,
　She croucheth close within her winding banks,
And creeps retreat into her peaceful palace ;
　Yet straight high-flowing in her female pranks
Again she will be wanton, and again,
By no means staid, nor able to contain.

[From *The Tears of Peace.*]

THE SPIRIT OF HOMER.

'I am,' said he, 'that spirit Elysian,
That in thy native air, and on the hill
Next Hitchin's left hand, did thy bosom fill
With such a flood of soul, that thou wert fain,
With exclamations of her rapture then,
To vent it to the echoes of the vale ;
When, meditating of me, a sweet gale
Brought me upon thee ; and thou didst inherit
My true sense, for the time then, in my spirit ;

And I, invisibly, went prompting thee
To those fair greens where thou didst English me.'
  Scarce he had utter'd this, when well I knew
It was my Prince's Homer ; whose dear view
Renew'd my grateful memory of the grace
His Highness did me for him ; which in face
Methought the Spirit show'd, was his delight,
And added glory to his heavenly plight :
Who told me, he brought stay to all my state ;
That he was Angel to me, Star, and Fate ;
Advancing colours of good hope to me ;
And told me my retired age should see
Heaven's blessing in a free and harmless life,
Conduct me, thro' earth's peace-pretending strife,
To that true Peace, whose search I still intend,
And to the calm shore of a loved end.

THE PROCESSION OF TIME.

Before her flew Affliction, girt in storms,
Gash'd all with gushing wounds, and all the forms
Of bane and misery frowning in her face ;
Whom Tyranny and Injustice had in chase ;
Grim Persecution, Poverty, and Shame ;
Detraction, Envy, foul Mishap and lame ;
Scruple of Conscience ; Fear, Deceit, Despair ;
Slander and Clamour, that rent all the air ;
Hate, War, and Massacre ; uncrowned Toil ;
And Sickness, t' all the rest the base and foil,
Crept after ; and his deadly weight, trod down
Wealth, Beauty, and the glory of a Crown.
These usher'd her far off ; as figures given
To show these Crosses borne, make peace with heaven.
But now, made free from them, next her before ;
Peaceful and young, Herculean Silence bore
His craggy club ; which up aloft, he hild ;
With which, and his fore-finger's charm he still'd
All sounds in air ; and left so free mine ears,
That I might hear the music of the spheres,

And all the angels singing out of heaven ;
Whose tunes were solemn, as to passion given ;
For now, that Justice was the happiness there
For all the wrongs to Right inflicted here,
Such was the passion that Peace now put on ;
And on all went ; when suddenly was gone
All light of heaven before us ; from a wood,
Whose light foreseen, now lost, amazed we stood,
The sun still gracing us ; when now, the air
Inflamed with meteors, we discover'd fair,
The skipping goat ; the horse's flaming mane ;
Bearded and trained comets ; stars in wane ;
The burning sword, the firebrand-flying snake ;
The lance ; the torch ; the licking fire ; the drake ;
And all else meteors that did ill abode ;
The thunder chid ; the lightning leap'd abroad ;
And yet when Peace came in all heaven was clear,
And then did all the horrid wood appear,
Where mortal dangers more than leaves did grow :
In which we could not one free step bestow,
For treading on some murther'd passenger
Who thither was, by witchcraft, forced to err :
Whose face the bird hid that loves humans best ;
That hath the bugle eyes and rosy breast,
And is the yellow Autumn's nightingale.

Helen on the Rampart.

[From *Iliad III.*]

They reach'd the Scaean towers,
Where Priam sat, to see the fight, with all his counsellors ;
Panthous, Lampus, Clytius, and stout Hicetaon,
Thymoetes, wise Antenor, and profound Ucalegon ;
All grave old men ; and soldiers they had been, but for age
Now left the wars ; yet counsellors they were exceeding sage.
And as in well-grown woods, on trees, cold spiny grasshoppers
Sit chirping, and send voices out, that scarce can pierce our ears

For softness, and their weak faint sounds ; so, talking on the tower,
These seniors of the people sate ; who when they saw the power
Of beauty, in the queen, ascend, even those cold-spirited peers,
Those wise and almost wither'd men, found this heat in their years,
That they were forced (through whispering) to say : ' What man
    can blame
The Greeks and Trojans to endure, for so admired a dame,
So many miseries, and so long ? In her sweet countenance shine
Looks like the Goddesses'. And yet (though never so divine)
Before we boast, unjustly still, of her enforced prize,
And justly suffer for her sake, with all our progenies,
Labour and ruin, let her go ; the profit of our land
Must pass the beauty.' Thus, though these could bear so fit
    a hand
On their affections, yet, when all their gravest powers were used,
They could not choose but welcome her, and rather they accused
The gods than beauty.

THE CAMP AT NIGHT.

[From *Iliad VIII.*]

          The winds transferr'd into the friendly sky
Their supper's savour ; to the which they sat delightfully,
And spent all night in open field ; fires round about them shined.
As when about the silver moon, when air is free from wind,
And stars shine clear, to whose sweet beams, high prospects,
    and the brows
Of all steep hills and pinnacles, thrust up themselves for shows,
And even the lowly valleys joy to glitter in their sight,
When the unmeasured firmament bursts to disclose her light,
And all the signs in heaven are seen, that glad the shepherd's
    heart ;
So many fires disclosed their beams, made by the Trojan part,
Before the face of Ilion, and her bright turrets show'd.
A thousand courts of guard kept fires, and every guard allow'd
Fifty stout men, by whom their horse eat oats and hard white corn,
And all did wishfully expect the silver-throned morn.

THE GRIEF OF ACHILLES FOR THE SLAYING OF PATROCLUS, MENOETIUS' SON.

[From *Iliad XVIII.*]

They fought still like the rage of fire. And now Antilochus
Came to Æacides, whose mind was much solicitous
For that which, as he fear'd, was fall'n. He found him near
    the fleet
With upright sail-yards, uttering this to his heroic conceit :
'Ay me, why see the Greeks themselves, thus beaten from
    the field,
And routed headlong to their fleet? O let not heaven yield
Effect to what my sad soul fears, that, as I was foretold,
The strongest Myrmidon next me, when I should still behold
The sun's fair light, must part with it. Past doubt Menoetius' son
Is he on whom that fate is wrought. O wretch, to leave undone
What I commanded ; that, the fleet once freed of hostile fire,
Not meeting Hector, instantly he should his powers retire.'

  As thus his troubled mind discoursed, Antilochus appear'd,
And told with tears the sad news thus : 'My lord, that must
    be heard
Which would to heaven I might not tell ; Menoetius' son lies dead,
And for his naked corse (his arms already forfeited,
And worn by Hector) the debate is now most vehement.'

  This said, grief darken'd all his powers. With both his hands
    he rent
The black mould from the forced earth, and pour'd it on his head,
Smear'd all his lovely face ; his weeds, divinely fashioned,
All filed and mangled ; and himself he threw upon the shore,
Lay, as laid out for funeral, then tumbled round, and tore
His gracious curls. His ecstasy he did so far extend,
That all the ladies won by him and his now slaughter'd friend,
Afflicted strangely for his plight, came shrieking from the tents,
And fell about him, beat their breasts, their tender lineaments
Dissolved with sorrow. And with them wept Nestor's warlike son,
Fell by him, holding his fair hands, in fear he would have done

His person violence ; his heart, extremely straiten'd, burn'd,
Beat, swell'd, and sigh'd as it would burst. So terribly he mourn'd,
That Thetis, sitting in the deeps of her old father's seas,
Heard, and lamented.

HERMES IN CALYPSO'S ISLAND.

[From *Odyssey V.*]

Thus charged he ; nor Argicides denied,
But to his feet his fair wing'd shoes he tied,
Ambrosian, golden ; that in his command
Put either sea, or the unmeasured land,
With pace as speedy as a puft of wind.
Then up his rod went, with which he declined
The eyes of any waker, when he pleased,
And any sleeper, when he wish'd, diseased.
This took, he stoop'd Pieria, and thence
Glid through the air, and Neptune's confluence
Kiss'd as he flew, and check'd the waves as light
As any sea-mew in her fishing flight
Her thick wings sousing in the savoury seas,
Like her, he pass'd a world of wilderness ;
But when the far-off isle he touch'd, he went
Up from the blue sea to the continent,
And reach'd the ample cavern of the Queen,
Whom he found within ; without seldom seen.
A sun-like fire upon the hearth did flame ;
The matter precious, and divine the frame ;
Of cedar cleft and incense was the pile,
That breathed an odour round about the isle.
Herself was seated in an inner room,
Whom sweetly sing he heard, and at her loom,
About a curious web, whose yarn she threw
In with a golden shittle. A grove grew
In endless spring about her cavern round,
With odorous cypress, pines, and poplars crown'd,

Where hawks, sea-owls, and long-tongued bittours bred,
And other birds their shady pinions spread ;
All fowls maritimal ; none roosted there,
But those whose labours in the waters were.
A vine did all the hollow cave embrace,
Still green, yet still ripe bunches gave it grace.
Four fountains, one against another, pour'd
Their silver streams ; and meadows all enflower'd
With sweet balm-gentle, and blue violets hid,
That deck'd the soft breasts of each fragrant mead.
Should any one, though he immortal were,
Arrive and see the sacred objects there,
He would admire them, and be over-joy'd ;
And so stood Hermes' ravish'd powers employ'd.
  But having all admir'd, he enter'd on
The ample cave, nor could be seen unknown
Of great Calypso (for all Deities are
Prompt in each other's knowledge, though so far
Sever'd in dwellings) but he could not see
Ulysses there within ; without was he
Set sad ashore, where 'twas his use to view
Th' unquiet sea, sigh'd, wept, and empty drew
His heart of comfort.

ODYSSEUS' SPEECH TO NAUSICAA.

[From *Odyssey VI.*]

                    All in flight
The virgins scatter'd, frighted with this sight,
About the prominent windings of the flood.
All but Nausicaa fled ; but she fast stood :
Pallas had put a boldness in her breast,
And in her fair limbs tender fear comprest.
And still she stood him, as resolved to know
What man he was ; or out of what should grow
His strange repair to them. And here was he
Put to his wisdom ; if her virgin knee

He should be bold, but kneeling, to embrace ;
Or keep aloof, and try with words of grace,
In humblest suppliance, if he might obtain
Some cover for his nakedness, and gain
Her grace to show and guide him to the town.
The last he best thought, to be worth his own,
In weighing both well ; to keep still aloof,
And give with soft words his desires their proof ;
Lest, pressing so near as to touch her knee,
He might incense her maiden modesty.
This fair and filed speech then shew'd this was he :
   ' Let me beseech, O queen, this truth of thee,
Are you of mortal, or the deified race ?
If of the Gods, that th' ample heavens embrace,
I can resemble you to none above
So near as to the chaste-born birth of Jove,
The beamy Cynthia. Her you full present,
In grace of every God-like lineament,
Her goodly magnitude, and all th' address
You promise of her very perfectness.
If sprung of humans, that inhabit earth,
Thrice blest are both the authors of your birth ;
Thrice blest your brothers, that in your deserts
Must, even to rapture, bear delighted hearts,
To see, so like the first trim of a tree,
Your form adorn a dance. But most blest he,
Of all that breathe, that hath the gift t' engage
Your bright neck in the yoke of marriage,
And deck his house with your commanding merit.
I have not seen a man of so much spirit,
Nor man, nor woman, I did ever see,
At all parts equal to the parts in thee.
T' enjoy your sight, doth admiration seize
My eyes, and apprehensive faculties.
Lately in Delos (with a charge of men
Arrived, that render'd me most wretched then,
Now making me thus naked) I beheld
The burthen of a palm, whose issue swell'd
About Apollo's fane, and that put on

A grace like thee ; for Earth had never none
Of all her sylvan issue so adorn'd.
Into amaze my very soul was turn'd,
To give it observation ; as now thee
To view, O virgin, a stupidity
Past admiration strikes me, join'd with fear
To do a suppliant's due, and press so near,
As to embrace thy knees.

The Song the Sirens sung.

[From *Odyssey XII.*]

'Come here, thou worthy of a world of praise,
That dost so high the Grecian glory raise ;
Ulysses ! stay thy ship, and that song hear
That none pass'd ever but it bent his ear,
But left him ravish'd, and instructed more
By us, than any ever heard before.
For we know all things whatsoever were
In wide Troy labour'd ; whatsoever there
The Grecians and the Trojans both sustain'd
By those high issues that the Gods ordain'd.
And whatsoever all the earth can show
T' inform a knowledge of desert, we know.'

Odysseus reveals himself to his Father.

[From *Odyssey XXIV.*]

All this haste made not his staid faith so free
To trust his words ; who said : 'If you are he,
Approve it by some sign.' 'This scar then see,'
Replied Ulysses, 'given me by the boar
Slain in Parnassus ; I being sent before
By yours and by my honour'd mother's will,
To see your sire Autolycus fulfil
The gifts he vow'd at giving of my name.
I'll tell you, too, the trees, in goodly frame

Of this fair orchard, that I ask'd of you
Being yet a child, and follow'd for your show
And name of every tree. You gave me then
Of fig-trees forty, apple-bearers ten,
Pear-trees thirteen, and fifty ranks of vine;
Each one of which a season did confine
For his best eating. Not a grape did grow
That grew not there, and had his heavy brow
When Jove's fair daughters, the all-ripening Hours,
Gave timely date to it.' This charged the powers
Both of his knees and heart with such impression
Of sudden comfort, that it gave possession
Of all to trance ; the signs were all so true ;
And did the love that gave them so renew.
He cast his arms about his son and sunk,
The circle slipping to his feet ; so shrunk
Were all his age's forces with the fire
Of his young love rekindled. The old sire
The son took up quite lifeless. But his breath
Again respiring, and his soul from death
His body's powers recovering, out he cried,
And said : ' O Jupiter ! I now have tried
That still there live in heaven remembering Gods
Of men that serve them ; though the periods
They set on their appearances are long
In best men's sufferings, yet as sure as strong
They are in comforts ; be their strange delays
Extended never so from days to days.
Yet see the short joys or the soon-fix'd fears
Of helps withheld by them so many years :
For if the wooers now have paid the pain
Due to their impious pleasures, now again
Extreme fear takes me, lest we straight shall see
The Ithacensians here in mutiny ;
Their messengers dispatch'd to win to friend
The Cephallenian cities.'

MICHAEL DRAYTON.

[MICHAEL DRAYTON was born at Hartshull in Warwickshire about the year 1563. He died on the 23rd of December, 1631, and lies buried in Westminster Abbey. In 1591 he published *The Harmony of the Church*, which was for some unknown reason refused a licence, and has never been reprinted till recently. It was followed by *Idea* and *The Pastorals*, 1593; *Mortimeriados* (the Barons' Wars), 1596; *The Heroical Epistles* (one had been separately printed 1598); *The Owl*, 1604; *Legends* of Cromwell and others, 1607–1613; *Polyolbion* (first eighteen books 1612, whole 1622); *The Battle of Agincourt*, 1626; besides minor works at intervals.]

The sentence which Hazlitt allots to Drayton is perhaps one of the most felicitous examples of short metaphorical criticism. 'His mind,' says the critic, 'is a rich marly soil that produces an abundant harvest and repays the husbandman's toil; but few flaunting flowers, the garden's pride, grow in it, nor any poisonous weeds.' Such figurative estimates must indeed always be in some respects unsatisfactory, yet in this there is but little of inadequacy. It is exceedingly uncommon for the reader to be transported by anything that he meets with in the author of the *Polyolbion*. Drayton's jewels five words long are of the rarest, and their sparkle when they do occur is not of the brightest or most enchanting lustre. But considering his enormous volume, he is a poet of surprisingly high merit. Although he has written some fifty or sixty thousand lines, the bulk of them on subjects not too favourable to poetical treatment, he has yet succeeded in giving to the whole an unmistakeably poetical flavour, and in maintaining that flavour throughout. The variety of his work, and at the same time the unfailing touch by which he lifts that work, not indeed into the highest regions of poetry, but far above its lower confines, are his most remarkable characteristics. The *Polyolbion*, the *Heroical Epistles*, the *Odes*, the *Ballad of Agincourt*, and the *Nymphidia* are strikingly unlike each other in the qualities required for successful treatment of them, yet they are all successfully treated. It is something to have written the best war song in a language, its best fantastic poem, and its only topographical poem of real value. Adverse criticism may contend that the *Nymphidia* and the *Polyolbion* were not worth the doing, but this is another matter altogether. That the *Ballad of Agincourt* was not worth the doing, no one who has any fondness for poetry or any appreciation of it will attempt to contend. In the lyric work of the *Odes*, scanty as it is, there is the same evidence of mástery and of what may be called thoroughness of workmanship. Exacting critics may indeed argue that Drayton has too much of the thoroughly accomplished and capable workman, and too little of the divinely gifted artist. It may be thought, too, that if he had written less and concentrated his efforts, the average merit of his work would have been higher. There is, at any rate, no doubt that the bulk of his productions, if it has not interfered with their value, has interfered with their popularity.

The Barons' Wars, which, according to some theories, should have been Drayton's best work, is perhaps his worst. The stanza, which he has chosen for good and well-expressed reasons, is an effective one, and the subject might have been made interesting. As a matter of fact it has but little interest. The somewhat 'kite-and-crow' character of the disturbance chronicled is not relieved by any vigorous portraiture either of Mortimer or of Edward or of the Queen. The first and last of these personages are much better handled in the *Heroical Epistles*. The level of these latter and of the *Legends* is decidedly high. Not merely do they contain isolated passages of great beauty, but the general interest of them is well sustained, and the characters of the writers subtly differenced. One great qualification which Drayton had as a writer of historical and geographical verse was his possession of what has been called, in the case of M. Victor Hugo, *la science des noms*. No one who has an ear can fail to recognise the felicity of the stanza in *Agincourt* which winds up with ' Ferrars and Fanhope,' and innumerable examples of the same kind occur elsewhere. Without this science indeed the *Polyolbion* would have been merely an awkward gazetteer. As it is, the 'strange herculean task,' to borrow its author's description of it, has been very happily performed. It may safely be assumed that very few living Englishmen have read it through. But those who have will probably agree that there is a surprising interest in it, and that this interest is kept up by a very artful admixture of styles and subjects. Legends, fancy pieces such as that of the Marriage of Thame and Isis, with its unmatched floral description, accounts of rural sports and the like, ingeniously diversify the merely topographical narrative. Had the *Polyolbion* been its author's only work, Goldsmith's sneer would still have been most undeserved. But the variety of Drayton's performance is almost as remarkable as its bulk. This variety it is impossible to represent fully either in this notice or in the extracts which accompany it. But to the foregoing remarks it may be added that Drayton was master of a very strong and at the same time musical decasyllabic line. His practice in Alexandrines and in complicated stanzas seems to have by no means injured his command of the ordinary heroic couplet. His series of Sonnets to Idea is perhaps his least successful work if we compare him with other men, just as *The Barons' Wars* is his worst performance if his own work only be considered. The *Nymphidia* has received higher praise than any other of his poems, and its fantastic conception and graceful tripping metre deserve this praise well enough. The curious poems of *The Owl* and *The Man in the Moon* show, if they show nothing else, his peculiar faculty of raising almost any subject to a certain poetical dignity by dint of skilful treatment. Lastly, his prose Prefaces deserve attention here, because many of them display the secret of his workmanlike skill. It is evident from them that Drayton was as far as possible from holding the false and foolish improvisation-theory of poetry, and they testify to a most careful study of his predecessors and contemporaries, and to deliberate practice in the use of the poet's tools of language and metre.

G. SAINTSBURY.

Queen Margaret to William de la Pool,
Duke of Suffolk.

What news (sweet Pool) look'st thou my lines should tell
But like the tolling of the doleful bell
Bidding the deaths-man to prepare the grave?
Expect from me no other news to have.
My breast, which once was mirth's imperial throne,
A vast and desert wilderness is grown:
Like that cold region, from the world remote,
On whose breem seas the icy mountains float;
Where those poor creatures, banished from the light,
Do live impris'ned in continual night.
No object greets my soul's internal eyes
But divinations of sad tragedies;
And care takes up her solitary inn
Where youth and joy their court did once begin.
As in September, when our year resigns
The glorious sun to the cold wat'ry signs
Which through the clouds looks on the earth in scorn;
The little bird yet to salute the morn
Upon the naked branches sets her foot,
The leaves then lying on the mossy root,
And there a silly chirriping doth keep
As though she fain would sing, yet fain would weep,
Praising fair Summer, that too soon is gone,
Or sad for Winter, too fast coming on:
In this strange plight I mourn for thy depart,
Because that weeping cannot ease my heart.
Now to our aid who stirs the neighb'ring kings?
Or who from France a puissant army brings?
Who moves the Norman to abet our war?
Cr brings in Burgoyne to aid Lancaster?
Who in the North our lawful claim commends
To win us credit with our valiant friends?

To whom shall I my secret griefs impart?
Whose breast shall be the closet of my heart?
The ancient heroes' fame thou didst revive,
As from them all thyself thou didst derive:
Nature by thee both gave and taketh all,
Alone in Pool she was too prodigal;
Of so divine and rich a temper wrought,
As Heav'n for thee perfection's depth had sought.
Well knew King Henry what he pleaded for,
When he chose thee to be his orator;
Whose angel-eye, by powerful influence,
Doth utter more than human eloquence:
That if again Jove would his sports have tried,
He in thy shape himself would only hide;
Which in his love might be of greater pow'r,
Than was his nymph, his flame, his swan, his show'r.

To the Cambro-Britons and their Harp, his Ballad of Agincourt.

Fair stood the wind for France,
When we our sails advance,
Nor now to prove our chance
    Longer will tarry;
But putting to the main,
At Caux, the mouth of Seine,
With all his martial train,
    Landed King Harry.

And taking many a fort,
Furnished in warlike sort,
Marcheth tow'rds Agincourt
    In happy hour;
Skirmishing day by day,
With those that stopp'd his way,
Where the French gen'ral lay
    With all his power.

Which in his height of pride,
King Henry to deride,
His ransom to provide
    To the king sending.
Which he neglects the while,
As from a nation vile,
Yet with an angry smile
    Their fall portending.

And turning to his men,
Quoth our brave Henry then,
Though they to one be ten,
    Be not amazed.
Yet have we well begun,
Battles so bravely won,
Have ever to the sun
    By fame been raised.

And for myself (quoth he),
This my full rest shall be,
England ne'er mourn for me,
    Nor more esteem me.
Victor I will remain,
Or on this earth lie slain,
Never shall she sustain
    Loss to redeem me.

Poitiers and Cressy tell,
When most their pride did swell,
Under our swords they fell,
    No less our skill is,
Than when our grandsire-great,
Claiming the regal seat,
By many a warlike feat
    Lopp'd the French lilies.

The Duke of York so dread
The eager vaward led,
With the main, Henry sped,
    Amongst his hench-men.

Exeter had the rear,
A braver man not there,
O Lord, how hot they were,
    On the false Frenchmen !

They now to fight are gone,
Armour on armour shone,
Drum now to drum did groan,
    To hear, was wonder ;
That with the cries they make,
The very earth did shake,
Trumpet to trumpet spake,
    Thunder to thunder.

Well it thine age became,
O noble Erpingham,
Which didst the signal aim
    To our hid forces ;
When from a meadow by,
Like a storm suddenly,
The English archery
    Stuck the French horses.

With Spanish yew so strong,
Arrows a cloth-yard long,
That like to serpents stung,
    Piercing the weather ;
None from his fellow starts,
But playing manly parts,
And like true English hearts,
    Stuck close together.

When down their bows they threw,
And forth their bilbos drew,
And on the French they flew,
    Not one was tardy ;
Arms were from shoulders sent,
Scalps to the teeth were rent,
Down the French peasants went,
    Our men were hardy.

This while our noble king,
His broad sword brandishing,
Down the French host did ding,
    As to o'erwhelm it,
And many a deep wound lent;
His arms with blood besprent,
And many a cruel dent
    Bruised his helmet.

Gloucester, that duke so good,
Next of the royal blood,
For famous England stood,
    With his brave brother;
Clarence, in steel so bright,
Though but a maiden knight,
Yet in that furious fight
    Scarce such another.

Warwick in blood did wade,
Oxford the foe invade,
And cruel slaughter made,
    Still as they ran up;
Suffolk his axe did ply,
Beaumont and Willoughby,
Bare them right doughtily,
    Ferrers and Fanhope.

Upon Saint Crispin's day
Fought was this noble fray,
Which fame did not delay
    To England to carry;
O when shall English men,
With such acts fill a pen,
Or England breed again
    Such a King Harry?

The Arming of Pigwiggen.

[From *Nymphidia*.]

(He) quickly arms him for the field,
A little cockle-shell his shield,
Which he could very bravely wield,
  Yet could it not be pierced :
His spear a bent both stiff and strong,
And well near of two inches long ;
The pile was of a horsefly's tongue,
  Whose sharpness naught reversed.

And put him on a coat of mail,
Which was of a fish's scale,
That when his foe should him assail,
  No point should be prevailing.
His rapier was a hornet's sting,
It was a very dangerous thing ;
For if he chanc'd to hurt the king,
  It would be long in healing.

His helmet was a beetle's head,
Most horrible and full of dread,
That able was to strike one dead,
  Yet it did well become him :
And for a plume a horse's hair,
Which being tossed by the air,
Had force to strike his foe with fear,
  And turn his weapon from him.

Himself he on an earwig set,
Yet scarce he on his back could get,
So oft and high he did curvet
  Ere he himself could settle :
He made him turn, and stop, and bound,
To gallop, and to trot the round,
He scarce could stand on any ground,
  He was so full of mettle.

FROM 'POLYOLBION.'

[Song xv. l. 147.]

The Naiads and the nymphs extremely overjoy'd,
And on the winding banks all busily employ'd,
Upon this joyful day, some dainty chaplets twine:
Some others chosen out, with fingers neat and fine,
Brave anadems do make: some baldrics up do bind:
Some, garlands: and to some the nosegays were assigned
As best their skill did serve. But for that Thame should be
Still man-like as himself, therefore they will that he
Should not be drest with flowers to garden that belong
(His bride that better fit), but only such as sprung
From the replenish'd meads and fruitful pastures near.
To sort which flowers, some sit, some making garlands were;
The primrose placing first, because that in the spring
It is the first appears, then only flourishing;
The azur'd hare-bell next with them they neatly mix'd,
T' allay whose luscious smell they woodbind plac'd betwixt.
Amongst those things of scent, there prick they in the lily:
And near to that again her sister daffodilly.
To sort these flowers of show, with th' other that were sweet,
The cowslip then they couch, and the oxlip for her meet:
The columbine amongst they sparingly do set,
The yellow kingcup wrought in many a curious fret,
And now and then among, of eglantine a spray,
By which again a course of lady-smocks they lay:
The crow-flower, and thereby the clover flower they stick,
The daisy, over all those sundry sweets so thick,
As Nature doth herself to imitate her right:
Who seems in that her pearl so greatly to delight,
That every plain therewith she powd'reth to behold:
The crimson darnel flowers, the blue-bottle and gold,
Which though esteem'd but weeds, yet for their dainty hues,
And for their scent not ill, they for this purpose choose.

Thus having told you how the bridegroom Thame was drest,
I 'll show you how the bride fair Isis was invest ;
Sitting to be attired under her bower of state,
Which scorns a meaner sort than fits a princely rate,
In anadems, for whom they curiously dispose
The red, the dainty white, the goodly damask rose ;
For the rich ruby, pearl, and amethyst, men place
In kings' imperial crowns, the circle that enchase.
The brave carnation then, with sweet and sovereign power
(So of his colour call'd, although a July flower),
With th' other of his kind, the speckled and the pale :
Then th' odoriferous pink, that sends forth such a gale
Of sweetness ; yet in scents as various as in sorts.
The purple violet then, the pansy there supports :
The marygold above t' adorn the arched bar :
The double daisy, thrift, the button-bachelor,
Sweet-william, sops-in-wine, the campion : and to these
Some lavender they put, with rosemary and bays :
Sweet marjoram, with her like, sweet basil rare for smell,
With many a flower, whose name were now too long to tell :
And rarely with the rest, the goodly fleur-de-lis.

JOSEPH HALL.

[JOSEPH HALL, successively Bishop of Exeter and Norwich, was born July 1st, 1574, at Bristow Park, near Ashby de la Zouch, in Leicestershire. His prose writings, which are very voluminous, have gained him the title of the Christian Seneca. His polemical works brought him into collision with Milton; his sermons rank among the most eloquent in our language; his characters of Virtues and Vices were the delight of Lamb; and his Occasional Meditations still maintain their popularity. He terminated a life of much usefulness and many troubles at Higham, near Norwich, September 8th, 1656, in the eighty-second year of his age. As a poet Hall is known only by his *Satires*, which were written when he was a very young man. They came out in two instalments, the first of which was entitled *Virgidemiarum, First three Bookes of Toothlesse Satyrs—Poetical, Academical, Moral*, and appeared in 1597; the second, entitled *Virgidemiarum, The three Last Bookes of Byting Satyrs*, were published in the following year. Both parts were reprinted in 1599, and again in 1602.]

Hall boasts that he was the first English satirist. This is not true. To say nothing of the fathers of our tongue, and of the satires of Barklay, Skelton, Roye, and Gascoigne, he had been anticipated in his own walk by Thomas Lodge, whose *Fig for Momus* appeared in 1593. Hall has however a higher claim to praise. He was the founder of a great dynasty of satirists. He made satire popular, and he determined its form. Marston immediately succeeded him as his disciple; the author of *Skialetheia*, the author of *Microcynicon*, and innumerable other anonymous satirists followed in rapid succession, till we reach Donne and Jonson, Wither and Marvel, Dryden and Oldham. In all these poets the influence of Hall is either directly or indirectly perceptible. Dryden had in all probability perused him with care, and Pope was so sensible of his merits that he not only carefully interlined his copy of Hall, but expressed much regret that he had not been acquainted with his Satires sooner.

Hall's abilities, not only as a satirist, but as a descriptive writer and as a master of style, are of a high order. His models were, he tells us, Horace, Juvenal, and Persius. With the first he has little in common ; he has none of his sobriety, none of his grace, none of his urbanity. To the influence of the third is to be attributed his most characteristic defect, obscurity, an obscurity which arises not from confusion or plethora of thought, but from affectation in expression, from archaic phraseology, from unfamiliar combinations, from recondite allusions, from elliptical apostrophes, and from abrupt transitions. To Juvenal his obligations were great indeed. He borrows his phrases, his turns, his rhetorical exaggerations, his trick of allusive and incidental satire, his reflections, his whole method of dealing with and delineating vice. But borrowing he assimilates. Hall's satire is distinguished by its vehemence and intrepidity. He has himself described the savage delight with which he applied himself to satirical composition, and every fervid page testifies the truth of his confession. He never seems to flag : his energy and fertility of invective are inexhaustible. He has in his six books bared and lashed every vice in the long and dreary catalogue of human frailty ; but the reader, soon surfeited, is glad to leave him to pursue his ungrateful task alone. Nor is Hall more attractive when painting the minor foibles of mankind ; for his humour is hard, his touch heavy, and his wit saturnine. As a delineator of men and manners he will always be interesting. His Satires are a complete picture of English society at the end of the sixteenth century. His sketches are vivid and singularly realistic, for he has the rare art of being minute without being prolix, of crowding without confusing his canvas ; and he united the faculty of keen observation to great natural insight. History is indeed almost as much beholden to him as satire.

His style is, for the age at which his poems appeared, wonderful. Though marred by the defects to which we have referred, it is as a rule at once energetic and elegant, at once fluent and felicitous, at once terse and ornate. He carried the heroic couplet almost to perfection. His versification is indeed sometimes so voluble and vigorous, that we might, as Campbell well observed, imagine ourselves reading Dryden. To cull one or two examples :—

> 'Fond fool! six feet shall serve for all thy store,
> And he that cares for most shall find no more.'

> 'Nay, let the Devil and St. Valentine
> Be gossips to those ribald rhymes of thine,
> And each day dying lives, and living dies.'

He is the first of our authors to evince decided powers of epi-grammatic expression, and to diversify the heroic couplet by the introduction of the triplet. It is much to be regretted that Hall's most vigorous and most successful writing is of such a character as makes it impossible to be presented to general readers in our day. The conclusion of the first satire of the fourth book, and of the fourth satire of the same book, are passages in question. In consulting the interests of propriety we are, we must add, not consulting the interests of Hall's fame as a satirist, though the shade of a Father of the Church will we trust forgive the injury.

Besides these Satires he was the author of a few miscellaneous poems, chiefly of a religious and elegiac character, but they are not of much value.

J. Churton Collins.

The Golden Age.

[From Book iii. Satire 1.]

Time was, and that was termed the time of gold,
When world and time were young that now are old
(When quiet Saturn swayed the mace of lead,
And pride was yet unborn, and yet unbred).
Time was, that whiles the autumn fall did last,
Our hungry sires gap'd for the falling mast
   Of the Dodonian oaks.
Could no unhusked acorn leave the tree
But there was challenge made whose it might be.
And if some nice and licorous appetite
Desir'd more dainty dish of rare delight,
They scal'd the stored crab with clasped knee
Till they had sated their delicious eye :
Or search'd the hopeful thicks of hedgy rows
For briery berries, or haws, or sourer sloes.
Or when they meant to fare the fin'st of all,
They lick'd oak-leaves bespread with honey-fall.
As for the thrice three-angled beech-nut shell,
Or chestnut's armed husk and hid kernell,
No squire durst touch, the law would not afford.
Kept for the court, and for the king's own board,
Their royal plate was clay, or wood, or stone :
The vulgar, save his hand, else he had none.
Their only cellar was the neighbour brook :
None did for better care, for better look ;
Was then no plaining of the brewer's scape,
Nor greedy vintner mix'd the strained grape.
The king's pavilion was the grassy green
Under safe shelter of the shady treen.
Under each bank men laid their limbs along,
Not wishing any ease, not fearing wrong,
Clad with their own as they were made of old,
Not feeling shame nor feeling any cold.

HOLLOW HOSPITALITY.

[From Book iii. Sat. 3.]

The courteous citizen bade me to his feast
With hollow words, and overly [1] request :
'Come, will ye dine with me this holiday?'
I yielded, though he hop'd I would say nay:
For I had maiden'd it, as many use ;
Loath for to grant, but loather to refuse.
'Alack, sir, I were loath—another day,—
I should but trouble you ;—pardon me, if you may.'
No pardon should I need ; for, to depart
He gives me leave, and thanks too, in his heart.
Two words for money, Darbyshirian wise :
(That's one too many) is a naughty guise.
Who looks for double biddings to a feast,
May dine at home for an importune guest.
I went, then saw, and found the great expense ;
The face and fashions of our citizens.
Oh, Cleopatrical ! what wanteth there
For curious cost, and wondrous choice of cheer?
Beef, that erst Hercules held for finest fare ;
Pork, for the fat Bœotian, or the hare
For Martial ; fish for the Venetian ;
Goose-liver for the licorous Roman ;
Th' Athenian's goat ; quail, Iolaus' cheer ;
The hen for Esculape, and the Parthian deer ;
Grapes for Arcesilas [2], figs for Pluto's mouth,
And chestnuts fair for Amarillis' tooth.
Hadst thou such cheer? wert thou ever there before?
Never,—I thought so : nor come there no more.
Come there no more; for so meant all that cost :
Never hence take me for thy second host.
For whom he means to make an often guest,
One dish shall serve ; and welcome make the rest.

[1] Superficial. [2] Plutarch, *Moralia* 668 a, calls Arcesilaus φιλόβοτρυς

A Coxcomb.

[From Book iii. Sat. 5.]

Late travelling along in London way
Me met, as seen by his disguised array,
A lusty courtier, whose curled head
With abron[1] locks was fairly furnished.
I him saluted in our lavish wise ;
He answers my untimely courtesies :
His bonnet vailed, ere ever he could think
The unruly wind blows off his periwinke.
He lights and runs and quickly hath him sped
To overtake his overrunning head.
The sportful wind, to mock the headless man,
Tosses apace his pitched Rogerian[2] :
And straight it to a deeper ditch hath blown ;
There must my yonker fetch his waxen crown.
I looked and laughed, whiles in his raging mind
He cursed all courtesy and unruly wind.
1 looked and laughed, and much I marvelled
To see so large a causeway on his head,
And me bethought, that when it first begon
'Twas some shrewd autumn that so bared the bone.
Is 't not sweet pride, when men their crowns must shade
With that which jerks the hams of every jade,
Or floor-strewed locks from off the Barber's shears ?
But waxen crowns well 'gree with borrowed hairs.

A Deserted Mansion.

[From Book v. Sat. 2.]

Beat the broad gates, a goodly hollow sound
With double echoes doth again rebound ;
But not a dog doth bark to welcome thee,
Nor churlish porter canst thou chafing see ;
All dumb and silent, like the dead of night,
Or dwelling of some sleepy Sybarite.
The marble pavement hid with desert weed,
With houseleek, thistle, dock, and hemlock seed :

[1] Auburn.   [2] A nickname for a false scalp.

But if thou chance cast up thy wondering eyes,
Thou shalt discern upon the frontispiece
ΟΥΔΕΙΣ ΕΙΣΙΤΩ[1] graven up on high,
A fragment of old Plato's poesy:
The meaning is, 'Sir Fool, ye may be gone,
Go back by leave, for way here lieth none.'
Look to the towered chimneys, which should be
The windpipes of good hospitality,
Through which it breatheth to the open air,
Betokening life, and liberal welfare ;
Lo there the unthankful swallow takes her rest,
And fills the tunnel with her circled nest ;
Nor half that smoke from all his chimneys goes
Which one tobacco pipe drives through his nose.
So rawbone hunger scorns the mudded walls,
And 'gins to revel it in lordly halls.

ADVICE TO MARRY BETIMES.

[From Book iv. Sat. 4.]

Wars, God forfend ! nay God defend from war ;
Soon are sons spent, that not soon reared are.
Gallio may pull me roses ere they fall,
Or in his net entrap the tennis ball,
Or tend his spar-hawk mantling in her mew,
Or yelping beagles' busy heels pursue,
Or watch a sinking cork upon the shore,
Or halter finches through a privy door,
Or list he spend the time in sportful game,
In daily courting of his lovely dame,
Hang on her lips, melt in her wanton eye,
Dance in her hand, joy in her jollity:
Here's little peril, and much lesser pain,
So timely Hymen do the rest restrain.
Hie wanton Gallio and wed betime,
Why should'st thou lose the pleasures of thy prime ?
Seest thou the rose leaves fall ungathered ?
Then hie thee, wanton Gallio, to wed.

[1] 'Let no man enter.'

JOHN MARSTON.

[MARSTON has been identified with an Oxford man of that name who was
admitted B.A. in 1593, and with Maxton or Mastone, 'the new poet' men-
tioned in Henslowe's Diary in 1599. But nothing is known of his private
life. He published *The Metamorphosis of Pygmalion's Image* and *Certain
Satires* in 1598, and *The Scourge of Villany, Three Books of Satires*, in the
same year. He was conjoined with Chapman and Jonson in the composi-
tion of the play called *Eastward Ho!* which had unpleasant consequences
for its authors, and he wrote several plays by himself, the dates of which
range from 1602 to 1613.]

If we were asked whether Marston should be classed as a satirist
or as a dramatist, it would be difficult to give a satisfactory answer.
His plays are full of satiric power, and his satires are not without
evidences of the dramatist's way of looking at life. The personages
of his dramas, though boldly and fully pourtrayed, are set up as
types of base or noble humanity, to be vehemently disliked or liked.
The author is far from being impartial in his exhibition of their
character ; the reader seems to be aware of him standing by with
a stern moral purpose to emphasize their vices and their virtues.
In his satires, on the other hand, he has a habit of turning round
upon himself which may truly be called dramatic. He rails, and
then rails at himself for railing ; pours forth torrents of abuse upon
the objects of his dislike,—dancing, fencing, sonnetteering dandies,
apish scholars, pedants, gulls, perfumed inamoratos,—the vices,
the effeminacies, the affectations of the time,—and then vituperates
himself no less roundly as a vile, snarling, canker-eaten, rusty
cur, who will rake everything into his tumbril, and cannot see
good in anything. The Elizabethan time was too large and full-
blooded, too full of sanguine aspiration, of prosperous bustle and
variety, to be favourable to the production of satire. It was not
sufficiently out of temper with itself to encourage the satirist.
Marston's so-called satires are rather wild buffooneries, than the

offspring of deep-seated and savage indignation. Though the language is strong enough to warrant the idea that he was much offended by the profligacy and apish fopperies of the gilded youth of the time, and he makes himself out to be a terrible cynic, 'who cannot choose but bite,' he does not really bite, but only belabours with a clown's cudgel of inflated skin.

The eloquence of Hall's satires makes one hesitate to say that the language had not then been developed into a fitting instrument for polished satire, but, however this may be, Marston made no attempt at rapier-like thrusts of cynical wit. He guffawed at Hall's 'worthless satires,' and the graceful archaism of his style, which seemed to him as contemptible as any of the minor vices which the satirist undertook to expose. Hall in one of his satires expressed a wish that he could use the freedom of speech of the ancient satirists. Marston gratified this wish without scruple, to such an extent that he has been stigmatised as the most filthy and scurrilous writer of his time. To the first of these epithets Marston has some claim, but to call him scurrilous conveys an imputation of ill-nature which would be most undeserved. That he could write better things than the coarse, rugged, furious, ribald, broadly-humorous couplets which he called satires, and which he estimated himself at their true value, when he took his 'solemn *congé* of this fusty world,' may be seen by any one who consults Charles Lamb's extracts from his plays, or better still, the plays themselves.

W. MINTO.

To Detraction.

Foul canker of fair virtuous action,
Vile blaster of the freshest blooms on earth,
Envy's abhorred child, Detraction,
I here expose to thy all-tainting breath
  The issue of my brain ; snarl, rail, bark, bite,
  Know that my spirit scorns Detraction's spite.

Know that the Genius, which attendeth on
And guides my powers intellectual,
Holds in all vile repute Detraction.
My soul—an essence metaphysical,
  That in the basest sort scorns critics' rage
  Because he knows his sacred parentage—

My spirit is not puff'd up with fat fume
Of slimy ale, nor Bacchus' heating grape ;
My mind disdains the dungy muddy scum
Of abject thoughts and Envy's raging hate.
  'True judgment slight regards Opinion,
  A sprightly wit disdains Detraction.'

A partial praise shall never elevate
My settled censure of my own esteem ;
A canker'd verdict of malignant hate
Shall ne'er provoke me, worse myself to deem.
  Spite of despite, and rancour's villany,
  I am myself, so is my poesy.

To Everlasting Oblivion.

Thou mighty gulf, insatiate cormorant !
Deride me not, though I seem petulant
  To fall into thy chops. Let others pray
  For ever their fair poems flourish may,

But as for me, hungry Oblivion
Devour me quick. Accept my orison,
  My earnest prayers, which do importune thee
  With gloomy shade of thy still empery
  To veil both me and my rude poesy.
Far worthier lines, in silence of thy state,
Do sleep securely, free from love or hate ;
From which this living ne'er can be exempt,
But whilst it breathes, will hate and fury tempt.
Then close his eyes with thy all-dimming hand,
Which not right-glorious actions can withstand ;
Peace, hateful tongues ; I now in silence pace,
Unless some hound do wake me from my place.
  I with this sharp, yet well-meant poesy
  Will sleep secure, right free from injury
  Of cankered hate, or rankest villainy.

SIR JOHN DAVIES.

[BORN at Tisbury, Wiltshire, and educated at Winchester and New College. Oxford. After a somewhat riotous youth, he gained the friend-ship and patronage of Lords Mountjoy and Ellesmere, and became Solicitor-and Attorney-General for Ireland under James. On the dismissal of Chief Justice Crew by Charles I in Nov. 1626, Sir John Davies, who had dis-tinguished himself by zealous championship of anti-popular views, was appointed his successor. He did not live however to enter upon the office, dying suddenly of apoplexy in the following month. The *Orchestra, or a Poeme of Dauncing* was licensed 1593, published 1596; *Nosce Teipsum* was published 1599; *Hymns to Astraea* 1599. Davies was a contributor to *England's Helicon* (1600) and to *Davison's Poetical Rhapsody* (1602). An edition of his works appeared in 1622, and a modern complete edition, con-taining hitherto unpublished matter, was made by Mr. Grosart in 1869 (republished 1876).]

Sir John Davies belongs to that late Elizabethan circle of courtly poets which still gathered round the declining age of the great Queen with apparently as much personal devotion as the circle of Sidney and Spenser had gathered round her prime. His *Nosce Teipsum*, published in 1599, was dedicated

> ' To that clear majesty which in the North
> Doth like another sun in glory rise ; '

and the *Hymns to Astraea*, which appeared in the same year, may be ranked as one of the most readable and freely written expres-sions of that complex sentiment toward the Queen of which each considerable Elizabethan poet became in turn the mouthpiece. This later group is to be distinguished on the one hand from the earlier lyrical and pastoral school, and on the other from the great dramatic circle which crowds the foreground of this second period. Its production was reflective and philosophical, and only occasion-ally and subordinately either lyrical or dramatic. It testified to revolt against pastorals and love poetry, but no member of it was possessed of a sufficiently great or pliant genius to achieve any important triumph outside the older and well-worn fashions. Lord Brooke in point of power reigns supreme among these philosophers in verse, but Sir John Davies' *Nosce Teipsum* enjoyed a wider contemporary reputation than anything of Lord Brooke's, and has been far more frequently read since. It is a strange performance, and is to be admired rather for the measure of victory it obtains over unfavourable conditions, than for any absolute poetical merits. Some handbook of Christian philosophy seems to have fallen in the author's way during a year of retirement at Oxford,—possibly the *De Natura Hominis* of Nemesius, of which Wither published an English translation in 1636,—and the text suited a sobered mood, while it offered an opportunity for rehabilitating a reputation shaken by youthful folly and extravagance. Accordingly the *Nosce Teipsum* was produced, an 'oracle expounded in two Elegies—(1) of Human Knowledge ; (2) of the Soul of Man and the Immortality thereof.' It is an exposition in the verse of *Gondibert* and the *Annus Mirabilis* of what Davies himself calls the 'received opinions,' the orthodox metaphysic of his time, and treats such topics as 'what the soul is ;' 'that the soul is more than the Temperature of the Humors of the Body ;' 'that the soul is created immediately by God ;' 'the vegetative or Quickening power ;' 'the power of sense, the Relations between wit and will,' &c. &c. All these interminable and tremendous subjects are indeed handled with admirable clearness and brevity. Where Lord Brooke would have wandered on to unmeasured length, thinking his way from cloud to clearness with laborious sincerity, Sir John Davies, a man of far inferior temper and morale, plays the artist with his inartistic material, clearly foresees his end, maps out his arguments and 'acclamations,' and infuses just so much imagination and so much eloquence as will carry the subject to the ears it is intended to reach. Hallam said of *Nosce Teipsum* that it scarcely contained a languid verse. It may be said of it with equal truth that it scarcely contains a verse of real energy, and that it shows not a spark of that genuine poetic gift which at rare intervals lightens the most heavy and formless of Lord Brooke's *Treatises*. Nothing in Davies' smoothly turned and occasionally eloquent introduction to his subject proper, ' The Elegy of Human Knowledge,' has the poetic flavour of such lines as these, which break the monotony of Lord Brooke's Treatise on the same subject :—

> 'The chief use then in man of that he knows,
> Is his painstaking for the good of all;
> Not fleshly weeping for our own-made woes,
> Not laughing from a melancholy gall,
> Not hating from a soul that overflows
> With bitterness, breathed out from inward th'all;
>   But sweetly rather to ease, to loose or bind,
>   As need requires, this frail fall'n human kind.'

Expression of this high and tender quality is not to be looked for in *Nosce Teipsum.* The poem deals with an eternally poetic subject, the longings, griefs, and destiny of the soul, in such a way as to furnish one more illustration of the futility of 'philosophical poetry,'—of the manner in which the attempt to combine poetry and science extracts all pathos and all influence from the most pathetic and the most potent of themes. From this judgment we may perhaps exclude the passages, quoted below, which deserve to live when the rest of *Nosce Teipsum* is forgotten.

Orchestra was a poem of the author's youth, 'a sudden rash half-capreol of my wit,' as he calls it in the dedication. It is unfinished and immature in style, but there is considerable charm in its wandering fancifulness. The graceful and delicate verse beginning 'For lo, the sea that fleets about the land' (p. 556), will remind a reader of well-known lines in the *Ancient Mariner.* In one or two other passages Sir John Davies may be suggestively matched with modern poets. The resemblance of his 38th Epigram to Wordsworth's *Power of Music* has been already pointed out, and a verse of another modern poem,—

> 'We see all sights from pole to pole,
>   And glance and nod and bustle by,
> And never once possess our soul
>   Before we die,'—

recalls a passage in the Elegy 'Of Human Knowledge':—

> 'We that acquaint ourselves with every Zone,
>   And pass both Tropics, and behold the Poles,
> When we come home are to ourselves unknown,
>   And unacquainted still with our own souls.'

MARY A. WARD.

The Soul compared to a River.

[From *Nosce Teipsum.*]

And as the moisture, which the thirsty earth
  Sucks from the sea, to fill her empty veins,
From out her womb at last doth take a birth,
  And runs a nymph along the grassy plains :

Long doth she stay, as loth to leave the land,
  From whose soft side she first did issue make ;
She tastes all places, turns to every hand,
  Her flowr'y banks unwilling to forsake :

Yet Nature so her streams doth lead and carry,
  As that her course doth make no final stay,
Till she herself unto the ocean marry,
  Within whose wat'ry bosom first she lay :

Even so the Soul which in this earthly mould
  The Spirit of God doth secretly infuse ;
Because at first she doth the earth behold,
  And only this material world she views :

At first her mother-earth she holdeth dear,
  And doth embrace the world and worldly things :
She flies close by the ground, and hovers here,
  And mounts not up with her celestial wings.

Yet under heaven she cannot light on ought
  That with her heavenly nature doth agree ;
She cannot rest, she cannot fix her thought,
  She cannot in this world contented be :

For who did ever yet, in honour, wealth,
  Or pleasure of the sense, contentment find?
Who ever ceas'd to wish, when he had health?
  Or having wisdom was not vext in mind?

Then as a bee which among weeds doth fall,
　Which seem sweet flowers, with lustre fresh and gay;
　She lights on that, and this, and tasteth all,
　But pleas'd with none, doth rise, and soar away;

So, when the Soul finds here no true content,
　And, like Noah's dove, can no sure footing take;
　She doth return from whence she first was sent,
　And flies to Him that first her wings did make.

THE SOUL COMPARED TO A VIRGIN WOOED IN MARRIAGE.

[From the Same.]

As a king's daughter, being in person sought
　Of divers princes, who do neighbour near;
　On none of them can fix a constant thought,
　Though she to all do lend a gentle ear:

Yet she can love a foreign emperor,
　Whom of great worth and power she hears to be;
　If she be woo'd but by ambassador,
　Or but his letters, or his pictures see:

For well she knows, that when she shall be brought
　Into the kingdom where her spouse doth reign;
　Her eyes shall see what she conceiv'd in thought,
　Himself, his state, his glory, and his train.

So while the virgin Soul on earth doth stay,
　She woo'd and tempted is ten thousand ways,
　By these great powers, which on the earth bear sway;
　The wisdom of the world, wealth, pleasure, praise:

With these sometime she doth her time beguile,
　These do by fits her fantasy possess;
　But she distastes them all within a while,
　And in the sweetest finds a tediousness.

But if upon the world's Almighty King
　She once do fix her humble loving thought;
　Who by His picture, drawn in every thing,
　And sacred messages, her love hath sought;

Of Him she thinks, she cannot think too much;
  This honey tasted still, is ever sweet;
  The pleasure of her ravished thought is such,
  As almost here she with her bliss doth meet:

But when in Heaven she shall His essence see,
  This is her sovereign good, and perfect bliss:
  Her longings, wishings, hopes all finished be,
  Her joys are full, her motions rest in this.

There is she crown'd with garlands of content,
  There doth she manna eat, and nectar drink;
  That Presence doth such high delights present,
  As never tongue could speak, nor heart could think.

ANTINOUS PRAISES DANCING BEFORE QUEEN PENELOPE.

[From *Orchestra, or A Poeme of Dauncing.*]

'For that brave Sun the Father of the Day,
Doth love this Earth, the Mother of the Night;
And like a reveller in rich array,
Doth dance his galliard in his leman's sight,
Both back, and forth, and sideways, passing light;
  His princely grace doth so the gods amaze,
  That all stand still and at his beauty gaze.

'But see the Earth, when he approacheth near,
How she for joy doth spring and sweetly smile;
But see again her sad and heavy cheer
When changing places he retires awhile;
But those black clouds he shortly will exile,
  And make them all before his presence fly,
  As mists consum'd before his cheerful eye.

    *   *   *   *   *   *

'And now behold your tender nurse the Air
And common neighbour that aye runs around;
How many pictures and impressions fair
Within her empty regions are there found;
Which to your senses Dancing do propound.
  For what are Breath, Speech, Echos, Music, Winds,
  But Dancings of the Air in sundry kinds?

'For when you breathe, the air in order moves,
Now in, now out, in time and measure true;
And when you speak, so well she dancing loves,
That doubling oft, and oft redoubling new,
With thousand forms she doth herself endue,
   For all the words that from our lips repair
   Are nought but tricks and turnings of the air.

'Hence is her prattling daughter Echo born,
That dances to all voices she can hear;
There is no sound so harsh that she doth scorn,
Nor any time wherein she will forbear
The airy pavement with her feet to wear;
   And yet her hearing sense is nothing quick,
   For after time she endeth every trick.

'And thou sweet Music, Dancing's only life,
The ear's sole happiness, the air's best speech;
Loadstone of fellowship, charming-rod of strife,
The soft mind's Paradise, the sick mind's leech;
With thine own tongue, thou trees and stones canst teach,
   That when the Air doth dance her finest measure,
   Then art thou born, the gods' and men's sweet pleasure.

'Lastly, where keep the Winds their revelry,
Their violent turnings, and wild whirling hays[1],
But in the Air's translucent gallery?
Where she herself is turn'd a hundred ways,
While with those Maskers wantonly she plays;
   Yet in this misrule, they such rule embrace,
   As two at once encumber not the place.

'If then fire, air, wand'ring and fixed lights
In every province of the imperial sky,
Yield perfect forms of dancing to your sights,
In vain I teach the ear, that which the eye
With certain view already doth descry.
   But for your eyes perceive not all they see,
   In this I will your Senses master be.

---

[1] country-dances.

'For lo the Sea that fleets about the Land,
And like a girdle clips her solid waist,
Music and measure both doth understand ;
For his great crystal eye is always cast
Up to the Moon, and on her fixèd fast :
   And as she danceth in her pallid sphere,
   So danceth he about his Centre here.

'Sometimes his proud green waves in order set,
One after other flow unto the shore ;
Which, when they have with many kisses wet,
They ebb away in order as before ;
And to make known his courtly love the more,
   He oft doth lay aside his three-forked mace,
   And with his arms the timorous Earth embrace.

'Only the Earth doth stand for ever still,
Her rocks remove not, nor her mountains meet,
(Although some wits enriched with Learning's skill
Say heav'n stands firm, and that the Earth doth fleet,
And swiftly turneth underneath their feet ;)
   Yet though the Earth is ever steadfast seen,
   On her broad breast hath Dancing ever been.

'For those blue veins that through her body spread,
Those sapphire streams which from great hills do spring
(The Earth's great dugs ; for every wight is fed
With sweet fresh moisture from them issuing ;)
Observe a dance in their wild wandering ;
   And still their dance begets a murmur sweet,
   And still the murmur with the dance doth meet.'

[From *Hymnes of Astraea, in Acrosticke Verse.*]

TO THE SPRING.

E arth now is green, and heaven is blue,
L ively Spring which makes all new,
I olly Spring, doth enter ;
S weet young sun-beams do subdue
A ngry, agèd Winter.

B lasts are mild, and seas are calm,
E very meadow flows with balm,
T he Earth wears all her riches ;
H armonious birds sing such a psalm,
A s ear and heart bewitches.

R eserve (sweet Spring) this Nymph of ours,
E ternal garlands of thy flowers,
G reen garlands never wasting :
I n her shall last our state's fair Spring,
N ow and for ever flourishing,
A s long as Heaven is lasting.

TO THE NIGHTINGALE.

E very night from even to morn,
L ove's Chorister amid the thorn
I s now so sweet a singer ;
S o sweet, as for her song I scorn
A pollo's voice, and finger.

B ut Nightingale, sith you delight
E ver to watch the starry night ;
T ell all the stars of heaven,
H eaven never had a star so bright,
A s now to Earth is given.

R oyal Astraea makes our day
E ternal with her beams, nor may
G ross darkness overcome her ;
I now perceive why some do write,
N o country hath so short a night,
A s England hath in Summer.

To the Month of September.

E ach month hath praise in some degree ;
L et May to others seem to be
I n sense the sweetest Season ;
S eptember thou art best to me,
A nd best doth please my reason.

B ut neither for thy corn nor wine
E xtol I those mild days of thine,
T hough corn and wine might praise thee ;
H eaven gives thee honour more divine,
A nd higher fortunes raise thee.

R enown'd art thou (sweet month) for this,
E mong thy days her birth-day is ;
G race, plenty, peace and honour
I n one fair hour with her were born ;
N ow since they still her crown adorn,
A nd still attend upon her.

JOHN DONNE.

[BORN 1573, in London; his mother being a descendant of Sir Thomas More. He studied both at Oxford and Cambridge, and also at Lincoln's Inn; travelled in Italy and Spain, 'and returned perfect in their languages.' He was afterwards in the service of Lord Chancellor Ellesmere and others, and in 1610 was persuaded by James I 'to enter into sacred orders.' In 1621 the king made him Dean of St. Paul's, and he held other benefices. He died in 1631. Izaak Walton's celebrated *Life* was prefixed to his *Eighty Sermons*, fol., 1640; and this *Life* asserts that 'most of his poems were written before the twentieth year of his age.' The *Poems* were collected and first published posthumously in 1633: but Harl. MS. 5110 (British Museum), is entitled, 'Jhon Dunne his Satyres anno domini 1593.']

Donne's contemporary reputation as a poet, and still more as a preacher, was immense ; and a glance at his works would suffice to show that he did not deserve the contempt with which he was subsequently treated.   But yet his chief interest is that he was the principal founder of a school which especially expressed and re-presented a certain bad taste of his day.   Of his genius there can be no question ; but it was perversely directed.   One may almost invert Jonson's famous panegyric on Shakespeare, and say that Donne was not for all time but for an age.

To this school Dr. Johnson has given the title of the Meta-physical ; and for this title there is something to be said. 'Donne,' says Dryden, 'affects the metaphysics not only in his Satires, but in his amorous verses where Nature only should reign, and perplexes the minds of the fair sex with nice speculations of philosophy when he should engage their hearts and entertain them with the soft-nesses of love.'   Thus he often ponders over the mystery of love, and is exercised by subtle questions as to its nature, origin, endurance.   But a yet more notable distinction of this school than its philosophising, shallow or deep, is what may be called its fantasticality, its quaint wit, elaborate ingenuity, far-fetched allusiveness ; and it might better be called the Ingenious, or

Fantastic School. Various and out-of-the-way information and learning is a necessary qualification for membership. Donne in one of his letters speaks of his 'embracing the worst voluptuousness, an hydroptic immoderate desire of human learning and languages.' Eminence is attained by using such stores in the way to be least expected. The thing to be illustrated becomes of secondary importance by the side of the illustration. The more unlikely and surprising and preposterous this is, the greater the success. This is wit of a kind. From one point of view, wit, as Dr. Johnson says, 'may be considered as a kind of *discordia concors* ; a combination of dissimilar images or discovery of occult resemblances in things apparently unlike. Of wit thus defined they [Donne and his followers] have more than enough. The most heterogeneous ideas are yoked by violence together ; nature and art are ransacked for illustrations, comparisons, and allusions ; their learning instructs, and their subtility surprises ; but the reader commonly thinks his improvement dearly bought, and though he sometimes admires is seldom pleased.'

And so in the following curious passage from Donne's Dedication of certain poems to Lord Craven it should be observed how 'wit' and 'poetry' are made to correspond : 'Amongst all the monsters this unlucky age has teemed with, I find none so prodigious as the poets of these late times [this is very much what Donne's own critics must say], wherein men, as if they would level undertakings too as well as estates, acknowledging no inequality of parts and judgments, pretend as indifferently to the chair of wit as to the pulpit, and conceive themselves no less inspired with the spirit of poetry than with that of religion.' Dryden styles Donne 'the greatest wit though not the best poet of our nation.'

The taste which this school represents marks other literatures besides our own at this time. It was 'in the air' of that age ; and so was not originated by Donne. But it was he who in England first gave it full expression—who was its first vigorous and effective and devoted spokesman. And this secures him a conspicuous position in the history of our literature when we remember how prevalent was the fashion of 'conceits' during the first half of the seventeenth century, and that amongst those who followed it more or less are to be mentioned, to say nothing of the earlier poems of Milton and Waller and Dryden, Suckling, Denham, Herbert, Crashaw, Cleveland, Cowley.

This misspent learning, this excessive ingenuity, this laborious wit seriously mars almost the whole of Donne's work. For the most part we look on it with amazement rather than with pleasure. It reminds us rather of a 'pyrotechnic display,' with its unexpected flashes and explosions, than of a sure and constant light (compare the *Valediction* given in our selections). We weary of such unmitigated cleverness—such ceaseless straining after novelty and surprise. We long for something simply thought, and simply said.

His natural gifts were certainly great. He possesses a real energy and fervour. He loved, and he suffered much, and he writes with a passion which is perceptible through all his artificialities. Such a poem as *The Will* is evidence of the astonishing rapidity and brightness of his fancy.

He also claims notice as one of our earliest formal satirists. Though not published till much later, there is proof that some at least of his satires were written three or four years before those of Hall. Two of them (ii. and iv.) were reproduced—'versified'—in the last century by Pope, acting on a suggestion by Dryden; No. iii. was similarly treated by Parnell. In these versions, along with the roughness of the metre, disappears much of the general vigour; and it should be remembered that the metrical roughness was no result of incapacity, but was designed. Thus the charge of metrical uncouthness so often brought against Donne on the ground of his satires is altogether mistaken. How fluently and smoothly he could write if he pleased, is attested over and over again by his lyrical pieces.

JOHN W. HALES.

Song.

Go and catch a falling star,
Get with child a mandrake root,
Tell me where all times past are,
Or who cleft the Devil's foot ;
Teach me to hear mermaids singing,
Or to keep off envy's stinging,
  And find
  What wind
Serves to advance an honest mind.

If thou be'st born to strange sights,
Things invisible go see,
Ride ten thousand days and nights
Till age snow white hairs on thee ;
Thou, when thou return'st, wilt tell me
All strange wonders that befell thee,
  And swear
  No where
Lives a woman true and fair.

If thou find'st one let me know,
Such a pilgrimage were sweet ;
Yet do not, I would not go,
Though at next door we might meet ;
Though she were true when you met her,
And last, when you wrote your letter,
  Yet she
  Will be
False, ere I come, to two or three.

A Valediction forbidding Mourning.

As virtuous men pass mildly away,
And whisper to their souls to go,
Whilst some of their sad friends do say,
'Now his breath goes,' and some say 'No';

So let us meet and make no noise,
No tear-floods, nor sigh-tempests move,
'Twere profanation of our joys,
To tell the laity our love.

Moving of th' Earth brings harm and fears,
Men reckon what it did and meant ;
But trepidation of the spheres,
Though greater far, is innocent.

Dull sublunary lovers' love,
(Whose soul is sense) cannot admit
Of absence, 'cause it doth remove
The thing which elemented it.

But we by a love so far refin'd,
That ourselves know not what it is,
Inter-assured of the mind,
Careless eyes, lips, and hands, to miss ;

Our two souls therefore, which are one,
Though I must go, endure not yet
A breach, but an expansion,
Like gold to airy thinness beat.

If they be two, they are two so
As stiff twin compasses are two,
Thy soul, the fix'd foot, makes no show
To move, but doth, if th' other do.

And though it in the centre sit,
Yet when the other far doth roam,
It leans and hearkens after it,
And grows erect as that comes home.

Such wilt thou be to me, who must
Like th' other foot, obliquely run,
Thy firmness makes my circle just,
And makes me end where I begun.

Song.

Sweetest love, I do not go
For weariness of thee,
Nor in hope the world can show
A fitter love for me ;
　　But since that I
Must die at last, 'tis best
Thus to use myself in jest
By feigned deaths to die.

Yesternight the Sun went hence,
And yet is here to-day,
He hath no desire nor sense,
Nor half so short a way ;
　　Then fear not me,
But believe that I shall make
Hastier journeys, since I take
More wings and spurs than he.

O how feeble is man's power,
That if good fortune fall,
Cannot ado another hour,
Nor a lost hour recall !
　　But come bad chance,
And we join to 't our strength,
And we teach it art and length,
Itself o'er us t' advance.

When thou sigh'st thou sigh'st not wind,
But sigh'st my soul away ;
When thou weep'st unkindly kind,
My life's blood doth decay.
　　It cannot be
That thou lov'st me, as thou say'st ;
If in thine my life thou waste,
Thou art the life of me.

O O 2

> Let not thy divining heart
> Forethink me any ill,
> Destiny may take my part
> And may thy fears fulfil;
> But think that we
> Are but laid aside to sleep:
> They who one another keep
> Alive, ne'er parted be.

FROM 'VERSES TO SIR HENRY WOOTTON.'

Be then thine own home, and in thyself dwell;
Inn anywhere; continuance maketh Hell.
And seeing the snail, which everywhere doth roam,
Carrying his own house still, is still at home:
Follow (for he's easy pac'd) this snail,
Be thine own palace, or the world's thy jail.
But in the world's sea do not like cork sleep
Upon the water's face, nor in the deep
Sink like a lead without a line: but as
Fishes glide, leaving no print where they pass,
Nor making sound, so closely thy course go;
Let men dispute whether thou breathe or no:
Only in this be no Galenist. To make
Court's hot ambitions wholesome, do not take
A dram of country's dulness; do not add
Correctives, but as chymics purge the bad.
But, sir, I advise not you, I rather do
Say o'er those lessons which I learn'd of you:
Whom, free from Germany's schisms, and lightness
Of France, and fair Italie's faithlessness,
Having from these suck'd all they had of worth
And brought home that faith which you carry'd forth,
I throughly love: but if myself I've won
To know my rules, I have, and you have, *Donne.*

The Will.

Before I sigh my last gasp, let me breathe,
Great Love, some legacies ; here I bequeath
Mine eyes to Argus, if mine eyes can see,
If they be blind, then Love, I give them thee ;
My tongue to Fame ; to ambassadors mine ears ;
    To women, or the sea, my tears ;
Thou, Love, hast taught me heretofore
By making me serve her who had twenty more,
That I should give to none, but such as had too much before

My constancy I to the planets give,
My truth to them who at the court do live ;
Mine ingenuity and openness
To Jesuits ; to buffoons my pensiveness ;
My silence to any, who abroad hath been ;
    My money to a Capuchin.
Thou, Love, taught'st me, by appointing me
To love there, where no love receiv'd can be,
Only to give to such as have an incapacity.

My faith I give to Roman Catholics ;
All my good works unto the schismatics
Of Amsterdam ; my best civility
And courtship, to an university ;
My modesty I give to shoulders bare ;
    My patience let gamesters share.
Thou, Love, taught'st me, by making me
Love her that holds my love disparity,
Only to give to those that count my gifts indignity.

I give my reputation to those
Which were my friends ; my industry to foes ;
To schoolmen I bequeath my doubtfulness ;
My sickness to physicians, or excess ;

To Nature, all that I in rhyme have writ;
　And to my company my wit;
Thou, Love, by making me adore
Her, who begot this love in me before,
Taught'st me to make, as though I gave, when I did but restore.

To him for whom the passing bell next tolls
I give my physic books; my written rolls
Of moral counsels I to Bedlam give;
My brazen medals, unto them which live
In want of bread; to them which pass among
　All foreigners, my English tongue,
Thou, Love, by making me love one
Who thinks her friendship a fit portion
For younger lovers, dost my gifts thus disproportion.

Therefore I'll give no more; but I'll undo
The world by dying; because love dies too.
Then all your beauties will be no more worth
Than gold in mines, where none doth draw it forth;
And all your graces no more use shall have
　Than a sun-dial on a grave.
Thou, Love, taughtest me, by making me
Love her, who doth neglect both me and thee,
To invent and practise this one way to annihilate all three.